After Kubrick

After Kubrick

A Filmmaker's Legacy

Edited by
Jeremi Szaniawski

BLOOMSBURY ACADEMIC
NEW YORK • LONDON • OXFORD • NEW DELHI • SYDNEY

BLOOMSBURY ACADEMIC
Bloomsbury Publishing Inc
1385 Broadway, New York, NY 10018, USA
50 Bedford Square, London, WC1B 3DP, UK
29 Earlsfort Terrace, Dublin 2, Ireland

BLOOMSBURY, BLOOMSBURY ACADEMIC and the Diana logo are trademarks of
Bloomsbury Publishing Plc

First published in the United States of America 2020
This paperback edition published in 2021

Copyright © Jeremi Szaniawski and Contributors, 2020 Volume Editor's Part of the
Work © Jeremi Szaniawski Each chapter © of Contributors

For legal purposes the Acknowledgments on p. vi constitute an extension
of this copyright page.

Cover design: Adrian Limoni
Cover photographs, from top to bottom: A Serious Man, 2009, Under the Skin, 2013,
Ex Machina, 2009, Interstellar, 2014, There Will Be Blood, 2007 © Collection Christophel /
ArenaPAL and Courtesy Everett Collection / Mary Evans

All rights reserved. No part of this publication may be reproduced or transmitted
in any form or by any means, electronic or mechanical, including photocopying,
recording, or any information storage or retrieval system, without prior
permission in writing from the publishers.

Bloomsbury Publishing Inc does not have any control over, or responsibility for, any
third-party websites referred to or in this book. All internet addresses given in this
book were correct at the time of going to press. The author and publisher regret any
inconvenience caused if addresses have changed or sites have ceased to exist,
but can accept no responsibility for any such changes.

Library of Congress Cataloging-in-Publication Data
Names: Szaniawski, Jeremi, editor.
Title: After Kubrick: a filmmaker's legacy / edited by Jeremi Szaniawski.
Description: New York: Bloomsbury Academic, 2020. | Includes
bibliographical references and index.
Identifiers: LCCN 2019034896 (print) | LCCN 2019034897 (ebook) | ISBN 9781501347641
(hardback) | ISBN 9781501347658 (epub) | ISBN 9781501347665 (pdf)
Subjects: LCSH: Kubrick, Stanley–Influence. | Kubrick, Stanley–Criticism
and interpretation.
Classification: LCC PN1998.3.K83 A64 2020 (print) | LCC PN1998.3.K83
(ebook) | DDC 791.4302/33092–dc23
LC record available at https://lccn.loc.gov/2019034896
LC ebook record available at https://lccn.loc.gov/2019034897

ISBN: HB: 978-1-5013-4764-1
PB: 978-1-5013-8355-7
ePDF: 978-1-5013-4766-5
eBook: 978-1-5013-4765-8

Typeset by Deanta Global Publishing Services, Chennai, India

To find out more about our authors and books visit www.bloomsbury.com and
sign up for our newsletters.

Contents

Acknowledgments   vi

Introduction: 1999–2019, and Beyond: A Post-Kubrickian Odyssey
    Jeremi Szaniawski   1

1. Stanley Kubrick's Prototypes: The Author as World-Maker
    Thomas Elsaesser   29
2. "Kubrick's Cube": Stanley Kubrick, Judaism, and His Jewish Heirs
    Nathan Abrams   51
3. Kubrick's Inheritors: Aesthetics, Independence, and Philosophy in the Films of Joel and Ethan Coen *Rodney F. Hill* 67
4. Blurring the Lines between Victim and Perpetrator: Yorgos Lanthimos and the Legacy of Stanley Kubrick *Pierre-Simon Gutman* 87
5. Glimpses of Eternity: Stanley Kubrick's Time Machines *Jeremi Szaniawski* 101
6. Kubrickian Dread: Echoes of *2001: A Space Odyssey* and *The Shining* in Works by Jonathan Glazer, Paul Thomas Anderson, and David Lynch *Rick Warner* 125
7. Excessive and Incomplete: Kubrick's Turing *Marta Figlerowicz* 147
8. Thus Spoke Kubrick: "Guide Pieces," Modes of Citation and the Rise of the Temp Track *Adrian Daub* 165
9. Fade to Crude: Petro-Horror and Kubrick's *The Shining* *Pansy Duncan* 179
10. The Anxiety of Interpretation: *The Shining*, *Room 237* and Film Criticism *Daniel Fairfax* 195
11. Political Opacity in the Films of Stanley Kubrick *John Pitseys* 213
12. Coping with the Unknown in *2001: A Space Odyssey* and *Interstellar* *Mircea Valeriu Deaca* 231
13. Biopolitical Abjection and Sexuation: Stanley Kubrick's Political Films *Seung-hoon Jeong* 243
14. Kubrick at the Museum: Post-Cinematic Conditions, Limitations, and Possibilities *Jihoon Kim* 263
15. The Dead Kitten: Sacrifice in *Barry Lyndon* *Alexander Nemerov* 281

Appendix: Interview with Gaspar Noé *Pip Chodorov*   295
List of Contributors   300
Index   305

Acknowledgments

I would like to thank all the people who have made *After Kubrick: A Filmmaker's Legacy* possible: first and foremost, my heartfelt thanks go to the fifteen contributors for their remarkable and thought-provoking scholarly contributions, and care during revisions.

I would also like to express my gratitude to the peer-reviewers for their positive feedback to the proposal as well as for raising pointed and helpful questions.

Several people made contributions to greater perfect this volume, assisting with the editing, putting the collection as a whole into the best possible shape:

Sally Shafto provided expert editorial assistance on my translations of two chapters.

Michael Cramer's help was invaluable, both in assisting with the editing of the collection's introduction and a couple of chapters (including my own) and in complementing and enriching them with his peerless insight.

A special shout-out goes also to Jennifer Stob for so generously and enthusiastically providing editorial assistance at the eleventh hour.

Adrian Limoni and Marie Fessol were incredibly helpful with the book's cover design, not least in designing the title font. Sula Danowski kindly provided further guidance for the back cover design and font.

Thanks go too to Gaspar Noé, who gave his time at Cannes in 2018 for a wonderful interview with Pip Chodorov about *2001: A Space Odyssey*, and who inspired me to make this volume about Kubrick's inheritors.

At Bloomsbury, I salute the work of all involved in making the book a reality, from editors to typesetters to graphic designers. Particular thanks go to Katie Gallof not only for her trust in the project and guidance, but also her generosity and patience. I also wish to thank Erin Duffy, Louise Dugdale, Joseph Gautham, and all who have helped with the preparation and production of the book.

Thanks go to CINEMATEK, the Belgian Royal Film Archive, for hosting a wonderful series of screenings in April and May 2019, around the twentieth anniversary of Kubrick's death and this book. I should single out Freddy Malonda and Micha Pletinckx for helping to prepare and curating the series, and Johan Vreys for advertising it most efficiently.

I would like to thank Dudley Andrew and Keith Wagner for their generous advice and moral support and Mary and Lee Faulkner for their friendship and kind hospitality.

I would like to single out two people who contributed in a significant way to this book, albeit many years ago, and perhaps unwittingly. Their benevolence and generosity went a long way toward inspiring me to take on the project: my father, Marek Szaniawski, was the first person to tell me of Stanley Kubrick's films and encourage me to watch them. It was my father who apprised me of Kubrick's passing in March, 1999.

At Yale, my dear friend Michael Kerbel, whose uncle, Manuel Gottlieb, was Kubrick's dentist in New York, was a well of insight and anecdotes about the master.

Together with Michael and the Cinema at the Whitney, Yale's erstwhile 35mm film club, we programmed *Dr. Strangelove, or How I Learned to Stop Worrying and Love the Bomb* as our second semester gala film, and later, in March 2009, a series of films (*The Killing, Paths of Glory, 2001: A Space Odyssey*) for the tenth anniversary of the director's death.

The final touches to this collection were applied for the most part in Istanbul, the City of the World's Desire. May its people, street cats and dogs, and the Bosphorus be held responsible in the most wonderful way for all the positive energy I found in them, and which helped me to complete the book's manuscript.

I dedicate this book to the memory of two dear friends who passed away in 2019: Andrée Simonis and Sevgi Sanlı.

Andrée, who in her capacity as a dermatologist had followed me since my prime infancy, was a consummate cinephile. Fittingly, if sadly, the last time we saw each other was during Alexander Nemerov's talk on *Barry Lyndon* in Brussels.

Sevgi was a translator into Turkish of William Shakespeare and G.B. Shaw among many other important English authors, who took me to some unforgettable theater performances in Istanbul.

I will greatly miss these two extraordinary women's wisdom, strength, and generosity–and their kind and forgiving smiles.

Introduction:
1999–2019, and Beyond: A Post-Kubrickian Odyssey

Jeremi Szaniawski

We're all children of Kubrick, aren't we? Is there anything you can do that he hasn't done?

Paul Thomas Anderson

And the stars look very different today.

David Bowie

Black Stars

In 1969, the song "Space Oddity," by a young artist named David Bowie, reached the top of the British charts. The hit single, telling of the misfortunes of Major Tom, sent on a mission to outer space from which he seems unlikely to ever return, was only the first major landmark among a vast number of cultural products referencing *2001: A Space Odyssey*, released a year earlier, and arguably the single most influential motion picture of all time. Not only did its England-based American director, Stanley Kubrick, change science fiction forever, but he also gave a concrete form to a zeitgeist marked by the encounter between lunar landings and the rather different kind of space travel offered by psychedelic substances. Pushing the boundaries of film technology, phenomenology, and philosophy, Kubrick captured the exhilaration and dread of an ebullient late capitalism, which was offering new possibilities at once promising and terrifying. One finds this same zeitgeist echoed in Bowie's song, as though Kubrick had hit upon a repeatable figuration of late-1960s utopianism and the dread that accompanied it. Both artists likewise offered art that was crystallizing challenging and mesmerizing ideas, bridging the gap between the popular and the highbrow. For Bowie, this ambivalent wonder at the scientific promise of the 1960s ended with a crash to Earth: on his 1981 album *Scary Monsters*, the singer, slowly recovering from a brilliant but alienating decade of substance abuse, mentioned Major Tom again ("a junkie strung out in heaven's high, leading an all time low").[1] Yet the spirit of *2001* had hardly exhausted its appeal: Bowie's son, Duncan Jones, would go on to direct *Moon* (2009), a feature film strongly borrowing from the imagery defined by Kubrick. In the music video to the title track of Bowie's final album, *Blackstar* (2015), released shortly before his death, the forlorn cosmonaut, now found lying lifeless on some distant planet, was summoned one final time. Bowie was announcing his own imminent passing in the song's lyrics:

> Something happened on the day he died
> Spirit rose a metre and stepped aside
> Somebody else took his place, and bravely cried
> I'm a Blackstar
> I'm a Blackstar

In many ways, these words also expressed the feeling that many aspiring artists, filmmakers, or simply regular film fans felt upon learning of Kubrick's death, on March 7, 1999. A bright star in the firmament of cinema had gone out—but its light kept on reaching the world. While he was hardly without his detractors, the auteur, household name, one-man studio, reclusive genius, and manic paranoid generated fascination, awe and admiration, and more often than not gratitude and even reverence of unparalleled proportion—feelings that have not abated since his passing (a similar sentiment accompanied Bowie's death in early 2016). His death left a void, marking the end of a heroic age of cinematic auteurism and quality mainstream filmmaking, and was immediately followed by a barrage of obituaries, articles, books, and retrospectives. The latter never fail to attract scores of spectators, including large numbers of film students, a sure marker of the quasi-mythical fascination exerted by Kubrick, and his aura, as it were. Warner Bros. and the Kubrick Estate hurried to capitalize on the director's fame, while also dispelling his reputation as a paranoid artist, surrounded by a cloud of conspiracy theories. Endeavoring to celebrate his life and legacy, closely overseeing the Stanley Kubrick Exhibition,[2] the publication of lavishly illustrated volumes (including selections from photo albums revealing Kubrick as a family man), and films (the concurrent release of *Stanley Kubrick: A Life in Pictures* [Jan Harlan, 2001] and rerelease of *2001: A Space Odyssey*), they ensured that Kubrick's work—and the Kubrick brand—will be a lasting, enduring project. Twenty years on, it is very much alive, with a dynamic Foundation honoring the master's memory as well keeping his work vibrant and relevant, and the vast Kubrick Archive, located in the University of the Arts London, open to anyone interested in researching Kubrick's life and oeuvre.

To be sure, if, before his death, the number of publications dedicated to Kubrick was already on par with those devoted to Alfred Hitchcock, Orson Welles, or Charlie Chaplin, he has since overtaken his "competitors" in this regard by a landslide, also courtesy of innumerable blogs, vlogs, and other online publications, a testament to both the canny and proactive work of the Foundation, and to the lasting appeal and relevance of the films themselves. One striking example of the quasi-religious and fetishistic devotion to Kubrick's work is Lee Unkrich's website http://www.theoverlookhotel.com/. Not only does it regularly post rare production stills and little-known pieces of information about *The Shining* (1980), it also documents all kinds of ancillary paraphernalia—toys, items of clothing, video games, and art projects—attesting to the film's cult status and continued influence in popular culture and the Western world, which came to discover it in "great waves of terror," through its successive releases in theaters and on television, home video, and VOD/online platforms.

In academia, Kubrick's work has been viewed and analyzed from just about every single angle, with scholarly approaches ranging from the theoretical to the empirical. Articles, collections, and monographs tackle his work with actors and his aesthetic of the grotesque (Naremore 2007); the reimagining of cinema and "cinema of loneliness" (Kolker 1980, 2016); the philosophy of existentialism to be found in Kubrick's oeuvre (Abrams 2009); the subsurface narrative of Jewishness to be found in his films (Cocks 2004, Abrams 2018); the new perspectives offered by the Kubrick Archive (Krämer, Ljulic and Daniel 2015); or, more generally, his motifs and methods of filmmaking (Michelson 1969, Ciment 2011, Chion 2001), his work with music (McQuiston 2013, Gengaro 2013), and his engagement with history and politics (Jameson 1990, Vidal 2005) or with time (Deleuze 1989, Pramaggiore 2017). This list barely touches on a corpus of hundreds of books and articles written all around the world about Kubrick. The director thus sits today at the top of a Mount Olympus of analysis and interpretation, but also of speculation and fanciful, if not outright demented, conspiracy theories, as the documentary *Room 237* (Rodney Ascher, 2012) demonstrates. Extending beyond the world of film and art (one may point out here the world of pop music, but also design and architecture), Kubrick's visionary imaginary has also inspired thought and discourse on artificial intelligence, coding, and even ethics. Yet surprisingly little has in fact been written, outside of fan journalism, about Kubrick's artistic influence on younger generations of filmmakers. It is this gap in Kubrick studies that this collection seeks to address, attending to the similarities between those films that bear Kubrick's influence and the implications of their citation of his work.[3] A filmmaker's ghost, his teaching, his aesthetic, and his moral and political legacy live on even beyond their commercial exploitation, and are transmitted or reinterpreted in scores of films, which are sometimes more than mere pastiche or derivative fare. In the world of film production, Kubrick has long been acknowledged by his peers for his high level of technical and artistic proficiency, for what we may call his visionary professionalism—even if it has been argued that Kubrick was hardly a visionary, but rather an autistic mind who endlessly studied, repeated, and rehearsed ideas, until they "clicked," hence his endless rewriting of the script on set, and fabled repetitions of the same take that far exceeded the industry standard. The Kubrickian "toolkit" has proved attractive to film students, and many of the filmmakers studied in this collection. Their desire being to emulate not even so much Kubrick's philosophy, as his degree of perfectionism and professional excellence. All the while, it is Kubrick the director who is celebrated, not the purportedly stingy producer (even if the two were probably inseparable sides, the latter enabling or facilitating the creative freedom conducive to the former). Also, while the reader will be familiar with most, if not all, contemporary directors dealt in this volume, it is important to note that they are, in their notable references to Kubrick, merely the tip of an iceberg: countless other practitioners, both professional and amateur, similarly channel Kubrick's work, spirit, and ideas, in a spectrum of attitudes ranging from awe and deference to immature borrowing and morbid fetishism, all Kubrickian "blackstars" the world over. Accordingly, the filmmaker's legacy is thus primarily considered here outside of its institutional, official life, approached obliquely via his followers' films and the spontaneous dialogues they instantiate with Kubrick, seeing in them his philosophical and intellectual, and also tonal, stylistic, and thematic/motivic impact.

Perhaps the key question at this juncture is: "Why (quote) Kubrick (and why now)." What is the point of looking at a filmmaker's influence on his peers? As will become clear in this introduction and through the chapters this collection comprises, there are several layers and modes involved in referencing a filmmaker, and several reasons for doing so: the first, and probably most superficial one, has to do with cultural cachet and cinephilia that filmic pastiche or empty citation seem to connote. The danger here, oft-encountered for instance in student and fan films or works by lesser craftsmen, is of clinging to a figure of reference as a useless buoy, and being overshadowed or dwarfed by the direct comparison that quoting (or trying to quote) Kubrick's films entails, a clumsy exercise bringing Kubrick to a terrain he most definitely abhorred: the middlebrow. At the same time, and conversely, there is perhaps something liberating and subversive in some appropriations of Kubrickian tropes, not least in the case of parody in other media (literary references, magazine articles, memes, online videos, etc.), which freely concoct a brew of Kubrickian citations. In these cases, Kubrick's films function as points of cultural memory, which can then be reworked productively or critically. Such practice is productive, not least in how it indirectly acknowledges the way Kubrick's own films renegotiated the gap between highbrow culture and popular art. Examples range from Jennifer Shiman's *Kubrick's The Shining in 30 Seconds (and re-enacted by Bunnies)*[4] to Michael Haneke's *Funny Games* (1998 and its 2007 remake). With its cleverly perverse reference to and subversion of the mechanisms of violence, cruelty, and identification from *A Clockwork Orange* (1971), *Funny Games* at once celebrates and contests Kubrick's legacy. In these pages, the extent to which Kubrick's influence has penetrated the collective subconscious will also be evident, generating networks of imagery now part of popular culture, much as they themselves channeled it (Jack Nicholson's "Heeere's Johnny," referencing Johnny Carson in *The Shining*'s most iconic moment being a case in point). Throughout, Kubrick appears as having been a master manipulator in a manner extending beyond his films, reaching into trends in popular culture and popular cinema, a fact evidenced by the way that his films themselves, as Thomas Elsaesser notes, often came after the crest of a given genre had been reached already (e.g., the horror film wave of the 1970s with *The Shining* and the Vietnam War film wave of the 1970s and early 1980s with *Full Metal Jacket* [1987]), so it is perhaps little surprise that popular culture should have adopted them in turn.

The most ambitious way of drawing upon Kubrick, instantiated by at least a few of the directors studied in this collection, would be to use his work as a starting point (in a manner echoing what Roland Barthes identified in *Sade, Fourier, Loyola* as an attempt to create a new language) for the expansion of cinematic grammar, the delimitation of new narrative and stylistic spaces, and the generation of new internal articulations to the medium and, perhaps, a "theatricalization" of filmic space.[5] This access to new means of filmic enunciation that these filmmakers try to obtain by way of Kubrick, whom they evidently perceive as a trailblazer, a cinematic Icarus, is a tall order. To succeed in the enterprise, as the director put it himself (upon accepting the D. W. Griffith lifetime achievement award), is akin to writing *War and Peace* in a bumper car. While the process is indeed of an Icaric nature, and well-nigh unattainable, the *jouissance* contained in achieving this feat ranks among the holy grails of filmmaking. More modest pleasures, and more frequent impotence or even frustration, substitute themselves for such ultimate creative *jouissance* in most cases of homage, reference, or pastiche of Kubrick's work.

But why should Kubrick constitute the benchmark by which one measures one's own cinematic achievement, whether it be an act of true creation or a mere surface citation? This question no doubt calls for a bit of historicizing: past the heyday of what Fredric Jameson identified as postmodern pastiche (roughly the 1970s to the late 1990s), we have now entered a global age wherein the question of identity is no longer tied only to a postindustrial context, but also to a digital economy and increased number of voices vying for attention and visibility. Unsurprisingly, then, Kubrick's towering figure as an auteur and individual(ist), who produced films that were also cultural events (even when their commercial success was not always immediately spectacular), carries another appeal: that of the lasting or cult phenomenon. It is thus unsurprising, that a lot of the auteurs who most identifiably claim Kubrick's influence seek not blockbuster fame, but instead seek to carve out a lasting cultural niche for their films, extending far beyond the latter's (often short or limited) theatrical releases. For example, Christopher Nolan, unquestionably the most commercially successful Kubrickian epigone, aims for a longer life span for his works and is largely successful in achieving it, as attested to by their perennial presence as "trending" films on online platforms after their successful global theatrical runs. Last but not least, as will be shown in the following pages, the wide range of ways in which Kubrickian tropes are being cited and recuperated speaks to a kind of match between his films—multilayered, complex, and calling for repeated viewing and multiple interpretations—and a world that has become exponentially, even numbingly or blindingly, complex; his films' concern with new technologies, alienation, and cultural anomie closely reflect our confusing and contradictory neoliberal (and soon trans-human?) global age.

Visible Traces, Invisible Signatures

Probably the first mainstream filmmaker to have paid homage to his idol, with his take on the painterly universe of *Barry Lyndon* (1975), *The Duellists* (1977), Ridley Scott serves as a fine example of the way Kubrick's legacy has seeped into the collective unconscious by way of his epigones' and admirers' productions. Scott, who was trained in the fine arts, and whose glossy images detract from actual cinematic pacing (his films always somewhat dull despite their beautiful cinematography), was attracted not only by Kubrick's unforgettable visual compositions but also by an unattainable sense of rhythm and epic breadth. Acknowledging his debt to the master, Scott explored a variety of genres, and we might see in *Gladiator* (2000) echoes of *Spartacus* (1960) or in *Alien* (1979) those of *2001: A Space Odyssey*: the aseptic, white interiors of the spaceship and hibernation pods are common to both films, while Scott's blending of sci-fi and horror echoes the prototypical work with genre that Kubrick had made his signature. In *Blade Runner* (1982),[6] Scott utilized front screen projection to make the replicants' eyes gleam like the leopard's in *2001*'s "Dawn of Man" sequence. He also turned to the mountain landscape footage from *The Shining*'s opening credits for the closing scene of the original theatrical release of *Blade Runner*—when Harrison Ford and Sean Young elope into idyllic, misty landscapes of the American wilderness (these scenes, imposed by the studio to provide a semblance of a happy ending to the film, were later removed from the director's cut release, alongside Ford's neo-noir voice-over narration). Scott also cast Joe Turkel, who had played in three of Kubrick's films (*The Killing* [1956], *Paths of Glory* [1958], and *The Shining*), for the part of Tyrell, the God-like inventor who ends up murdered by his artificial human creation.[7] In turn, Kubrick seemingly acknowledged *The Duellists*, creating a game of back and forth cinematic referencing: Jack Nicholson frozen in the labyrinth at the end of *The Shining* echoes similarly frozen Napoleonic soldiers in a scene from Scott's film. Considering Kubrick's massive borrowing from genre films for his gothic epic (including Robert Wise's *The Haunting* [1963] and Richard Donner's *The Omen* [1976]) and life-long fascination with Napoleon (see Castle), it is likely that the nod was very deliberate—as though to say: this is how you freeze a character in time.

Through the last decades of the twentieth century, Kubrick's followers, like Scott, but also like John Carpenter or James Cameron, mostly indulged in what Fredric Jameson has branded pastiche, or blank parody. This nostalgic gesture, typical of postmodernity, may be the most playful, but also, again, the least interesting aspect of Kubrick's legacy. It remains nonetheless arresting when located in films taking place in the future, as is evidently the case with science fiction films, which are in turn combined with the noir or horror genre, as in Scott's case. Still, even such visions of the future serve the same nostalgic purpose, only to better disguise it: "It is by way of so-called nostalgia films that some properly allegorical processing of the past becomes possible: it is because the formal apparatus of nostalgia films has trained us to consume the past in the form of glossy images that new and more complex 'postnostalgia' statements and forms become possible" (Jameson 1991, 287). With more or less humor, wavering between the blank parody of pastiche and more jocular instantiations, John Carpenter's debut, *Dark Star* (1974), features a clear parody of *2001*'s super computer HAL 9000. And in his horror-sci-fi masterpiece *The Thing* (1982), as Rick Warner identifies, Carpenter references *2001* and *The Shining*, both through an overall sense of Kubrickian dread, and through literal quotes: the film's credits, which use the exact same font as the one in the "Dawn of Man" section in *2001*; the chess game between MacReady (Kurt Russell) and the computer; the scientists standing around the rectangular hole in the ice; and the breaking through the door with the ax by Childs (Keith David). Devising a sequel to Scott's horror/sci-fi classic, James Cameron—a keen and overt admirer of Kubrick (see Hughes 2000)—made the high-concept *Aliens* (1986), which also heavily and reverently quotes Kubrick.

Using special effects strongly informed by *2001*, the opening scene shows a small spacecraft approaching and docking with a larger one, where the protagonist, Ripley, lies in deep sleep inside a cryogenic pod. After evoking Krzysztof Penderecki's music over the opening titles, here James Horner's score pastiches the delicate adagio from Aram Khachaturian's ballet suite *Gayane*, famous for having illustrated the opening of the "Mission to Jupiter" segment, and the majestic, floating motion of the Discovery One ship in outer space.[8] Cameron, admittedly the most successful cinema entrepreneur of the last thirty years, took his cue from the master from at least two perspectives: first, in playing with generic boundaries in an attempt to probe the frontiers of commercial cinema, turning each new film, even beyond its blockbuster nature, into an event. But unlike Kubrick, Cameron's high-concept films—in typical popular, postmodern fashion—blend horror, war film, and sci-fi auspiciously, as they do the period drama and the action film, but fail to elevate these genres to art-house status.[9] Contrary to HAL 9000's murder of the Discovery's crew, which resonates with deep philosophical echoes, *Aliens* is merely filled with a populist denunciation of corporate greed and the military-industrial complex, and when the alien species coveted as a military weapon turns against humans, it is not philosophy so much as commingling of various substances (oil, blood, alien goo, and acid) which ensues. It is as though slime were a necessary element of even the most earnest homage—an impression confirmed by such fare as Panos Cosmatos' obsessive, nightmarish trip into *2001*'s imagery, *Beyond the Black Rainbow* (2010)—all style and no substance whatever.[10]

A modernist by any account (albeit, as Jameson and Elsaesser indicate, of a belated kind), whose films, unlike popular postmodernist fare, resist simple consumption and commodification, Kubrick, like Alfred Hitchcock before him, was a master experimenter of the film form, playing with genre cinema conventions to transcend or deflect them, and whose influence spans multiple areas of filmmaking, as is plain to see. But whereas the most gifted of Hitchcockian inheritors (it suffices to think of the takes on *Vertigo* [1958] by Michelangelo Antonioni, Chris Marker, and Brian De Palma) managed to appropriate his films' deeper meanings and lessons in filmmaking, all the while borrowing his motifs (the vanishing woman, the blonde/brunette nexus, the trope of voyeurism, etc.), to do the same with Kubrick seems like a daunting task. The reason, here as elsewhere, is of a historical nature. Indeed, the aforementioned filmmakers borrowing from Hitchcock still operated within an "industrial" (if technically already postindustrial or late capitalist) world, their act of allusion and citation already tainted with the implications of postmodernity but still capable of articulating a dialogue between the pre-Second World War sensibility Hitchcock carried from Europe to the United States and the zeitgeist of postwar Europe and America. Kubrick's lesser acolytes, meanwhile, tend to reduce their citations to the level of pastiche or pure surface-level quotation, succumbing to the exhaustion of forms characteristic of the postmodern era, but perhaps, more importantly, to its inability to see the past as anything else other than a kind of surface or "style." As Fredric Jameson writes

> in a post-industrial world, as the sheer difference of increasingly distinct and eccentric individualities turns under its own momentum into repetition and sameness, as the logical permutations of stylistic innovation become exhausted,

the quest for a uniquely distinctive style and the very category of "style" come to seem old-fashioned. . . . The result, in the area of high culture, was the moment of pastiche in which energetic artists who now lack both forms and content cannibalize the museum and wear the masks of extinct mannerisms. (82–83)

And indeed, those craftsmen who still borrowed from Kubrick or Hitchcock in the 1980s and the 1990s (the neo-noir, Phil Joanou's *Final Analysis* [1992], etc.) were too far removed, too entrenched already in the neoliberal moment, to summon in any productive way the philosophy of the master of suspense, indulging instead in a score of clichés. Kubrick's more recent followers, coming themselves at least twenty, and usually thirty, forty, or fifty years later, handle cliché and pastiche from at least two general positions. Some, indeed like the Hitchcockian epigones of the 1990s, indulged very much in gestures of empty citation and pastiche of themes and subjects, as for instance in the man-ape motif, as exemplified by such grotesque and derivative films as *Kong: Skull Island* (Jordan Vogt-Roberts, 2017) (apparently, you must quote Kubrick one way or the other when making a film involving weapon-wielding apes!); others attempted somehow to go deeper, trying to summon Kubrick's ghost, spirit, and worldview: Matt Reeves' overambitious reflection on evolution and survival, *War for the Planet of the Apes* (2017), blends *2001*'s evolving apes, a snowy mountain resort akin to *The Shining*'s Overlook Hotel and the militarist, de-humanizing imagery of *Full Metal Jacket*, all the while attempting to convey a deeper message about the future of mankind. A third, most productive position, is embodied by an auteur of the ilk of David Lynch, a successful heir to Hitchcock and Kubrick in equal part, able to channel and sublate their art and to turn it into his own. As has been noted frequently, Lynch has often revisited and rehearsed Hitchcockian tropes and motifs (his obsession with the blonde-brunette motif in *Lost Highway* [1996] a case in point). What is less known is that, thrilled that Kubrick commended his *Eraserhead* (1977), Lynch has since kept on discreetly quoting the American master as well. This can be seen for instance, as Rick Warner points out, in the atom bomb mushroom cloud and Penderecki's music in *Twin Peaks: The Return* (2017). But we also find Kubrickian echoes in *Wild at Heart* (1990), a film that freely blends entire chunks of American film history: in one scene, Marietta Fortune (Diane Ladd) plasters her face with red lipstick to an ominous, rumbling tune, alluding to *The Shining*'s "REDRUM" scene, also channeling the demented vibe of the film's last act. As for Bobby Peru's (Willem Dafoe) seduction of Lula (Laura Dern) in a seedy motel room, it obliquely evokes the encounter and "seduction" of Delbert Grady and Jack Torrance, two characters from two different realms—the sort of interpenetration which Lynch's cinema has made its "dread and mutter." Summoning more than motifs, indeed channeling and re-appropriating Kubrick's spirit in terms of tone and atmosphere, as Warner illustrates, Lynch borrows "a suspenseful atmosphere of dread," different in essence from Hitchcockian suspense, directly from Kubrick: "[Lynch's] practice of environmental dread and suspense is Kubrickian, not so much because of obsessive nods to certain Kubrick films . . . but because of elective affinities between artists whose styles overlap." "With both Lynch's and Kubrick's immersive lightshows," Warner goes on, "dread involves—on top of acute uneasiness and disorientation—a sense of awe. This tonal complexity revives an archaic meaning of "dread," wherein fear of something powerful inspires reverence and surrender." This is a late updating of the sublime, to which spectators of Kubrick's and Lynch's films are accustomed: "In short, the aesthetics of Kubrickian dread partake in the first movement of the sublime without giving us the subsequent uplift of regained superiority over our environment," with a sensation of "dissolution of the self" attached to it, accounting for the vertiginous fascination and attraction generated by the films—a mysterious and enthralling call of the void. Lynch's approach differs from those filmmakers who explicitly quote Kubrick without pursuing the deeper meaning of the affect that his films carry. In this, Lynch is also much closer to Kubrick as an auteur in terms of bridging the popular/art divide.

Motivic and tonal approaches, which also include stylistic quotations (camera movements and special effects), are only one visible way of channeling an auteur, as Lynch's work illustrates, though it would make sense that the visual would govern such approaches in the case of Kubrick. Yet the essence of Kubrick's cinema and its ultimate appeal lies beyond, touching upon something ineffable, invisible, and coded deeply into the texture of sounds and images. A photographer himself before he became a film director and influenced by the works of Weegee and Diane Arbus, Kubrick devised striking images whose unsettling strangeness remains imprinted in the minds of film directors and informs their aesthetics, accounting for the often vapid or sterile attempts at quoting them (the appeal of their "weird" or "cool" nature). Those filmmakers and film students who do only this, however, are oblivious to the fact that the power of images such as Arbus's and Kubrick's do not come from the striking physical appearance of their subjects or the uncanny emotion they summon, but from their unknowability that nonetheless calls itself to our affective or intuitive attention. As Arbus put it: "A photograph is a secret about a secret. The more it tells you, the less you know." Kubrick, who refused clear-cut endings and, in true modernist fashion, cultivated polysemous, multilayered narratives and obliqueness in his films, resisting simple interpretation and inviting repeated viewing, understood this. Edgar Reitz, who oversaw the dubbing of *Eyes Wide Shut* (1999) in German, put it very similarly: "Kubrick's theme is something invisible. Th[is] makes him a true artist, it shows how he understands that the art of film is never about the visible, although the camera is always fanatically grasping for the world of stimuli that can be grasped by the senses and is constantly trying to bring these within its ambit and draw satisfaction from it" (248). In short, while Kubrick's visual imprimatur is a key to entering his universe, it is his deeper understanding of the medium's power and capabilities that account for his deep, lasting influence.

The reason for the depth and the invisible nature of the real authorial signature in Kubrick also has to do with the monumental amount of research and thought that went into his work, imbuing it with an almost palpable temporal and material density (not least through the fabled excessive or mind-numbing repetition of the same take). This allows for the creation of more than images and sounds, but outright diegetic worlds and universes, demonstrating the need for a vast, immense, seemingly senseless or uneconomical expenditure of energy and human work—a sacrifice, no less—to be invested and consented to in order to allow, as Alex Nemerov puts it in his study of the concert scene in *Barry Lyndon*, for a single, singular "Moment of Truth" to emerge. Such moments, the fruit of a long and rich artistic and literary tradition before being expressed through film by Kubrick, will, in turn, resonate deeply with the viewer's own life and experience (not least in the case of Nemerov, who is Diane Arbus's nephew), allowing for a sense of belonging in a greater intellectual and spiritual whole that art expresses and encompasses. Key moments in Kubrick are, thus, despite their recognizability or quotability, embedded in a whole that goes beyond them, gesturing beyond themselves, which is yet another reason why their superficial citation often rings so hollow and fetishistic, as though reducing a whole world to the status of a single ad-like cliché. At their best, Kubrickian followers—David Lynch, who is also a talented painter, but also Paul Thomas Anderson, are cases in point—manage to avoid this problem, accomplishing a similar feat to the master himself.

Kubrick's Tune

Kubrick's noted fascination with war, destruction, and technological progress clashed with his romantic individualism, expressed among other things through his love of classical music ("Never has a committee written a symphony," as he put it himself [in Reitz, 249]). The use of music as motif and as a strong carrier of philosophy and affect distinguished Kubrick in many ways from his contemporaries—his work with temp tracks, as Adrian Daub illustrates, which were kept for the final soundtrack, endowing the films with a choreographic, sometimes operatic, and even epic quality—and has inspired countless filmmakers since. Daub shows how a musical, flux-like sensitivity characterized Kubrick's method: "the distinct modes of deploying music, and of integrating music into the process of assembling a film, would come to structure Kubrick's oeuvre going forward—and to inaugurate a whole new musical vocabulary for composers composing for art films, one that entwined original composition, explicit pastiche and citation in ways that allowed the audience to participate in the process by which film-music makes meaning."

To name but a few (ranging from apt but artless craftsmanship to quirky, ironic artistry) post-Kubrickian directors working with temp tracks, we find the operatic opening of *Melancholia* (Lars von Trier, 2011), staging in slow motion the deadly ballet of planets to the sound of Richard Wagner, a clear riff on the spaceship ballet of *2001*. Back on earth, honoring Kubrick's hospitality to pop music, the exciting drums of Iggy Pop's "Lust for Life" and the beats of Blondie and Damon Albarn animate Danny Boyle's *Trainspotting* (1996), a film which quotes and tries to update *A Clockwork Orange*'s disaffected youth for 1990s Scotland.[11] Elsewhere, the director's *Sunshine* (2007) explicitly references *2001*'s visuals, but does not follow Kubrick's musical lead. Terrence Malick, meanwhile, uses music to suggest that love, mercy, and compassion are keys to the meaning of life on Earth, and the only way to reach toward a form of transcendence, if not eternity (as the mother tells her sons in *The Tree of Life* [2011]: "Unless you love, your life will flash by"). This simple philosophy undergirds Malick's trademark moments of epiphany, wrapped in whiffs of the Emersonian sublime (see also *The Thin Red Line* [1998], *The New World* [2005], and *Song to Song* [2017]) and reinforced by a mix of classical tunes very much in keeping with the tradition of the temp track championed by Kubrick, but without any of the latter's rigor or irony, and therefore often bordering on (if not lapsing into) kitsch. It should also be noted that both Boyle and Malick resort to voice-over(s) in ways that also owe much to Kubrick's work with reinventing what had become, by the 1960s and the 1970s, a hackneyed technique. Reverent nods to Kubrick's unforgettable work with music are also reprised in the form of pastiche, be it in postmodern fashion, as in James Horner's aforementioned score to James Cameron's *Aliens*, or in a more refined and complex idiom—as in Jonny Greenwood's work for Paul Thomas Anderson, which borrows from Krzysztof Penderecki and Bob Harris (whose music Kubrick used in *The Shining* and *Lolita* [1962], respectively). In both Anderson's and Kubrick's films, the use of music is a factor of aesthetic pleasure as well as of irony, producing a rich, double discourse.[12]

Enter the Brain

Kubrick's phenomenological import to cinema, particularly the psychedelic, abstract imagery of *2001*, and its correlation to the intake of hallucinogenic drugs, constitutes another important part of his legacy. This aspect of his work relates to its concern with subjective states and with the "expandable" status of the mind more broadly; it aligns with another motif dear to the director, as Thomas Elsaesser indicates, namely that of characters confronted with radical dilemmas and extreme situations (and the violence implicit to cinema). Ken Russell's flawed but intriguing *Altered States* (1980) conducted a similar experiment, following in Kubrick's footsteps—but literalizing the experimentation with psychedelic drugs and showing the protagonist failing to achieve superman status: not becoming a Star Child, but rather first regressing to the state of man-ape. More recently, Gaspar Noé, who holds *2001* above any other film, has eagerly recreated the film's psychedelic journey throughout his filmography, which constitutes a vast enterprise in the phenomenology of narcotics and probing of the limits of subjectivity: *Irreversible* (2002), *Enter the Void* (2009), and *Climax* (2018) all feature direct quotes of *2001*, including one of the film's posters seen in the characters' bedroom, and an aborted fetus meant to evoke the Star Child. The psychedelic dimension of Kubrick's film is also referred to in Ciro Guerra's *Embrace of the Serpent* (*El abrazo de la serpiente* [2015]), a somewhat glossy and derivative, but not altogether uninteresting, evocation of experiential limits. In its final sequence, the film abandons its Herzogian tale of a European man lost in the Latin American wilderness for a hallucinatory scene expressing an immaterial journey: following the consumption of some potent drugs, the explorer's soul leaves his body, and the film moves from black and white cinematography to a smorgasbord of colorful, kaleidoscopic aerial shots.

As Gilles Deleuze indicated, some filmmakers lay on the side of the body, while others on that of the brain—Kubrick serving of course as the epitome of the latter tendency. Instances of brain allegory, Deleuze notes, abound in the films (the war room in *Dr. Strangelove, or, How I Learned to Stop Worrying and Love the Bomb* [1964], the maze in *The Shining*, etc.), albeit closely connected to bodily imagery (the sexual humor, the bleeding hotel, etc.). Kubrick also correlated the theme of psychedelic experience with overall interiority and cerebrality (*2001* as the "ultimate trip" and a "mind expanding" experience). What is depicted in Kubrick's films is thus, like the psychedelic experience, a world that is already a mental construct rather than some kind of ostensibly shared external reality; yet this does not mean in any way that they reveal some kind of underneath or "inner truth." The brain remains the hidden organ, separated from the world by a membrane, or the skull, a form of separation that Kubrick's films attempt to translate into filmic terms; this recalls the import Arbus assigns to the invisible, which governs Kubrick's films from behind the visible surface. This points to the lineage between his oeuvre and the work of all cerebral or hyperintellectual filmmakers, and their shared love of systems and algorithmic thinking, which push the very limits of human cognitive abilities (think of Shane Carruth's *Primer* [2004] and *Upstream Color* [2013]). But the cerebral all too often carries associations of coldness, a charge that has been leveled against Kubrick and his films, and led to mistaken alignments of his oeuvre with that of, say, David Cronenberg: the Canadian filmmaker's works are all too often overly intellectual and detached from the brain/body nexus, for all their investigation of the "new flesh" promoted by disease, accidents, drugs, or scientific experiments. By the same logic, it would also be a mistake to detect too much of a Kubrickian influence on filmmakers on the "body" side, such as Quentin Tarantino (even though the latter has explicitly borrowed from Kubrick, just as he has from countless other filmmakers). Conversely, obsessiveness and systemic, mathematical approaches, inspired by Kubrick among others, can be detected in Darren Aronofsky's early work, as in the "systems" of *Pi* (1998) and *Requiem for a Dream* (2000), but also, if more allegorically, in *mother!* (2017), a film informed deeply by Kafkaesque absurdism and a sense of menace straight out of Harold Pinter, but also featuring echoes of Kubrick (the bleeding house trope). In this *huis clos*, which represents the artist's dark inner space, Aronofsky demonstrates how the protagonist writer's compulsive desire for inspiration (the muse he ends up consuming over and over again) and, further, to master time is acquired through a repetition of the creative act. Conversely, the film shows how the mastery of creative act comes about through the mastery of time and repetition. Of course, this also applies in the case of filmmaking, and so *mother!* illuminates Kubrick's concern with systems and repetition (the infamous hundreds of takes driving actors to exhaustion and to the verge of nervous breakdown) as a key to perfection, but not without its thankless, dehumanizing side. On a less sinister note, and while, besides his constant and stimulating experimenting with genre, he cannot directly be correlated to Kubrick, Steven Soderbergh ranks nonetheless among the most cerebral contemporary mainstream auteurs (not least in his manifest thirst for problem-solving and quasi-scientific innovation in his mise-en-scène and storytelling). Also, while he did not list it in his "top ten," Soderbergh, like Noé, has held a clear fascination for *2001*, enough that he conducted a labor of love experiment consisting in an entire re-editing of the film, entitled *The Return of W. De Rijk* (2015). In it "Soderbergh streamlines things, while offering a more fragmented structure. HAL 9000 appears intermittently throughout and is more directly linked to the monolith" (Rick Warner, email exchange with the editor).[13] This, in and of itself, is as strong a testament as any to a deep investment in and obsession with the film, and the Deleuzian "brain as screen" as one could think of.

Dark Side of the Brain: Kubrick's Polysemous Cinema

There is a dark side to the brain, as there is to any celestial orb, no doubt: the systemic, technological, "Kabbalistic" intricacy of Kubrick's cinema, coupled with his wish for privacy (and consequent aura of secrecy), have led to a score of conspiracy theories surrounding his oeuvre, attributable less to the director's lifestyle and more to the mystery, dual nature, complexity, or obscurity of the films (the flip side of their luminous popular appeal), which feeble or paranoid minds see as part of some dark, secret project. This conspiratorial thinking has perhaps reached new levels due to a phenomenon that in some senses repeats in macrocosmic terms what occurs in Kubrick's films on a microcosmic level, namely one enabled by the internet, through which sheer density of information only seems to strengthen the need to appeal to some hidden logic or agent behind it all—in short, to become paranoid. *Room 237* offers a small digest of these theories, from the faux moon landing of the Apollo spacecraft, presumably directed by Kubrick on a studio set, to the "code" revealing in *The Shining*, the director's "deal" with the US government to do so, to the disturbing secret societies imagery *of Eyes Wide Shut*.[14] As Daniel Fairfax interrogates and elucidates at one and the same time,

> why is it that [*The Shining*] in particular should incite such a multitude of interpretation, whose perpetual accumulation shows no signs of abating, even now, nearly four decades after its initial release? What is it about Kubrick, what is it about his film, that leads scholars, critics, enthusiasts and conspiracy theorists alike to produce such a voluminous outpouring of analysis?

Fairfax attributes the film's maze-like appeal to the way its many narratives and subtextual strands "often merge together in the mind of the spectator, particularly on an initial viewing, transforming their disparate standpoints into a pleonastic stew of film interpretation." The epitome of a film calling for and resisting Jamesonian cognitive mapping at one and the same time, *The Shining* is, quite simply, a hall of mirrors and maze of a film, uniting thought experiment and the appeal of the cinema of attraction. This combination is rare enough that it would necessarily invite excessive or esoteric analyses, which have certainly become more culturally prevalent across the board in the age of the internet.

A thick and unsavory bone in the Kubrickian "stew," allegations of conspiracy theory have died hard ever since becoming a currency, shortly following the release of *Eyes Wide Shut* and the strange mockumentary *Dark Side of the Moon* (*Opération Lune*, William Karel, 2002). This "rogue spirit" of Kubrickian exegesis has been replayed in two very different ways of late: *Under the Silver Lake* (David Robert Mitchell, 2018) channels numerous Kubrickian (but also Hitchcockian, Lynchian, and many other) tropes and motifs to represent a paranoid character (Andrew Garfield) slowly losing his mind in a sea of misinterpreted codes—an interesting postmodern riff, if anything, on the conundrum of dealing with the human mind's failing to deal with the internet, algorithms, and artificial intelligence, rather than on the misdeeds of some obscure evil force. Much the opposite happens in the case of *Hereditary* (Ari Aster, 2018), a film that attempts to reiterate the feats of *Rosemary's Baby* (Roman Polanski, 1968) and *The Shining* in reinventing the horror genre. The film endorses a dark, nihilistic worldview, wherein simple folk are merely pawns in the hands of a Satanist cult and are sacrificed for the realization of the latter's dark project, a "new world order" of sorts ("Hail Paimon!"). But there too the film may evoke the anxiety procured, in our restless global political unconscious, by the supplanting of humanism by trans-human and nonhuman agencies. For John Pitseys, at any rate, the conspiratorial streak seen by many in the films of Kubrick is pure drivel: indeed, Pitseys argues in a Cartesian manner that everything in Kubrick that is to be known is in plain sight, right on the surface, under our very noses. There are no conspiracies, no grand architects of the universe, no secret codes or societies any more than there ever was a faked moon landing, no access to a real world that remains outside of our purview or grasp, Pitseys explains, elsewhere than in paranoid or overactive spectators' imaginations. Kubrick's films are not about implicit transactions, but about explicit rules of the game, even as the latter may be ignored or misunderstood by some, as is the case of *Barry Lyndon*'s upstart protagonist. That they generate an aura of mystery has to do with their artistic complexity and cinematic mastery, and not with some dark force or hidden acts. While some would disagree with Pitseys, perhaps Edgar Reitz's insight is helpful here in order to distinguish the hidden from the invisible: "Kubrick's film is about the secret that is hidden behind the eyes, beneath the skin's surface, behind the tenderness of the beloved, . . . the true voyeuristic aspect of film art" (248–49). Not that Pitseys's and Reitz's views are irreconcilable: reasonable and rational minds will engage with the world in a reasonable, rational and methodic manner—as Kubrick himself did no doubt.

Pansy Duncan illustrates how, without a hint of conspiratorial thought, the layered and complex nature of Kubrick's films always calls for productive additional readings, like an unending well of interpretation. "Oil is murder!" screams Duncan's account of *The Shining*, in which blood can be equated with oil in Kubrick (Paul Thomas Anderson replays this analogy literally in *There Will Be Blood* [2007]), the gore of the film becoming a commentary on the economic angst of the 1970s. Duncan contends that, torrents of blood notwithstanding, the sense of dread famously induced by the film converges not around blood, but around crude oil. "In this respect, *The Shining* moves beyond . . . 'human fear in a human world' to connect with . . . the 'energy unconscious,' tapping into contemporary anxieties about Western petrocultures' radical dependence on oil." An affect studies scholar of note, Duncan attends to the film's "material register rather than to its representational register, identifying moments of substitution in which petroleum or petroleum derivatives take the place of blood as the object of what Linda Williams refers to as horror's signature scenes of 'gross display.'" *The Shining* thus achieves two effects:

> On the one hand, it speaks to contemporary anxieties about Western petrocultures' reliance on a resource whose availability, by the late 1970s, was increasingly in question and whose environmental effects seemed increasingly nefarious. On the other, it retroactively reframes the familiar logic of the 1970s "New Regime" horror, of which the film appeared to mark the generic apotheosis, as a genre awash in oil.

Perhaps Nathan Abrams, who here assesses some of Kubrick's "Jewish heirs"—Mike Leigh, the Coen Brothers, David Mamet, and Darren Aronofsky—has given us one of the most illuminating interpretive keys to understanding the double and layered nature of Kubrick's cinema, his dual popularity as a high modernist and commercially successful filmmaker, and to solving, at least temporarily, the conundrum of the intimations of a hidden message in his cinema. Abrams argues here and in his *Stanley Kubrick: New York Jewish Intellectual* (2018) that alongside each surface narrative in his films, Kubrick offered, through his signature method of misdirection, another subsurface narrative, centered on his Jewish identity. Kubrick may not have been religious, but the impact of Judaism is apparent in his films obliquely, typically via analogies and metaphors that incorporate extensive biblical and other Jewish and Hebrew imagery. Abrams' analysis allows us, for instance, to at last better understand the appeal of Jack Torrance in *The Shining*: what on paper was a horrible and despicable character appears to be a complex self-portrait of Kubrick himself. Parallels between Nicholson and Kubrick emerge in the documentary directed by Vivian Kubrick about the film's making (including Kubrick's very real bullying of Shelley Duvall on the set). Since Kubrick was a secular Jew, Abrams tells us, so is Torrance: he has *kopf*, is sensitive and intuitive, yet doomed to a cruel fate in the end. It is in Torrance's dual nature (as the murderous madman and as the failed mensch), more so than in Nicholson's screen charisma, that we can understand the complexity and strange fascination for the character. Through Torrance, Kubrick spoke about himself and about themes that preoccupied him, from the Holocaust (see Cocks) to his own preoccupations as a father and husband (see Ciment), and as a tormented thinker and artist haunted by ghosts—past and present—yet not any less human for all that. And, admittedly, like Jack in the labyrinth, Kubrick worked himself to death, a Theseus not following Ariadne's thread toward an exit but indeed intent on wrestling the Minotaur again and again, ever led by a perfectionist's unquenchable obsession to get the job done. In the end, Kubrick tells us, we are all double, brain and body, man and beast, at the same time.

Kubrick's Post Mortem: Contemporary Heir Apparent Auteurs

The lion's share of this collection is dedicated to contemporary "global auteurs," Kubrick's cinematic heirs of sorts in the twenty-first century, who have been channeling him most consistently and explicitly, both through motivic quotations and like-minded experimentations with genre, affect, and cinematic time. Kubrick's imprint, as many of the earlier examples suggest, was elevated and commodified, translated into musical or visual quotes, but also, more surreptitiously, into a mood, tone, or worldview, already in his lifetime. Following his death, he has acquired a quasi-prophetic aura, and these filmmakers have become his wayward disciples. While some of these have already been discussed earlier, we might add some other names, while also returning to the likes of Nolan and Anderson, in both cases considering their relationships with some of the aspects of Kubrick's work discussed thus far.

Jonathan Glazer qualifies perhaps as the master's most devout epigone, who moved from the world of commercial and music videos[15] into the cutting edge, art-house feature film scene, injecting most of his productions with a dose of obscure Kubrickian imagery. In his sophomore feature *Birth* (2004) alone, Glazer references *2001* in the jogging in the snow which opens the film; *Barry Lyndon* in the brawl during the chamber music concert; *The Shining* in the very Nicholsonian performance and features of Danny Huston, the wintry Central Park, or the doorman throwing a ball at the wall; and *Eyes Wide Shut* in the upper-class NYC setting. The director also cast two actors who had worked with Kubrick—Nicole Kidman and Arliss Howard—as brother and sister. *Under the Skin* (2013) follows suit, as its opening scene depicts the creation of Scarlett Johansson's eyeball, echoing the spaceship Discovery (while her repeating and learning words on the soundtrack mirrors the training that Keir Dullea had to undergo ahead of starring in *2001*). "I've picked [Kubrick']s pockets, really," Glazer freely admits. "People politely say 'homage,' but I probably stole his wallet" (in Giroux). Although deemed insufficiently "Talmudic" in method and spirit to merit the term of Kubrickian Jewish heir, Glazer surely pursues the project of subsurface Jewishness delineated by Abrams: think only, in *Birth*, of the very Jewish Upper East Side family, with Lauren Bacall as the lesbian matriarch Eleanor, towering over the proceedings with much ironic humor and (mutter)wit(z). The film thus obliquely speaks, like Kubrick's, to the predicament of many Jews in the early twentieth century, who, be it in California or in New York, had to parade as WASPs and celebrate Christmas to be integrated in the establishment, repeating a similar practice loaded with prejudice in Europe through the late modern period.

Such feelings of pervasive anti-Semitism, which Kubrick mentioned at times (not least in view of meeting his uncle-in-law, Nazi filmmaker Veit Harlan), no doubt resonates in the case of the cruel and acerbic humor of the Coen Brothers, whom Rodney F. Hill considers as perhaps the clearest heirs to Kubrick, pointing to direct quotations of *The Shining* in *Barton Fink* (1991) or of *Dr. Strangelove* in *Raising Arizona* (1987). "While the Coens—and Stanley Kubrick for that matter—have generally avoided, even spurned, questions regarding philosophy or any other 'deep meanings' in their films, those elements are unmistakably present throughout both bodies of work. These philosophical similarities," Hill writes, "arguably the most substantial connection between the Coens and Kubrick, relate back to the other ties, [such as] the grotesque and such willingness to question and revise one's attitude or outlook at the heart of the philosophical enterprise." "Furthermore," Hill goes on, "the uncommon level of independence achieved by Kubrick and the Coen Brothers in their respective careers is the very quality that has allowed their distinctive aesthetics and world-views to emerge." It is also worth noting how, as secular Jewish artists, the Coens share with Kubrick their status as cultural outsiders in a predominantly Christian America. This "disconnect" contributes to their ironic, distanced approaches to humor and absurdity; it further manifests itself in a wary distrust of authority and power structures (perhaps also stemming from their Jewish roots and the historical precedent of persecution of Jewish immigrant populations), evident not only in their plots but also in their relationships to the mainstream film industry, as they oscillate between more mainstream and more independent modes. The resulting parallel is found in an ethos of artistic and intellectual independence that sits alongside commercial viability. As a result, Kubrick and the Coens have managed the feat of creating distinctive cinematic works of art across various genres, with consistent aesthetic and philosophical leanings. The caveat, in the case of the Coens, is that their overpowering misanthropy and cynicism all too often overtake and obscure the deeper implications of their films. When at their finest, however, as in the wickedly funny and deeply moving *A Serious Man* (2007), the brothers have managed to recreate a blend of Jewish humor (seldom did cinema better illustrate the Yiddish saying "Der mentsh trakht un Got lakht!"—[man plans, and God laughs!]) and pessimistic humanism that endows their best films with the same universalism, dark irony, and rich ambiguity that Kubrick's films possess.[16]

Most recently, the enfant terrible of the Greek "weird wave," Yorgos Lanthimos, was hailed by the mainstream global media as channeling Kubrick when *The Favourite* (2018) drew attention to its costumes, décors, cinematography, and narrative of an upstart's ambitions to power, all very reminiscent of *Barry Lyndon* and thus "post-Kubrickian." Yet, as Pierre-Simon Gutman argues, Lanthimos had been peppering his films with unambiguous Kubrickian quotations for a while: think of the two sisters from *Dogtooth* (*Kynodonthas*, 2009) posing in a similar way to the Grady twins' ghosts in *The Shining*; the monochrome, silhouetted, black and white posters for *The Lobster* (2015), which evokes *The Shining*'s black and yellow ones; or, most pointedly, the use of Nicole Kidman and steadicam tracking shots[17] in *The Killing of a Sacred Deer* (2017), whose medical convention scene is lit and shot in a way reminiscent of *Eyes Wide Shut*'s new year's party at the Zieglers. Lanthimos' biggest concession to the mainstream and most readily consumable film, *The Favourite* (a kind of quality demographics "upgrading" of those British TV shows about royalty such as, say, *Victoria*), also boasts, next to the "Lyndonian" setting, slow cross-dissolves similar to those that rendered space and time ambiguous and uncanny in *The Shining*, and the wide-angle lens shots that reinforced *A Clockwork Orange*'s psychedelic pop-art aesthetic and spirit of cool. Yet, in what constitutes a clear sign of the times, with its entertaining critique of parliamentary politics, representing a principled but perfidious right-wing (Rachel Weisz) opposed to a wanton upstart left (Emma Stone) vying to control a decaying power figure (Olivia Colman), the film owes its satirical bent more to *Dr. Strangelove* and *Lolita* (with which it shares the aesthetic of the grotesque as analyzed by James Naremore) than to the humanism of *Paths of Glory* and the simple yet deep philosophical questions (on life, on art, and on expenditure) of *Barry Lyndon*. Gutman rightly compares and distinguishes Kubrick from Lanthimos in their humanism, taking his cue from Marcello Walter Bruno; whereas, for Bruno, Kubrick adopted the point of view of the victim, Lanthimos seems to assume that of the perpetrator, a reflection of a neoliberal age marked by less than romantic, cutthroat individualism and a waning of humanism, not least in the Greek director's economically depressed country.

Looking at the four filmmakers most extensively discussed in this collection—Christopher Nolan, Gaspar Noé, Jonathan Glazer, and Paul Thomas Anderson—I argue that Kubrick's work with time may be his important and medium-specific contribution to cinematic art. As a modernist auteur in the post-atomic age par excellence, Kubrick engaged with time in all of its aspects—psychological, chronological, and quantum. Taking my cue from Maria Pramaggiore, I argue that Kubrick's films enable the viewer to think with and about time, and that, at their best, his heirs come close to a similar effect. While a strictly postmodern pastiche approach flattens and spatializes time, the auteurs I discuss generate a new idiom of "space-time" for the neoliberal age, challenging both the reduction of the work of art to a commodity, in modernist fashion, and contemporary global cinema's war on time as Bergsonian *durée*. The complex, layered time that they create cannot be reduced to one dimension, and thus opposes neoliberalism's attempts to flatten or reduce our sense of historical contingency by promoting modes of experience through which the world appears to be a rapidly changing yet somehow eternal present, in which the past and other forms of understanding or experiencing time are brutally liquidated on a daily basis. Seen thus, the multiple experiments with cinematic time in Gaspar Noé's and Christopher Nolan's films, including of course the reverse structure of *Memento* (1999) and *Irreversible*, but also in Jonathan Glazer's and Paul Thomas Anderson's films discussed here, are eminently Kubrickian: moving past the mere use of techniques (such as slow motion, which Kubrick used so deliberately [*The Shining*, *Full Metal Jacket*, and *A Clockwork Orange*], the jumbled narration of *The Killing*, and the dissolution of a referential, "calendar" time in *The Shining*, etc.), time-distorting effects in these cases do more than underscore the intensity of the moment and suggest psychological time. When looked at as form, and from a more philosophical and political perspective, time allows for the exploration of zones of uncertainty about the stability and essentiality of our modes of existence and experience and their relationship to capitalism. Furthermore, at their finest, these filmmakers even summon Deleuzean "crystals," images of pure time, which is one of cinema's most specific capacities.

It is mostly through their play with time that Christopher Nolan's films—even as they suffer from severe screenwriting deficiencies—remain another impressive testament, in their bravura and quixotic ambition, to the lasting power of Kubrick's oeuvre. In his chapter, Mircea Deaca looks at the cognitive conundrum ("coping with the unknown") the spectator is confronted with when dealing with science fiction films, distinguishing between Nolan's and Kubrick's takes on the genre: in *Interstellar* (2014), separate instances of a lifetime coexist in a single tesseract maze that displays time in spatial terms, while also accounting for the way Nolan proposes love as the key to solving the gravity equation in the film. "Movement is hypostasized as emotion. Emotion is what moves us," Deaca writes. "Whereas for Kubrick, the Renaissance moment is figured as an epistemic leap of humanity, for Nolan, the dawn of a new era is conceived as the recovery of romantic love (love between father and daughter, son and mother, man and woman)." Reconnecting with the hypothesis whereby Kubrick's import has to do with something invisible or unknowable, Deaca's cognitive studies approach shows how "*2001* insists over and over again on the aesthetics and mysticism of movement in order to make tangible the 'unknown.'"

Their obvious differences notwithstanding, parallels between *2001* and *Interstellar* are inescapable: Nolan seems to have wanted to update Kubrick's masterpiece for the twenty-first century, with its narrative of salvation of mankind from the brink of extinction. As Hans Zimmer's score lifts the final organ chord of Richard Strauss' *Thus Spoke Zarathustra* and lets it persist on the soundtrack, however, it is as though the echo of *2001* reaches us from a distant, faraway galaxy, light-years away—a no longer retrievable world. This does not seem too far-fetched a theory: as John MacKay has observed, *Interstellar* may be using practical special effects (as opposed to computer-generated ones) and be shot on film (as opposed to digital), the film nonetheless allegorizes the shift from the age of analog to digital cinema. The journey inside the tesseract evokes a digital editing station rather than a moviola, and the protagonist communicates with the past and his daughter using Morse—a binary/digital, code. While Nolan may be nostalgic for the age of 35mm (the presence of dust in the film equated with analog film grain by MacKay) and may critique a non-sustainable world, his film nonetheless suggests that salvation and redemption must come about through a recreation of the world, not a restoration of the old planet Earth. The digital world is thus our "redemption," and that of a cinema on the brink of technological obsolescence and limitations, or outright redundancy. In this sense, it is both logical and ironic that Nolan was involved in the (un)restoration of *2001*, a brand new print of which was supposed to screen in great pomp at Cannes 2018 for the film's fiftieth anniversary. The ambition misfired: the 70mm print ended up being a formerly circulated copy—and a slightly scratched one, at that.

Such Icarus-like vying for the status of Kubrick's *epigone primo* is not Nolan's province alone, and quite a few of the directors mentioned here probably wish they could receive this badge of honor, even as most end up failing due to an excess of hubris. Here, it is impossible not to identify a fetishistic desire, the reifying of a legacy and even a human relationship, in the case of Steven Spielberg: a self-proclaimed friend of Kubrick's, the erstwhile New Hollywood wonder boy not only took it upon himself to adapt Brian Aldiss's "Super-Toys Last All Summer Long" into his *A.I. Artificial Intelligence* (2001), disregarding a large part of Kubrick's desiderata and indications in the process (for instance, Kubrick insisted that music from Strauss's *Der Rosenkavalier* be used in the film), even as he quotes him elsewhere (Gigolo Joe's pas-de-dance mimicking that of Alex in *A Clockwork Orange*). Spielberg returned to Kubrick once again more recently, finding inspiration in 3D computer game experiments and repurposing the space of the Overlook Hotel as a VR "ultimate horror" location, in a very odd yet intriguing scene of *Ready Player One* (2018).[18] While the two men no doubt maintained a close correspondence over the years, and both revolutionized Hollywood cinema through the 1970s, it is fair to say that their sensibilities and idioms were entirely different, if no less epochal and defining for the industry. No doubt the latter scarcely feels nostalgic for a time rife with such idiosyncratic individuals. Neoliberalism and corporate capitalism have made sure to get rid of visionary mavericks, sapping the creativity and genius of the likes of Spielberg and other New Hollywood filmmakers, now turned into corporate drones, obeying laws devised by trans-humanist doctrines and financial algorithms, and revering data rather than man, a situation which Spielberg's, ironically enough, *A.I.* tried to represent from a humanist perspective.

A Man and His Times, and Ours

Stanley Kubrick was born in 1928 in the Bronx, into a secular Mitteleuropean Jewish middle-class family. He grew up in a world of promises: the America of the New Deal, of industrial capitalism, and the form of entrepreneurship attached to it. His life as a young adult was marked by the dual heritage of the Second World War and the Allies' victory, evident in his deep fascination with war; the horror of the Holocaust witnessed from afar; the miracles and dangers of an accelerating, computerized, and automated society; the geopolitical East-West binary structure of the Cold War; and the euphoria of economic growth in the Western bloc under the constant threat of all-out nuclear war. Accordingly, he was a product of this era, at one and the same time a consummate businessman, filmmaker, disenchanted humanist (says Ciment: "a disillusioned romantic turned dis-illusionist" [146]), and modern master evolving in an increasingly postmodern and neoliberal environment from which he gradually retreated in his English life. From this complex substrate, coupled with superior intellectual abilities, Kubrick derived a series of epochal films, which remain at one and the same time points of reference in cinematic and technological accomplishment, and portraits of an era.

Born into quite a different world (that of a neoliberal economy, increasing degradation of the planet's resources, and disillusionment *tout court*), tired of postmodernity but marked by it, or, conversely, riding the wave of neoliberal aesthetics, the contemporary filmmakers mentioned earlier indulge with more or less ambition in gestures of pastiche, tribute, and even invocation, both of the genius or the outright mystery of Kubrick's films, or, through his films, of a bygone era in which they emerged. Some of these directors desperately grapple with Kubrickian motifs in search of some answer to some obscure question. Perhaps some of them were trapped at an early age, in front of their TV set, in the metaphorical labyrinth from which they could never extricate themselves: Being exposed to Kubrick's maze-like genius is no small matter, and not all revelation is necessarily a gift. In this sense, even if there is always value in expanding one's purview, the danger of reverence or idolizing (or some sort of sublime-induced awe, distrust, and dread) is never far when engaging with Kubrick (whether as a scholar or as a filmmaker). Perhaps dimly aware of this, in essence, and barring a few exceptions, all filmmakers quoting Kubrick are for the most part performing a safe, nostalgic, and ultimately reactionary gesture, even though yearning for good cinema in times of deep crisis of the medium is understandable, to a point. Yet at the same time, the insistence on referencing Kubrick generates new layers of historical complexity, connecting the twentieth and twenty-first centuries by raising once again, at a time when environmental threats (turned into Hollywood spectacle by the likes of Spielberg and Nolan) and artificial intelligence threaten to put an end to humanist ideology, the questions his cinema poses—about human beings, their place in the world, and their potential and limits. Kubrick's cinema thus reveals itself, in a way, as having anticipated the obsolescence or transcendence of both its medium and the category of the human itself that is now underway, refusing nostalgia through its insistence on the transience and fragility of any ontological or moral certainties.

Therefore, no assessment of Kubrick's legacy in the twenty-first century could be remotely comprehensive without a take on artificial intelligence and its trans-humanist implications. Reprising Kubrick's quote about how a committee never wrote a symphony, it is worth noting that at the time of the release of this collection, algorithms are not yet able to write a scholarly chapter, but can "compose" baroque pieces à la Bach, albeit rather uncanny and elevator music-like ones. Kubrick's vanguard work with artificial intelligence, from HAL 9000 to the unrealized brilliance of *A.I.*, has spawned countless narratives about singularity, cybernetics, and trans-humanism, often in their more dystopian, pop, and B instantiations—from James Cameron's *The Terminator* and Verhoeven's (and Ed Neumeier's) *Robocop* (1987) to Alex Garland's *Ex Machina* (2014) and its mainstream updating of the Turing test. Tracing this lineage of artificial intelligence, Marta Figlerowicz notes the intersubjective and "interspecies" dialogue proposed by Kubrick:

> In Kubrick's work and in the work of later directors influenced by him, . . . thinking machines are challenged to deepen their immersion in the human sensory field. Such embodied computers critique naïve views of thinking and awareness as associated with disembodied autonomy, a release from social ties and inborn wants. Indeed, they suggest that a great part of our alienation from ourselves comes not simply from the machines we create, but from the misguided hopes of detachment we place in them.

Surely the spate of films dealing with artificial intelligence released over the last fifty years all find a putative if wayward progenitor in HAL 9000, even as it is in fact, as recent scholarship has come to realize (and the darkest speculation on the subject has quickly made grist for its dystopian mill, too), the inscrutability of the black monolith's "signal" that may define the real relationship between humans and algorithms, once the latter create their own mode of communication and turn the human brain from the highest manifestation of cognitive and analytical ability to junk in the scrap yard of evolutionary history. Yet therein lies perhaps the central contradiction of Kubrick's cinema, for all the irony and humor of the master: the tension between the terrifying need to overcome humanity's limitations (the imperative of technological progress) and the attachment to humanist values. As a result, his films deliver a layered worldview, and messages that some may consider objectionable or disturbing.

The issue of intersubjectivity dealt with by Figlerowicz raises the question of encounter with the other (be they alien or algorithm), but also with the self. Kubrick's humanism is at times difficult to reconcile with a form of sadism and prejudice perceived by some in his films: despite P. T. Anderson's claim serving as this introduction's incipit, not all see themselves as "children of Kubrick," and many will frown, for instance, at his seeming homophobia (surely he throws a measure of ridicule on LGBT characters: an inmate trying to seduce Alex during service in *A Clockwork Orange*, the two soldiers bathing and cavorting gaily in *Barry Lyndon*, or the hotel clerk in *Eyes Wide Shut*); the cruelty of his filmic situations involving the suffering of the elderly, women, and children; and the rather implacable and systemically imprisoning worldview his cinema instantiates. As Robert Kolker notes, the dismemberment of female mannequins in the midst of a fight between two men in *Killer's Kiss* (1954) represents a textbook example of every charge of misogyny ever leveled at film noir, and Kubrick remains, for all intents and purposes, a very phallic, patriarchal filmmaker. In this context, it is unsurprising to note the very masculine character of the range of filmmakers covered here, as Kubrick does not seem to have inspired women filmmakers until now, even if his films always contain their own internal critique. For instance, watching *The Shining* today puts the emphasis on neoliberal precarious and fluid labor and its relationship to domestic violence: the master may have been cold, calculating, and cerebral to the extreme, but he privileged cinematic emotion over pure ratiocination, and was far too sophisticated and informed a mind to propose a simplistic or unequivocally misogynistic worldview.

Suggesting another way to approach these issues, Seung-hoon Jeong reads Kubrick as illustrating realities of power rather than paying lip service to discursive humanism, seeing his representations of beleaguered and sometimes ridiculed sexual or racial groups as disillusioned rather than prejudiced. Jeong shows how the absurdist and existentialist Kubrick (as a product of his era) today deserves less attention than the biopolitical Kubrick. "What he highlights more than the subjective experience of the absurd world," Jeong argues,

> is the objective structure of how power generates, controls, and abandons subjects under and beyond the law. Here, biopolitics concerns not only Foucauldian biopower that governs the regulation of populations and the subjugation of their bodies to the nation-state, but primarily Agambenian sovereignty that creates the boundary between subjectivized bodies in the State and mere bodies cast out of it.

It is on this biopolitical ground, established and sustained by sovereignty, that inner-state political games are played out. In short, Kubrick looks at the world through a biopolitical lens, Jeong argues, and his gaze upon minorities is more sympathetic than meets the eye or than his literal representations suggest.

If we follow Jeong's lead, we may consider two more contemporary representations of biopower in relation to Kubrick, both of which represent seemingly ideal, truly gender-equal, and race/color-blind societies: one is "softly" totalitarian, as imagined by neoliberalism with its society of spectacle; the other is in a populist, militarist, fascist vein of biopolitical extremes. The former scenario finds expression in Peter Weir's

The Truman Show (1998), a film showing how a society of information and surveillance becomes its own absurd nightmare. Kubrickian echoes are conveyed through subtle references to *The Shining*, as when Marlon, the "best friend," looking for Truman, asks, in Jack Torrance fashion "come out, come out, wherever you are." As for Christoph, the sinister, God-like, all-seeing perfectionist, scrutinizing every movement of his "child," he is a rendition of Kubrick's obsession with control (rigging his house with cameras, etc.). The film also instantiates a feedback loop of image consumption of Baudrilliardian simulacra ever unbroken, even as Truman escapes the studio set in the end. Another grotesque version of such "ideal" society, equal in terms of gender but never in terms of class, can be found critiqued in Paul Verhoeven's *Starship Troopers* (1997), which combines and revisits the space opera of *2001* and the military training of *Full Metal Jacket*, filtering them through an ironic, misanthropic lens. Verhoeven's films, when at their best, cleverly enmesh biopolitics and stories of greed and ambition, wherein humans—particularly the other (the woman, the neighbor, and the queer figure)—are consistently *abjectified*, left with few other options but to "waste" their enemies, or "fuck" with their spouses. Yet, while the surviving protagonists of *Starship Troopers*, like Alex in *A Clockwork Orange* and Private Joker at the end of *Full Metal Jacket*, seem fearless and happy, Jeong asks provocatively: can we claim the same?

A Dead Star's Light

Hardly ever eliciting sheer indifference, Kubrick and his films invite myriad responses and assessments; they are infinitely rich, complex, and not devoid of shadows. This complexity and contradictory quality only fuels the mystery and fascination that his oeuvre continues to arouse. As Michel Ciment wrote, one feels somewhat powerless or defeated when trying to tackle the complexity of Kubrick.[19] This is not least the case for this collection, which explores the complexity of the network of implications of his legacy—extending in all directions, and multiplying like the rhizomatic and monstrous yet hypnotic hallucinations of Oscar in *Enter the Void*. One has to accept the limitations of one's approach, hoping it contributes to a greater enterprise.

This assessment of Kubrick's legacy, and of a certain idea of cinema, is occurring at a moment when VOD platforms such as Netflix are causing commercial cinema to rethink its goals, in a challenge perhaps even greater than that posed by commercial television in the 1960s, which was one of the factors that led to the collapse of the studio system. Jean-Luc Godard, an admirer of the early Kubrick, then a cautious skeptic of his later works, closes his paean to cinema, life, and the Arab world, *Le livre d'image* (2018), with a quote from the notorious dance scene from Max Ophüls's *Le Plaisir* (1952), where an older man dons a mask to pretend he can still cavort like his younger self, before collapsing to the floor in exhaustion. The implied reference is of course to Godard himself, but also, perhaps, an indirect nod to Kubrick, who much admired Ophüls (and indeed delved into the Austrian milieu beloved by the latter through his adaptation of Schnitzler's *Traumnovelle* with *Eyes Wide Shut*, which of course also prominently features masks). An artistic, stylistic, and philosophical legacy is measured as much by the achievements of its offspring as it is by the shadow of their (sometimes half-forgotten) forebears, whose actual height may be properly assessed only once they have fallen down, like Ophüls's exhausted dancer. Since his death, Kubrick's legacy has perhaps reached its apex, its highest level of visibility and relevance (his films acknowledged as masterpieces and generating ample emulation among his peers, critics, and film students). Only time will tell if this is actually a good thing and a sign of a promising future for cinema—or, conversely, if the master's legacy is a dangerous, poisonous or sterile one. Only after Kubrick joins Ophüls in being absorbed and filtered into a socio-cultural substrate, operating in more removed, subtle ways, having at last attained a geological, sediment-like status, can the legacy be properly assessed at last, even if Kubrick's cultic following may delay or resist this process. For now, like the dead star, Stanley Kubrick's oeuvre seems to live on and shine more than ever before. For all its contradictions and problematic or ideologically objectionable aspects, it retains a vital quality, generating thought in and on film, a dark dialectics that is vibrant and momentous just as it is filled with pitfalls and dead ends. Kubrick's oeuvre and legacy are akin to a maze that we may find maddening and terrifying, but that we may also learn to map and explore again and again, understanding the ultimate joy found in such exploration, or, for some, in attempts to devise their own cinematic labyrinths.

Notes

1. Elsewhere, David Bowie used Wendy Carlos's music from *A Clockwork Orange* ahead of his Spiders from Mars tour (as shown in D. A. Pennebaker's documentary of the final concert [1973]). As Rod Munday notes, Bowie also used the word "yarbles" from the "nadsat" dialect invented by Anthony Burgess for the novel, and reprised by Kubrick in the film, in his song "Girl Loves Me" (2016).
2. Perhaps the most significant and conspicuous manifestation of this project of enshrining Kubrick as part of the world cultural canon, the Exhibition opened in 2004, and is still touring the world to this day. It displays a large amount of props, documents, annotated scripts, archival notes, and equipment the filmmaker worked with, drawing massive crowds wherever it is held. In his discussion of the Exhibition, Jihoon Kim elects to turn a blind eye to the somewhat morbid nature of the otherwise indeed impressive post-cinematic phenomenon of a migration from "the black box to the white cube." Instead, Kim analyses how the Exhibition partakes in the "the exhibition of cinema," distinguished here from "the cinema of exhibition," both of which arose around the time of the director's death. Kim illustrates how, while never a gallery artist himself (unlike a few other masters of cinema), Kubrick has been an inspiration not only for his peers, but also for artists in other fields, such as video and installation art (works by Jennifer Steinkamp, Jane and Louise Wilson, Brice Dellsperger).
3. For a study of Kubrick's more direct legacy, and the way his films are being shown, reassessed or re-appropriated in the twenty-first century, see Broderick (2019).
4. In her presentation during the Stanley Kubrick Life and Legacy conference held at the Lorentz Center in Leiden in July 2019, Kate McQuiston proposed examples of

feminine reappropriation and implicit critique of Kubrick, ranging from Shiman's bunnies video, or the pointed references to Kubrick's films to be found in the novel *Goldfinch* by Donna Tartt, to the memoir *M train* by Patti Smith.

5   Thanks go to Joy McEntee, Daisy Baxter, Elisa Pezzotta, Eugeni Ruggero, as well as all the other participants of the "reception" panel I chaired at the Kubrick Legacy conference in Leiden, for their comments and suggestions, which went a long way toward informing this section of the introduction.

6   Scott was of course not the only filmmaker to borrow from the revolutionary aesthetics and effects of *2001*: the vast majority of "serious" sci-fi films made since have been informed by Kubrick's film, from the recent *Moon*, *Oblivion* (Joseph Kosinski, 2013) or *Arrival* (Denis Villeneuve, 2016), all the way back to classics of the 1970s of the New Hollywood—think of *THX 1138* (1971), the first film by George Lucas, who would later enlist several of Kubrick's collaborators, including Colin Cantwell, on *Star Wars* (1977).

7   Steven Spielberg did something similar a few years later, when, in *Indiana Jones and the Temple of Doom* (1984) he cast Philip Stone, most famous for his roles as *A Clockwork Orange*, *Barry Lyndon* and *The Shining*.

8   *Aliens*' opening titles are accompanied by rumbling, ominous chords, reminiscent of those heard in Krzysztof Penderecki's *The Awakening of Jacob* (used by Kubrick in *The Shining*).

9   It is interesting to note how the war and action scenes in *Aliens*, with marine corps wielding heavy weaponry, anticipates the Vietnam section of *Full Metal Jacket*, particularly the Animal Mother character. Both films were produced almost concomitantly, in or near London.

10   Oft-encountered in failed student films, such winks at the audience through an audiovisual reference of a masterpiece are meant to create some sort of community of cinephiles, a badge of good taste or of being with the in crowd, and possibly a way to elevate and redeem what is otherwise garish and immature stuff. The increasing numbers of Hollywood films functioning through such superficial gimmicks, and the indirect statements about the horizons of cinema and humanism which these empty, mindless and dark films make are sobering indeed.

11   Another British film to channel Kubrick's film was *The Great Ecstasy of Robert Carmichael* (Thomas Clay, 2005), with its deeply revolting rape and murder of a bourgeois couple by the disaffected youth (one of whom shares with Kubrick's Alex an interest in classical music).

12   For an in-depth discussion of the irony, referentiality and playfulness of Kubrick's use of music, becoming "musicology" in its own right, see McQuiston (2008: 116–18).

13   The film sadly was removed from Soderbergh's website because of copyright complaints.

14   This Faustian pact—and the price to pay in order to access to celebrity or some other status—is intriguingly rehearsed in Brady Corbet's *Vox Lux* (2018). Whether Corbet did this deliberately or not, and although he dedicates it to the memory of Jonathan Demme, his film is first and foremost rife with Kubrickian echoes. As Conner Reed notes: "Lol Crawley's camerawork feels focus-grouped to elicit Stanley Kubrick comparisons," not least in the opening tracking shots over cars and the way the first meeting with the studio representative is framed, straight out of *The Shining*. Elsewhere, we find the mask Celeste wears in a music video, strongly reminiscent of

Eyes Wide Shut, and Willem Dafoe's ironic commentary, an ornate, grotesque version of *Barry Lyndon*'s voice-over narration.

15 Noted music video director Mark Romanek is another Kubrick aficionado, once poised to direct a prequel to *The Shining*, the as of yet unproduced *The Overlook Hotel*. Kubrick's work with music and visual rhythm no doubt explains his lasting appeal with the music video art scene. Another example is Michel Gondry, whose music video for Lenny Kravitz, *Believe* (1993), channels *2001*, a film Gondry later "sweded" in his feature film *Be Kind Rewind* (2008).

16 Another inheritor of Kubrick's mood and worldview, albeit a more discreet one than the Coens, is Alexander Payne, whose disenchanted yet bittersweet humanism counterbalances cynicism and has been a staple of his films, some of which have on occasion directly referenced Kubrick: *About Schmidt* (2002) rekindled an image of Jack Nicholson as an actor worthy of attention (a status he lost after *The Shining*, the remainder of his career degenerating into a vast enterprise in self-indulgent pastiche), while the flawed but nonetheless under-appreciated *Downsizing* (2017) quotes *The Shining* (the aerial view of the car ride), *Full Metal Jacket* (the shaving of Matt Damon's head) and *2001* (the dome protecting the downsized community, seen from ground level, evocative of the worm-eye view shots of the monolith), as undergirding reference points, or beacons, in Payne's ironic reevaluation of environmentalist doctrine, precarious labor, the shortcomings of a philosophy of progress and the neoliberal myth of a classless society.

17 On the subject of tracking shots, it is worth noting that David Fincher's signature tracking shots at ground level, perhaps the most interesting feature of his films, owe a great deal to Kubrick's camera movements from *Paths of Glory* and *The Shining*. In both directors, the camera movement evokes a pointed sense of anticipation, or even dread, correlated as they are with a sense of revelation or even transgression.

18 This literal quotation and 'recycling' of imagery from *The Shining* in mainstream cinema (more precisely, a recycling of images from locations seen in the film—all characters are impersonated by new actors) coincides with the film's recent 4K restoration/transfer (which screened at Cannes in 2019). The recent trailer to the film *Doctor Sleep* (2019), based on Stephen King's eponymous sequel to *The Shining*, features no less than twelve images lifted from Kubrick's classic, such as the aerial shots of the ride (now taking place on a snowy night), Danny on his tricycle by room 237, or the blood gushing from the elevator, to the tune of Wendy Carlos's *Dies Irae*. This is very ironic, as though King were re-appropriating and 'subverting' material from a film he publicly criticized (indeed he produced his own TV mini-series remake in the 1990s). Judging by the trailer, the film is both an adaptation of King's novel and an unauthorized sequel to Kubrick's film (it features the hotel, which was destroyed in the novel; and the maze, which did not feature in it). It is quite certain that Kubrick would never have allowed for this, had he been alive. While it is sobering to see that Warner Brothers (or any other studio) would have few scruples about making a profit on their back catalog in such a manner, the 'desecration' has an empowering, liberating side—a sense that nothing is sacred; it seems not so much that we are children of Kubrick, but rather that he belongs to all of us, for better or for worse.

19 "Every critic [...] who has attempted to come to terms with Kubrick's work has been made painfully aware of the limits of his own discourse . . . His is an oeuvre that both demands and defies analysis." (Ciment 2011: 3)

Works Cited

Abrams, Jerold J. 2009. *The Philosophy of Stanley Kubrick*. Lexington, KY: University Press of Kentucky.
Abrams, Nathan. 2018. *Stanley Kubrick: New York Jewish Intellectual*. Rutgers, NJ: Rutgers University Press.
Barthes, Roland. 1989 [1974]. *Sade, Fourier, Loyola*, trans. Richard Miller, Berkeley, CA: University of California Press.
Broderick, Michael, ed. 2019. *The Kubrick Legacy*. London: Routledge.
Bruno, Marcello Walter. 2017. *Stanley Kubrick*. Rome: Gremese.
Castle, Alison. 2011. *Stanley Kubrick's Napoleon: The Greatest Movie Never Made*. London: Taschen.
Chion, Michel. 2001. *Kubrick's Cinema Odyssey*, trans. Claudia Gorbman. London: BFI.
Ciment, Michel. 2011. *Stanley Kubrick*. Paris: Calmann Lévy.
Cocks, Geoffrey. 2004. *The Wolf at the Door: Stanley Kubrick, History, and the Holocaust*. New York: Peter Lang.
Deleuze, Gilles. 1989. *Cinema 2: The Time-Image*, translated by Hugh Tomlinson and Robert Galeta, Minneapolis: University of Minnesota Press.
Gengaro, Christine. 2013. *Listening to Stanley Kubrick: The Music in his Films*. Toronto: Scarecrow Press.
Giroux, Jack. 2014. "Jonathan Glazer On 'Under the Skin,' Kubrick's Influence and How the Easiest Part of It Was Getting . . .," *Film school rejects*, April 4, 2014. https://filmschoolrejects.com/jonathan-glazer-on-under-the-skin-kubrick-s-influence-and-how-the-easiest-part-of-it-was-getting-c7a3383e78e3.
Hughes, David. 2000. *The Complete Kubrick*. Virgin Books: Virgin Complete Directors.
Jameson, Fredric. 1990. "Historicism in *The Shining*" (1981), in *Signatures of the Visible*. New York and London: Routledge.
Jameson, Fredric. 1991. *Postmodernism: or the Cultural Logic of Late Capitalism*. London: Verso.
Kolker, Robert P. 1980. *A Cinema of Loneliness: Penn, Kubrick, Coppola, Scorsese, Altman*. New York: Oxford University Press.
Kolker, Robert P. 2016. *The Extraordinary Image: Orson Welles, Alfred Hitchcock, Stanley Kubrick, and the Reimagining of Cinema*. New Brunswick, NJ: Rutgers University Press.
Krämer, Peter, Tatiana Ljulic, Richard Daniels, eds. 2015. *New Perspectives*. London: Black Dog Publishing.
MacKay, John. 2014. "On Interstellar (2014)," https://www.academia.edu/9240536/On_INTERSTELLAR_2014 (accessed March 5, 2019).
McQuiston, Kate. 2008. "Value, Violence, and Music Recognized: A Clockwork Orange as Musicology," in Gary D. Rhodes, ed., *Stanley Kubrick Essays on His Films and Legacy*. Jefferson, North Carolina, London: McFarland, 105–22.
McQuiston, Kate. 2013. *We'll Meet Again: Musical Design in the Films of Stanley Kubrick*. Oxford: Oxford University Press.
Michelson, Annette. 1969. "Bodies in Space: Film as 'Carnal Knowledge,'" Artforum, February.
Naremore, James. 2007. *On Kubrick*. London: British Film Institute.
Pramaggiore, Maria. 2015. *Making Time in Stanley Kubrick's Barry Lyndon: Art, History, and Empire*. New York, London: Bloomsbury.

Reed, Conner. 2019. "*Vox Lux* and the Price of Greatness." Little White Lies. https://lwlies.com/articles/vox-lux-the-price-of-greatness-natalie-portman-brady-corbet (accessed August 10, 2019).

Reitz, Edgar. 2004. "Our Work Was an Exception. Directing the Dubbing of *Eyes Wide Shut*." In *Stanley Kubrick*. Kinematograph 20. Frankfurt am Main: Deutsches filmmuseum, 244–49.

Vidal, Jordi. 2005. *Traité du combat moderne. Films et fictions de Stanley Kubrick*. Allia.

1

Stanley Kubrick's Prototypes: The Author as World-Maker

Thomas Elsaesser[1]

Kubrick is like the black slab in 2001: a force of supernatural intelligence, appearing at great intervals amid high-pitched shrieks, who gives the world a violent kick up the next rung of the evolutionary ladder.

David Denby, in Baxter (1997: 233)

A Filmmaker of Extremes and of Contradictions

Stanley Kubrick (1927–1999) was a director of extremes. Extremes in his person: the "control freak" who had to interfere in every detail, down to the color of the ink people could use when writing to him; the "demented perfectionist" who drove his employees into white rages or year-long diets of tranquilizers.[2] Against this reputation as a meddling maniac endowed with uncanny ubiquity, there is the image of the taciturn recluse who since 1963 had rarely left his walled-up fortress in rural England,[3] and the man who issued gagging orders to journalists as well as putting nondisclosure contracts on anyone who worked for him.[4] Yet this need for privacy and secrecy is again confounded by his habit of not only interminable transatlantic phone conversations to friends and intimates but also early morning calls to prospective collaborators who had never met him.[5] The long-distance communicator of a thousand faxes,[6] in turn, is contradicted by reports of his vast kitchen-living room area, where people came and went all day, while a gregarious and witty Kubrick held court, giving extensive interviews to his biographer Michel Ciment.

Extremes also in his films, each of which probed the limits of some aspect of the human condition: sexuality and death, natural aggression and man-made violence, warfare and the military mind, the audible silence of space and the inaudible screams inside the nuclear family. They were nothing less than deep philosophical issues, but often packed into banal, stereotypical, or barely existent plots. Extremes, finally, in the critical opinions aroused by his films. Since the controversies sparked off by *Lolita* (1962), the drug-busts during screenings of *2001: A Space Odyssey* (1968), and the media-scandal—at least in Britain—around *A Clockwork Orange* (which eventually led to the director withdrawing it from exhibition), each film polarized the critics, making some of them unforgiving even beyond Kubrick's death. Next to an early and faithful admirer, such as Alexander Walker in London, he had, in New York's David Denby and Pauline Kael, two implacable and persuasion-proof opponents.[7] In his obituary of the director, David Edelstein could not help writing: "I'll despise Kubrick forever for associating Beethoven's Ninth Symphony, Singin' in the Rain,' and some of the most glorious works of Handel and Purcell with sadomasochism and man's inhumanity to man" (Edelstein 1999). That all these critics were willing to grant Kubrick the distinction of having been a "visionary" or "dark genius" hardly lessened the confusion either about his status as a world-famous director or the meaning of his films.

Yet these colorful contradictions, accumulating around his person(a) and his working methods—especially because they are so predictably and ritually invoked—should give us pause. They are even a little irritating in their clichéd inevitability, unless one sees them as something other than mere perversity.[8] The extremes, for instance, point to the effort required in the latter half of the twentieth century to control one's image, if one wished to remain (in and for the film industry) that totemic individualist par excellence, the Director as Auteur, and to retain the name of Artist in the wider public realm. Both opened the necessary space for Kubrick to build a very special "brand-name" and to keep its market value, under conditions when a new "Kubrick" took up to five years to appear, causing gaps much longer than the average cinemagoer's attention span. That an element of parody or pastiche should creep into such self-presentation is thus not so much a personal foible or character trait, as a structural given of "late capitalist" cultural production.

Kubrick's mythology of self-contradictions and extremes has furthermore to be seen in the context of his decision, taken around 1962, to become a one-man-studio, and to relocate this operation to Britain, a country at that time experiencing a modest revival of its indigenous filmmaking, both "new wave" (Tony Richardson, Lindsay Anderson, John Schlesinger, and Karel Reisz) and commercial (the James Bond series, for instance, successfully launched in 1963).[9] The move to Britain nevertheless did not dent Kubrick's resolve to be an American mainstream (rather than a European art cinema) director.

This focuses attention on Hollywood itself, and on the changes that intervened in the studio system in the 1960s and early 1970s. The traditional studios, as is well known, went into steep decline, beginning in the late 1950s with the rise of television, but accelerating dramatically in the 1960s. Huge losses on prestige projects such as *Hello, Dolly!* (1969), *Paint Your Wagon* (1969), or *Dr. Dolittle* (1967) had by the late 1960s led to widespread bankruptcy and the sell-off of assets, such as real estate and film libraries. Kubrick's own position did not remain unaffected, since MGM, the studio for which he had produced and directed *2001*, his most successful film, was one of the major casualties. MGM's demise forced the director, among other things, to abandon his long-nursed project to make a film about Napoleon.[10] The deal he was subsequently able to strike with Warner Brothers-Seven Arts, reputedly unique within the annals of Hollywood—complete freedom to choose his subjects; unlimited time and almost unlimited money to develop them; and retaining total control over the execution, final shape, and manner of distribution of the finished film—has to be seen within the context of the major transformations that American industrial filmmaking underwent in the period between 1968 and 1975.[11] While not contradicting the exceptionality of Kubrick's position, the Hollywood context relativizes its uniqueness. It helps, for instance, to locate the economic reasons and institutional circumstances that made such an arrangement possible, when comparing Kubrick to fellow filmmakers of his generation—most of whom during this crucial period produced box-office successes bigger than his—such as Arthur Penn (*Bonnie and Clyde* [1967]), Mike Nichols (*The Graduate* [1967]), Robert Altman (*M*A*S*H* [1972]), Roman Polanski (*Rosemary's Baby* [1968]), or William Friedkin (*The French Connection* [1971] and *The Exorcist* [1973]).

Kubrick follows in the footsteps of the first generation of author-producers after the decartelization decision (the Paramount Decree of 1948), such as Otto Preminger and Alfred Hitchcock, and the establishment of actors as producers (Warren Beatty, Robert Redford or, of course, Kirk Douglas, for whom Kubrick directed *Spartacus* [1960], after Anthony Mann was sacked). While Preminger went under, and Hitchcock managed to survive for a few more years, mainly thanks to the protective cover of Lew Wasserman at Universal, Kubrick, like Woody Allen, straddled the age divide, becoming one of the directors of the next generation (together with Martin Scorsese and Steven Spielberg) who established, via their own registered companies, a long-term professional relationship as well as a personal bond with one or two key figures in the newly re-conglomerated studios. For Kubrick, at the now Kinney-controlled Warner Brothers, these key figures were the new and flamboyant CEO Steve Ross (also a close friend of Steven Spielberg, when one remembers that *Schindler's List* [1993] is dedicated to Ross); his then deputy, Terry Semel; and Warner's man in London, Julian Senior, with whom Kubrick had worked closely since *A Clockwork Orange*. After the death of Ross, it was Semel at Time-Warner who became the recipient of Kubrick's all-hours-of-the-day-and-night phone and fax messages.[12] In addition, many of these American *auteurs* had a career-long association with a trusted executive producer. In the case of Woody Allen, for instance, it is Charles H. Joffe (continuously since *Take the Money and Run* [1969]), and for Kubrick it became Jan Harlan, descendant of Veit Harlan, who also happened to be Kubrick's brother-in-law. Concurrent, and possibly also a consideration for Warner's, was the fact that the British film industry, while unable to mount significant productions itself after the brief boom period in the 1960s, did become a major infrastructural resource for the New Hollywood in the 1970s and in 1980, not only in the case of the apparently "British," but in truth Italo-American, *James Bond* film franchise but also for such typically Hollywood blockbuster productions as *Star Wars* (1977) or *Close Encounters of the Third Kind* (1977).[13] It made Kubrick's apparent eccentricity of filming in London part of a sound Hollywood economic strategy, and put him in this respect level with director-producer-superstars such as Spielberg and George Lucas.

Kubrick's Authorship: Between One-Offs and Prototypes

If Kubrick's position was thus not quite as unique as the myth would have it, and much more embedded in the transformations of New Hollywood than his recluse "exile" existence suggested, the particular forms his "authorship" took deserve brief comment. For instance, as a way of valorizing American commercial directors, such as John Ford, Howard Hawks, or Hitchcock, the auteur theory had peaked in the mid-1960s and had started being attacked by the time Kubrick the author came to prominence (in 1968, after *2001*). So much was heard about his "death" that, according to the structuralist doctrine of the time, the author was a mere effect of the text, quite unconnected to the biographical person or even the artist with a "body" of work.[14] Unlike Altman or Allen, the Kubrick recognition effect initially attached itself not to his person, or to his work as the evolving stages of an unfolding project, but was focused on individual films, as if they were one-offs: notably *2001: A Space Odyssey*, which received scores of detailed studies, but only few of which analyzed the film in reference to Kubrick's preceding ones, which would have been the typical move of the auteurist critic.[15]

However, these one-offs can be seen in relation to another "crisis" of the Old-New Hollywood, namely, that around genre. In view of the fact that traditional genres, such as the Western, the musical comedy, the epic, and even the thriller, no longer seemed to attract the "baby boomers," Hollywood was seeking new "formulas" to woo these different (younger) audiences, and was willing to experiment with untried directors (Dennis Hopper and Bob Rafelson), untried actors (Jack Nicholson and Robert de Niro), and untried genres (the Road Movie, for instance). Kubrick's one-offs, it can be argued, fit into this strategy, and would thus become more like "prototypes." In other words, the perceived characteristics of Kubrick's working method—namely, that from film to film, he moved not only to different themes and subject matter[16] but also to different styles, forms, and techniques—did have a strategic value to his employer also, as Warner Brothers, like every other studio, was casting around for the winning combination, which could revitalize and re-energize what in spite of these transformations remained an essentially stars-and-genre-based way of making mainstream cinema.

This distinguishes Kubrick from the European author, such as Federico Fellini, Ingmar Bergman, Michelangelo Antonioni, or even R. W. Fassbinder and Wim Wenders, each of whom developed not only his own style and recurring thematics but his own genre (often helped by key actors or stars: Marcello Mastroianni, Max von Sydow, Liv Ullmann, Monica Vitti, Hanna Schygulla, and Rüdiger Vogler). By contrast, a Kubrick film rarely carries a key player over from one film to the next, and insofar as he can be associated with genres, these were once more Hollywood genres rather than auteurist genres. But even here, Kubrick's work shows interesting anomalies. He certainly pioneered a new kind of war film with *Paths of Glory* (1958), and *A Clockwork Orange* dramatically changed our idea of the Swinging London films

(Richard Lester's films with The Beatles) or the pop-art-anarchic-mayhem strand of the 1960s British Film Renaissance (John Schlesinger's *Billy Liar* [1963], and Lindsay Anderson's *If...* [1968], from which Kubrick took Malcolm McDowell), not to mention the changes *A Clockwork Orange* rang on the genre of the musical. And there is almost universal consensus that with *2001,* Kubrick re-invented the modern science fiction film, taking it definitely out of the disreputable 1950s B-genre category.

But already with *Barry Lyndon* (1975), and then again with *The Shining* (1980), the genre question becomes more complicated. To these (and other) films, Fredric Jameson has applied the label "meta-genre" films, whose typical mode is "pastiche":

> Pastiche seems to have emerged from a situation of two fundamental determinations: the first is subjectivism, the over emphasis and over-evaluation of the uniqueness and individuality of style itself—the private mode of expression, the unique "world" of a given artist, the well-nigh incomparable bodily and perceptual sensorium of this or that new claimant for artistic attention. But as individualism begins to atrophy in a post-industrial world, as the sheer difference of increasingly distinct and eccentric individualities turns under its own momentum into repetition and sameness, as the logical permutations of stylistic innovation become exhausted, the quest for a uniquely distinctive style and the very category of "style" come to seem old-fashioned.... The result, in the area of high culture, was the moment of pastiche in which energetic artists who now lack both forms and content cannibalize the museum and wear the masks of extinct mannerisms. (Jameson 1990: 82–83)

Jameson goes on to argue that, evidently, pastiche in mass culture is different from that in Thomas Mann or in Joyce. But he sees the revival of B-film genres, the mimicry of past (high culture) idioms, such as classical paintings and costume drama, and the technologically manufactured (zoom lens, light sensitive stock, and steadicam) cult of the self-consciously beautiful, "glossy" image[17] as symptoms either of what he calls elsewhere a "nostalgia for the present" or as a boredom with "the aesthetic" itself, ambiguously poised between symptom and critique of this very same facile perfection, wrought by the technologies of vision and imagining:

> Beauty and boredom: this is then the immediate sense of the monotonous and intolerable opening sequence of *The Shining*. [Kubrick's] depthless people, whether on their way to the moon [in *2001*], or coming to the end of another season in the great hotel at the end of the world, are standardized and without interest.... If Kubrick amuses himself by organizing a counterpoint between this meaningless and obligatory facial benevolence and the ghastly, indeed quite unspeakable story the manager is finally obliged to disclose, it is a quite impersonal amusement which ultimately benefits no one. Meanwhile, great swathes of [Berlioz] pump all the fresh air out of *The Shining*'s images and enforce the now familiar sense of cultural asphyxiation. (Jameson 1990: 82, 83)

I shall come back to Jameson's modernism-postmodernism periodization scheme and the place he sees for Kubrick within it. But evidently, the dilemma or the dialectic of the one-off and the prototype within Hollywood itself that I tried to sketch, adds another historical-economic layer to Jameson's critique, and with it, may give a different meaning to the peculiar temporality or a-synchronicity that emerges. What Jameson calls "nostalgia," I am more tempted to identify with a Freudian term "Nachträglichkeit"—deferred action. For it looks as if the logic of Kubrick's reformulation of genres also implied a certain risk—that of having been "too soon" to benefit commercially from a "cycle," or having been "too late" in the life span of such a cycle. Thus, if *2001* came "too soon" to reap the enormous financial windfall that came with the blockbuster marketing strategies, which Lucas exploited for the *Star Wars* saga, and *Barry Lyndon* (as a revised *Tom Jones* [Tony Richardson, 1963]) missed out on the subsequent vogue for costumed classics adaptations on (BBC or PBS) television, one could argue that both *The Shining* and *Full Metal Jacket* (1987)] were completed when the crest of their respective waves (horror: *The Exorcist*, *The Omen* [1976], and *Halloween* [1978]; Vietnam film: *Apocalypse Now* [1979] and *Platoon* [1986]) had already peaked or broken. In fact, it is known that Kubrick, who usually nursed his projects for up to twenty years, abandoned or set aside certain films because he sensed that they would have arrived after another prototype had become the defining blockbuster. This was the case with Brian Aldiss' story "Super-Toys Last All Summer Long" a.k.a. "Pinocchio" and "Artificial Intelligence," which Kubrick put aside after the success of *Star Wars*, and the abandonment of "The Aryan Papers" (based on Lewis Begley's *Wartime Lies*), which would have been released after Spielberg's *Schindler's List*.[18] What one can say is that the prototypical aspects of Kubrick's work highlight—besides the oblique relation to authorship and genre—an oblique relation to "influence." So many of his films were met with indifference and incomprehension, and only later, with hindsight, revealed their place in a given generic history, as if there *had* to be a delay or a deferral before the prototypical features became apparent or the films imposed themselves as classics. In this sense, they are the opposite of the blockbuster with its sudden, immediate, but also ephemeral, impact. "Kubrick's films," as one of his temporary collaborators put it, "seem to be out of time." (McWilliam 1999)

Kubrick's Modernism or (His Critique of) Postmodernism

This feature of Kubrick's films—their a-temporality as masterpieces and unique works—in turn modifies the more industrial logic of the one-off and the prototype. It would, however, also indicate that Jameson is right in seeing Kubrick as essentially a "modernist"—but at the moment in time where cinematic modernism, too, became aware of its own "exhaustion" (if that is the right word). The fact that Kubrick the stylist is both technically innovative and generically eclectic, while his "themes" shift from film to film, makes him fit the model of the late-modernist artist who adopts particular styles as pastiche or mimicry. But the modernist line in literature that stretched from Gustave Flaubert to Thomas Mann via Joseph Conrad and James Joyce is not only characterized by the mask of genre pastiche. It also cultivates the narrational style of irony, or the studied neutrality and impersonality of an "absent God." As Flaubert put it: "The writer has to be in his work like God in his creation: nowhere to be seen and everywhere to be felt," to which Joyce famously added: "The artist, like the God of the creation, remains within or behind or beyond or above his handiwork, invisible, refined out of existence, indifferent, paring his fingernails" (Joyce 1916). Such references to Flaubert's impersonal style ("free indirect") and to Joyce's multiple layers of citations, puns, and riddles can put into a literary-historical perspective much of the irritation felt with Kubrick for seemingly never showing his hand. The whole debate, for instance, about Kubrick's supposed lack of a moral—but also lack of a narratological—point of view can be located in this cultivation of an absence, which would then not be a lack at all, but a precious pointer to the fact that in Kubrick—as, say, in the Anglo-Irish theatrical tradition derived from Joyce, such as Beckett or Pinter—the absence signifies a presence, the unseen is as important as the seen, and silences are more eloquent than words. This does not mean that Kubrick is feigning to possess some kind of suprahuman objectivity. Rather, his effort to establish and sustain a position both inside and outside, polemically committed and ironically aloof, passionately human but also machine-like inhuman, is itself one of the keys to his identity and "signature" (Jameson) as a modernist.

However, one could also argue that Kubrick is, as Jameson implies, already a full-blown postmodernist, where instead of a carefully studied impersonality, the director impersonates, pastiches, and mimics styles and poses, but in such a way that the parodic intent is often muted to the point of invisibility, and the irony seems so remote that the usual contract that parody has with the viewer—namely, that of complicity or eye-winking knowingness—has no shared space in which to establish itself. Jameson refers to this as blank irony, a deliberate flattening out, or even one-dimensionality, which makes certain culturally saturated, recognizable signs available for new contexts, such as the space vehicle spinning to the strains of the Blue Danube waltz (*2001*), of Beethoven and masturbation, "Singin' in the Rain" and rape (both in *A Clockwork Orange*), the Road Runner and horror-hauntings, television-presenter Johnny Carson and homicidal mania (both in *The Shining*).

In Jameson's scheme, as we saw, postmodernism is characterized by a clear recognition that "the uniqueness and individuality of style itself" has been overvalued. Already in 1960, Kubrick voiced a similar view, namely, that the emphasis on being "original" in the movies is exaggerated:

> I haven't come across any recent new ideas in film that strike me as being particularly important and that have to do with form. I think that a preoccupation with originality of form is more or less a fruitless thing. A truly original person with a truly original mind will not be able to function in the old form and will simply do something different. Others had much better think of the form as being some sort of classical tradition and try to work within it. (Kubrick 1960)

The statement balances the "classical" definition of Hollywood authorship—to be creative within an established tradition rather than break with a form for the sake of originality—with an already postmodern disdain or fatigue with "the new" for its own sake. To these features can be added the "invisible ink" aspect of Kubrick's authorial signature, marked by a refusal to invest his work with the semblance of individual biography or personal touches—a refusal that has earned him the attribute "calculating" from so many critics, and has also baffled audiences.

A second point of postmodernist style is the refusal of depth, the attachment to surface, and here too one recognizes an often-voiced complaint about Kubrick, namely, that the glossy surface of his films not only repels contact, empathy, and identification but also mirrors the glib moral judgments and facile symmetries in his stories (which Robert Hughes regards as assets). Third, postmodernism is anti-psychological, and it is true that Kubrick in his films often destroys psychological motivation (notably in *2001*, *A Clockwork Orange*, and *The Shining*), substituting instead such typically "postmodern" surrogates as magic, the supernatural, comedy, or horror conventions, without a corresponding commitment of believing in any of them.

But if Kubrick is—in this as in other respects—a typical postmodernist, one might with equal justice argue that he already "overcomes" postmodernism—the only question being whether he does so from a modernist perspective or from a post-postmodernist point of view, in which his (absent) perspective has to be imagined as being located somewhere else—either in the "future," or outside these space-time coordinates altogether, and in some other ("third") political-discursive space. For instance, if critics have spoken of *Dr. Strangelove, or, How I Learned to Stop Worrying and Love the Bomb* (1964), *2001*, and *A Clockwork Orange* as his futurist trilogy, then his films about sexuality, couples, and the family (*Lolita*, *The Shining*, and *Eyes Wide Shut* [1999]) could be said to probe the contours of a post-bourgeois society, and his films about military or para-military institutions (*Fear and Desire* [1953], *Paths of Glory*, and *Full Metal Jacket*) see masculinity from the perspective of highly problematic post-patriarchal "male bonding." And while he kept audiences shocked and the critics divided with his determined effort that each of his films should take up a burning and controversial issue, it seems clear that his aim was not only the strong response he usually received but also to ensure that the values espoused by his characters, in all their conflicting extremity, could not be attributed to him or be used to pin down his own moral point of view. The opposite of neutrality, this courting of a strong response, in the absence of identifying the author as their moral origin, points not to the postmodernist, but to the modernist. In particular, it would make Kubrick a modernist who does not wear either the mask of impersonality or of pastiche, but who cultivates a "cold persona" and, more specifically in the case of Kubrick, a cold persona in the face of (or because of) some very hot subjects. It would indicate that the critics, who so often applied the label "cold" to Kubrick, were on to something, but not to what this chilly mission was finally about.[19]

For what characterizes the cold persona? Rather than to the blank irony and pastiche discussed under postmodernism, it would refer to the dilemma of the human observer, who in the face of suffering, inhumanity, and violence cannot act other than to armor himself with "coldness" for protection, self-protection, and camouflage.[20] The notion was developed to typify the post-traumatic literary response to the First World War in otherwise such politically opposed figures of German modernism as Bertolt Brecht and Ernst Jünger, whose "expressionist" angst turned into the perhaps no less troubled, but outwardly expressionless "cool" of the New Sobriety.[21] While Brecht dismantled his animalistic "Baal" into the socio-technical cyborg Galy Galy in *Mann ist Mann*, Jünger's *Storms of Steel* combined the point of view of the militarized-technological eye (the precision optics of war photography and the vision machinery of the motion picture camera) with the dispassionate-dissecting eye of the entomologist, itemizing and describing society, in peace and war, as he would beetles, ants, or a butterfly. With reference to the former, Kubrick's Alex from *A Clockwork Orange* turning into his "Private Pyle" from *Full Metal Jacket* would be the analogy to Brecht's Baal/Galy Galy transformation, while in the case of Jünger, one can trace an affinity with Vladimir Nabokov's particular cool, and whose own entomological fascination would in turn, via *Lolita*, take us also to Kubrick. For him, one has to add as part of the "cold persona" the point of view of the no-longer human, the extraterrestrial (*2001*—HAL 9000 the Computer), but also the not-yet human, as in the hominid ape in *2001*, as well as the child (Danny, in *The Shining*).

The perspectives of the extraterrestrial and of the child might be starting points for exploring more closely the enigmatic relationship that existed between Spielberg and Kubrick. Spielberg acknowledged influence and precedence when he said of Kubrick: "He copied no one, yet all of us were scrambling to imitate him." Even without comparing details or speculating about the differences between Kubrick's *A.I.* and the film Spielberg eventually made (in 2001), in memory of and as homage to the director, their fundamentally different personas can be gauged when remembering how Spielberg systematically and obsessively re-inscribes everywhere—including his extraterrestrial figures—the "child" in search of the good father (*E.T.* [1982], *Empire of the Sun* [1987], *Jurassic Park* [1993], and *A.I.*), while Kubrick's "children" have to find their way, lose their way, or retrace their steps all by themselves, in a (dangerously, but also daringly) post-Oedipal universe.

Second, with the cold persona in mind, one can return to the question of Kubrick's "influence" also in the sense of his films as delayed or deferred prototypes, because what now comes into view is a whole range of directors who—mostly associated with postmodernism—appear to have not so much adopted the cold persona as extracted or subtracted from it a different "cool." They, too, try to stay cool in the face of hot subjects, but they invest their cool with precisely those traits of personality, individuality, and idiosyncrasy that the modernist Kubrick had taken out of it. I am thinking of David Lynch (the entomological point of view in *Blue Velvet* [1986]), of David Cronenberg (the vantage point of the virus in *Shivers* [1975], the perspective of cold surface metal in *Crash* [1996], or of the mutant organisms in *Naked Lunch* [1993] and *eXistenZ* [1999]), but also of David Fincher's Tyler Durden in *Fight Club* (1999). And last, but not least, Quentin Tarantino, whose heroes in *Reservoir Dogs* (1992) and *Pulp Fiction* (1994) might be said to be self-consciously "cool" versions of Alex and his Droogs from *A Clockwork Orange*. Danny Boyle's *Trainspotting* (1996) and *Sunshine* (2007) stand as updated versions of Kubrick's prototypes for an age of cool immanence.

The Regime of the Brothers

The argument would be that *A Clockwork Orange*, possibly even more than *2001* or *The Shining*, is Kubrick's most enduring, but also perhaps most enigmatic, prototype film, less for giving rise to a particular genre and its cycles, as for this persona and its psycho-social constellation. Ostensibly a film about individual freedom and the state's right to engineer goodness in its citizen, the film can today be most usefully read as a defining statement about the crisis of masculinity so often invoked, whether elaborated psychoanalytically, around the post-oedipal "culture of narcissism" (C. ash), the "enjoying superego" (S. Žižek) and the "regime of the brother" (J. Flower-McCannell), or anti-psychoanalytically, around "discipline and punish" (M. Foucault) and the "control society" (G. Deleuze). In each case, what is implied is the demise of the efficacy of the symbolic order, represented by classical bourgeois individualism and its patriarchal identity formation, in regulating the male's entry into society. What makes Kubrick's contribution so special within this rather broad horizon of cultural critique and analysis is how accurately he has located the fault-lines and breaking points, the ambivalences and irreducible aporias of these shifts in gender-roles and symbolic functions, notably the sociopolitical formation of the all-male group, impersonating the father's prohibiting function, without accepting the law of castration. To recapitulate briefly how the psychoanalytical argument might go, by recalling the three paradigmatic scenes with which *A Clockwork Orange* opens: the scene of the Irish tramp in the underpass who defiantly says to his aggressors that he no longer wants to live in this world, because there is no respect for law and order; the scene where Alex and his gang enter the home of the writer, tie him up, and in front of his eyes, cut up and gang-rape his wife; and the scene where Alex wakes up the next day, to see his social worker sit on his father's bed. He berates and threatens Alex, but mainly in order to blackmail him into granting sexual favors.

While these acts and reactions are in each case the consequence of Alex's behavior, who has been displaying the kind of unbridled violence he and his gang are capable of, they can also be read as their retro-active "causes," responsible for Alex's (lack of) socialization. In this sense, Alex's subsequent journey is determined by another gang: not the rival youth gang of Billy-Boy whom Alex's Droogs cheat out of their prey, but the gang of "obscenely enjoying" superego fathers, starting with the social worker and continuing through to the prison warder, the government minister, even the prison chaplain and the abused writer who himself becomes a moral crusader. Most revealing in the present context is probably the figure of the writer. Also called Alex(ander), he is transformed from a left-leaning liberal into a rabid advocate of law and order. Having to helplessly witness the rape of his wife casts him in the role of the humiliated father, which according to Žižek is one of the key conditions for the post-oedipal male to emerge. This graphic scene, combined with the direct address to the camera, is a defining moment of modern cinema, not only shattering the "illusionist" space of classical cinema, by calling attention to the ordinary voyeurism that goes "unpunished" every time we go to the movies, but also naming one of the most unstable power-relations in the social symbolic: that of the son, no longer rebelling against the father, but still capable of humiliating him, and thus demonstrating his own inability to enter into the symbolic order other than through feelings of shame and, its obverse, exhibitionist violence.

The impotent father figures, representing the symbolic order and the law, on the other hand, flaunt their extreme libidinal investment in exercising this law. Against Alex's rights as a citizen, here defined as the right to do evil and then face just punishment, the state now plays the role of the enjoying superego. As Žižek has so often pointed out, this reverses the Kantian categorical imperative, by putting the subject into a double bind. No longer is the individual free to "choose" the personal good, in view of its compatibility with the general good: when goodness is imposed on the individual by the state, it may be good, but it is no longer ethical. Conversely, if the symbolic order extracts pleasure out of knowing itself to be "good," it may be representing the general good, but it does not act ethically. The response of Alex, mirroring the "enjoyment" of the superego fathers, may itself become the more authentically ethical act.[22]

The appropriate Foucault reference to the universe of Kubrick's films and its particular sociopolitical inscription would be Gilles Deleuze's "Postscript on the Societies of Control," where, following Foucault, he outlines a number of key sites of modernity that have started to mutate in the late twentieth century:

> Foucault['s] disciplinary societies . . . reach their height at the outset of the twentieth century. They initiate the organization of vast spaces of enclosure. The individual never ceases passing from one closed environment to another, each having its own laws: first the family; then the school ("you are no longer in your family"); then the barracks ("you are no longer at school"); then the factory; from time to time the hospital; possibly the prison, the pre-eminent instance of the enclosed environment.... Now we are in a generalized crisis in relation to all these environments of enclosure—prison, hospital, factory, school, family. The family is an "interior," in crisis like all other interiors—scholarly, professional, etc. The administrations in charge never cease announcing supposedly necessary reforms: to reform schools, to reform industries, hospitals, the armed forces, prisons. But everyone knows that these institutions are finished, whatever the length of their expiration periods. It's only a matter of administering their last rites. (Deleuze 1992: 4)

One can see how *A Clockwork Orange* responds very precisely to the crisis identified by Deleuze, and especially its notion of institutional enclosure, which in the film extended to the enclosure of the body itself via the Ludovico treatment, hinted at by Deleuze, and certainly prominent already in Foucault. At the same time, the idea of looking at disciplinary practices not as part of an antiauthoritarian moral critique, but from the perspective of what is in the process of replacing them, makes *Full Metal Jacket* even more of a follow-up of *A Clockwork Orange* by detailing the discursive and physical violence necessary to both insert males into social institutions (here, the Marines), and to break them out of the "regimes of brothers" with their mutual dependence via shame, complicity, humiliation, and the sharing of guilty secrets (as happens in both *A Clockwork Orange* and *Full Metal Jacket*).

But as Kubrick also points out, when at the end of *Full Metal Jacket* we hear the "Mickey Mouse Club" theme tune, the move to control societies has a purpose well beyond new kinds of warfare and combat: it signals a broad range of changes of psychic ("psychotic") processes, setting free different kinds of "energies" once tied up in the disciplinary regime of the classical bourgeois state and now needed to regulate the processing of sensory stimuli and the professional flexibilization demanded by postindustrial societies of its "productive" members as well as of those whose most socially useful task is consumption. The ambivalences attached to the portrayal of Alex, confusing audiences and so resented by the critics, can be seen as the necessary corollary of Deleuze's dictum about

> the ultra-rapid forms of free-floating control that replace the old disciplines operating in the time frame of a closed system. There is no need to invoke the extraordinary pharmaceutical productions, the molecular engineering, the genetic manipulations, although these are slated to enter the new process. There is no need to ask which is the toughest regime, for it is within each of them that liberating and enslaving forces confront one another. (Deleuze 1992: 4)

Les extrêmes se touchent

So the extremes, with which I began, do seem to meet after all, and, in the work, they even describe a trajectory of sorts. For while Deleuze's control society furnishes an apposite description of what links *A Clockwork Orange* to *Full Metal Jacket* and both to *The Shining*, one can—in the light of Kubrick's last film *Eyes Wide Shut*—add another dimension, where Žižek and Deleuze complement each other and are at the same time given a further twist or reversal. *Eyes Wide Shut* is first of all a film about fantasy, or rather, the devastating effect of having a fantasy and of not having a fantasy. It strikingly confirms Žižek's claim: you have to have a fantasy (a "symptom") in order to function at all in everyday reality or in a human relationship, lest you be overwhelmed by the Real. In this reading, *Eyes Wide Shut* would be the story of Bill Harford, a man who has no fantasy to sustain his (sense of) reality. This is in contrast to his wife, who has "healthy" sexual fantasies to support her role as caring mother and loving, sexy wife. Bill is thus the victim of other people's fantasies, or, as Deleuze famously said: if you are living in someone else's dream, then you are *foutu*—lost, "screwed." And so he is, several times over, having to seek out the fantasies of others, where he promptly and abjectly loses himself—be they those of his wife, those of the two women, or those of the "enjoying" super-fathers (his "friend" Victor Ziegler as much as Milic, the lewd, pimping costume lender). Bill, almost begging to be admitted to their fantasies, ends up in the most terrible forms of enclosure at the orgy. Here it is (sexual) fantasy itself that is the institution "disciplining" the male, while Kubrick makes the viewer aware of the "naked" violence that frames not just this fantasy enclosure but all "institutionalized fantasy," as we know it from the entertainment industries and experience economies. In *Eyes Wide Shut*, violence and fantasy become the recto and verso of each other, as had already been the case in *A Clockwork Orange*. This film—prototype and key film—it would thus seem—also for Kubrick's own subsequent work—can now be re-read across *Eyes Wide Shut* as already outlining the twin boundaries of the control societies and their post-oedipal identities: violence and fantasy are equally "complete," sealed worlds, promising neither freedom nor release, because they are as self-referential as they are self-policing.

This self-policing self-referentiality points straight in the direction of Hollywood—the old Hollywood of censorship and the Hays Code, with which Kubrick conflicted in his early work, such as *Lolita*; the New Hollywood of the 1970s, with its apparent "freedoms," which Kubrick tested with *A Clockwork Orange*; and the blockbuster Hollywood of the 1990s, whose strategy consists of dividing the "real world" into a series of self-contained zones, each one isolated from the others, and yet each supplied with the same "fantasy worlds." The strategy has its analogy in politics and warfare: When television reports about a conflict area, its coverage follows strict generic rules, permitting some kind of discourses ("terrorism," "peace-keeping," and "civilian casualties") and excluding others (the causes of poverty, the class structure or ethnic divides, and the role of foreign investment or local corruption). Similarly, a tourist hotel during the off-season, a fashionable domestic interior of an artist-writer, or a president's war room also have their generic boundaries, next to which, as Kubrick showed in film after film, lie as many kinds of madness as there are decors to trigger them. In this way, Kubrick is able to relate the fantasy worlds of Hollywood movies to the real worlds of "zoning"—in suburban London or downtown Manhattan, in bombed-out Hue or Parris Island—where genres provide the interface of these different enclosures, thereby also giving a clue to the paradox of his own recluse existence that encompassed the expanse of infinite space.

Kubrick, in other words, was the director of serious extremes, because they alone capture our lived reality. His persona and lifestyle finally allegorized not just Hollywood, but the "worlds" it has helped to put into the world.[23] If the prototypes he created were too unique for Hollywood mass production and rarely achieved mass consumption, their deferred action may still propel those who are willing to be kicked up (or down?) the evolutionary ladder.

The Legacy

The "Kubrickian ladder," be it evolutionary or otherwise, seems quite packed.[24] Twenty years following the director's death, his films—their imagery and atmosphere, but also his work method and position within the industry—inspire a veritable tribe of filmmakers, as attested indeed by the present collection. Let us look, in closing, at how the aspects dealt with in the present chapter—the obvious or inevitable manic perfectionism aside—have been picked up and revisited by figures otherwise as diverse as the Coen Brothers, Paul Thomas Anderson, Gaspar Noé, or David Robert Mitchell, all in a double quest to create cinematic worlds of their own and beyond, and to fill Kubrick's shoes. But first, to state the obvious: the "reclusive one-man studio" profile and unprecedented authorial and creative independence deal struck by Kubrick with Warner Brothers are quite simply no longer conceivable in our day and age of hyper-corporatized, global studio consortium system coupled with the intrusive quality of new technologies, including, of course, the internet.

Kubrick quipped once, "No committee ever wrote a symphony." And while, circa 2020, we witness algorithms writing music pieces à la Bach or Mozart that are less and less deeply entrenched in the "uncanny valley," it is the ideal of the individual auteur that most of Kubrick's "inheritors" are still very much attached to. At best, however, in their vying for a degree of independence and directorial control, they can be found "pitching" themselves according to three scenarios, each of which has the auteur staunchly enshrining his name as a brand: the first one, mostly found in Europe, has auteurs navigating a state and region funding-based system, responding to the EU's need for more synergies and obligatory coproduction schemes, managing these from a centralized position within their own production company, and handling the majority shares of the funding (Lars von Trier being a case in point).

Another scenario has auteurs take advantage of cheaper new technologies, operating from the fringe on low budgets (sometimes "crowdfunded" through the internet). If the ephemeral Dogme 95 movement that von Trier initiated comes to mind, as does Gus Van Sant's experiment with a minimal crew on the film *Gerry* (2002), an even more compelling example would seem to be Shane Carruth, who directed two feature films on shoestring budgets (*Primer* [2004] and *Upstream Color* [2013]), which rapidly achieved cult status and, to boot, are strongly Kubrickian in spirit, not least with their mathematically sublime play on time.

The third possibility of surviving as an "independent" auteur in the West has established figures—especially those who emerged in the heyday of the phenomenon (the early days of Sundance and Miramax, . . . and of deregulated hedge funds)—alternating between "independent" films (with budgets varying between $3 million and $12 million on average), video-on-demand, and films or series produced by streaming platform studios (Netflix and Amazon), and, at times, outright blockbusters ("one for the family, one for the firm" or "one for me, one for the industry"). Seen thus, Steven Soderbergh's constant play with generic conventions and adaptation to industry financing trends constitutes one extreme of the "independent" (indeed self-effacing) auteur-filmmaker spectrum. On the other end, we can see the recent multiplying of productions by Terrence Malick, once a director of an output even rarer than Kubrick himself, and, like him, a notoriously secretive, reclusive figure with an inevitable auteurist signature. While Soderbergh tends to erase his authorial signature (and for good reason. Says the filmmaker: "The fact that I am not an identifiable brand is very freeing, because people get tired of brands and they switch brands. I've never had a desire to be out in front of anything, which is why I don't take possessory credit."), resurging where one would least expect it (*Unsane* and *Logan Lucky*), in a rather playful way, Malick indulges in introspective epics about the meaning of life and other such profound and for some, deeply touching matters. Both auteurs, much as Kubrick, have capitalized on their aura of "mystique," attracting scores of stars intent on discovering their method and hopeful to be part, alternately, of a quirky, humorous sleeper (Soderbergh) or of yet another important, serious film—in short, a "masterpiece" bereft of irony (Malick).

Perhaps we can add yet another type, namely, that of the blockbuster filmmaker with a declared auteur bend. This version of the auteur, Christopher Nolan being the prime example, invokes Kubrick as a landmark warranting a quixotic hubris ("No one told me it was impossible, so I did it."). The obsession with being an "independent" yet also a commercially viable director comes with other forms of cinephile fetishizism in Nolan's case (obsession with time and promoting the use of celluloid film—be it regular 35mm or even 70mm or Imax as was the case with *Interstellar* [2014] and *Dunkirk* [2017]) as a badge of cinematic honor. Not surprising, then, that Nolan made a point of supervising the restoration of *2001: A Space Odyssey*, a brand new 70mm print of which was to be screened at the 2018 Cannes film festival. Unfortunately—and the anecdote is telling!—the restored print could not be ready on time, and an older print (and a scratched one, at that) was shown instead.

Even more canny are the Coen Brothers, heirs of Kubrick in more ways than one. They have managed to retain a great deal of authorial independence over the years, alternating privately fundraised projects with studio-produced ones, keeping production costs low, and attracting star power at preferential rates. Like Kubrick, the Coens have alternated film genres with apparent ease, their directorial control and precision undisputed; unlike Kubrick, they have often been criticized for a seeming excess of levity and adolescent humor. This no doubt has contributed to the tag "postmodern" being applied to their films, although, as with Kubrick, the exact degree of pastiche and philosophical depth the Coens' respective projects can be difficult to assess. Likely, we may discern a form of cool in both, meant to put a distance between vivid emotions and the self, or a form of pessimism and entomological cynicism animating highly sophisticated, mathematical minds (think, in both instances, of *A Serious Man* [2009]). Surely the Coens have come closest to Kubrick when evoking the ineffable, when their films' real message was not one delivered on the surface but one that combined their dry wit and irony with a more profound statement about the meaning(lessness) of existence.

Of the names discussed so far, however, I have not yet mentioned the directors that have most knowingly cultivated a persona close to Kubrick's: Paul Thomas Anderson, Jonathan Glazer, Gaspar Noé, and David Robert Mitchell. The first has managed to get projects off the ground seemingly on the value of his name and status as a masterpiece-maker alone. Emulating Kubrick as a creator of cinematic one-offs and prototypes—Anderson's films are seldom commercially viable (at least by twenty-first century standards)—they do provide their studio with a cachet of cultural respectability, often reaping critical acclaim and acquiring cult status, just as Kubrick did with Warner Brothers. To be sure, Anderson has honed his Kubrickness knowingly, including a reputation as a reclusive, distant artist, with a form of inscrutability ("what are his films really about?"), despite providing articulate and courteous responses in interviews.

None of "PTA's" many characters fits the model of the histrionic, capricious, and ultimately lonely and reclusive figure better than the ones created for Anderson by Daniel Day-Lewis in *There Will Be Blood* (2007) and *Phantom Thread* (2017), respectively. The films, among other things, allegorize the project of the misunderstood but prestigious "genius" in whose madness a method must be detected, thereby enshrining the modernist ideal of individual style and voice ... even as the films of Anderson, if only by virtue of the socio-historic context of their production, are rather post-postmodernist in essence, rather than a revival of a modernist impetus, blending the two in a manner very reminiscent of Kubrick. In short, Anderson's allegories of film directing in the twenty-first century are what Kubrick's films might have mutated into, had they indeed come too late.

Freely borrowing from Kubrick's stock imagery and stylistic devices even more greedily than Anderson, Jonathan Glazer has designed an oeuvre that can be quite readily aligned with postmodernism, through its repeated use of pastiche, if, again, a belated form thereof. But his films resonate more with the notion of deferral than with nostalgia, which Jameson considered to be the primary mode of postmodernism. Glazer's films, even as they endow the early twenty-first century with an inescapable passé (indeed, 1970s) feel, seem somewhat muted and ghostly, in their visuals as in the spirit animating their narratives. They are acts of mourning, or so it would seem, that perform an unwitting critique of the solitude that befalls the alienated subject in the twenty-first century Western world. Hence the melancholia pervading entire universes crafted by Glazer, destroying loving couples (*Birth* [2004]) and affecting even alien creatures (*Under the Skin* [2013]). This melancholy mood that can be equally related to socioeconomic concerns (a Marxist reading) as well as to the post-oedipal and post-disciplinary societies, as suggested earlier.

As if in reaction to this new world of control dreaded by Gilles Deleuze, Gaspar Noé has developed an oeuvre admittedly entirely fixated on his experience of discovering *2001: A Space Odyssey* at the ripe young age of eight (see Chodorov and Szaniawski), and which expands on a constant investigation of the sublime aesthetics and camera movement devised by Kubrick, which Noé seems to clutter with the most regressive topics. Yet, there too, there is method to the apparent madness, and a deeper and more intelligent vision behind the extreme close-ups of body parts and graphic rape. Psychopathology is cannily foiled in Noé, even when on the surface his scripts over-determine certain themes (sex, violence, and death) as the source of all events—the emphasis on sodomy and STDs in *Irreversible* (2002) being a case in point. This notorious film, like Noé's more recent *Climax* (2018), pursues Kubrick's critique and representation of exhibitionist violence amid a repressive bourgeois society, interrogating the role of failed superego fathers and ethics of direct action. *Irreversible*'s gay S&M nightclub—le Rectum—is a locus of grotesque excess escaping traditional societal rules (an outlet, literally). There, the power dynamics of domination and submission are more explicitly and, Noé would argue, more truthfully stated, just as the male characters present therein are monstrous sons to monstrous fathers (suggesting that anal rape is descended in a patrilinear fashion), and humiliation and violence, as in Kubrick, solve nothing, yet propel the story, and the world, further, in leaps and bursts, which in the case of *Irreversible* are ironically constructed backward. In *Climax*, an opening dance number involving an elaborate choreography of some twenty dancers gives way to chaos after one of them, unbeknownst to the rest, drugs the entire troupe. Here Noé devises a psychosexual and social experiment, positing an obvious critique of the dangers, in a postindustrial society, of freeing energies once tied up in the bourgeois order, which (self-) destruct when this order starts unraveling.

Noé's cinema, with its liminal situations and dizzying camera movements, is one of extremes, where characters' fantasies and the reality of the diegetic worlds they explore are at a great risk of merging and collapsing into a nightmarish Real (the Rectum club and the underpass in *Irreversible*; the bad trip of the ghost in *Enter the Void* [2009]), which is the stuff of the director's own dark fantasy. In a more detached, indeed postmodern, way, David Robert Mitchell explores the condition of a paranoid subject lost in someone else's fantasy— in short, Hollywood's own fantasy of itself—in *Under the Silver Lake* (2018). This film performs quite transparently, parapractically one is tempted to say, the act of retracing the steps of some erstwhile pioneer, trying to make sense of a system, and finding a "code" to map and read Los Angeles and what lies beneath its glossy veneer. Film noir and hallucinatory perambulations blend freely, and the failure of the film as such is also its modest metafilmic victory: it exposes the limits of probing and exploring a universe as hermetically sealed and ungrounded as the movie world, which Kubrick (and besides him, maybe only David Lynch) mastered.

It is this tantalizing mastery that is much coveted by the filmmakers I mentioned (and there are many more!), which inevitably must entail much tripping along the way—be it by trying to climb the ladder in oversized shoes or getting lost in dark corners, barefoot. For one, creating total worlds, as Kubrick's epigones find out the hard way, falters the moment the timing is off, the abyss becomes too literal, or the horror is too hokey—missing that crucial element of deferral. Kubrick's privileged and contradictory position was that of being out of place and yet in the right time. His followers are left with the dubious honor of attempting to fill the void he left—knowing their belatedness, but nonetheless staking their claim. Then, the second revelation, deriving directly from the first, may be the most painful: in our day and age, it would seem that all conditions (socioeconomic, technological, and philosophical) conspire to prevent an emphasis on this most modernist artistic accomplishment: to summon an emotion not by what is said and shown, but by the invisible. Kubrick caught his time by the skin of its teeth, like that horse jawbone, thrown across the universe into intergalactic space. If reviving such a frisson of an instant would seem nigh impossible, we may still wish to appreciate and salute the efforts of those attempting to climb the ladder all the more.

Notes

1. A version of this chapter originally appeared in *Kinematograph* 20, 2004, under the title "Evolutionary Imagineer." It has been updated and edited for the needs of this collection.
2. See the John Alcott and Garrett Brown interviews in Falsetto (1996: 214; 273). Note also http://www.wendycarlos.com/kubrick.html and Frederic Raphael's book about his experience with Kubrick, *Eyes Wide Open* (1999). Raphael commented in *The Observer*, Sunday, July 11, 1999: "The thing about Kubrick is he was a serious reclusive. Whether that was a form of drawing attention by not drawing attention, I don't know. [But] I think he wasn't interested in himself."
3. His official address was Childwickbury Manor, Harpenden, Hertfordshire. Some visitors thought it was grand, while others, like Sara Maitland, were surprised rather than impressed: "He lived, rather unromantically between Luton and St Albans, in the house originally built for the founder of Maples furniture store: an Edwardian pomposity set in large grounds" (Maitland).
4. "His name has become an adjective for over-control. It is said that Kubrick sent his scripts—or pages thereof—around in plastic bags, to be read by the intended recipient and then returned via hovering messengers" (Edelstein 1999).
5. "One morning in 1995 the telephone rang. I answered and a gruff voice said, 'This is Stanley Kubrick. Would you like to write a film script for me?' Assuming this was a joking friend, I replied, 'And this is Marilyn Monroe and I've been dead 30 years.' He laughed. It really was Stanley Kubrick" (Maitland).

    Candia McWilliam was another such contributor. She also noted "I could not bear the idea of contact with other people to the degree that Stanley, in his professional life, had it."
6. According to Steven Spielberg, Kubrick was a "great communicator. . . . When we spoke on the phone, our conversations lasted for hours. He was constantly in contact with hundreds of people all over the world."
7. These were some of the comments by New York critics about *2001*: "It's a monumentally unimaginative movie" (Pauline Kael, *Harper's magazine*); "A major disappointment" (Stanley Kaufman, *The New Republic*); "Incredibly boring" (Renata Adler, *The New York Times*); "A disaster" (Andrew Sarris, *The Village Voice*).

    Variety wrote, prior to its release: "2001 is not a cinematic landmark. It compares with but does not best, previous efforts at film science-fiction; lacking the humanity of *Forbidden Planet*, the imagination of *Things to Come* and the simplicity of *Of Stars and Men*. It actually belongs to the technically slick group previously dominated by George Pal and the Japanese" (Ciment 2003).
8. Other extremes and contradictions: "While his movies are thought of as huge (they are certainly hugely expensive), Kubrick's crews were legendarily tiny—in many cases no more than fifteen people—and the director himself would go around arranging the lights in the manner not of a deity but of an electrician or plumber.

Where most people think of Kubrick's films as having been storyboarded to death—pre-digested—others report that he often wandered his sets with a camera lens, groping for shots on the spot. He spoke in an engaging nebbishy Bronx-Jewish accent that was always a shock to hear—like the voice of the unmasked Wizard of Oz, it didn't belong. On his sets he wore the same outfits; it is said that, like Einstein, he had five or more of each lined up on hangers. The act of making choices was clearly excruciating to him; that's why the choices he made are so memorable" (Edelstein).

9   The context is relevant to Kubrick, however short-lived this renaissance should prove to be, and however little he finally participated in it—in contrast to that other expatriate US self-exiled director in Britain, Joseph Losey, if one thinks of his collaboration with Harold Pinter.
10 See Joseph Gelmis, "Interview with Kubrick," in Falsetto (1996: 29–32), and a chapter in Baxter.
11 See Cook (2002).
12 "I received hundreds and hundreds of phone calls and thousands of faxes [during our 30-year collaboration]. I guess you could say he was unrelenting." Terry Semel, at the Warner Brothers Kubrick memorial service.
13 See Walker 1974.
14 See Barthes (1977), and Peter Wollen (1972).
15 Dennis Bingham highlights this aspect in "The Displaced Auteur—A Reception History of *The Shining*" (in Falsetto 1996: 284–306).
16 "Ten feature motion pictures, each one totally different from the others in both content and style. He has never twice made the same film" John Alcott (in Falsetto 1996: 124).
17 "Is it ungrateful to long from time to time for something both more ugly and less proficient or expert, more home-made and awkward, than those breathtaking expanses of sunlit leaf-tracery, those big screen flower-bowls of an unimaginably intense delicacy of hue, that would have caused the Impressionists to shut up their paint boxes in frustration?" (Jameson 1990: 83).
18 "After an initial bout of work on *AI* with Aldiss in the early 70s, it was shelved, partly in response to *Star Wars*. So The Aryan Papers was the frontrunner after Kubrick finished *Full Metal Jacket* in 1987. "Kubrick always wanted to do a film on the Holocaust, but he never got a good script," says Harlan. He had tried to commission an original screenplay from the novelist Isaac Bashevis Singer (who turned it down on the grounds that he knew nothing about the Holocaust), before settling on an adaptation of the novel *Wartime Lies*, by Lewis Begley. "We were very committed to do this film," Harlan recalls. "We had done enormous amounts of research and preparation, but there came a point when he and Warner boss Terry Semel decided it would be better to do *AI* first. It had to do with *Schindler's List*," he said. "It was such a good film and so successful, and Stanley's film would have come out about a year later. He'd already had this experience with *Full Metal Jacket*, which came out the year after *Platoon*, and that hurt us, there's no question about it." So in 1995, The Aryan Papers was abandoned and Kubrick returned to *AI*" (Rose 2000).
19 "An obituary in the *New York Times* used the word *cold* three times, and for good measure added *chilly*, *icy*, *bleak*, and *grim*. Kubrick the Cold is a cliché that cropped

up in the columns of Pauline Kael and now serves as a comfy sofa for those who don't want to deal with Kubrick's ambition" (Alex Ross 1999).

20 Frederic Raphael noted in *Eyes Wide Open*: "Stanley was so determined to be aloof and unfeeling that my heart went out to him. Somewhere along the line he was still the kid in the playground who had been no one's first choice to play with." The latter may or may not have been the case, but the "cold persona" evidently only begins (and ends) as an aesthetic construct, if this "kid" becomes an artist.

21 See Lethen (2002), whose book identifies this "cold persona" as a "survival strategy" among some prominent writers, philosophers and artists of the postwar (the First World War) generation in Germany.

22 Slavoj Žižek devotes part three of *The Ticklish Subject* ("Whither Oedipus"), to "The Demise of Symbolic Efficiency." There, he details instances of the falling apart of the double paternal function, from False Memory Syndrome to the Moral Majority Promise Keepers, from the obsession with code-crackers and hackers, to the reason why there is no sex between the protagonists in the *X-files*. Žižek also points to the return of what he calls "ferocious Superego figures," with their command to enjoy!, or their own display of obscene enjoyment, either by inhibiting male identity formation under the sign of consumerist self-indulgence, or unleashing infantile rage or "tightening the Master-Slave matrix of passionate attachments," as in films that try to re-inscribe the non- phallic father, such as *La Vita e bella* (Žižek 2000: 374).

23 Perhaps only Kubrick himself was fully aware of the double-edged praise in a sentence like "Stanley Kubrick does not simply create films—he creates entire worlds." "Photographing Stanley Kubrick's *Barry Lyndon*," *American Cinematographer* (March 1976), 268.

24 This final section owes much to an extended email exchange with the editor, Jeremi Szaniawski, and benefited from his incisive views on contemporary cinema.

Works Cited

Barthes, Roland. 1977. "The Death of the Author" (1968), in Stephen Heath (ed. And trans.), *Image, Music, Text*. New York: Hill & Wang., 142–48.
Baxter, John. 1997. *Stanley Kubrick: A Biography*. New York: Harper Collins.
Ciment, Michel. 2001. *Kubrick, the Definitive Edition*. London: Faber and Faber.
Cook, David A. 2002. *Lost Illusions: American Cinema in the Shadow of Watergate and Vietnam, 1970–1979*. Berkeley: California University Press.
Deleuze, Gilles. 1992. "Postscript on the Societies of Control," *October* 59.
Edelstein, David. 1999. "Kubrick take 1 take 2," *Slate*, March 8.
Falsetto, Mario. 1996. *Perspectives on Stanley Kubrick*, New York: G.K. Hall.
Hughes, Robert. 1971. "The Décor of Tomorrow's Hell," *Time Magazine*, December 27.
Jameson, Fredric. 1990. "Historicism in *The Shining*" (1981), in *Signatures of the Visible*. New York and London: Routledge.
Joyce, James. 1916. *A Portrait of the Artist as a Young Man*. New York: Huebsch, 249.
Kubrick Stanley. 1960. Kubrick Interview, *The Observer*, December 4. Cited at http://www.archiviokubrick.it/english/words/interviews/1960directorsnotes.html.
Lethen, Helmut. 2002. *Cool conduct*. Berkeley: University of California Press.
McWilliam, Candia. 1999. "Remembering Kubrick," *The Guardian*, March 13.

Raphael, Frederic. 1999. *Eyes Wide Open*. New York: Ballantine.
Rose, Steve. 2000. "Kubrick, Spielberg and the AI project" *The Guardian*, May 5.
Ross, Alex. "A Tribute to Stanley Kubrick," *Slate* March 8, 1999.
Walker, Alexander. 1974. *Hollywood UK: The British Film Industry in the Sixties*. New York: Stein and Day.
Wollen, Peter. 1972 (1969). "The Auteur Theory," in Peter Wollen, *Signs and Meaning in the Cinema*. London: Secker & Warburg, 74–115.
Žižek, Slavoj. 2000. *The Ticklish Subject*. London: Verso.

2

"Kubrick's Cube": Stanley Kubrick, Judaism, and His Jewish Heirs

Nathan Abrams

Rarely thought of as a Jewish director (whatever that may mean), Kubrick never denied his ethnicity but neither did he follow any religion. His parents, Jacques and Gertrude (née Perveler), were both Jewish, but they *did* not practice much religion at home. Kubrick did not have a bar mitzvah and said very little about the subject in his lifetime; however, a version of the traditional mourner's Kaddish was performed at his funeral. Yet, despite the voluminous research into Kubrick, his photography, and his films, little of it has been based on exploring his Jewish ethnicity either as biography or as influence. Few have bothered to dig deeper into his socioeconomic, intellectual, cultural, and ethnic-religious context. Nor have any deemed it fit to place Kubrick's unique approach to his art in the wider context of Jewish culture, liturgy, religion, and history beyond the Holocaust, which is especially surprising given how much of his work is strewn with allusions and themes drawn from normative Judaism. Such an approach that fails to consider Kubrick's Jewish background does not recognize that Kubrick did not just spring from nowhere. At the same time, Kubrick's signature technique of misdirection simultaneously expressed his Jewishness while distracting many from recognizing it. Given the willingness of scholars, critics, and fans to ignore Kubrick's origins and ethnicity that played a part in shaping his view of the world, many (quasi-religious) commentaries have arisen interpreting his oeuvre from a myriad of perspectives.

By contrast, Geoffrey Cocks' ground-breaking research illuminated Kubrick's life and work by revisiting it in a context that has until now been minimized or overlooked by biographers, scholars, fans, and critics (2004). Cocks' research has shown how his Jewishness had a significant effect upon Kubrick, manifested, in part, by his desire to make a film about the Holocaust. Kubrick may not have been religious, but the religious framework of Jewishness and Judaism that surrounded him, however diluted, influenced his films. The impact of the director's ethnicity is apparent in his films obliquely, rarely explicitly, typically via analogies and metaphors that incorporated extensive biblical and other Jewish and Hebrew imagery.

Building upon Cocks' work, my own original approach to Kubrick explores his films in an intensive process of textual analysis akin to Talmudic study to elucidate and elaborate upon their deeper or hidden meanings beneath the surface, that is, beyond the literal reading or representation in his films. Kubrick's films invite us to look deeper, to embark on a journey of interpretation that takes us beyond the story. My book *Stanley Kubrick: New York Jewish Intellectual* redefined the interpretation of his films, encouraging viewers to go back and re-watch them. To take just one example, *2001: A Space Odyssey* (1968) is possibly Kubrick's most elliptical film. He described it as a six-million-dollar religious film, insisting that "the God concept" lay at its heart and that in it he had tried to achieve "a scientific definition of God." Paradoxically, many have seen it both as Kubrick's most secular and most religious film. While fans, critics, and scholars alike have picked up its religiosity, or lack of it, their interpretations have been overwhelmingly Christian. An alternative approach, however, reveals a distinctly Jewish understanding of the universe, especially in its use of imagery drawn from the Hebrew Scriptures, Talmud, liturgy, and Kabbalah.

This methodology is equally applicable to Kubrick's other films. For instance, *Dr. Strangelove, or, How I Learned to Stop Worrying and Love the Bomb* (1964) can be read as a Jewish version of the apocalypse, bringing into its purview the mythical legend of the Golem (something also shared with *2001*). *A Clockwork Orange* (1971) is perhaps his most theological film, dealing with the nature of evil from the perspective of Jewish normativity. *The Shining* (1980) can be understood as Kubrick's contribution to the centuries-old discussion of that shocking story from Genesis 22, The Binding of Isaac, and the problem of blind obedience to authority in the twentieth century.

This fruitful method has demonstrated that Kubrick's work can be approached as the work of a mind immersed in the same processes that produced the Talmud, that body of religious civil and ceremonial law central to Rabbinic Judaism. The Talmud is a dense compendium filled with commentaries, debates, and references outside the text itself. Like the web, it is hypertextual and intertextual, containing multiple and multifarious coexisting arguments that contend with each other in a form of debate arrived at through intense textual analysis (known as "pilpul"). It has been often described as "the sea of the Talmud." The Talmud is not chronological. It need not be started at the beginning because it was not written in a stepwise fashion. As Norman Solomon has put it, "Talmud is essentially an activity, not a book; you engage in it, rather than read it as you would a piece of literature. The word *Talmud* means 'study,' and stands for the creative study of Torah" (2009: xviii). One must bring to its study, "wit and an inquisitive and open mind" (xii). Like a Rubik's Cube, with its endless permutations, the Talmud can be turned over and over.

Alongside Talmudic interpretation lies a system of exegesis (interpretation) known by the acronym *PaRDeS* (in Hebrew this is pronounced "Pardes," which also means "paradise" or "orchard"). The ancient Jewish exegetes saw it as their challenge to unlock the Bible's messages, to reveal the inner significance of the text, and this approach enabled them to penetrate beneath the surface of the text. It is realized through four layers of seeing. First, *Peshat* (lit. "plain" or "simple") is the attempt to establish the literal or plain meaning of the text, primarily through the process of defining precisely the grammatical functions and structures of its language, the story (in some ways very similar to film language and grammar). The second layer, "*Remez*" (lit. "hints"), operates by the belief that even the most commonplace word in the Bible is a container of deeper meaning, which the interpreter is required to decode. The third level, "*Derash*" (comparative meaning, from Hebrew *darash*—"to inquire" or "to seek"), relates to the ancient tradition and oldest form of Bible interpretation known as Midrash: a kind of formal or informal elaboration on Jewish scripture, as a form of commentary, in order to elucidate or elaborate upon its hidden meanings; a method of interpreting biblical stories that goes beyond simple distillation of religious, legal, or moral teachings. It fills in many gaps left in the biblical narrative regarding events and personalities that are only hinted at in the text. As Gerald Bruns explains, "What matters in midrash is not only what lies behind the text in the form of an originating intention but what is in front of the text where the text is put into play. The text is always contemporary with its readers or listeners, that is, always oriented towards the time and circumstances of the interpreter" (1990: 191). Midrash thus seizes upon any repetition, of a word, or even a single letter, as intended to convey a meaning. At the same time, it can be highly metaphorical—not intended to be taken literally. Rather, it may sometimes serve as a key to particularly esoteric discussions to make the material less accessible to the casual reader. The final level is *Sod* (lit. "secret"). This equates to the tradition known as *Kabbalah* (lit. "received"), which believes that the Hebrew language has two alphabets, one revealed, and one hidden. Furthermore, in a Kabbalistic method known as *Gematria*, whereby the Bible is interpreted by calculating the numerical value of words, based on the values of their constituent letters, the secrets of Hebrew words can be deciphered from the cumulative sum of the numerical value of each letter, and certain numbers have profound significance.

The exegetical approach underpinning the Talmud is, arguably, a perfect fit for Kubrick's canon. Kubrick's style of filmmaking can certainly be described as "Talmudic." First, like any Talmudic scholar or *yeshiva bochur* (a picture of one appears in a photograph he took for *Look* magazine), he was an assiduous scholar, albeit not in any institutionalized setting like a seminary. He pored over his subjects, researching them deeply; he *cared*. To take one example, just look at the volume of material he read for his film about Napoleon, including possibly every book written on him in English. He compiled a series of index cars chronicling every day of Napoleon's life. As Jeremi Szaniawski has put it, such an image "summons a very Talmudic, *shule* context: reading, reading, reading, discussing, interpreting, interpreting . . . an [seemingly] endless process."[1] When he was not reading, Kubrick the filmmaker was interrogating his collaborators, absorbing their ideas, almost to the point of, sometimes, sucking them dry. His thirst for knowledge was insatiable.

Second, the way Kubrick researched his material was, like the Talmud, interlinked and associative. The catalogue of the Stanley Kubrick Archive at the University of the Arts London might categorize Kubrick's research by project, but this archival approach separates into discrete units rather than overlapping interests whereby ideas worked up for one film frequently found their way into others. A line from *Lolita* (1962), "LOLITA, light of my life," for example, ends up in *The Shining* used by Jack about Wendy (Shelley Duvall). My book on *Eyes Wide Shut* (1999) shows how Kubrick thought about adapting Arthur Schnitzler's *Traumnovelle* for the remainder of his feature filmmaking career, from the early 1950s onwards (Kolker and Abrams 2019). Ideas from that novella thus influenced much—perhaps all—of his output. Similarly, Kubrick sought and began, but ultimately failed, to make a movie about the Holocaust. In between, his fascination with Napoleon preoccupied him—and it found its way into *A Clockwork Orange* and *Barry Lyndon* (1975)—but he never abandoned his desire to make that film.

Third, Kubrick drafted and redrafted his screenplays that he then refined further in a form of Talmudic disputation (*pilpul*), back and forth, with his cast, crew, and creative collaborators. It has become abundantly clear from researching his working method that there was an almost endless process of back and forth until Kubrick was given what he did not know, and that which he was looking for in the first place. His signature technique was to encourage actors to improvise around the script, which was then rewritten as production progressed, often involving multiple takes and, in the case of *Eyes Wide Shut*, complete reshoots with a new set of actors. He wrote and rewrote while a film was in production. We see this in the only extant footage of Kubrick at work—the documentary *Making "The Shining"* (1980) by his daughter Vivian—where Jack Nicholson explains the different colors used to code the different screenplay drafts and how he only read the one produced that day. We even see Kubrick typing away, on set, while shooting is progressing. Consequently, during preproduction, and shooting itself, he generated a range of script documents.

Kubrick also generated a range of artefacts, costumes, and other possibilities, leaving behind him an archaeology of many different iterations and versions of what his films could be. This creative process and the resulting screenplay texts, as well as possible set-ups, locations, scenes, and so on, formed, like the Talmud, a palimpsest—an ancient text that was repeatedly used, then washed, and even scraped clean to be written on again. These gestures are only partially preserved; however, they are subsequently overwritten themselves, as the palimpsest becomes a tissue that reveals the layers of past and present.

Kubrick then indulged himself in editing—perhaps his favorite part of the entire filmmaking process—tinkering, and tweaking in a process of refinement, redaction, codification, and condensing of the greater whole into a summa of the preceding process, a précis. We know he even did this while a film was beginning its release, most notably with *2001* and *The Shining*. Some argue it would have happened with *Eyes Wide Shut*, too. For Kubrick, then, a film—like the Talmud—was a living thing.

Fourth, like the Talmud, Kubrick's orbit was wide-ranging and freewheeling. We know he covered many genres in the films he made and considered many more for the unplanned ones. He read and researched widely when making these films, immersing himself in the technical, scholarly, and historical literature surrounding nuclear disarmament, space travel, evolution, behavioral conditioning, the Vietnam War, the Holocaust, artificial intelligence, and Napoleon, to name just a few topics.

Fifth, his films formed a coherent canon with extensive cross-referencing, self-reflexivity, and self-referentiality. Allusions to his *Look* magazine photography can be found in many of his movies—too many to mention here. There are even more explicit references including, but not limited to, the record sleeve of music from *2001* that appears in *A Clockwork Orange*. The recurrence of the alphanumeric sequence CRM-114, which first appears in *Dr. Strangelove* but finds its way in various other forms into *A Clockwork Orange* (Serum-114) and *Eyes Wide Shut* (the morgue is location on C-wing, Room 114), is one example; the name Ludovico, which appears in *A Clockwork Orange* and *Barry Lyndon*, is another. *Eyes Wide* Shut, being the summa of his filmmaking and photographic career, is chock-full of references to his previous works. The way that the ending of Kubrick's films sometimes dovetailed into the beginning of the next has also been noticed. Finally, here, is the recurrence of actors across his oeuvre, including Joe Turkel and Philip Stone (three films apiece), Peter Sellers, Leonard Rossiter, and Steven Berkoff, not to mention his daughter, Vivian Kubrick (she appears in *2001*, *The Shining*, and *Full Metal Jacket* [1987]).

Finally, as mentioned earlier, Kubrick's films embrace the spirit of Talmudic study. They are some of the most cerebral and intellectual films ever made because Kubrick did his research and filled his films with its results. His works contain ideas and lots of them. As I argued in my 2018 book, Kubrick was a New York Jewish Intellectual, responding to the key concerns and debates of the day. Furthermore, he did not tell his audiences what to think; rather, he gave them the tools with which to think. Kubrick made the viewer work hard to engage with the meanings of his films. In the way that they are made, and the way that they play out on-screen, Kubrick's films embrace the spirit of the Talmud. Just as with the Talmud, in Kubrick's films, nothing is rendered easily or lightly, and the viewer must work hard to decode the deeper meanings and ideas. They can be turned over and over—perhaps we could call this Kubrick's Cube.

Consequently, Kubrick's work stimulates great interest, and his thirteen feature films are pored over with a Talmudic assiduousness, what we may call "Kubrickian exegesis," to appropriate a term from this volume's editor. This outpouring, or deluge—millions of words written by thousands of people—has reached an "almost Biblical level of exegesis" according to K. J. Donnelly (2018: 104), giving his films the status of some of the most scrutinized films of all time. His canon—*2001*, *The Shining*, and *Eyes Wide Shut* in particular—are studied at universities, chronicled in books, and have generally inspired levels of academic and fan analysis rivaled by the work of Talmudic scholars. Their studies reflect Bruns's aforementioned observation about Midrash, but is just as apt for Kubrick that what matters in his films is not only what lies behind the text in the form of an originating intention, but what is in front of the text where the text is put into play; the text is always contemporary with its readers or listeners, that is, always oriented toward the time and circumstances of the interpreter. They share a sort of Talmudic faith in the omniscient intentionality of the films' creator. Kubrick has been canonized as an "infallible perfectionist" with "overwhelming, God-like control and agency" (Donnelly 2018: 16), whereby every ambiguity, continuity error, prop, and artistic decision is interpreted as a coded message and analyzed for hidden meaning. Shawn Montgomery has called it "Crypto-Kubrology." Even Kubrick's death was treated as another secret to be unlocked. Witness the huge interest in Rodney Ascher's 2012 documentary *Room 237*, which uses a form of Talmudic and Midrashic exegesis to uncover whether Kubrick's film is about the genocide of the Native Americans, the Holocaust, faked NASA moon landings, or the Minotaur. Videos uncovering hidden secrets in Kubrick's films proliferate on the internet and YouTube. At the time of writing, the "I'm sorry Dave" scene has over two million views on YouTube alone. The Stanley Kubrick Appreciation Society, The Kubrick Society, and alt.movies.kubrick Facebook Groups—three English-language sites—currently have a combined total of more than 25,000 members. An exhibition of Kubrick memorabilia has been touring the world since 2004, drawing large crowds in a diverse range of geographical locations, including the Americas, Europe, and Asia. The exhibition arrived in the United Kingdom in 2019 for the first time, marking the twentieth anniversary of Kubrick's death and the release of *Eyes Wide Shut*.

But given that recognition of the import and impact of Kubrick's Jewishness, combined with his Talmudic and Midrashic style of filmmaking, has only arrived relatively recently, is it possible to assess his legacy and influence on similar Jewish directors? Here, I will suggest that five Jewish filmmakers—Mike Leigh, David Mamet, Joel and Ethan Cohen, and Darren Aronofsky—sensed and in turn were influenced by Kubrick's Talmudic and Midrashic method, applying it to their own work, and hence creating cerebral and intellectual works that can be turned over and over—in a form of Talmudic disputation or Kubrickian exegesis—in search of hidden and deeper meanings.

A Talmudic Method: Mike Leigh

Kubrick's working method resembled that of another Jewish director whose work Kubrick admired, Mike Leigh. Like Kubrick, Leigh was the son of Jewish doctor whose father had come to England from continental Europe. In addition, like Kubrick, all of Leigh's grandparents were Yiddish-speaking immigrants. There the youthful similarity ends, for Leigh grew up in a kosher and Zionist home in Manchester, England, by contrast to Kubrick's parents who, as far as we know, did not practice any ostensible religion. Leigh's parents strived "to be as English as possible" (qtd. in Bochenski 2008: 18). Where we still do not know where Kubrick stood on Israel, Leigh was a member of the Labor Zionist youth group Habonim (literally, "the builders"), but he left the movement in 1960 after becoming disenchanted with Israel's policies toward the Arabs. He only returned to Israel in 1991. Despite his ambivalence toward Israel, Leigh is proud of his Jewish heritage, but he only began to speak about it openly in the mid-1990s. Ray Carney and Leonard Quart explain how Leigh was neither traditionally religious nor, as an adult showed any interest in or formal identification with Jewish communal and cultural organizations. Despite these feelings, his Jewish roots are an undeniable part of who Leigh is, though they are a private rather than public aspect of his life. Those roots are also a factor that, he admits, has contributed to his being an outsider and rebel. Jewishness, however, has never been the subject of his art (excepting the unpleasant, middle-class Jewish characters in *Hard Labour* [1973], who live in a house only two doors from where the director grew up), although he has talked vaguely of making a film about the world of his parents and grandparents. Still, the shouting and general tumult of a certain type of Jewish family life has affected how he depicts family interaction in his work. Further, Leigh holds that there cannot be anything more Jewish than the tendency of his films both to posit questions rather than provide answers and to take pleasure in both lamenting and laughing at the human predicament (2000: 1–2).

Significantly, Leigh was one of the few fellow film directors to be invited to Kubrick's funeral in March 1999.[2]

Like Kubrick, Leigh also appeared to be consciously avoiding any reference to Judaism, and hence did not tend to insert any Jewishness into his films in any direct or explicit fashion. Indeed, at the time of writing, Leigh has made only one film—*Hard Labour*—with any overt reference to his or anyone else's Jewishness in his films. Where he has done so, he did it onstage in 2005 in his play *Two Thousand Years*, which has not made it onto either the big or the small screen. While Leigh feels "it's possible to see a certain kind of Jewish influence," he thinks, "it would be wrong to label these films 'Jewish,'" as "it could be distracting and distorting" (qtd. in Movshovitz 2000: 76). Furthermore, he has added, "at the most fundamental and obvious level it would be perfectly wrong to read my films as being primarily in any way about Jewishness ... for years and years I shut up about the whole thing, because you don't want to be labelled and the whole thing has a different currency in the English dimension" (qtd. in Movshovitz 2000: 90). Thus, it seems that Leigh has taken the same route that Kubrick had traveled before him, namely, to universalize his Jewishness out of the public sphere.

Nevertheless, Leigh has gone on record to describe his approach to filmmaking as "Talmudic." Influenced by his youthful participation in Habonim, and compounded by visits to, including a brief sojourn in, Israel, Leigh embraced a "collectivist" creative process in his practice as a director. "Having that leadership experience," Leigh subsequently reflected, "was great and has absolutely informed not only how I am but also how I've worked. Everybody was open and democratic and working together towards a goal, a spirit of which goes right the way through my productions and the way I work" (qtd. in Raphael 2008: 6). Leigh's screenplays emerge from a process of *pilpul* with his cast. Working intensely with a group of individual selected actors, they developed the characters and narratives, typically via a form of improvisation. Only Leigh, at the center, orchestrating the action, knows how these interconnected lives will result. Like Kubrick, this can take months of collaboration and rehearsal. Unlike Kubrick, however, Leigh drafts the final script, which is then scrupulously followed and eventually staged (or filmed) without further revision. Tellingly, Leigh has described this much-discussed but still mysterious method as "a rebbe surrounded by Talmudic students, talking things out." He seeks "in a Talmudic way, to raise questions and posit possibilities" (qtd. in Inverne 2005). As the critic John Lahr nicely observes, "The question mark is what Leigh's films are all about" (1996: 50). He then invites his audiences to sit round the table and to say, "'Maybe it's this. Maybe it's that. We don't know.' Which is a Talmudic investigation that doesn't arrive at any conclusions, basically." And, like the older Kubrick, "with his full beard and deep, expressive eyes [Leigh resembles] a wonder-working Hasidic rabbi, able to examine the most intimate secrets of the soul" (Turan 1996: 7).

Using a form of Talmudic investigation, Donald Weber argues, persuasively in my opinion, that Leigh's *Secrets and Lies* (1996) is his "exemplary Jewish film, a more apt representation of what Leigh has described as the 'Jewish spirit in my work'" (2016: 158).

He continues to say that "Mike Leigh's 'Jewish' soul remains more powerfully—indeed, most provocatively—revealed . . . in his deeply moving film about lost souls searching for family ties, for a way of salving the pain of living in a topsy-turvy multicultural Britain, where everyday people, feeling apart and uprooted, seek alternative modes of filiation, of connecting with a tribe to call their own" (2016). Leigh explained, "I wanted to do a film that in some way was about the need we all have to deal with our roots, to assert our identities and to know who we are, and to share and be truthful" (2016: 169). "In this respect," concludes Weber, "*Secrets and Lies* might be considered Leigh's more deeply Jewish work: Jewish, that is, in its 'tragic-comic' tones (the 'Jewish' influence that Leigh invariably acknowledges when asked about his relation to Jewishness), its sounding of the human heart, above all in its soul-searching powers of empathy" (2016).

Secrets and Lies is a film about the need to search for "roots" and "identity" in contemporary society.³ Hortense (Marianne Jean-Baptiste) is a black middle-class optometrist in search of her birth mother who, it is revealed, is the white working-class Cynthia (Brenda Blethyn), sister of Maurice Purley (Timothy Spall). Both Maurice's given name and chosen profession—a portrait photographer—can be read as Jewish. After all, Kubrick had an uncle named Maurice and began his career as a photographer for *Look* magazine. Indeed, Leigh modeled Maurice on his Russian immigrant grandfather Mayer Leibermann, who made a modest living as a portrait photographer in Leigh's native Salford.

"Thus at some level the figure of Maurice seems to channel Leigh's still vivid Jewish family memories" (Weber 2016: 170). Maurice even reveals himself to be Jewish, argues Weber, through his "comic tone of Jewish ironic understatement" and use of the words *schlep* when he says, "It's a bit of a schlep, isn't it?" (2016: 172). "At this moment," says Weber, "Maurice seems positioned as a hidden Jew in *Secrets [and Lies* . . .] Maurice appears to declare his ethnicity, to 'out' himself as a 'Jew' through his coded, 'insider' question to Hortense, even if the familiar Yiddish word 'schlep' has, for the most part, acquired a universal meaning" (2016). Thus, as Weber reveals, a Talmudic approach with a Talmudic filmmaker like Leigh reveals deeper secrets (and lies), in a mode akin to Kubrick's method and analysis of his work.

Talmudic Linguist: David Mamet

Another director whom Kubrick admired was David Mamet, who, in turn, admired Kubrick. Mamet described *The Killing* (1956) as "the world's greatest film noir" (2008: 149) and "Kubrick's team for the one last job is the greatest compilation of tough talent known to man" (2008:150). Influenced by *The Killing*, Mamet went on to make *Heist* (2001), possibly his most direct homage to Kubrick. Born in 1947, almost two decades after Kubrick, Mamet is much more open about his Jewishness, even having embraced the study of the Torah. Being more comfortable in his Jewish skin, Mamet sprinkles his work with Yiddish cadences and phrases as well as biblical and Jewish references and Talmudic allusions. As befitting a director who began his professional life as a playwright and a novelist, Mamet's Jewishness, arguably, is rendered through a taut and precise use of language—what might be called "Jewish syntax." In comparison to Kubrick's near wordlessness at times, he revels in beats, rhythms, and speech patterns and vocabulary of his subjects whose "particularized portrayals invite identification as Jews" (Kane 1999: 3). As Leslie Kane argues, "In language that juxtaposes the profane and mundane, the quotidian and the mythic, the vulgar and the spiritual, colloquial and sacred texts, Mamet, drawing on a six-thousand-year tradition of argument, paints a broad canvas of civilized arguers who dispute with each other about everything that matters" (Kane 1999). While Kubrick's "particularized portrayals invite identification as Jews," perhaps the closest Kubrick comes to such language use is the precise grunt-speak of *Full Metal Jacket*.

Impressed by Mamet's skills, Kubrick considered Mamet as a possible screenwriter (even if he eventually settled on Frederic Raphael) for *Eyes Wide Shut*. In 1993, he had scribbled a note to himself: "David Mamet—Rhapsody" (Abrams 2018: 242; Kolker and Abrams 2019: 39). Kubrick told Raphael that he admired David Mamet's *House of Games* (1987), where a successful psychiatrist, Margaret Ford, feels unfulfilled and is led on an odyssey by a patient named Billy Hahn—did the names Billy and Ford inspire Bill Harford? In its use of delusion and deception, its blurring between confidence game and reality, and its stilted use of language, one can see parallels between *House of Games* and *Eyes Wide Shut*.[4]

In a fruitful method that influenced my own reading of Kubrick, Kane (1999) has demonstrated how Mamet's work is rich in biblical allusion and scriptural exegesis, including Kabbalah and Gematria. For example, his *Homicide* (1991) deliberately employs coded languages, including a numerical one, making frequent reference to twos and fives. Mamet makes the task easier for us for, like Mike Leigh, but unlike Kubrick, he has been on record about his Jewish studies. He even includes direct references to the Book of Esther. At the same time, however, he is less concerned as to whether most of his audiences would recognize the Jewish symbolism within his work. Paraphrasing the great Jewish scholar Maimonides, he replied, "Those that do, do; those that do not, do not" (Mamet, qtd. in Kane 1999: 362 n. 40).

As Leslie Kane has pointed out in terms of Mamet's work specifically, but which is just as apt for Kubrick, "His response underscores the coded nature of the work, accessible on many levels" (Kane 1999).

"A Grand Unifying Theory of Coen-ness": Joel and Ethan Coen

The "two-headed monster," as long-time collaborator John Turturro affectionately calls brothers and film-directing partnership Joel and Ethan Coen, emerged from nowhere in 1985 with *Blood Simple*. In this volume, Rodney F. Hill sees them as the clearest heirs to Kubrick, evidenced by their range of genres and their direct homages to *Dr. Strangelove* in *Raising Arizona* (1987) and *The Shining* in *Barton Fink* (1991), respectively (although their prolific output, having gone on to make sixteen more movies, distinguishes them from Kubrick).

Adam Nayman sees *Burn After Reading* (2008) as a political satire in the mode of *Strangelove* (2018: 232). To this can be added the homage paid to both *Killer's Kiss* (1955) and *Lolita* (1962) in *The Man Who Wasn't There* (2001). Indeed, Kubrick was and continues to be a major influence on the Coens' work, and his presence looms large over their films. As critic and programmer Kent Jones notes, Stanley Kubrick is "one of the few filmmakers whose shadow falls over Joel and Ethan's playground" (qtd. in Nayman 2018: 14). On *Barton Fink*, for example, they would say, "Think Kubrick!" (Nayman 2018: 253). One could also consider their use of Homer's *The Odyssey* in *O Brother Where Art Thou?* (2000). Surely, John Goodman's overblown performance of Walter Sobchak in *The Big Lebowski* (1998) owes something to the exaggerated performances of some many of Kubrick's leading men (Paul Mazursky, Peter Sellers, George C. Scott, Jack Nicholson, and Lee Ermey). As for the blank that is Barton Fink, he could possibly be seen as a combination of Keir Dullea and Ryan O'Neal (minus their looks).

Nevertheless, it is in their Talmudic and Midrashic filmmaking that the Coens really deserve the "Kubrickian" moniker. As Hill states, "Although it is possible to enjoy these films simply on the level of entertainment and narrative engagement, they offer a deeper level of ambiguity, metaphor, and symbolism than does the typical Saturday-night diversion." Nayman adds, "They also produce artworks that seem perfectly formed and impenetrable, and yet also prove—like Kubrick's superficially anal-retentive masterpieces—to be wide open to rigorous analysis and desperate speculation alike" (Nayman 2018: 14). An image from their *A Serious Man* (2009), which stands as a microcosm of their entire oeuvre, illustrates this. In it, untenured physics professor Larry Gopnik (Michael Stuhlbarg) stands before his lecture class, dwarfed by an enormous chalkboard, covered in its entirety by a convoluted mathematical proof. This "single most indelible frame in any movie by the Coen brothers," Adam Nayman argues, sums up the "cosmological complexity" of their universe, a dizzying array of intertextual, self-referential, and hypertextual associations that loop back and forth across their movies, creating a "Grand Unifying Theory of Coen-ness" (2018) One wonders if there could be such a thing as a "Grand Unifying Theory of Kubrick-ness."

Taken together, the Coen Brothers' films can accurately be described as "Talmudic." Like Kubrick, whose words and works are intricately analyzed and debated in Talmudic fashion, scholars have applied similar levels of infallibility to the Coens. Adam Nayman argues "they are obsessives who calibrate their frames and soundscapes down to the millimeter" (14). "The next visibly imprecise camera placement or sloppy dialogue cue in their work," Nayman avers, "will also be the first" (2009). Moreover, as any Talmudic scholar knows, fully getting the Coen Brothers' films requires immersion in film lore and film history.

The Coen Brothers' *A Serious Man* is possibly the film that is closest, in spirit, to Kubrick's Talmudic film style. Although it is explicitly Jewish—something Kubrick never managed to achieve in his lifetime—it contains an abundance of unexplained religious references rooted in Jewish lore. The film opens with an epigraph from the medieval Jewish sage and commentator Rashi: "Receive with simplicity everything that happens to you." Are the Coens being disingenuous here? Or are they warning us merely to enjoy the experience and not think about it too deeply? It certainly shows their knowledge of Jewish philosophy (recall that Walter Sobchack's dog in *The Big Lebowski* was called "Maimonides" and "Jew by choice" Walter was fond of quoting the originator of Zionism, Herzl). The film then launches into a subtitled Yiddish-language prologue set in the past, in a Polish *shtetl* concerning the spirit of a dead person known in Yiddish as a *dybbuk* (an evil spirit or demon possessing a human being).[5] This prologue may or may not have a connection to that which proceeds it. The person in question may or may not be a *dybbuk*. In a Kubrickian move, we are never entirely clear. In a fashion mirroring the match cut in *2001* that projects us four million years into the future, the Coens fast-forward us into the 1960s, where the next language heard is untranslated Hebrew. And while English dominates the dialogue thereafter, it is punctuated with further untranslated Hebrew and Yiddish phrases (*goy*, *Hashem*, and *get*). On one level, *A Serious Man* is a reworking of the Book of Job, just as *2001 is*, on one level, a reworking of Homer's *Odyssey* (itself revisited by the Coens in *O Brother*). Just like its *schlemiel* protagonist, Larry, as he undergoes his own personal odyssey, shuffling from rabbi to rabbi to make sense of what is happening to him, we end the film none the wiser. A parable about a goy's teeth—much like the prologue—goes nowhere. Or maybe it does. We just never know if it is meant to or if the Coens are messing with us in a form of Kubrickian misdirection.

Barton Fink has been read as the movie nearest in look and subject to Kubrick. In its tale of a blocked Hollywood studio-era screenwriter, holed up in a hotel, struggling to produce, it certainly mirrors the situation of Jack Torrance (Jack Nicholson) in *The Shining* and Kubrick when he was not making a film. Barton is a "schmuck with an Underwood," just as Jack is an asshole with an Adler. However, using the form of analysis that Geoffrey Cocks applied to *The Shining*, we can begin to see that a series of clues combine to allow, albeit not with certainty, a subsurface haunting of the film by the specter of the Shoah. While Cocks' book was not published until 2004, the Coens sensed in *The Shining* what Cocks later analyzed. *Barton Fink* was conceived while the Coens were working on *Miller's Crossing* (1991) in which John Turturro played the wandering Jew-type, Bernie Bernbaum. During *Miller's Crossing*, Bernie is led to a wooded area outside of town where he is to be executed, SS-style. Joel Coen remarked, "People objected to the fact that the character was Jewish and about the way Gabriel Byrne takes him out to the woods to shoot him. It's such a stretch to take this old Chicago gangster behavior and turn it into a train ride to Auschwitz[?]" (qtd. in Bergan 2001: 45). Written while the Coens were making *Miller's Crossing*, *Barton Fink* cannot help but refer back to their earlier film; at the same time, it provides baggage that is almost immediately carried over from one film to the next, particularly in their near simultaneity.

Firmly grounded in the "Golden Age" of studio-era Hollywood, which reached its zenith between 1930 and 1945, the film is shot through with stylized, 1930s and early 1940s period architecture, look, and set design. Fink's heavy overcoat, his hat, his dark, drab suits, all come realistically out of the 1930s, and recall the clothing of so many of those murdered during the Holocaust. Indeed, at the end of the film, as he prepares to leave the Hotel Earle clutching a mysterious package, he resembles a deportee. Furthermore, the Coens deliberately chose to locate the film in 1941, on the eve of the bombing of Pearl Harbor and one year prior to the implementation of the Final Solution, but at a point when hundreds of thousands of Jews had already been murdered, invoked by the pairs of shoes, seemingly ownerless, lining the corridor of the sixth floor of the Hotel Earle.[6] It is the film's denouement that the Holocaust clues are most noticeable by their relative abundance, particularly as the hotel is consumed by fire—the original meaning of the term "Holocaust"—but then again, is it? Yet like Kubrick, the significant thing about *Barton Fink* is in its refusal to use the Holocaust to any edifying or other effect. The Coens were deliberately evasive on the question of whether the import of such references was readily decoded or whether they proved too subtle for re/viewers. Critics were certainly puzzled by the ending. While the Holocaust hovered as a phantom-like presence over the film, *Barton Fink* has been interpreted in several ways, but which proves especially resistant to definitive interpretation. In this way, the Coens definitely are heirs to the Kubrickian Talmudic tradition of producing films that are rich and polysemous in nature, but which defy simple analysis.

Kubrick's Heir Apparent: Darren Aronofsky

Perhaps the closest Jewish heir to Kubrick is independent filmmaker Darren Aronofsky. Born in 1969, he grew up with what he described as a "classically hypocritical high holiday Jewish upbringing" (Adams 1998: 2) in Brooklyn, New York, not too far from Kubrick's childhood home of the Bronx. When he was eighteen years old, he went to Israel to work on a Kibbutz before attending Harvard University. While in Israel, he took what he described as "one of those crash courses on Judaism; there was a lot of Kabbalah in it, and that got my mind sparked" (qtd. in Desser and Friedman 2004: 314). While the religious appeal of Hassidism passed him by, he was drawn to what David Desser and Lester D. Friedman describe as "the more intimate relationship between mathematical equations and the Kabbalah" (Desser and Friedman 2004), which he spent much time exploring during his time at college. Consequently, as Jeremi Szaniawski (2019) has pointed out, Darren Aronofsky's early work embodies Kubrick's "obsessiveness and systemic, mathematical (and Kabbalistic)" approach, especially his early features *Pi* (1998) and *Requiem for a Dream* (2000).

Aronofsky presents other similarities to Kubrick. He began his feature filmmaking career in black and white. He is not prolific, having made only seven major features between 1998 and 2017 (strikingly close to Kubrick's nine features between 1953 and 1972), and has covered a range of genres, including science fiction, family melodrama, psychological drama, biblical epic, and sport. His *Black Swan* (2010) very much echoes Kubrick's obsession for doppelgangers and even ballet (Kubrick's second wife, Ruth Sobotka was a ballet dancer who choreographed and performed the ballet sequence in his *Killer's Kiss*). Like Kubrick, who cast his three wives in his films—Toba Metz in *Fear and Desire* (1953), Sobotka in *Killer's Kiss*, and Christiane Harlan in *Paths of Glory* (1958), Aronofsky has directed his: Rachel Weisz in *The Fountain* (2006). Similarly,

Aronofsky's body of work forces its viewers to work hard to decode its meanings. His most elliptical films, *The Fountain* and *mother!* (2017) resemble Kubrick's *2001*, and likewise have often been criticized as obscure or incomprehensible.

Jadranka Skorin-Kapov has referred to Aronofsky's interests as resembling "Kubrick's excess visible in the human condition and leading us toward the limit of existence in obsession or madness" (2015: 66).

However, where Kubrick's works can be mined for their Jewish meanings—Talmudic, Midrashic, Kabbalistic—Aronofsky's are much more explicit in their use of these exegetical techniques. As befitting a younger Jewish director, perhaps more comfortable in his Jewish skin in latter-day Hollywood, Aronofsky deals with more explicit Jewishness than Kubrick was ever able to do. Where *Spartacus* (1960) feels like a biblical epic, recreating the Exodus from Egypt, but using another historical event, *Noah* (2014) is an unambiguous reworking of the biblical story, drawing upon Genesis, Midrash, and the Book of Enoch. And where I have argued that one can detect the influence of Kabbalah in Kubrick's *2001*, but only beneath its surface (Abrams 2018), Aronofsky's *Pi* is explicit in its use of Kabbalah to structure the movie in which a group of Jewish scholars are engaged in mathematical research, deriving from the belief that the Torah is really a string of numbers that form a code sent by God. They are thus searching the text for the 216-digit number they believe is the true name of God. Whether intentional or not, this gematric approach mirrors that which Geoffrey Cocks applied to Kubrick's oeuvre in uncovering iterations of the number forty-two (which he argues is a signifier for the Final Solution) and its multiples of seven. Like *The Killing*, *Pi* also seeks to answer what David Desser and Lester D. Friedman describe as the "age-old question of whether the universe is but a series of random, chaotic events or does some hidden design exist that makes rational sense" (315). It also explores the nature of institutions—here religious and financial—in much the same way that Kubrick explored hierarchies and organizations in his work.

The Fountain seems to be attempting to do something vaguely like what Kubrick did in *2001*.[7] Indeed, Glenn Kenny (2006) of *Premiere* compared Aronofsky's direction in this film to Kubrick's "in terms of conceptual audacity and meticulousness of execution." Like its predecessor, *The Fountain* is a cerebral science fiction film that aims to push the boundaries of the genre while dealing with the big philosophical questions regarding life, death, and eternity. Just as Kubrick described *2001* as a search for the scientific definition of God, Aronofsky described his film as "the search for God, the search for meaning" (qtd. in Linder 2001). The six years it took Aronofsky to make the film parallels some of the timeframes in which Kubrick made his. If *2001* opens with a segment that paraphrases the Fall of Man in Genesis, *The Fountain* opens with a direct quote from it (Genesis 3:24). Thereafter, the film is designed around the Sefirot of Kabbalah.

Like *2001*, *The Fountain* contains multiple storylines set in different time periods, which Aronofsky has stated are open to interpretation; its intricacy is "very much like a Rubik's Cube, where you can solve it in several different ways" (qtd. in Kolakowski 2006). It, too, is composed of three stories set in three time periods in which the protagonist metamorphoses through different stages of human evolution. Tomas Creo

(Hugh Jackman) is a conquistador, sent by Isabella, Queen of Spain (Rachel Weisz), to find the fabled Tree of Life in New Spain to save her from death at the hands of the zealous Inquisitor. In the present, neuroscientist Tommy Creo struggles to use a strange substance derived from a South American tree to cure his dying wife's cancer (also played by Weisz). In an unspecified future, Tommy is an astronaut traveling in a womb-like enclosure not dissimilar to that of the Star Child that ends *2001* to take a gigantic tree holding the fading soul of his dead wife to Xibalba, the Mayan underworld that exists as a dying star surrounded by a nebula.

If *The Fountain* proved opaque, it was nothing in comparison to Aronofsky's most recent film, *mother!*. This film, like *2001*, has divided audiences, even earning loud boos as well as applause. Marketed by Paramount Pictures as a horror film, it defies genre conventions and audience expectations. Possibly it is in a genre all of its own: allegorical biblical movie, building upon the Midrashic mode evidenced in *Noah*. A poet called Him (Javier Bardem) and his unnamed wife (Jennifer Lawrence) are renovating his childhood home. A series of uninvited guests arrive—graciously received by Him, much to her consternation—leading to death, mayhem, carnage, and an all-consuming fire (*olah* or *shoah*) in which all but Him die.

The film ends as it begins: on an image of a woman awaking in bed, repeating the cycle. One can see many parallels with Kubrick's work here. Like the Torrances in *The Shining*, Him is blocked, and mother is doing all the restorative work—like Wendy (Shelley Duvall), she is the "caretaker." The film is explicitly allegorical in the way that Kubrick intended *Fear and Desire*. The nonlinear storyline recalls *The Killing*, while the cycle and reincarnation reflects both *The Shining* and *2001*. The senseless killing emulates *A Clockwork Orange*, *Spartacus*, and *Full Metal Jacket*. It becomes clear that the film, at least its first half, is a retelling of Genesis—the Fall of Man, Cain and Abel, and the Flood—in much the same way as the "Dawn of Man" sequence in *2001*. The second half, in its critique of Catholicism, echoes Kubrick's fascination with religion and religious iconography, particularly as it appeared in his first three documentaries, but recurred in subsequent films (*Paths of Glory*, *A Clockwork Orange*, *Barry Lyndon*, *Full Metal Jacket*, and *Eyes Wide Shut*). Aronofsky's willingness to produce such mystical, elliptical incomprehensible texts, particularly when so much of their meaning may be lost on his audiences and in the face of studio pressure, but which draw upon traditional Jewish sources, clearly resembles Kubrick's.

Conclusion

While this chapter has taken a narrow focus on five film directors, there are many more who could be considered. I have barely touched the range of Jewish filmmakers and their films that Kubrick admired, including but not limited to Steven Spielberg, Woody Allen, Roman Polanski, and David Cronenberg. Consider for example, the contemporaneity and similarity of *Eyes Wide Shut*, Polanski's *The Ninth Gate*, and Cronenberg's *eXistenZ* (Jennifer Jason Leigh who was meant to appear in *Eyes Wide Shut* ended up starring in this film), which all came out at the same time (1999). Or how Kubrick recommended Allen's *Husbands and Wives* (1992) to Frederic Raphael while working on a film with remarkably similar themes and even starring the same actor (Sydney Pollack). Then there are those who have followed in his wake, such as Charlie Kaufman, Spike Jonze, and Jonathan Glazer. This latter director is particularly interesting—in his borrowings from Kubrick's work and in only making three films in two decades with barely a hint of Jewishness in them, which seemingly emulates Kubrick. Furthermore, in *thematic* terms, his *Sexy Beast* (2000)—one last job/heist—*Birth* (2004)—marriage and childhood precocity—and *Under the Skin* (2013)—an outsider in an alien world—resemble *The Killing*, *The Shining/Eyes Wide Shut*, and *2001/Barry Lyndon*, respectively. Stylistically, Glazer draws liberally from across Kubrick's oeuvre when crafting his films. Perhaps where Glazer and some of his contemporaries fall down is that they lack the depth—the cerebral, intellectual element that makes them less susceptible to Kubrickian exegesis—to be turned over and over like a Rubik's Cube. While Talmudic and Midrashic analysis can be applied to a vast panel of Jewish (and non-Jewish) filmmakers, arguably, not all of those filmmakers are Talmudic in the way Kubrick and his films were.

Notes

1 Jeremi Szaniawski, email to author, March 4, 2019.
2 According to Kubrick's daughter, Katharina, he was a fan of Leigh's 1977 film *Abigail's Party* (Wrigley 2018).
3 A title that could be just as apt for *Eyes Wide Shut* if a bit too on the nose for Kubrick.
4 Later (in 1995), it was reported that Mamet had been working on a *Lolita* screenplay.
5 It is worth noting here, given what will be discussed below, that "Dybbuk" was the codename that Mossad gave Adolf Eichmann, one of the chief architects of the Holocaust. Furthermore, the prologue in which this dybbuk appears is a reminder of the world which Nazis like Eichmann destroyed.
6 Here, we can see a link to the hair on the floor of the barbershop as the new recruits are being shaved in *Full Metal Jacket*, an equally powerful echo of Auschwitz and the Nazi death camps.
7 Aronofsky indirectly acknowledges the influence of *2001* in his choice of name for his protagonist, Tommy: Major Tom in David Bowie's song *Space Oddity* itself inspired by Kubrick's film.

Works Cited

Abrams, Nathan. 2018. *Stanley Kubrick: New York Jewish Intellectual*. New Brunswick, NJ: Rutgers University Press.
Adams, Sam. 1998. "Pi Brain." *Philadelphia City Paper*. July 23.
Bergan, Ronald. 2001. *The Coen Brothers*. London: Phoenix.
Bochenski, Matt. 2008. "Who's Happy Now?" *Curzon Cinemas* 7. March/April.
Bruns, Gerald L. 1990. "The Hermeneutics of Midrash," in Regina M. Schwartz (ed.), *The Book and the Text*. Oxford: Blackwell, 189–213.

Carney, Ray and Leonard Quart. 2012. *The Films of Mike Leigh*. Cambridge: Cambridge University Press.

Cocks, Geoffrey. 2004. *The Wolf at the Door: Stanley Kubrick, History and the Holocaust*. New York: Peter Lang.

David Desser and Lester D. Friedman. 2004. *American Jewish Filmmakers*. Urbana-Champaign: University of Illinois Press.

Donnelly, K.J. 2018. *The Shining*. New York: Columbia University Press.

Hill, Rodney. 2019. "Kubrick's Inheritors: Aesthetics, Independence and Philosophy in the films of Joel and Ethan Coen," in Jeremi Szaniawski (ed.), *After Kubrick: A Filmmaker's Legacy*. New York and London: Bloomsbury Academic.

Inverne, James. 2005. "'Like Having a Muslim in the House.'" *The Jerusalem Report*. October 17.

Kane, Leslie. 1999. *Weasels and Wisemen: Ethics and Ethnicity in the Work of David Mamet*. Basingstoke and London: Macmillan.

Kenny, Glenn. 2006. "The Fountain," *Premiere*. November 22.

Kolakowski, Nick. 2006. "Director Darren Aronofsky: A 'Fountain' Quest Fulfilled." *Washington Post*, November 24.

Kolker, Robert and Abrams, Nathan. 2019. *Eyes Wide Shut: Stanley Kubrick and the Making of His Final Film*. New York: Oxford University Press.

Lahr, John. 1996. "This Other England." *The New Yorker*. 72. September 23.

Linder, Brian. 2001. "Aronofsky, Pitt Team for Sci-Fi Epic." *IGN*. April 5.

Mamet, David. 2008. *Bambi vs. Godzilla: On the Nature, Purpose, and Practice of the Movie Business*. New York: Vintage.

Movshovitz, Howie. 2000. *Mike Leigh: Interviews*. Jackson, MI: University Press of Mississippi.

Nayman, Adam. 2018. *The Coen Brothers—This Book Really Ties the Films Together*. New York: Abrams Books.

Raphael, Amy. 2008. *Mike Leigh on Mike Leigh*. London: Faber and Faber.

Skorin-Kapov, Jadranka. 2015. *Darren Aronofsky's Films and the Fragility of Hope*. New York and London: Bloomsbury Academic.

Solomon, Norman. 2009. *The Talmud*. London: Penguin.

Szaniawski, Jeremi. 2019. "After Kubrick (1927–1999): a Cinematic Legacy." Senses of Cinema. March. http://sensesofcinema.com/2019/feature-articles/after-kubrick-1927-1999-a-cinematic-legacy (accessed May 13, 2019).

Turan, Kenneth. 2000. "The Case for Mike Leigh" [1996], in Howie Movshovitz (ed.), *Mike Leigh: Interviews*. Jackson, MI: University Press of Mississippi, 84–97.

Weber, Donald. 2016. "*Peckhlach*: Mike Leigh's Jewish Soul," in Nathan Abrams (ed.), *Hidden in Plain Sight: Jews and Jewishness in British Film, Television, Popular Culture*. Evanston, IL: Northwestern University Press, 157–79.

Wrigley, Nick. 2018. "Stanley Kubrick, cinephile." February 8. https://www.bfi.org.uk/news-opinion/sight-sound-magazine/polls-surveys/stanley-kubrick-cinephile (accessed May 13, 2019).

3

Kubrick's Inheritors: Aesthetics, Independence, and Philosophy in the Films of Joel and Ethan Coen

Rodney F. Hill

Classic "auteur" criticism has had a tough time dealing with Stanley Kubrick, who, unlike Hitchcock, Hawks, Ford, and others, essentially "never made the same film twice." That is, it is difficult to spot prima facie connections between such disparate works as *2001: A Space Odyssey* (1968), *A Clockwork Orange* (1971), and *Barry Lyndon* (1975)—to say nothing of *Lolita* (1962)—and to recognize them all as being "Stanley Kubrick films." As Kubrick told Michel Ciment in 1971: "There is no deliberate pattern to the stories that I have chosen to make into films. About the only factor at work each time is that I try not to repeat myself" (Ciment 2001: 153).

Similarly, Joel and Ethan Coen have prided themselves on trying to achieve "something different" with each new film, often radically shifting tone and genre from one film to the next—a tendency that emerged from the very beginnings of their career, with such wide-ranging works as *Blood Simple* (1984), a low-budget film noir; the "hayseed comedy" *Raising Arizona* (1987); *Miller's Crossing* (1990), a polished, period gangster drama; the generically unclassifiable *Barton Fink* (1991); and *The Hudsucker Proxy* (1994), a studio-financed screwball comedy. This pattern of generic variation continues to the present day, as evidenced in their most recent efforts: the western, *True Grit* (2010), an adaptation of Charles Portis's 1968 novel (and pointedly *not* a remake of the 1970 John Wayne movie); *Inside Llewyn Davis* (2013), a character study of a struggling folk singer; and *Hail, Caesar!* (2016), an affectionate spoof of 1940s Hollywood. Even *The Ballad of Buster Scruggs* (2018) illustrates this tendency, consisting of six short segments that are vastly different in aesthetics and tone, despite their generic kinship as "westerns." If we are to consider the Coen Brothers as *auteurs*, as with Kubrick, we must look beyond their surface-level narratives and delve deeper into their approach to film style and philosophy ("the life of the mind," as it were), in order to see how such an odd assortment of films fits together.

This level of generic disparity (that is, the fact that the filmmakers have not been pigeonholed into particular types of films that they are *expected* to make) may stem in part from another commonality shared by Kubrick and the Coens: their remarkable degree of independence.

Perhaps the most astonishing thing about Kubrick's debut feature, *Fear and Desire* (1953), is that it saw the light of day at all—as an American independent film before there was any institutional support for truly independent work (outside of niche markets such as the avant-garde, the so-called race films of the 1910s–1940s, etc.). Previously, the term *independent producer* had denoted someone such as David O. Selznick, who was not attached to a particular studio but still worked well within the studio system, with all of its resources. (Hitchcock would later follow this same model.) Only after the 1948 Supreme Court decision in the Paramount Case, which weakened to some extent the oligopoly of the Hollywood studios, did the possibility arise for truly independent American filmmakers to secure mainstream distribution and exhibition for their films.

At the forefront of that phenomenon, Stanley Kubrick emerged as just such an independent; and he seems to have understood from the outset the potential of genre pictures—in the case of *Fear and Desire*, the war film—to explore fundamental aspects of the human psyche and thus, hopefully, to find an audience with whom such a film would resonate, even without a big budget or top stars. The biggest "name" in *Fear and Desire* (as with the subsequent *Killer's Kiss* [1955]) is the "B" actor, Frank Silvera. Although *Fear and Desire* was not a commercial success, it did receive a respectable distribution—playing in multiple major markets—and some good reviews, including praise from James Agee, who told Kubrick, "There are too many good things in the film to call it 'arty'" (Phillips 2002: 112). It also served as a "calling card" for Kubrick, along with *Killer's Kiss*, allowing him to progress to the next level in his career. In these respects, we may see *Fear and Desire* as a daring, early entry in what would become the "American independent cinema"; and decades later, the films of the Coen Brothers, among others in the resurgence of American indies, owe a debt to the pioneering work of 1950s mavericks such as Kubrick, Morris Engel, and a few others, who demonstrated that it was possible to make potentially successful films outside "the system."

Like *Fear and Desire*, the Coens' first feature, *Blood Simple*, is a modest genre piece, financed independently and made entirely outside the structures of the Hollywood system, at a time when blockbusters ruled the day. As with Kubrick's early work, the film boasts no stars, the biggest "name" being the character actor, M. Emmett Walsh (Frances McDormand was unknown at the time). Ethan Coen has noted the problems in getting such a project into the public eye: "The difficult part was interesting an American distributor. They said it's too bloody to be an art movie and too arty to be an exploitation movie" (Mottram 2000: 25). Yet, just as Kubrick had found a champion for his directorial debut in the maverick independent distributor Joseph Burstyn, the Coens fell in with visionary distributor/producer Ben Barenholtz, who saw in *Blood Simple* a perfect candidate for his innovative, "midnight-movie" approach to handling "Amer-indies." Although the film just barely broke even in its initial American theatrical run, it set the Coens on a three-film deal with Barenholtz and established them as new, independent voices with whom critics and the industry would have to reckon.

Another key point of comparison is that, like Kubrick's films, those of the Coen Brothers cry out for interpretation. Even the seemingly light, cartoonish comedy, *Raising Arizona*, leaves us with an ambiguous ending worthy of Kubrick, as the character of Hi (Nicolas Cage) awakens from the film's final dream, intoning in voice-over, "I don't know . . . maybe it was Utah." Indeed, dreams and dreamlike imagery pepper the entire film; and the shadowy, villainous figure of the "lone biker" seems to be born directly out of Hi's nightmares, that is, out of his unconscious, clearly inviting Freudian or Jungian interpretation. Similarly, throughout *Miller's Crossing*, Tom's (Gabriel Byrne) hat is emphasized as a visual symbol of something; but of what? On such points the Coens remain stubbornly silent. Although it is possible to enjoy these films simply on the level of entertainment and narrative engagement, they offer a deeper level of ambiguity, metaphor, and symbolism than does the typical Saturday-night diversion. That is to say, like Kubrick, the Coens straddle the boundary between classical Hollywood and art cinema, occasionally stepping boldly over that line, as with *Barton Fink* (and in Kubrick's case, *2001: A Space Odyssey*). As popular-culture scholar Lynnea Chapman King points out, in describing her experiences during a public screening of *No Country for Old Men* (2007):

> After the final image of Tommy Lee Jones had cut to black [on the enigmatic line, "And then I woke up"], there were audible exclamations from the patrons around me: "That's it?" "What happened?" This twelfth film by Joel and Ethan Coen evoked the same response that the brothers' films have been eliciting for over two decades: stunned silence, confusion, disappointment, and perhaps even hostility or disgust from viewers accustomed to tidily packaged cinematic narratives. (2009: v)

Of course Kubrick's films, especially his mature work from *Dr. Strangelove, or: How I Learned to Stop Worrying and Love the Bomb* (1964) onward, often have garnered similar levels of confusion and misunderstanding from audiences and critics alike, even those predisposed to admire his work. As Sydney Pollack observed: "I can't remember any Stanley Kubrick movie that was released where there wasn't controversy. *2001* I remember very well—I remember Pauline Kael's review of *2001*—they were not good reviews. And then ten years goes by, and they're all classics" (Harlan 2001). Kubrick's adaptation of *The Shining* (1980), from Stephen King's best-selling novel, is another case in point, described in Jan Harlan's documentary, *Stanley Kubrick: A Life in Pictures* (2001), as "a film that would both satisfy him artistically and meet the demands of the box office." As with almost all of Kubrick's work, *The Shining* was greeted with both praise and consternation. Noted cinematographer Allen Daviau was impressed with the steadicam shots that follow Danny (Danny Lloyd) on his Big-Wheel through the hallways of the Overlook Hotel, especially with "the sense of movement that [it] gave that picture inside of this very, very foreboding place" (Harlan 2001). On the other hand, Martin Scorsese, another staunch admirer of Kubrick as an artist, recalls his initial bafflement: "At first I was taken aback by some of the performance; and then, after the third or fourth viewing, I understood the level of intensity of what Nicholson was doing" (Harlan 2001).

Given that his films were so often misunderstood by audiences and critics, it seems surprising that Kubrick usually demurred when asked to explain his work. For instance, in a 1987 interview, Kubrick dismisses the critical impulse to interpret a flaming piece of rubble featured prominently in *Full Metal Jacket* (1987), in the scene just after Cowboy (Arliss Howard) has been shot (Figure 3.2). The shape of the object, combined with the Marines' placement in front of it, unmistakably calls to mind the monolith from *2001: A Space Odyssey* (Figure 3.1); but Kubrick refused to explain or even admit such a connection: "It just happened to be there. . . . I'm sure some people will think that there was some calculated reference to *2001*, but honestly, it was just there" (Cahill 1987: 194).

While the Coens on balance seem to grant more interviews than Kubrick did, they can be equally cagey in refusing to explain themselves. Take, for example, this exchange with *IndieWIRE* from 1998:

> INDIEWIRE: You majored in philosophy at Princeton. What is your philosophy of filmmaking?
> ETHAN COEN: Oooh—I don't have one. I wouldn't even know how to begin. You've stumped me there. None that I've noticed. Drawing a blank on this one. (Stone 1998: 87)

According to *Vogue* critic, Tad Friend, "They told one reporter that Jennifer Jason Leigh was actually 'bald as a cue ball' and wore a wig throughout filming [*The Hudsucker Proxy*], and that she showed no embarrassment about taking out her false teeth and swishing them around in a glass" (Friend 1994: 65). Friend noted that "the Coens are a legendarily tough interview," as he discovered when he asked if there were differences between the two brothers in their approach to filmmaking:

> There was an excruciating silence. "No . . . nah . . . no, no, no . . . not really," Ethan finally said. "It's a terrible question, a terrible thing to do . . ." Joel mumbled. "It's

Figure 3.1 Huddling before the monolith (*2001: A Space Odyssey*, 1968), copyright Warner Bros.

Figure 3.2 Huddling before the monolith in *Full Metal Jacket*. Kubrick: "Honestly, it was just there." (*Full Metal Jacket*, 1987), copyright Warner Bros.

> like you're on *The Dating Game*," Ethan said. "Yeah," Joel said. "You're going to find a real resistance to talking about ourselves as opposed to talking about the movies.... On the one hand, we want to talk about the movies..." "But the movies speak for themselves," Ethan concluded. (66)

And so, even with questions about their movies, the Coens can be equally evasive, as in this exchange with French critic Jean-Pierre Coursodon, regarding *Miller's Crossing*:

> Q: The hat is more than an accessory in the film, it's a recurrent theme as soon as the credits start, with that hat blown by the wind in the forest. What is the significance?
> JOEL: Everybody asks us questions about that hat, and there isn't any answer really. It's not a symbol, it doesn't have any particular meaning...
> ETHAN: The hat doesn't "represent" anything, it's just a hat blown by the wind.
> JOEL: It's an image that came to us, that we liked, and it just implanted itself. It's a kind of practical guiding thread, but there's no need to look for deep meanings. (Coursodon 1991: 44)

Curiously, one interviewer who *has* been able to get the Coens, as well as Stanley Kubrick, to open up about their work has been Michel Ciment. The noted French critic interviewed Kubrick extensively and on several occasions for the newspaper *L'Express* and the journal *Positif*, eventually republishing those exchanges in a volume simply titled *Kubrick* (1980). When the 1982 English translation of that book went out of print, it became highly sought-after, even a high-priced collectible, as an indispensable resource for those seriously interested in Kubrick's work.[1] What makes Ciment's interviews so valuable is the openness and candor with which Kubrick responds to the thoughtful, engaging inquiries, as with this exchange from 1971:

> [Ciment]: Since so many different interpretations have been offered about *A Clockwork Orange*, how do you see your own film?
> [Kubrick]: The central idea of the film has to do with the question of free-will. Do we lose our humanity if we are deprived of the choice between good and evil? ... Alex represents the unconscious; man in his *natural* state. After he is given the Ludovico *cure* he has been *civilized*, and the sickness that follows may be viewed as the neurosis imposed by society. (Ciment 2001: 149; emphasis in original)

So, while Kubrick disdained the sort of superficial, vapid, "fan-magazine" interviews expected of most successful filmmakers, here he seems to welcome the opportunity to open up to someone of Ciment's intelligence, who so clearly took the work seriously.

Perhaps it is that selfsame quality of Ciment's that has allowed him to elicit serious and thoughtful responses in multiple interviews with Joel and Ethan Coen, who otherwise seem to take perverse pleasure in toying with popular critics. For example, in the following exchange Ciment and Hubert Niogret get the Coens to discuss one of their films on a symbolic level, something they almost never do:

> Q: *The "folk tales" have some importance to* Raising Arizona, *like that of Davy Crockett?*
> ETHAN: We decided definitely to have a bond with the imaginary, that the movie wouldn't be a slice of life.
> JOEL: When we'd spoken with the cinematographer, Barry Sonnenfeld, regarding the look of the movie, we talked about opening it like a book of stories, with colors that had a certain vibration. That was part of the visual style.
> ...
> Q: *The character of the motorcyclist comes from a dream* ...
> JOEL: We tried to imagine a character who didn't correspond specifically to *our* image of an "Evil One" or a nightmare become reality, but rather to the image that Hi would have. Being from the Southwest, he'd see him in the form of a Hell's Angel.
> ETHAN: We also tried to connect the characters through the music. Holly sings a lullaby in the movie, and we asked the composer to introduce it into the musical theme that accompanies the bounty hunter. (Ciment and Niogret 1987: 26–29)

Eleven years later, Ciment and Niogret pull off another difficult feat, in drawing out the Coens on a philosophical subject regarding *The Big Lebowski* (1998):

> Q: *The three nihilists are Germans. Do you think your movie could also be qualified as nihilistic? What is its moral point of view?*
> JOEL: Certainly not. For us, the nihilists are the bad guys, and, if there's a preferred moral position, it'd be that of Jeff Bridges, though it's difficult to define! In a curious way, you could say he has the moral code of the private eye. But in his case, it's very fluid! What you can say with certainty is that the movie leads to a reconciliation between the Dude and Walter despite their difficult relationship. In a detective movie, there's a line of clear conduct, a much more solid spine, even if it's never explicit. That's not the case with the Dude. (1998, 105)

Fittingly, it is also Ciment who has most often asked the Coens about their affinity for Stanley Kubrick, starting as early as 1987:

> Q: *What American filmmakers of the last twenty years . . . do you like?*
> JOEL: Scorsese, Coppola, David Lynch . . .
> Q: *Kubrick?*
> JOEL: Yes.
> Q: *Kubrick's black humor?*
> JOEL: Yes, *Dr. Strangelove*. (Ciment and Niogret 1987: 35)

Later, Ciment and the Coens noted that the lineage of *Barton Fink* goes back not only to Roman Polanski, but also to *The Shining* (Ciment and Niogret 1991: 50); Ciment even finds a point of comparison in *Fargo* (1996): "A little like Kubrick with *Dr. Strangelove*, you begin with a quasi-documentary presentation, then gradually, with a cold humor, everything becomes dislocated and absurd" (1996: 75).

Specific, undeniable references to Kubrick can be found throughout the Coens' body of work, and it is worth noting a few of them here. About a third of the way through *Raising Arizona*, their second feature film, the bounty hunter, Leonard Smalls (Randall "Tex" Cobb), bursts through a men's room door on his Harley, in his pursuit of two escaped convicts. In the few seconds before Smalls (also known as the "lone biker of the Apocalypse") knocks down the door, an alert viewer may notice that it is covered in graffiti, with the series of letters, P.O.E./O.P.E. (Figure 3.3). Fans of Stanley Kubrick's *Dr. Strangelove* will recognize these letters as variations on the "recall code" that Mandrake (Peter Sellers) finally discovers and uses to abort General Ripper's (Sterling Hayden) apocalyptic mission of the B-52 bombers sent to attack the Soviets (Figure 3.4). What may seem at first glance to be a "throwaway" reference to *Dr. Strangelove*—in the way of the "empty pastiche" that is often attributed to the Coens, erroneously, as I will argue below—is rather the first direct clue that the Coens offer to their affinity for Kubrick (the first of many, one might add). Fittingly, the reference

Figure 3.3 O.P.E./P.O.E. in a *Raising Arizona* dream sequence, a sly reference to ... (*Raising Arizona*, 1987), copyright 20th Century Fox.

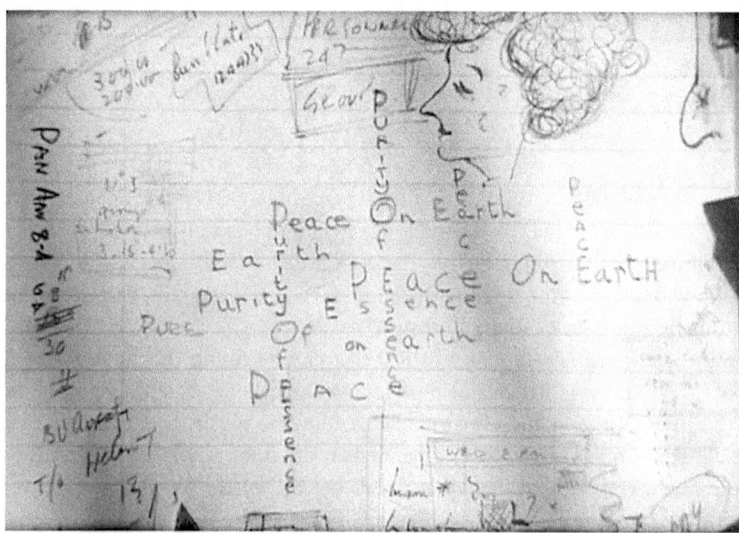

Figure 3.4 The recall code in *Dr. Strangelove*. (*Dr. Strangelove, or, How I Learned to Stop Worrying and Love the Bomb*, 1964), copyright Warner Bros.

also establishes the biker himself as an "apocalyptic" figure, while also alluding to a puzzle to be solved (in this case, not only the prison escape but also the kidnapping of Nathan Arizona, Jr.).

A more extended example comes much later in their career, as the Coens offer another unmistakable, though subtle, nod to Kubrick in the opening sequence of

No Country for Old Men: as Sheriff Ed Tom Bell (Tommy Lee Jones) narrates, we see a series of twelve arid landscapes, taking us from dawn to mid-morning. While nothing in this sequence directly copies the opening of *2001: A Space Odyssey*, with its series of twelve landscapes at or near sunrise (the beginning of the "Dawn of Man" sequence), some of the images do offer striking visual rhymes with Kubrick's film (Figures 3.5 and 3.6).

Again, more than a superficial moment of postmodernism, this oblique reference to *2001* suggests that *No Country*, too, will present a narrative that is to be taken on an epic, mythological, and even metaphysical level; but while *2001* offers one of the most optimistic visions of humanity's future prospects (Bowman's evolutionary leap/transformation into the Star Child), the Coens present us with one of the darkest.

Similarly in *Barton Fink*, the sickly green bathtub in Barton's hotel room—a striking anachronism, given the film's 1930s setting—obliquely calls to mind the modern,

Figures 3.5 and 3.6 Two images from *No Country for Old Men* (2007, copyright Miramax Films) that evoke *2001: A Space Odyssey*.

haunted green bathroom in *The Shining*.² Of course, Barton's bathroom is multivalent, as is usually the case with the Coens' intertextual references—it alternately calls to mind *Psycho* (1960), *The Conversation* (1974), and David Lynch—but *Barton Fink*'s kinship with Kubrick and *The Shining* goes deeper. It presents the story of a frustrated writer, holed up in a creepy hotel with supernatural undertones and an uncanny visual aesthetic (as with the gooey, peeling wallpaper, the floating, "disembodied" camera wandering through the eerily symmetrical hallways, and the extreme performances). Furthermore, just as Lloyd the bartender (Joe Turkel) and Delbert Grady (Philip Stone) in *The Shining* may be read as external manifestations of Jack's troubled psyche, Charlie (John Goodman) seems to emerge out of Barton's unconscious. Such a bold, unconventional narrative tactic is not unknown to the Coens, who offer a similar "monster from the id" with the lone biker in *Raising Arizona*. Barton's overly familiar, homoerotic relationship with Charlie ("We're men! We wrestled!") also calls to mind Humbert's (James Mason) uncomfortable kinship with his doppelganger, Clare Quilty (Peter Sellers), in *Lolita*, as evidenced in Quilty's highly suggestive dialogue outside the Enchanted Hunters Hotel: "It's great to see a normal face, 'cause I'm a normal guy. It'd be great for two normal guys like us to get together and talk about world events, you know, in a normal sort of way."

Other (albeit fleeting) examples abound, such as the bathtub scene between Billy Bob Thornton and Frances McDormand in *The Man Who Wasn't There* (2001): as he tenderly takes her leg in his hand, lathers it with soap, and begins to shave, one is reminded of the iconic toenail-painting shot that opens *Lolita*. The same film has Thornton's character, a barber, describing various haircuts, as we see a montage of men and boys in his barber's chair. Lest we miss the subtle visual cue to the opening of *Full Metal Jacket*, with its series of new recruits being shorn of their hair and their individuality, the Coens cement that reference for us with a shot of the barber sweeping up the hair clippings, just as we see in the Kubrick film. Notably, one of the hairstyles that ended up "on the cutting room floor," as it were (shown in the "bonus features" of the DVD release of *The Man Who Wasn't There*), is described by the barber as "the Timberline"—perhaps named in homage to Oregon's Timberline Lodge, the location of the iconic exterior of *The Shining*'s Overlook Hotel. In *O Brother, Where Art Thou?* (2000), the scene in which our three protagonists infiltrate a Klan rally offers a parodic riff on Bill Harford's encounter with "Red Cloak" (and Harford's ultimate unmasking) in *Eyes Wide Shut* (1999); and more significantly, *O Brother* is among the most overtly mythical works in the Coens' oeuvre, as a loose adaptation of Homer's *Odyssey* ("adapted" even more loosely by Kubrick with *2001*).

Such pervasive intertextuality has led some critics to dismiss the Coens' films, as Clark Buckner (2014) has noted, "as the blank parody of postmodern pastiche," with their abundant references to other filmmakers as well as literary figures, including Alfred Hitchcock, Vittorio Storaro, Raymond Chandler, and, yes, Stanley Kubrick. However, their affinity for Kubrick goes deeper than mere superficial "in-jokes" aimed at an audience of fellow cinephiles who will be "in the know" regarding such references. Much of the critical derision leveled at the Coens for their so-called "postmodernist" tendencies rests on the unconvincing assertions that their films are devoid of meaning and that their cinematic, literary, and cultural references ring hollow. It would seem as though such critics were determined to force the Coens' films wholesale into Frederic Jameson's conception of postmodernism, forgetting the actual films themselves in the process. Jameson offers a fairly clear entry point into understanding postmodernism, "as an attempt to think the present historically in an age that has forgotten how to think historically in the first place" (1991: ix). Perhaps in that sense, and only in that sense, we may in fact recognize something of the postmodern in the Coens' work, given the fact that they do—through no fault of their own—operate in "an age that has forgotten how to think historically." But Jameson further distinguishes between modernist and postmodernist concerns with "shifts and irrevocable changes in the representation of things and the way they change," suggesting:

> The moderns were interested in what was likely to come of such changes and their general tendency: they thought about the thing itself, substantively. . . . Postmodernism is more formal . . . and more "distracted," as Benjamin might put it; it only clocks the variations themselves, and knows only too well that the contents are just more images. In modernism . . . some residual zones of "nature" or "being," of the old, the older, the archaic, still subsist; culture can still do something to that nature and work at transforming that "referent." (ix)

It seems to me that the films of the Coen Brothers, especially if viewed as a "body of work," *do* hang onto some substantive referents to be found underneath all the seemingly superficial intertextuality—which I hope to show in my subsequent discussion of the philosophical bent in their work. So, rather than buying into the popular critical characterizations of the Coens as vapid postmodernists, I prefer to think of them as something else—if not practitioners of high modernism, then maybe "neo-modernists"?

Jeremi Szaniawski suggests, "What the Coens have done is a combinatory swing between postmodern entertainment (*The Big Lebowski, Intolerable Cruelty* [2003], *The Ladykillers* [2004], *Burn After Reading* [2008], *Hail Caesar!*, even) and high postmodernism (which is essentially nothing more than a continuation of modernism in its attempts at being 'writerly,' etc.)" (Note to author, Sept. 2018). For now, I would simply suggest that a great deal of substance is to be found in the Coens' work—ironically tying it still further to Kubrick—notably in terms of its broad aesthetic and philosophical approaches.

One of the most illuminating treatises on the films of Stanley Kubrick, James Naremore's *On Kubrick* (2007) argues that the director's body of work consistently employs the aesthetic of "the grotesque," that is, the sharp contrast of competing emotional experiences for the viewer, for example, the fearsome juxtaposed with the ludicrous. We find perhaps the most iconic example of this tendency in the scene from *A Clockwork Orange* where Alex (Malcolm McDowell) and his "droogs" (Warren Clarke, *et al*) attack the writer (Patrick Magee) and his wife (Adrienne Corri) in their home: in costumes that might be read as comical or playful, were it not for the obscenely protruding, phallic noses on the clown-like masks, the gang members brutalize their victims while laughing among themselves, as Alex offers up an impromptu song-and-dance performance of "Singin' in the Rain." The results are disturbing to say the least, not only because of the narrative content of the scene (the attack itself), but primarily because of Kubrick's aesthetic approach to the material, the aesthetic of the grotesque.

Naremore devotes his entire book to exploring—quite compellingly—that aesthetic impulse across all of Kubrick's films, and his analysis is especially illuminating with regard to *Lolita*. An iconic example of the grotesque from that film comes in the transition out of the scene where Humbert agrees to rent a room available in the home of Charlotte Haze (Shelley Winters). When Charlotte asks what was the deciding factor in his decision, Humbert glances at her teenaged daughter, Lolita (Sue Lyon) and responds with one of the film's most salacious double-entendres: "I think it was your cherry pies." After a knowing glance from Lolita, Kubrick cuts abruptly to the next scene, with a close-up of the monstrous Christopher Lee from *The Curse of Frankenstein* (1957), musically accompanied by a loud brass line emphasizing the horror of that moment from the Hammer film. Charlotte, Humbert, and Lolita are watching the movie at a drive-in, all in a row in the front seat of a car, with Humbert in the middle. Kubrick immediately goes from horror back to humor, as Lolita grabs Humbert's right hand, then Charlotte grabs his left, and finally all of their hands end up in a tangle, spoiling the moment between Humbert and Lolita. These rapid shifts, from humor to horror and back, reflect the tone of the entire film, with its disturbing subject matter (a middle-aged man in lustful pursuit of an underage girl) combined with a biting, often hilarious satire of upper-middle-class, suburban American life (Naremore 2007: Part Three, Chapter III).

A similar aesthetic of the grotesque pervades the films of Joel and Ethan Coen, which consistently blend the darkest of human impulses with the broadest of comedic treatments. Their funniest films, including *Raising Arizona*, *Burn After Reading*, *The Big Lebowski*, and *The Hudsucker Proxy*, delve into such dire subject matter as kidnapping, blackmail, suicide, and murder; and even their grimmest visions, such as *No Country for Old Men*, contain moments of humor that make them all the more unsettling. A pointed example from *True Grit* operates in a similar fashion to the scene from *Lolita* described earlier: fairly early in their quest to find Chaney (Josh Brolin), Rooster Cogburn (Jeff Bridges) and Maddie (Hailee Steinfeld) come upon a cabin with two preadolescent Native American children sitting on the edge of the front porch. As Rooster moves to enter the cabin, he abruptly throws the older of the two into the yard and then literally kicks the other one off the porch. The slapstick nature of the staging, together with a repetition of the gag when Rooster exits the cabin, seems calculated to induce laughter and guilt simultaneously in the audience. As if relying upon some feeling of shame in the viewer, having laughed at Rooster's blatant racism, the film follows up with Rooster and Maddie discovering a dead body hanging from a tree as they ride through "Indian country." That stark image immediately calls to mind America's ugly history of lynchings, as if to point up the disgusting, logical end of the racism that was played for laughs in the preceding scene. A bit later, Rooster and Maddie encounter another (or is it the same?) dead body, this one in the possession of a traveling "medicine man" and "dentist," himself a grotesque figure blending threat and comedy (he is large and foreboding, dressed in a bearskin complete with head), who offers to sell them the body: "I have taken his teeth; I will entertain an offer for the rest of him."

Perhaps the most perfect balance of these competing tendencies (the grim and the humorous) occurs in the Coens' dark comedy about kidnapping and murder, *Fargo*. Consider, for example, the uncomfortably comical interactions between Jerry (William H. Macy), Carl (Steve Buscemi), and Gaear (Peter Stormare) as they make arrangements for the kidnapping of Jerry's wife, Jean (Kristin Rudrüd). The abduction scene itself mixes the horrific (the black-masked figure of Carl creeping up onto the back deck of the Lundegaard home) and the laughably absurd (Jean watching, transfixed, like a "deer in the headlights," until the moment when Carl smashes a window with the tire iron he's carrying). The further interactions between the kidnappers and Jean veer on slapstick comedy, with Jean running wildly through the house, wrapped in (and blinded by) a shower curtain, finally tumbling down the stairs in a stunt-gag worthy of Buster Keaton or Jackie Chan. Such twisted humor is repeated when Carl and Gaear arrive at their hideout with a blindfolded Jean: her pathetic attempts to run away—stumbling, even running into a tree—elicit howls of laughter from Carl, and perhaps from the audience as well (but in the latter case accompanied by cringes of discomfort). As I have argued elsewhere:

> Such a balancing act between polar opposites is the stuff of mythology, and critics have noted the mythological—at times even epic—dimensions of the Coen Brothers' *oeuvre*. At the same time, their work is often characterized by a postmodernist, self-aware sense of irony that undercuts a mythologized view of "American life," even as it enacts that very mythos. Such is the dynamic of *Fargo*. (Hill 2017)

In Stanley Kubrick's work, as well as that of the Coen Brothers, this systematic deployment of the grotesque keeps us off guard, unsure of how to respond to any given moment or scene, or to the film as a whole, often causing an emotional and intellectual doubling-back of sorts, in a process of repeated reevaluation of those responses. Such ambiguity of response dovetails perfectly with the ambiguity in outlook offered in Kubrick's and the Coens' approaches to philosophy in their films. Philosophy is at the center of Kubrick's and the Coens' work. However, in neither case do the films present us with a particular philosophical *outlook*. Rather, Kubrick invites his viewers to ponder large philosophical questions (without providing us with clear answers); and the Coens present us with characters facing philosophical crises of various stripes, seemingly unaware of their own inconstant worldviews, also without resolving those dilemmas.

As early as *The Killing* (1956), critics have identified philosophical underpinnings in Kubrick's work, as Richard Schickel observed: "It is an existential movie. Existentialism basically posits that we define ourselves by doing and that chance is the one thing that we can never quite fully comprehend" (Harlan 2001). That is, despite all the meticulous planning of Johnny (Sterling Hayden) and his fellow conspirators to rob the racetrack, despite the timetables plotted out to the minute—as emphasized in the complex flashback structure and accompanying voice-of-God narration—it only takes the slightest mistake (an inadequate suitcase), or a seemingly inconsequential element of chance (a yapping little dog) to bring about the dissolution of the whole plan, with the loot in the end literally dissipating into thin air. Still, the film is not necessarily *positing* an existentialist philosophy; rather, it leaves us with a problematic philosophical, perhaps nihilistic, question, articulated in Johnny's final line of dialogue: "What's the difference?" That is, if one accepts the tenets of existentialism—which had taken the Western intellectual world by storm following the end of the Second World War—then why pursue any concrete goals or plans at all? Kubrick does not seem to have an answer for this dilemma, but *The Killing* is perhaps his way of sharing his own philosophical conundrum with his audience. We might go so far as to see the end of *The Killing* as a modernist query on the continued viability of traditional narrative structures in films, which are so dependent upon the setting (and achieving) of goals by their protagonists. Thus the film foreshadows the modernist questioning to come in virtually all of Kubrick's work.

Similarly in his later films, Kubrick was disinclined to offer clear philosophical *observations*, in favor of raising philosophical *questions* in his viewers. Although we might be tempted to misread *A Clockwork Orange* in terms of its overt "message" of morality, I have argued elsewhere that the film (more so than the 1961 source novel by Anthony Burgess) offers a more complex rumination on the nature of morality in relation to power structures (Hill 2002). Ultimately, the film seems far more interested in the problem of fascism than in simple questions of good and evil, offering a perplexing lack of resolution in which we are left to ponder what Alex's final "cure" really implies—again, an ambiguity not present in Burgess's novel, with its famed "Chapter 21" in which Alex "grows up." Kubrick would revisit similar questions—of the problematic relationships between humanity and structures of class and power—in all of his subsequent films: *Barry Lyndon* is the tragic tale of a naïve interloper who underestimates the ruthlessness of the upper classes to which he recklessly aspires; similarly, Jack Torrance in *The Shining* is willing to sacrifice everything, including the lives of his family, to the upper-class world—albeit a phantom one—that the Overlook Hotel represents; in *Full Metal Jacket*, Private Joker is able to hang onto something of his humanity by not surrendering to the killer instinct that the military has systematically tried to unleash in the film's other major characters; and in *Eyes Wide Shut*, Bill Harford barely escapes "the most dire consequences" for himself and his family as he, like Redmond Barry, fails to see (until it is almost too late) the brutality that lies just beneath the rich, tempting veneer of the power elites.

Dare we suggest yet another philosophical film in Kubrick's canon, by way of *2001: A Space Odyssey*? Here, Kubrick and co-writer Arthur C. Clarke do not provide any answers to the very large questions they posit—indeed, the biggest questions there are—about the nature of the universe and humanity's place in it. Rather, as Clarke explained:

> I respect [and] am in awe of the mystery of the universe. Something Einstein often said was, "Anyone who isn't awed by the universe, well, they haven't any soul." So,

from my earliest days, the wonder of space and time has intrigued me; and Stanley and I tried to put something of this feeling into the film. . . . We didn't intend a "message" specifically. Stanley wanted to create an *experience*, and people get different "messages" from it according to their own individual philosophies and outlooks. (Harlan 2001)

In one of the earliest (1969) scholarly essays on *2001: A Space Odyssey*, Annette Michelson similarly suggests that the film brings about an introspective position in the spectator, as the outward journey of Discovery in the film engenders an inward journey of discovery for the viewer. Like the monolith's impact on the characters within the film, for Michelson the film itself engenders epiphany and "converts the theatre into a vessel and its viewers into passengers; it impels us, in the movement from departure to arrival, to rediscover the space and dimensions of the body as theatre of consciousness"(63). She sees *2001* as a highly modernist work, whose subject ultimately is the experience of cinematic art.

While the Coen Brothers have yet to produce anything quite so revolutionary as *2001: A Space Odyssey*, I would argue that they do achieve in most of their work a level of high modernism on par with Kubrick. This claim flies in the face of much of the criticism mentioned earlier, which derides the Coens as mere practitioners of empty, postmodernist pastiche. The aforementioned scenes described from *True Grit*, for example, put the spectator in a "double mode" of viewing, similar to that described by Michelson with respect to *2001*, in which we are aware of the film's narrative strategies and how they manipulate our expectations, forcing us to backtrack and re-evaluate prior emotional responses. At times, the Coens take the cinema itself as their subject, as in *Barton Fink* (which is all about the inner processes of creative writing) and *Hail, Caesar!* (which seems really to be about the Coens, erstwhile "indie" outsiders, coming to grips with, and even embracing, the traditions of classical Hollywood).

Also in a similar vein to Kubrick, the Coen Brothers' films consistently explore philosophical and moral questions, as well as psychological symbolism, while rarely offering any but the vaguest of answers. In *No Country for Old Men*, Anton Chigurh (Javier Bardem), one of the most chilling villains ever to haunt the screen, seems bemused by the lack of philosophical integrity in all of his victims. Just as he is about to kill the bounty hunter Carson Wells (Woody Harrelson), Chigurh chides him for having no defensible moral code: "If the rule you followed led you to this, of what use was the rule?" On the other hand, Chigurh himself seems to adhere to the fatalistic moral system of fortune's spinning wheel, taking setbacks in stride, and showing mercy only when dictated by the flip of a coin. Curiously, he is another dark figure in the Coen universe who may or may not be real: Is he a ghost? Is he a manifestation of the Jungian shadow? Or is he Death incarnate? As the Coens close their darkest narrative (closely following their literary source from Cormac McCarthy), they leave us with no answers to these and other questions—only a dream narrated by Sherriff Ed Tom Bell in which he encounters his long-dead father out on the trail. The father rides on ahead to some unnamed destination (the land of the dead, perhaps?) and Bell concludes: "I knew that when I got there, he'd be there. And then I woke up"—a perplexing ending worthy of the best Kubrick films.

Perhaps the most overtly philosophical of the Coens' films is *A Serious Man* (2009), in which the protagonist, a physics professor named Larry Gopnick (Michael Stuhlbarg) feels abandoned by God and searches in vain for answers to age-old questions—which, predictably, are not forthcoming. Repeatedly turned away by the elder rabbi (Alan Mandell) at his synagogue, Larry must make do with the banal homilies offered by the much younger assistant rabbi (Simon Helberg), who encourages him to see the beauty in life's struggles. Meanwhile, Larry's career and family seem to be unraveling all around him, exacerbating his inability to understand "God's plan" for him.

Ironically, while Larry seeks—even expects—clarity and certainty from his would-be spiritual advisers, in his own role as a professor he flounders in attempting to convey to his students the tenets of quantum physics. In a classroom scene, Larry furiously scribbles mathematical equations on the blackboard, assuming erroneously that his students are following along. He concludes with the muddled observation: "So, if that's that, then we can do this! And that's Schrodinger's paradox: is the cat dead, or is the cat not dead?" Later, the scene repeats in a more exaggerated (and it turns out, nightmarish) form, in which we see a colossal chalkboard filled with innumerable calculations, all of which demonstrate, as Larry puts it, "the uncertainty principle: it proves we can't ever really know what's going on."

Yet Larry seems to lack the courage of his convictions when it comes to questions of uncertainty, not only as they relate to the metaphysical (his quest for answers from first one rabbi, then another), but also in a moral dilemma involving one of his students. The young man, Clive (David Kang), has surreptitiously left a bribe on Larry's desk in an unmarked envelope, implicitly in exchange for a passing grade. Clive denies leaving the envelope, but Larry insists that its meaning is clear. Clive's stone-faced response is, "Mere surmise, sir; very uncertain."

Returning to the image of the chalkboard (Figure 3.7), it provides a condensed illustration of Gopnick's philosophical inconsistency: it is an absurdly convoluted (practically infinite) and paradoxical attempt at a mathematical proof (which implies certainty) of uncertainty. Like a few other Coen protagonists—notably "the Dude" in *The Big Lebowski*—Gopnick espouses a philosophy of sorts that he himself does not follow. He teaches the uncertainty principle by way of Schrodinger's mercurial "cat" paradox; but in his argument with Clive he admits, "Even I don't understand the cat." Yet he expects clear answers from God.

K. L. Evans, a specialist in English and philosophy at Yeshiva University, argues that the film may be seen as a retelling of the Book of Job, whose ultimate lesson is that God does not owe humanity any answers for anything. Beyond that rather bleak outlook, though, the Coens offer a couple of alternative, not entirely tongue-in-cheek, observations on philosophy. The first comes from the epigraph that opens the film, in which the Coens quote the medieval French rabbi, Rashi: "Receive with simplicity everything that happens to you." Evans explains that this observation comes from Rashi's commentary on the Book of Deuteronomy and carries the sense of "awaiting or expecting God, as opposed to trying to figure out the world using divination" (Evans

Figure 3.7 In *A Serious Man* (2009), Prof. Gopnick (Michael Stuhlbarg) offers this elaborate (and dryly hilarious) "proof" that "nothing is knowable." Copyright Relativity Media, StudioCanal, Working Title Films, Mike Zoss Productions.

2012: 292). The other comes from Jefferson Airplane, in lyrics repeated at various points throughout the film: "When the truth is found to be lies / and all the hope within you dies / somebody to love? / . . . . You'd better find somebody to love." Ironically, while the rabbi is always "too busy" for Larry, he does confer with Larry's son, Danny (Aaron Wolff), after his *bar mitzvah*, repeating some of the lyrics above, and admonishing him to "be a good boy." Such is the extent of the wisdom that the rabbi has to offer—wisdom that Larry no doubt would reject were it offered to him.

Even *The Big Lebowski*, which on its surface might appear to justify the label, "postmodernist pastiche" so often applied to the Coens, has a consistent preoccupation with philosophy, by way of its varied cast of characters. In their essay "Takin' 'er Easy for All Us Sinners: Laziness as a Virtue in *The Big Lebowski*," Matthew K. Douglass and Jerry L. Walls argue that key characters in the film represent different, competing philosophical outlooks. As mentioned previously, a group of villains in the film identify themselves as "Nihilists," but ironically (and humorously) they do not fully adhere to that philosophy. To "the Dude," a.k.a. Jeffrey Lebowski (Jeff Bridges), Douglass and Walls attribute a sort of armchair Buddhism that they cleverly label "Dude-ism," a central tenet of which is that "one should accept life as it is and learn to be content" (147–48). Bunny Lebowski (Tara Reid), the supposed kidnapping victim, they posit as a hedonist, while her husband, "the Big Lebowski" (David Huddleston) subscribes to the philosophy of rugged individualism or social Darwinism (151, 153). Crucially, the Dude's best friend, Walter (John Goodman), seems dedicated to Kant's "categorical imperative," the notion that reason dictates adherence to the law for its own sake—a position diametrically opposed to "Dude-ism" (154). One could argue that all of the Dude's troubles in the film result from his failure to follow his own philosophy, in going along with Walter's insistence on obtaining justice for damages done to a throw-rug in his home—an offense that "Dude-ism" would deem utterly insignificant.

One could go on, film by film, demonstrating the philosophical and psychological complexities of the Coen Brothers' supposedly "empty" films; luckily that work has been done for us. *The Philosophy of the Coen Brothers*, edited by Mark T. Conard, presents a wide range of essays by scholars in film studies and philosophy, examining most of the Coens' work up to 2010, chiefly from a philosophical perspective. This should hardly come as a surprise: after all, as mentioned earlier, Ethan Coen majored in philosophy at Princeton. And while the Coens—and Stanley Kubrick for that matter—have generally avoided, even spurned, questions regarding philosophy or any other "deep meanings" in their films, as previously noted, for the careful, analytical viewer, those elements are unmistakably present throughout both bodies of work.

These philosophical similarities, arguably the most substantial connection between the Coens and Stanley Kubrick, relate back to the other ties noted in this essay. We have already considered the notion that an aesthetics of the grotesque may lead viewers to doubt and re-evaluate their own responses to a given film as it unfolds; and such willingness to question and revise one's attitude or outlook is at the heart of the philosophical enterprise. Furthermore, the uncommon level of independence achieved by Kubrick and the Coen Brothers in their respective careers is the very quality that has allowed their distinctive aesthetics and worldviews to emerge. Apropos of that independent spirit, we might also note in closing that, as secular Jewish artists, the Coens also share with Kubrick their status as cultural outsiders in a predominantly Christian America. This "disconnect" contributes to their ironic, distanced approaches to humor and absurdity; and it further manifests itself in a wary distrust of authority and power structures (perhaps also stemming from their Jewish roots), evident not only in their narrative plots, but also in their relationships to the mainstream film industry. As independent yet commercially successful filmmakers, who have managed to create distinctive cinematic works of art across various genres with consistent aesthetic and philosophical leanings, Joel and Ethan Coen stand today among the closest heirs to Stanley Kubrick's cinematic legacy.

Notes

1 Thankfully, it was republished yet again in an expanded version, as *Kubrick: The Definitive Edition*, after Kubrick's death.
2 In this context, the men's room from *Raising Arizona*, noted above, takes on a similar, uncanny quality, and the red graffiti also echoes *The Shining*'s "REDRUM" lipstick inscription.

Works Cited

Buckner, Clark. 2014. *Apropos of Nothing: Deconstruction, Psychoanalysis, and the Coen Brothers*. Albany: State University of New York Press.

Cahill, Tim. 1987. "The *Rolling Stone* Interview: Stanley Kubrick," in Gene D. Phillips (ed.), *Stanley Kubrick: Interviews*. Jackson: University Press of Mississippi, 189–203.
Ciment, Michel. 2001. *Kubrick: The Definitive Edition*. New York: Faber and Faber.
Ciment, Michel, and Hubert Niogret. 1987. "Interview with Joel and Ethan Coen," in William Rodney Allen (ed.), *The Coen Brothers: Interviews*. Jackson: University of Press of Mississippi, 25–35.
Ciment, Michel, and Hubert Niogret. 1991. "A Rock on the Beach," in William Rodney Allen (ed.), *The Coen Brothers: Interviews*. Jackson: University Press of Mississippi, 46–54.
Ciment, Michel and Hubert Niogret. 1996. "Closer to Life than the Conventions of Cinema," in William Rodney Allen (ed.), *The Coen Brothers: Interviews*. Jackson: University of Press of Mississippi, 72–80.
Ciment, Michel and Hubert Niogret. 1998. "The Logic of Soft Drugs," in William Rodney Allen (ed.), *The Coen Brothers: Interviews*. Jackson: University Press of Mississippi, 100–8.
Conard, Mark T., ed. 2012. *The Philosophy of the Coen Brothers*. Lexington: University Press of Kentucky.
Coursodon, Jean-Pierre. 1991. "A Hat Blown by the Wind," in William Rodney Allen (ed.), *The Coen Brothers: Interviews*. Jackson: University Press of Mississippi, 41–45.
Evans, K.L. 2012. "How Job Begat Larry: The Present Situation in *a Serious Man*," in Mark T. Conard (ed.), *The Philosophy of the Coen Brothers*. Lexington: University Press of Kentucky, 289–305.
Friend, Tad. 1994. "Inside the Coen Heads," in William Rodney Allen (ed.), *The Coen Brothers: Interviews*. Jackson: University of Press of Mississippi, 63–71.
Harlan, Jan, dir. 2001. *Stanley Kubrick: A Life in Pictures*. Burbank, CA: Warner Bros. DVD disc.
Hill, Rodney F. 2002. "A Clockwork Orange," in Gene D. Phillips and Rodney Hill (eds.), *The Encyclopedia of Stanley Kubrick*. New York: Checkmark Books, 51–63.
Hill, Rodney F. 2017. "Fargo." *Senses of Cinema*. http://sensesofcinema.com/2017/cteq/fargo (accessed January 2019).
Jameson, Fredric. 1991. *Postmodernism, Or, the Cultural Logic of Late Capitalism*. Durham: Duke University Press.
King, Lynnea Chapman. 2009. "Preface: Too Smart for Mainstream Media?" in Lynnea Chapman King, Rick Wallach and Jim Welsh (eds.), *From Novel to Film: No Country for Old Men*. Lanham, MD: Scarecrow Press, v–viii.
Mottram, James. 2000. *The Coen Brothers: The Life of the Mind*. Dulles, VA: Brassey's Inc.
Naremore, James. 2007. *On Kubrick*. London: BFI.
Phillips, Gene D. 2002. "Fear and Desire," in Gene D. Phillips and Rodney Hill (eds.), *The Encyclopedia of Stanley Kubrick*. New York: Checkmark Books, 111–13.
Stone, Doug. 1998. "The Coens Speak (Reluctantly)," in William Rodney Allen (ed.), *The Coen Brothers: Interviews*. Jackson: University of Press of Mississippi, 87–89.

4

Blurring the Lines between Victim and Perpetrator: Yorgos Lanthimos and the Legacy of Stanley Kubrick

Pierre-Simon Gutman[1]

In 2017, the Cannes premiere and subsequent release of *The Killing of a Sacred Deer*, coming on the heels of *The Lobster* (2015), confirmed the improbable international discovery of Greek filmmaker Yorgos Lanthimos. One year later, the critical triumph of *The Favourite* (2018) confirmed the astonishing breakthrough of the forty-something Hellenic director. While Greece continues to suffer from what his compatriots laconically call "The Crisis" (η κριση), whose consequences submerged that country in near bankruptcy, Lanthimos has emerged as the nation's biggest artistic and commercial success since Theo Angelopoulos. His very real accomplishments are indeed remarkable: a true auteur purposely out of sync with the exigencies of popular cinema, who not only directs three international productions back-to-back, with world stars Colin Farrell, Emma Stone, and Nicole Kidman, but also comes close to winning at the Oscars. His trifecta of films alone merits our undivided attention. Still, Lanthimos's tour de force may have made us overlook the most crucial aspect in his unfolding oeuvre: the gradual change in his approach and mise-en-scène. This metamorphosis has happened coincidentally with the director's move into English and the sphere of global filmmaking.

Confronted with *The Killing of a Sacred Deer* and *The Favourite*, critics and spectators were quick to recognize both a vivid aesthetic and a thematic influence of the Stanley Kubrick model. Tracking shots and symmetrical compositions have firmly placed Lanthimos in the congested camp of Kubrick's heirs. In moving away from his homeland and the "weird wave" movement, which he practically founded alongside Athina Rachel Tsangari and a few other young Hellenic talents,[2] the director exposed himself, suddenly revealing a more direct and visible influence. Are we witnessing a mutation, or was the Kubrick's influence unconsciously present for longer than it seems in Lanthimos's work? Neither restricted nor restrictive in nature, this question conveys essential elements for a global understanding of the Greek director's work and, beyond that, the very meaning of Kubrick's legacy in contemporary auteur cinema.

The critical reception of *The Killing of a Sacred Deer* triggered a veritable spate of comparisons between Lanthimos and Kubrick. It is true that the film itself prompts such an exercise. By multiplying perfectly geometrical tracking shots that unfold in often white corridors, the Greek director seems intent on quoting the aesthetic lessons of the master. The fact that such a referential process is embedded in his first true American film is hardly anecdotal. *The Lobster* was already a transnational work, with a cast close to a classic Hollywood global blockbuster (Farrell, Rachel Weisz, Ben Wheatley, Léa Seydoux, and John C. Reilly). The film depicts a dystopia, set in an indefinite future and abstract place. By making the mysterious hotel the locus of the main plot, Lanthimos employs a setting of deliberately vague geography and nationality, one where English, French, Greek, and American actors meet in an allegorical somewhere compounded of all these nations, which by a natural process, ultimately becomes a nowhere. *The Killing of a Sacred Deer*, conversely, was unambiguously set in America—one of those large Midwestern cities (the film was shot in Cincinnati), with its financial district, downtown high-rises, and various shades of suburbia—from the protagonist family's mansion to the antagonist's modest white trashy home. For the first time, Lanthimos poses the question of (cultural) displacement, in a country and a culture foreign to what had hitherto fed his cinematic imaginary (while still relying on classical Greek tragedy for his central narrative dilemma).

From there, a first possible hypothesis to account for the "Kubrickian markers" to be found in the film may have something to do with what Redmond Barry did to be accepted by the British aristocracy in *Barry Lyndon* (1975): a process of recognition and assimilation to a cinematic environment that is not one's own, as a way of integrating America formally, recognizing its difference, following in the aesthetic footsteps of one of its major auteurs.

This rather convenient interpretation, however, casts the first part of Lanthimos's filmography—the Greek part—as a blank slate of sorts, a mere prologue to the sudden appearance of instant Kubrickian roots, spontaneously shooting out in all directions. Obviously such an explanation is neither satisfactory, nor accurate. For one thing Lanthimos would have taken seriously the lessons of Barry's sorry fate.

Already as the patron saint of the "weird wave" in the days of *Alps* (2011) and *Dogtooth* (*Kynodontas*, 2009), Lanthimos's visual obsessions, evident in *The Killing of a Sacred Deer*, were already very much on display, as indeed were certain direct references to Kubrick's films. Ironically, by reintegrating the same mise-en-scène patterns into a distinctly Hollywood setting, Lanthimos made visible to critics and viewers alike references that were in fact there from the beginning. If *The Killing of a Sacred Deer* is considered Kubrickian, then *Dogtooth* and *Alps* should be too. Nevertheless, the American opus distinguishes itself by a specific element that has encouraged comparisons. From the relative static nature of the camera in his first feature films, Lanthimos in *Sacred Deer* has resorted extensively to steadicam shots, which follow or precede the protagonists up and down hallways.

Naturally, such shots immediately inspired multiple comparisons with one Kubrick film in particular, namely, *The Shining* (1980). This is hardly incidental when one considers its very special place in Kubrick's filmography. For a long time *2001: A Space Odyssey* (1968) clearly dominated his corpus. Over time, in the tiny playground of film-buff, cultural history, *The Shining* has been reassessed, gradually catching up to its

Figure 4.1 The two sisters standing side by side in Lanthimos's *Dogtooth* (2009), copyright Boo Productions.

Figure 4.2 Inevitably echo the Grady twin sisters in *The Shining* (1980), copyright Warner Bros.

older brother. Entire films are being dedicated to it (e.g., Rodney Ascher's *Room 237* [2012]); books and online video essays are devoted to its semantic richness, and this analytic attention includes the original Stephen King novel and the dubious remakes, just as its sequel, Mike Flanagan's *Doctor Sleep* (2019), is about to be released. And Steven Spielberg has pushed his devotion to *The Shining* to include the Overlook Hotel space, in a scrupulously faithful homage and sacrilegious *détournement*, in his recent blockbuster, *Ready Player One* (2018).

Much more than just a film classic, *The Shining* is now considered by many academics and film historians as the prototype of the contemporary "brain" film. As such, it is an essential work that has heralded and spawned the work of David Lynch, David Cronenberg, the Coen Brothers, and many more. For Gilles Deleuze, the brain-film is a part of the time-image:

> For, in Kubrick, the world itself is a brain, there is identity of brain and world, as in the great circular and luminous table in *Doctor Strangelove*, the giant computer in *2001: A Space Odyssey*, the Overlook hotel in *The Shining*. The black stone of *2001* presides over both cosmic states and cerebral stages: it is the soul of the three bodies, earth, sun and moon, but also the seed of the three brains, animal, human, machine. Kubrick is renewing the theme of the initiatory journey because every journey in the world is an exploration of the brain. The world-brain is *A Clockwork Orange*, or again, a spherical game of chess where the general can calculate his chances of promotion on the basis of the relation between soldiers killed and positions captured (*Paths of Glory*). But if the calculation fails, if the computer breaks down, it is because the brain is no more reasonable a system than the world is a rational one. (Deleuze 1989, 205–6)

In *The Killing of a Sacred Deer*, Lanthimos does cite *The Shining* (and the former's motifs—a bourgeois couple composed of a doctor and his wife played by Nicole Kidman, going through a marital crisis—also strongly echo *Eyes Wide Shut* [1999], [Figures 4.3 and 4.4]), but does Lanthimos really practice the kind of "brain cinema" theorized by Deleuze? Perhaps, if we remember that this link between the world-trip and the brain-trip is potentially evident already in *Dogtooth*, the Greek director's third feature and first international success. It speaks of a universe re-created; more precisely, it speaks of a universe in its totality but in a state of artificial reduction: for the three children of the family, the universe is limited to a house and garden—a place continually reworked and explored by the protagonists, including linguistically (words are given arbitrary meaning by the parents in their twisted socio-anthropological experiment). And what does this "world-house" correspond to, if not to the will of a brain—the father's—wishing to reduce the universe as a whole for his offspring, containing all hazards of life, and relegating them to the borders of this well-defined habitat?

From there, as Deleuze predicted, the world, the program imagined by the father, ends up breaking down, precisely because the brain is not merely a rational system (Deleuze reminds us that the brain *feels* as much as the body *thinks*), and the place imagined by said brain ends necessarily in malfunctioning/short-circuiting.

Figure 4.3 Nicole Kidman and her doctor husband (Tom Cruise) at a party in *Eyes Wide Shut* (1999), copyright Warner Bros.

Figure 4.4 Nicole Kidman and her doctor husband (Colin Farrell) at a party in *The Killing of a Sacred Deer* (2017), copyright 20th Century Fox.

Figure 4.5 Lord Bullingdon (Leon Vitali) about to fire his pistol in *Barry Lyndon* (1975), copyright Warner Bros.

The driving question here is the point of view of the author, his position within the story/film/brain. As for Kubrick, he clearly chose his camp. In a study of the American filmmaker, Italian scholar Marcello Walter Bruno (2017) observes that

> Kubrick's humanism is expressed rather through his fundamental choice, as a director, to observe the violent events from the point of view of the victims: think of the subjective framing of the dead, scattered in *Full Metal Jacket* or, to come back to *Spartacus*, to the anti heroic account of the battle of the Metaponte from the beginning knows the tragic outcome at the expense of gladiators. (96)

Does Kubrick's humanism, as described by Bruno—ultimately adopting the point of view of the victims—correspond to Lanthimos's? That is the question before us.

While the tracking shots in *The Killing of a Sacred Deer* and the decadent and painstaking reconstruction in *The Favourite* naturally encourage comparisons with Kubrick, whose films they openly quote (in *The Favourite*, besides the setting à la *Barry Lyndon*, we find the wide-angle shots and quick pans straight out of *A Clockwork Orange* [1971], see Figures 4.5 and 4.6), it is obvious that *The Lobster*, Lanthimos's first international film, should also not be overlooked. Its critical success was pivotal in orienting the career path of the director, as he moved onto the stage of "global auteur" (to quote the useful formula of Seung-Hoon Jeong and Jeremi Szaniawski [2016]). *The Lobster* is Kubrickian in its very narrative project, not only for its ominous hotel but also for its treatment of the grotesque in view of James Naremore's seminal work on this topic in the American director. Naremore describes the grotesque as a complex

Figure 4.6 Lady Sarah (Rachel Weisz) about to fire her pistol in *The Favourite* (2018), copyright Fox Searchlight Pictures.

mixture of sudden shifts in tone and register, between dread and caricature, to be apprehended and obtained:

> Its defining feature is what Philip Thompson describes as an *"unresolved"* tension between laughter and some unpleasant emotion such as disgust or fear. In effect, it fuses laughing and screaming impulses, leaving the viewer or reader balanced between conflicting feelings, slightly unsure how to react. . . . The most common understanding of the term, however, involves deformed and disgusting representations of the body—especially when they place exaggerated emphasis on the anus, the vagina, or other orifices, or when they depict bodily secretions or fluids. The same could be said of images that mix the human anatomy with something alien—the head of an animal, the legs of a puppet, and so forth. In the cinema, the grotesque can be created with masks, makeup, wide-angle close-ups, or simply with the casting of actors who seem grossly fat, emaciated, or ugly in ways that make their faces potentially both comic and frightening. (27–28)[3]

In the grotesque, which courses through all Kubrick's films from *Killer's Kiss* (1954) to *Eyes Wide Shut*, Naremore distinguishes a central element of the Kubrickian aesthetic. Here is Naremore again analyzing its presence at the beginning of *Full Metal Jacket* (1987):

> Whether or not the opening sequence of *Full Metal Jacket* is . . . a "modern-art masterpiece," it probably aspires to that condition. All its visual and verbal techniques are aimed at maintaining an exact style and a convincing picture of military life while at the same time making us cringe and laugh uncomfortably, feeling uncertain about the film's ultimate purpose. In the last analysis, it can be understood both as a meta-commentary on Kubrick's art and as a systematic demonstration of how the grotesque, whether in life or in movies, messes with our minds. (39)

It is easy to find common points between the grotesque, as outlined by Naremore, and the operation of the hotel in *The Lobster*, and especially the fate of its dwellers. The animal evolution (or involution) of the characters, this transformation inflicted on those unable, in due time, to find their soulmate, seems to be located in this complex of droll humor and dread, a social caricature, an absurd mixture, freely blending man and beast that is the very essence of the grotesque. And it is possible to detect traces of a different and yet similar process both in *The Favourite*, where the director mixes ridiculous and decadent visions of aristocratic games from the period (an animal presence comes into play here too between the rabbits, dogs, horses, Indian runner ducks, and the undignified behavior of the human protagonists) with a factual description of the beatings and cruelties that the members of this world are willing to inflict upon each other, in a sly game of survival of the fittest (and most perfidious).

Thus, Lanthimos belongs to the Kubrickian aesthetic tradition. And Naremore's conclusion is equally relevant and timely for our study, since it contrasts the formal coldness often attributed to Kubrick with a vision of compassion that the grotesque may conceal, without diminishing:

> The chief irony of the sequence is that even though Pyle's reaction to Hartman seems to be slow-witted, it is more likely to be a bewildered mingling of fun, fear, and disgust that turns suddenly into outright shock. In contrast with the stony looks on the faces of the other recruits, Pyle's reaction is sensitive and sane; only when forced to deny a suicide. His confusion and bewilderment, are moreover, are built into the very structure and texture of the film, which is designed to create a world that is both absurd and verisimilar. This is the world Kubrick repeatedly tried to represent. If some people look at it as cold, it can be because it allows the comfort of secure responses. The emotions are primal but mixed; the fear is one of humor and the laughter is both liberating and defensive. (40)

Clearly, Naremore is not far off here. Seeing beyond Kubrick's cynicism and will-to-provoke, he perceives that humanism of which Bruno wrote, a humanism that in turn emphasizes the point of view of Kubrick's victims, as they are confronted with the absurdity and violence of the universe.

How does this "humanist" point of view compare to that of Lanthimos? *The Lobster* remains the best starting point to try to address this issue. It is indeed in this film that the extreme formal rigidity of Lanthimos's cinema, thanks to the dystopian nature of the narrative, joins the entire organization and building of a world. It allows us to question the place that the filmmaker wishes to occupy within this world. What dominates the strange hotel at the center of the film's making is the extremely geometric dimension of most of the shots. Freely breaking the rule of two-thirds, Lanthimos organizes almost all his frames around a perfect, highly structural symmetry.[4] Such a voluntary deviation from the good rules of pictorial composition, inherited from the golden ratio and present in almost all the professional manuals of filmmaking, has a direct effect on the viewer's mind, who inevitably takes it into account, albeit unconsciously.

This departure from the rules of traditional cinematic composition directly echoes *The Shining* and also *Eyes Wide Shut*.

In her study devoted to Kubrick's last feature film, Diane Morel notices the way in which the director employs tracking shots and often geometric compositions to emphasize a cinematic version of the Freudian uncanny. Morel reminds us that for Freud, this feeling of the uncanny arose largely from a phenomenon of resurgence: "The disturbing strangeness born of repressed complexes is more resistant than, it remains in the literature as strangely disturbing as in the lived" (Freud 1985, 256). Morel (as well as Le Bihan 2017) recognizes this resurgence in the extensive and repetitive use of identical tracking shots as well as shot compositions, transforming the geometry into a mirror effect:

> The fascination that the film can exert is very much due to its rigor. . . . Cyril Neyrat, in a short article analyzing this game of forms, emphasizes both the abundant and spectacular use of tracking shots, the obsession with quadrangular geometry, and the centering of bodies in the frame. (Morel 2002, 166)

In breaking an image principle anchored in the eye of the spectator in *The Shining* and *Eyes Wide Shut*, Kubrick posits and formalizes the idea of an underlying anxiety, and generates a destabilizing effect capable of quickly escalating into anxiety. It is this very peculiar and effective conception of cinematic unease that Lanthimos reclaims in *The Lobster*. Behind the veneer of auteur cinema, he thus delivers a film that borrows the specific grammar of high horror, impregnated with a Freudian legacy.

In *The Killing of a Sacred Deer* Lanthimos amplifies this process, in terms of both formal and thematic borrowings. The narrative genre itself, which abandons an absurd dystopia for a mythological plot set in contemporary urban American Midwest, is at the crossroads of the fantastic and the thriller. It is much more influenced by the elements of the horror genre practiced in *The Shining*. The sometimes surreal atmosphere of *The Lobster* leaves room, in *Sacred Deer*, for a story much more loaded with traditional elements of the genre, with a threat to the family unit; an intrusive young man—both cajoling and threatening; not to mention of course the strange illness that befalls the children of the Farrell and Kidman couple. Borrowings from *The Shining* can apparently be considered within the more classic framework of quotations to reproduce the very precise impact that a genre film has on the public. However, the difference is significant: while *The Shining*'s tracking shots followed young Danny within the confines of a hostile and disturbing terrain (the Overlook Hotel), in *The Killing of a Sacred Deer* the tracking shots follow the protagonists through areas well known to them and already invested, marked out, and at first sight devoid of any unknown capable of propagating anxiety.

In this sense, Lanthimos also distances himself from *The Shining*'s cousin, *Eyes Wide Shut*, with its rituals and ceremonies (described by Morel) as well as its geometry and the mirror effects (described by both Neyrat and Le Bihan). If the similarities are there, the differences are equally glaring. At first glance, Lanthimos seems to adopt several of Kubrick's directorial "tics." Upon closer inspection, we realize that he reproduces them with an impeccable virtuosity in order to subordinate them to his own narrative and thematic stakes. And if Kubrickian tracking shots are also less present in *Alps* or *Dogtooth*, the formal work on anxiety and symmetry nevertheless remains. However, it does so with a major twist: the victims' point of view, which both Walter Bruno and Naremore describe in Kubrick, will now become that of the perpetrators.

Seen thus, *Dogtooth* is undoubtedly the real turning point in Lanthimos's work. While *Kinetta* (2005), his second feature film, may be read as the manifesto of the Greek "weird wave," *Dogtooth* represents the logical next step, bringing with it the movement's scheduled end. In the plot's narrative program, we find elements that link it to a pure form of Greek tragedy, obviously culturally significant and deeply resonant for Lanthimos. The father is indeed a form of god, all powerful in the arrangement of his (small) universe. His children are his heroes and victims, subject to the whims of a parent who creates, guides, and controls their destinies. The young man of *The Killing of a Sacred Deer* may certainly not be a powerful father figure, but he is still closer to the gods, subjecting humans to the blows of fate, and capable of cursing the family and having a mysterious and incurable disease befall them. He holds a mysterious power, which remains unaccounted for until the end. He uses it to torment the family and creates very literally the tragedy by imposing an impossible choice, which results in the death of a child. Kubrick staged similar iniquitous tragedy (think of the mock execution in *Paths of Glory* (1958), or the way the hand of some absent entity blows away the banknotes at the end of *The Killing* (1956) before a mystified and resigned Sterling Hayden), and this generates another telling echo compared to that haunting presence in Lanthimos's films. Kubrick's heroes are similarly struck by forces that push them to the breaking point; in Kubrick we witness the destruction of self and others, whether it be Barry Lyndon, Jack Torrance, or Gomer Pyle. But destiny has many countenances, or none at all. Sometimes the protagonists perpetrate their own torments—victims and perpetrators at one and the same time. The American filmmaker's humanism is also present in his way of looking at the victim, even in the executioner (*A Clockwork Orange*).

In contrast, Lanthimos seemingly separates victims and executioners, even if he sometimes plays, as in *The Favourite*, on the viewer's assumptions regarding their true identity (how we pity Emma Stone's character at first!). Tragic forces for the younger director assume a body, a face, an identity. And, like the father in *Dogtooth*, they can sometimes take the first place in the work, its story, and its mise-en-scène. This pure aesthetic dimension of domination can thus be read in the choice of frames and composition. In *Dogtooth*, formal rigidity and oppression, engendered by the geometrical radicality of the shots, becomes very much a principle. It is not a question of establishing a system of filmmaking that generates anguish, discomfort, or any other element potentially necessary for the reception of the film, but, on the contrary, to make this system an end in itself, marrying perfectly the will of the demiurgic parents of *Dogtooth*, possessed by their dream—that of creating a micro-society perfectly controlled and managed from all angles by them. *The Favourite* extends and enriches this system. Organized around the ferocious rivalry of two women vying for the queen's affection, and thus for power within the English court, the film has us witness two forces that will each maneuver to take control of space, the plan to try to seize the seat of English power, to appropriate and, if necessary, to reinvent it. Such ambition can be problematic and dangerous. In reality, it is not unlike that confronted by directors on their own film sets.

Considered thus, Lanthimos (reputedly a perfectionist of manic precision) echoes Kubrick almost parodically. The legendary rumors about the American director's need for control and his paranoia are legion, and it would be tedious to enumerate them all. Bertrand Tavernier's recollection will here suffice. For a while Kubrick's press attaché in France, Tavernier disapproved of his employer's compulsive need to spy indiscriminately on relatives and associates who visited him at his home—a close relative of the obsessive, closed universe in *Dogtooth*:

> To visit him was to enter a kind of little Fort Knox, or little Xanadu. The house was not extraordinarily luxurious, but it was surrounded by all sorts of signs, or warnings: *Do not Enter, No trespassing, Beware the dog*. Finally, you were not to touch the doorknob, because everything was connected to the police. It was a hell of protection, and I wonder how he could have died.[5]

There were also Kubrick's maniacal inspections, famous for checking the projection conditions of theaters screening his films. And this need for control not surprisingly extended to his treatment of his actors. Malcolm McDowell (2011) explains Kubrick's lack of interest in actors thus:

> His intelligence drove him to want to control everything. He was more interested in the technique of staging than in directing actors. If I asked him a question, I had a wall in front of me. The truth is that Kubrick will only be happy when he has programmable robots at will instead of overly human actors.

Jacques Rivette summed up Kubrick as a machine filming machines and considered *2001* to be his only masterpiece, with the computer HAL 9000 as the ultimate Kubrickian hero.[6] Despite his perspicacity, Rivette is slightly off the mark here: a need for control and manic obsessiveness were for Kubrick a means to achieve his goals, not an end in themselves.

When the filmmaker wished to project himself, he chose Napoleon, the titular emperor mirroring his own extravagant artistic ambitions. Commenting on the Taschen compendium edited by Alison Castle (2009) and devoted to Kubrick's archive on the ultimately abandoned "Napoleon" project, Laurent Joffrin remarks on the director's apparent identification with the emperor and concludes:

> The reader of the Taschen book comes quickly to this bright hypothesis: Kubrick was not content with loving the Emperor. In his rage to appropriate the supreme subject, he had identified with him. Kubrick, in fact, saw himself as the Napoleon of cinema. Like his model, he had quickly mastered all aspects of his art. Napoleon knew how to maneuver a regiment, lead a platoon to the assault, organize a siege

artillery, point a gun, gauge a new process of firing. He rode among his troops, counted the rifles, commanded the laces for the *grognards*' shoes, organized the refueling himself and planned the Grand Army's movements step by step, lying on his cards, stitching small colored pins on the roads to figure the battalions on the march. This minutia was combined with an exceptional imagination, which allowed him to design the wildest projects by applying the most rigorous execution. In the same way, Kubrick practiced all the trades of cinema: editing, assistance, synchronizing, lighting, manning the camera, the perfection of the lenses, the direction of actors or the material organization of the shoot, the accommodation of the team, all the way to the composition of their meals. Just as it was for Napoleon, this passion for detail was at the service of the wildest ambitions. (Joffrin 2000)

Kubrick regarded Napoleon's Russian campaign as a doomed blockbuster and texts on the aborted film clearly indicate the director's will and desire to articulate all possible commonalities, obvious or improbable, between subject and author. Napoleon wanted to conquer Europe; Kubrick was an absolute king of cinema, able to impose his whims and fancies on the most powerful Hollywood studios. Lanthimos' case is at once similar and very revealing in its profound differences. There are certainly resemblances in behavior and trajectory: an undeniable artistic ambition that has transported him from the confines of the Greek weird wave, auteurist cinema to the heart of Hollywood and the planetary star system. Lanthimos's perfectionism and thirst for control are equally visible in the rigorous composition of his frames, mise-en-scène, and obsession with control—less pronounced than Kubrick's no doubt, but nevertheless well known within the circles of Greek cinema.

But the most pronounced contrast is there as well, simple and significant: while Kubrick's demiurgic will as an instrument in the service of his artistic and personal ambitions allowed him to bring Hollywood to its knees and to acquire an unprecedented artistic independence, Lanthimos has placed his own ambitions at the heart of his topics and his cinema.

The owners of the hotel as well as the rebels of *The Lobster*, united in their will to master all actions or human impulses, the strange troop in *Alps*, the parents in *Dogtooth*, the courtesans in *The Favourite*: most of Lanthimos's films are in fact about taking control. These concerns are at the center of this devouring desire for mastery, perfectly conveyed by the filmmaker's geometric frameworks and symmetrical compositions, which betray the way in which a particular part of his artistic personality is in harmony with the strange universes portrayed. Having thus assumed Kubrick's mantle, Lanthimos overthrows it by making his films a perpetual interrogation of the manipulative perfectionism so dear to the American filmmaker, and which becomes a disturbing reality principle in the work of the Greek filmmaker. Here, the victims' point of view has completely been reversed. By removing the humanism, which is sometimes underestimated in Kubrick's art, Lanthimos questions not just the place, but the very moral and political nature of the spectator.

The mystery surrounding much of his daily life and personality has sometimes played a self-conscious role in Kubrick's mystique and success. It was also far from being anecdotal, as it referred to important elements in the filmmaker's work and his own relationship to cinema. More precisely, this refers to his will to sometimes relentlessly emerge, on a private and autobiographical level, in his own films, approaching each of them with the obsessive coldness of a machine—an aspect criticized by Rivette and also Jean-Luc Godard. Lanthimos is not exactly Arnaud Desplechin or François Truffaut in his self-projection inside his characters. His translation of Kubrick's legacy involves a fresh interrogation of his position as an artist, which distances him from the traditional direct autobiography, but is nonetheless intensely private. Lanthimos's approach takes on another meaning when we place it in the sociopolitical reality of contemporary Greece. If the now London-based filmmaker remains under-appreciated in his homeland,[7] his position as a remote prophet cannot evacuate so simply the predicament of Greece and the way in which it, consciously or not, has influenced the art of its most famous contemporary auteur.

In the media as well as in political debates, Greece in recent years has often assumed the role of victim, of the IMF and of Europe—a victim having paid dearly for its own mistakes, especially when joining the European Union. As we have seen, whether in his relationship to Kubrick's cinema or to a certain genre cinema, Lanthimos totally refuses, in his mise-en-scène, the condition or point of view of the victim. It is thus perhaps not so surprising to register his lack of recognition in his native land. From *Dogtooth*'s parents to the ambiguous hero of *The Lobster*, to the manipulative courtesans of *The Favourite*, and to the young man of *The Killing of a Sacred Deer*, the director never hesitates to put himself in the position of the demiurge and control-freakish characters who try to order the world instead of enduring it. That this cinema and its questions come from a Greek author interrogates us even more, as if Lanthimos had refused the too-easy parade of the small country caught in the nets of powerful and faceless institutions. His choice to move away from Kubrick's humanism while retaining the master's aesthetics takes on a more intriguing experimental national value: that of an artist who, through the sheer force of his directing, tries to question the other side of the mirror, the gaze, the one who inflicts and bends the real. In so doing, the Greek filmmaker goes beyond his own particular case to engage in a more global examination of an entire contemporary cinema, which he questions aesthetically, but also morally and politically. Through this interrogation, it is perhaps a whole chapter of cinema that Yorgos Lanthimos will close or even soon surpass.

Notes

1 Translated from the original French by Sally Shafto and Jeremi Szaniawski.
2 Journalist Steve Rose (2011) first coined the term "weird wave."
3 See also Naremore 2006.
4 Here for instance is an excerpt from an online guide to filmmaking: "Without entering into the mathematical details, know that the rule of two-thirds is a simplification of the rule of the golden mean. You trace lines that divide the image into three horizontal and three vertical parts. If the subject is placed dead center an overly emphatic symmetry is

created, which becomes monotonous and uninteresting to the viewer" www.faire-un-film.fr.
5   Tavernier (1999) (length: 2'20 seconds).
6   Dixit Rivette (2001): "Kubrick is a machine, a mutant, a Martian. He has no human feeling whatsoever. But it's great when the machine films other machines, as in *2001*."
7   Here is the *Courrier International* on the appreciation of Lanthimos among his compatriots: "In Greece too, the . . . director is far from being universally liked. Why? A journalist at *Protagon* hypothesizes that it's because of 'this tension that overtakes us when one of us escapes the tight borders of Greece.' Perhaps also because of his 'attitude almost as snobbish as the shots in his films,' even if it is not so much 'the mystery of his films as the mystery of his behavior that disturbs and provokes.'"
    "Cannes 2017. En Grèce qui (n')aime (pas) Yorgos Lanthimos?" *Courrier International*, May 23, 2017. https://www.courrierinternational.com/article/cannes-2017-en-grece-qui-naime-pas-yorgos-lanthimos.

Works Cited

Bruno, Marcello Walter. 2017. *Stanley Kubrick*. Rome: Gremese.
Castle, Alison, ed. 2009. *Stanley Kubrick's "Napoleon": The Greatest Movie Never Made*. Cologne: Taschen.
Deleuze, Gilles. 1989. *Cinema 2. The Time-Image*, trans. Hugh Tomlinson and Robert Galeta. Minneapolis: University of Minnesota Press.
Freud, Sigmund. 1985. "L'inquiétante étrangeté" (1919) *L'inquiétante étrangeté et autres essais*, Folio Essais. Paris: Gallimard.
Joffrin, Laurent. 2000. "Napoléon de Kubrick: Le Chantier de la gloire," *Libération*, November 18. https://next.liberation.fr/cinema/2009/11/18/napoleon-de-kubrick-le-chantier-de-la- gloire_594189.
Le Bihan, Loïc. 2017. *Shining au miroir. Surinterprétations*. Pertuis: Rouge profound.
McDowell, Malcolm. 2011. "Kubrick voulait tout contrôler," interview by Stéphanie Belpêche, *Journal du dimanche*, May 21. Last modified June 19, 2017. https://www.lejdd.fr/Culture/Cinema/Malcolm-McDowell-evoque-Orange-mecanique- 317507-3232919.
Morel, Diane. 2002. *Eyes Wide Shut ou l'étrange labyrinthe*. Paris: PUF.
Naremore, James. 2008. *On Kubrick*. London: BFI.
Naremore, James. 2006. "Stanley Kubrick and the Aesthetics of the Grotesque," *Film Quarterly* 60(1 Fall): 4–14.
Rivette, Jacques. 2001. *The Captive Lover*: An Interview by Frédéric Bonnaud, trans. Kent Jones, Senses of Cinema, no. 79. September.
Rose, Steve. 2011. "*Attenberg, Dogtooth*, and the Weird Wave of Greek Cinema," *The Guardian*, August 26. https://www.theguardian.com/film/2011/aug/27/attenberg-dog tooth-greece-cinema.
Tavernier, Bertrand. "Réaction à la mort de Stanley Kubrick de Bertrand Tavernier," *Journal télévisé de France* 2, March 7, 1999.

5

Glimpses of Eternity: Stanley Kubrick's Time Machines

Jeremi Szaniawski

Whoever the director may be, and however perceptively he has filmed and edited his movie, he can never have the same experience that the audience has when it sees the film for the first time. The director's first time is the first reading of the story, and the impressions and excitement of this event have to last through to the final work on the movie.

Stanley Kubrick (in Ciment 2001: 154)

Of all the many elements cinema comprises—many of which he had learned to master—Stanley Kubrick perhaps developed the most lasting and profound relationship with the medium's very essence: time. Kubrick thought about time, played with time, and, when possible, used it to his advantage, and not always to everyone's liking. In his short memoir *Kubrick* (2000), Michael Herr quotes critic Anthony Lane's reprimand of the director's "almost insolent approach toward the demands of chronology" (43). Herr himself characterized the director's approach to "time itself [as] meaningless, except as something to be kept on your side" (4). Kubrick took all the time he needed, Herr reminds us, not least in the preparation for his films, and his by now legendary extensive phone conversations with his collaborators. Accordingly, the director must necessarily have been more interested in an endless supply of time than of monetary funds. It is this far more ineffable and quixotic pursuit that allowed him to twist the studio's arms to have unprecedented amounts of time, more so even than money, to explore the possibilities of the films he was making. But besides the quest for the perfect effect or take through many repetitions (often regarded as manically perfectionist or even sadistic), one could argue that Kubrick was replaying the fantasy of eternity. As Arthur C. Clarke noted (see Ciment 2001: 136), Kubrick was obsessed with the notion of immortality. While he paradoxically likely died of exhaustion caused by a race against the clock—to complete his final film on time—this fixation on unlimited time allowed him also to endow his films with a density that accounts for their lasting appeal, their ability to stand up to multiple, indeed countless, viewings, and the way that they constantly generate new meanings and interpretations (this is also how they resist a term that has acquired currency under neoliberalism, namely, obsolescence). Stanley Kubrick could not conquer death, nor was he aiming to do so. Yet his films and their engagement with time constitute, like all works of modernist art, a way of allowing us glimpses of eternity.

In our increasingly trans-humanist age, this drive and desire to live eternally seems less technologically unlikely than it was twenty years ago, just as it raises ethical and moral questions of great magnitude, ones that would have certainly fascinated Kubrick. This technological change, meanwhile, should remind us of the rapidity with which time now seems to pass, and the fact that later filmmakers inspired by Kubrick do not by any means operate in a world in which time has the same meaning, even if, in many ways, it remains central to the film industry and has grown to be an increasingly prominent subject of films themselves.[1]

One might think, for example, of James Cameron, a director who was clearly inspired by Kubrick (see Hughes 2000), and who, like him, is well aware of the fact that time, for a filmmaker, is money. Keeping this adage close to heart causes it to turn into a concern of epic, engulfing proportion, one that goes beyond the practice of pushing budget limits while remaining economical, and which is allegorized by the stretching of the limits of conceivable diegetic time. Cameron's films, however, always moving at a sustained pace, deploy this diegetic time in a rather different way than Kubrick's, rejecting their balletic elegance and slow pace. In this, one can perhaps begin to detect fundamental changes not only in the way time is deployed in cinema (whether formally or thematically) but also in how these changes might signal a broader shift in society's relationship to time, one that we might grasp in phenomenological terms (the rhythm of films keeping pace with the accelerated barrage of stimuli that surround us in daily life), or in historical ones (as a symptom of the neoliberal world that developed after Kubrick had already won himself the ability to work at his preferred slow pace, and which would have likely made it impossible for him to achieve what he did).

Like Kubrick, Cameron started out directing clever B movies (*Piranha 2: The Spawning* [1981] and *The Terminator* [1984]). But—again a product of his time—he left behind Kubrick's sustained efforts at scientific verisimilitude, modernist rigor, and his demand for viewers to experience temporalities markedly different than those of everyday life, replacing them with the rapid stimulation of overblown action set pieces, schlocky special effects and gore, and, yes, time travel. This narrative device, absurd and nonsensical though it may be, has been a viable device for postclassical commercial and auteur cinema, either as a playful attraction and pretext for channeling nostalgia (the *Back to the Future* series [Robert Zemeckis, 1985-1990] a case in point) or dabbling in quantum physics (*Donnie Darko* [Richard Kelly, 2000] and *Primer* [Shane Carruth, 2004]). The difference between the modernist auteur and the postmodern craftsmen is fundamental: for the former, time is a dimension and matter in its own right; for the latter, time is just conceived as another dimension of space. Cinema's ability to explore time thus becomes blunted, reduced largely to a narrative tool in a way that corresponds, to follow Fredric Jameson's work on postmodernism, to a broader liquidation of history and an inability to conceive of forms of temporality outside of a kind of eternal present.

At the same time, Cameron's engagement with cinematic time derives from an understanding of the medium's affinity with all things time-based, starting of course with suspense. He also understands the usefulness of incorporating condensed/intensified psychological time in key scenes. This, however, Cameron conveys through the most hackneyed technique used to suggest the mind's working under the effect of an adrenaline rush, namely slow motion. This happens at a crucial moment in both *Terminator* movies or in *Aliens* (1986) when, upon being revived from her decades-long sleep in the pod, Ripley panics and screams as an alien starts to make its way through her abdomen in what turns out to be a nightmare scene. This, I argue, is a subtle and layered quote of *The Shining* (1980) and its heightened sense of suspense and dread. (Figures 5.1, 5.2) One can see the parallel between Ripley's horrified face and Wendy Torrance's as Jack's ax bursts through the bathroom door. While Kubrick himself refrained from using any slow motion in said scene, he famously toyed with time elsewhere in the film, from the *déjà vu* experienced by Jack early on to the encounter with ghosts from a 1920s ball to the infamous vision (in slow motion) of blood gushing forth from the hotel's elevator doors. The film lists a series of temporal indicators in intertitles ("Closing Day," "Wednesday," "4 PM," etc.) only to better make the passing of time inscrutable and uncanny, leading to a kind of questioning or relativizing of the way it is usually experienced. In the end, Jack Torrance is frozen in the space of the labyrinth as he is in time (his inclusion in the 1921 ball picture). While both Kubrick and Cameron, as producers and entrepreneurs, kept the adage "time is money" close to heart (hence the prevalence of diegetic time-based concerns in big budget films), Cameron halts before the threshold of film art, only using time effects for suspense and entertainment purposes, whereas Kubrick works with cinematic time as philosophical matter. This difference though, is not simply one between commercial filmmaking and art cinema, nor between art and the commodity, but rather a symptom of a broader

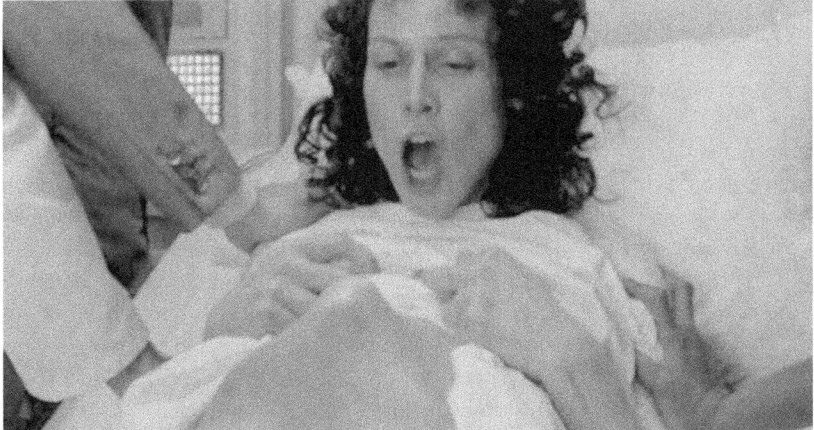

Figure 5.1 Ripley (Sigourney Weaver) watches in horror as an alien makes its way through her stomach in *Aliens* (1986), copyright Orion Pictures.

Figure 5.2 Wendy Torrance (Shelley Duvall), watches in horror as Jack's ax makes its way through the bathroom door in *The Shining* (1980), copyright Warner Bros. Pictures.

shift in our relationship with time and temporality under neoliberalism and in an age of new computational and communication technologies.

Before turning to several filmmakers who seize upon Kubrick's work on time in ways that both overlap with and diverge from what we see in Cameron (in part due to their closer affiliation with a "higher-brow" form of cinema), and who likewise provide us with telling symptoms of broader historical and technological shifts, it will be useful to consider the existing scholarship on Kubrick and time. While his work has been noted and analyzed from just about every single aspect of film theory and production, and despite attention rightfully given to Kubrick's engagement with history (Fredric Jameson, Robert Kolker, Geoffrey Cocks, etc.), few scholars, however, have studied Kubrick's remarkable take on cinematic time. Gilles Deleuze, of course, dedicated a few seminal pages to Kubrick's films in *Cinema 2: The Time-Image* (1989), enshrining him as a major American postwar filmmaker. Annette Michelson and James Naremore point to the slow pace of the spacecraft in *2001* and its experimental implications. Robert Stam notes how the director uses "cinema's capacity for mingling apparently contradictory times and temporalities" (2000: 60). Michel Ciment observes the uncanny spatiotemporal phenomenon at play in *The Shining*: "The gradual compression of 'objective' space and time (from the mountains to the hotel, from the hotel to the labyrinth; from months to days, from days to hours) is allied to a corresponding expansion of 'inner' time and space" (135). And Thomas Elsaesser (2004) aptly deconstructs the understanding of Kubrick as a postmodernist, rightly associating his films' odd chronological positioning in generic waves with the notion of *nachtrachtlichkeit* or deferred action, a concept that cuts both ways: Kubrick emerges as a figure out of time, timeless and untimely at one and the same time.

While time is nothing short of complex in his cinema, Kubrick himself did not, to my knowledge, theorize about it (nor was he particularly keen on theorizing *tout court*). But he did in his interviews discuss time on occasion: twice in his interviews with Ciment he went at length into the conundrum faced by the filmmaker, for whom it is impossible to watch one's own film for the "first time" (153–54; 193). He also marveled at the "acceleration" of events in wartime, in which life and death decisions have to be taken in the blink of an eye, quite unlike the way humans experience time in everyday life. In this, war becomes a perfect topic for narrative, Western, classical continuity-driven cinema, from which pauses, "dead" time, and so on. are usually elided. A cursory review of techniques and stylistic devices allows us to appreciate how keen Kubrick was on experimenting with cinematic time and time-related techniques. I just mentioned *The Shining*, but this is a ubiquitous phenomenon: Maria Pramaggiore (2015) notes an interest with time already at play in Kubrick's photographs and short films. The encounter of the soldiers with their alter egos at the end of his feature debut *Fear and Desire* (1953) surely hinted at an interest in temporal paradox. But it wouldn't be until later, in *The Killing* (1956), with its deconstructed narrative temporality and repeating timeline, that Kubrick (drawing on Orson Welles and Akira Kurosawa's time experiments, among others) would explicitly illustrate cinema's capacity to play with time. In this film noir, Kubrick creates tension between linear time and circles of repetition (this would later inspire Quentin Tarantino in *Pulp Fiction* [1994] and *Jackie Brown* [1997]). The fabled million-year ellipsis from bone to spacecraft in *2001: A Space Odyssey* constitutes another landmark in play with time, as do the balletic slow-motion and accelerated actions of *A Clockwork Orange* (1971). *Full Metal Jacket* (1987) resorts to slow motion punctually, in a scene of the private corps training in the mud and when the Vietnamese sniper shoots at Private Joker at the film's end. And already in a 1970s interview with Ciment, Kubrick spoke of what would become *Eyes Wide Shut* (1999), an exploration of the "sexual ambivalences of a *happy marriage*" (156), that is the tension, in a couple, between a desire for stability, security, repetition and order in one's lives, and a tendency to want to break away from it, to have adventures and to be destructive. In other words, Kubrick opposes two coexisting timelines: that of the protagonists' daily routines ("reality") and that of their erotic fantasies ("the sexual dreams and *might-have-beens*"). In the finished film, slow, obsessive zooms dilate and condense time in an oppressive and hypnotic manner, always timed to perfection to the music chosen by Kubrick, which in the end not only illustrates or reinforces the images but also provides a parallel diegetic universe and temporality to double that of the narrative per se. In all of these cases, play with time is not used for narrative suspense, or merely to convey a psychological state (although it can do this too), but to explore the complexity of time itself in its multiple forms.[2]

The short list given here barely touches the surface of Kubrick's engagement with cinematic time, and one can also certainly dwell at greater length on any individual film, drawing out philosophical, political, and aesthetic implications. In *Making Time in Stanley Kubrick's Barry Lyndon: Art, History, and Empire* (2015), Maria Pramaggiore analyzes the manifold ways in which *Barry Lyndon* (1975) engages with, represents, plays with, and combines strands of time, allowing us to think about time through film. The author's own experience watching "jet setters" Ryan O'Neal and Marisa Berenson transported into a recreation of the eighteenth century (8), and the powerful impression conferred upon her by the film, not so much of revisiting the past, but of "having relinquished all participation in the forward march of time" (8–9), are only just the first two initial time-related encounters with the film that compelled Pramaggiore to study the way in which it "produces temporality" (9), working toward the creation of an "aesthetic time." By aesthetic, the author immediately stresses, she intends not an idealist escape that is referred to or yearned for, but instead a "thoughtful and engaged social practice" (9).

> Kubrick's competing temporal modes carry both aesthetic and political implications. They set the stage for a process that elicits both cognitive processing and emotional engagement, a combination of types of attention that produces aesthetic time. This experience, which allows for the synthesis of affect and judgment, should not be confused with the aesthetics of the Romantic sublime: the encounter with the overwhelming and the formless, which produces the "unreasoning delight" of John Dennis, the "negative pain" of Edmund Burke or the subjectivity-destroying boundlessness of Kant. The ability to combine affect and judgment in the process of watching Kubrick's films is a matter of timing: it derives precisely from the way the films orchestrate various and competing temporalities and both establish and undercut narrative expectations. (Pramaggiore 2015: 39)

Time in Kubrick is thus not only aesthetic but also political and ethical, rich and multilayered, with additional layers of complexity added through Kubrick's concern with historical change, progress, and representation; the temporality of music in relation to that of the pictorial; and the question of rhythm. In addition to all these considerations relating to the film itself, Pramaggiore also discusses the question of the untimely and asynchronous, borrowing from Fredric Jameson and Friedrich Nietzsche, but also Jonathan Gil Harris: "The untimely is that which is out-of-time, inhabiting a moment but also alien to it. By resisting absorption into a homogeneous present, it also brings with it the difference that portends the future even as it conjures the past" (Harris para 12). Furthermore, Pramaggiore raises the question of physics—T-symmetry—"which claims that, at the microscopic level, the laws of physics are invariant under the condition of time reversal—Kubrick's work often, and sometimes scandalously, implies that the direction of 'time's arrow' might be merely academic and that the difference between moving backward and forward is not always so easy to ascertain" (18). This concept has been toyed with, as attested to in Rodney Ascher's *Room 237* (2012), by a video artist playing *The Shining*'s original cut forward and backward, yielding fascinating overlaps.[3]

Needless to say, Pramaggiore's study calls for similar ones of each and every Kubrick film. Perhaps the author's most important or comprehensive point about Kubrick is how his films help us to engage with and experience time, both on an emotional and an intellectual level: "the film offers viewers a way of thinking through the emotions provoked by aesthetic experience, rather than treating thought as an intellectual act divorced from affect" (10). Pramaggiore provides us with a crucial reminder of the way in which emotion and thought "find a place in the rhythms of [Kubrick's] films" (10). This is a key elaboration upon the already existing consensus in Kubrick studies, asserted by the director himself in his interviews with Ciment, namely that his films are not meant to be didactic, but rather to speak to the unconscious/subconscious and to emotions. In addition, Pramaggiore underlines the importance of a cognitive mapping, to borrow Jameson's term, when engaging with Kubrick's films.

No wonder Gilles Deleuze associated Kubrick's cinema with that of the brain, a cold and possibly cruel realm wherein all conceivable temporalities can be conceptualized, but also experienced ("There is as much thought in the body as there is shock and violence in the brain" [Deleuze, 205]). Just as a thought always contains a variety of *arrière-pensées* and afterthoughts, there is always more to any moment in a Kubrick film, always an added layer of time: the expert treatment of psychological time and the play with Newtonian time are merely the beginning of a vast enterprise. The ellipsis, for example, is a brain-cinema device par excellence: think again of the bone-to-spaceship cut in *2001: A Space Odyssey*, where fast-forward motion is not so much elided but instead acquires, quite literally, the speed of thought. The memorable and uncanny slow cross-dissolves of *The Shining* perform something similar, not only marking a transition between different spaces and times but also suggesting the working of the brain, and the relativity of chronological, Newtonian time. And the "all work and no play" moment in *The Shining* is another thought experiment that is also a temporal contraction/condensation, opening up onto more philosophical considerations.

In view of all the aforementioned points, expanding on Deleuze's masterful identification and discussion of the role of the brain in Kubrick's films, and nodding to David Rodowick's book (1997) repurposing the conceptual tools laid out by Deleuze, I argue that Kubrick's films are literally time machines that confer us with visions (or glimpses) of pure time, of Deleuzean/Bergsonian duration, of platonic eternity, even. The time that they reveal, however, is hardly essential or eternal, but instead always historically specific: associating cyclical and linear time with precapitalist practices, Pramaggiore expounds how *Barry Lyndon*, a product of postwar cinema, creates a self-enclosed space-time realm, yet at the same time is marked by a powerful feeling (shared by the author and many other viewers at least) of untimeliness as a product of 1970s. I am more interested, however, in seeing how Kubrick, a modernist auteur, has offered an avenue for later filmmakers to escape the pure "spatialization" of time (in and outside of cinema) that is characteristic of postmodernism and the neoliberal era. As Dan Hassler-Forest reminds us (2016), neoliberalism wages a pointed "war on time" (among other things, capitalism attempts to abolish the notion of mortality through senseless consumption, itself the engine of its unsustainable ideological backbone: economic growth). Hassler-Forest illustrates how, from the early *Dazed and Confused* (1993) to *Boyhood* (2014) and the *Before* trilogy (1995, 2004, and 2013), even a filmmaker as deeply preoccupied with cinematic time as Richard Linklater has gradually retreated from a critique of nostalgia (which is demonstrated by pitting *Dazed* against George Lucas's *über* nostalgic *American Graffiti* [1973]) to a model that adopts a perspective in which there is only a perpetual present.

The way in which contemporary filmmakers treat time and space, particularly when drawing upon Kubrick, may thus reveal deeper cultural and political tendencies, but also set up a kind of relay between past and present through their engagement with past modes of representing temporality. This can be a mystificatory or purely ideological practice (i.e., in the case of nostalgia), but also a productive or generative one, which at least gestures toward the possibility of other forms of time and other ways of conceiving of and experiencing it. Some contemporary filmmakers have taken it upon themselves not only to reference Kubrick but also to pursue experimenting with cinematic time in a way less sophisticated, but nonetheless intriguing and exciting, sometimes coming close to summoning—albeit in derivative ways—the time-images that Kubrick mastered, and thus upholding the spirit of a postwar capitalism that hadn't quite yet commodified time entirely. It is with this in mind that I want to look at a few of Kubrick's most important followers: Christopher Nolan, Gaspar Noé (both of whom have made a film constructed backward—*Memento* [2000] and *Irreversible* [2002]), Jonathan Glazer, and Paul Thomas Anderson. Instead of wallowing in tales of time travel as the latest (and possibly final) frontier to justify neoliberalism's wasteful ideology, promoting a fully ahistorical, spatialized time, their films allow for the manifestation of different kinds of "space-time."

Christopher Nolan: Time as Space

Since his breakthrough high-concept neo-noir thriller *Memento*, Christopher Nolan has practiced a filmmaking bent on temporal experiments (often verging on the gimmick): while *Memento* is constructed backward, thereby evoking the amnesia of its protagonist as he tries to solve the mystery of his wife's murder, *The Prestige* (2006) combines teleportation and more traditional sleight of hand to alter our understanding of diegetic time (although the latter remains linear and stable for the most part). In *Inception* (2010), time is dilated as one plunges deeper and deeper into levels of consciousness. In *Interstellar* (2014), the protagonists find themselves on a planet near a black hole, whose gravity causes one hour spent there to be the equivalent of ten years on planet earth. Later, the main protagonist is swallowed by a black hole, going beyond an event horizon and discovering a dimension in which time appears as three-dimensional space and can be navigated accordingly. And in *Dunkirk* (2017), three time lines (one unfolding over an hour, the other over a day, and the third over several days) are edited in parallel, engaging with what Stam has described as cinema's ability to play with apparently contradictory temporalities, creating an odd temporal paradox. Returning to the work of dilating time and generating suspense through crosscutting, a hundred years after D. W. Griffith, Nolan's films exhibit the artificiality, malleability, and relativity of cinematic time (and our perception of it), updating and upgrading crosscutting for the twenty-first century.

In *Interstellar*, Nolan's quixotic obsession with emulating *2001: A Space Odyssey* couldn't be more evident: the science fiction film was shot with many practical effects similar to those in Kubrick's film and, as in the 1968 opus, all scenes taking place in space are absolutely silent in terms of diegetic sound, to often poetic effect. While Hans Zimmer's score lifts the Straussian closing organ note from *Thus Spake Zarathustra* (as though to suggest that *Interstellar* picks up where *2001* left off), and the fake moon landing conspiracy theory is played with to amusing effect early on in the film, it is the character of time here that is the most profound, if not most evident, Kubrickian legacy. Yet this does not lie in Nolan playing with relativity or "bending" time through gravity, as characters on earth age by decades while the protagonists only spend a couple hours on an inhospitable planet. Instead, time is conveyed to us negatively, as pure nostalgia (for John MacKay [2014], the film's obsession with dust is an unconscious allegory of the passing of analog cinema and the grainy image of celluloid), with the house in the middle of the corn fields not evolving at all between the time when the pilot leaves earth and years later when we see the climax of the film in crosscutting: after the protagonist has been into the black hole and into the tesseract, he awakens in a recreated earth environment—a huge gyroscopic satellite—where his home is now a museum facsimile with monitors playing testimonies of old earth denizens reminiscing about the conditions shortly before resources on earth went extinct. Everything has to change so that everything can remain the same: the film, in this sense, reconnects with Nolan's desire to produce a brand new restored 70mm print of *2001*, just as it serves as an allegory for the film industry shift from analog/celluloid film to digital capture and projection as default values.

Despite his ambition, which, like Cameron, pushes him to attempt to transcend commercial cinema's boundaries, Nolan's fetishizing of both Kubrick and time yields no time-image or Deleuzean "crystal" per se. These films, indeed, turn time into space, in pure postmodern fashion. Furthermore, this navigable fourth dimension is a rather flat and ultimately incoherent and unimaginative space, used mostly as a narrative ploy. Nolan's films, though seemingly mind-bending and twisted or "impossible" (think again of the apparently inexplicable tricks of the twins in *The Prestige*), even as they make no sense, are ultimately governed by a sensory-motor schema, remaining subservient to what Deleuze would have characterized as the movement-image.[4] Not that there is fault in this, in and of itself. Surely Nolan's films are among the few blockbusters to come close to summoning the excitement and bravura of the classical western, with the motif of the frontier deeply at its core, upgraded to the age of the mind-game and thought experiment genre, and so they do sweepingly conquer one form of time—that in which otherwise a spectator's mind and body slip irretrievably into boredom for lack of proper intellectual stimulation.

Gaspar Noé: Enter the (Time of the) Brain

Like Nolan, Gaspar Noé conducts experiments with time with most if not all of his films, yet rejects the former's reduction of time to the dimension of the movement-image. In Noé, the conceit always stems from the phenomenology of narcotics, reviving the "ultimate trip" experience proposed by *2001: A Space Odyssey*, admittedly the French director's all-time favorite film (see Chodorov 2018, Appendix), which he quotes from film to film, thereby endowing his oeuvre with a real sense of continuity, not unlike the continuity, from film to film, found in Kubrick's.

Noé has produced one of the great experiments in cinematic phenomenology. Fascinated with the intake of drugs and other substances, he has weaved an oeuvre in which each film is preoccupied, tonally, formally, and thematically, with being a case study of the images and affects left on the brain and the nervous system—and, by extension, the body—by those very substances, and the way they alter our perception of time. The films then open up onto more philosophical considerations around the notion of time. For instance, *Irreversible* signals its interest in time from the outset, opening with the Schopenauerian motto[5] "Le temps détruit tout" ("time destroys all things"). But one can also argue, in vitalist terms, that time is the measure and place of creation rather than of destruction in the film. David Sterritt, in an early piece of scholarship in defense of Noé's work, writes the following: "*Irreversible* is not, in fact, simply a story told backward, but a complex study of the nature of time. Its director is less interested in cause and effect than in the form of time itself." This, Sterritt goes on, distinguishes it from other "reverse chronology" narratives such as Nolan's *Memento* (186–87). Sterritt is keen to suggest that the story told backward carries greater weight in Noé than it does in Nolan. To be sure, Noé boasts the self-aware "philo-pop" literary credentials to go along with this assertion. Indeed, in the last scene of the film, just before the image turns to a stroboscopic abstraction, we see Alex, lying in a park, unaware of her pregnancy and the fact that she will soon be raped and murdered, reading J. W. Dunne's *An Experiment with Time* (1927), which characterizes her as both a soul-searching and pseudo-intellectual hipster, in an ironic jab of sorts (the book, Sterritt notes, has been taken up "not by the academy but by dilettantes and dabblers, mystics and bedroom psychics" [189]), and sheds a measure of light on the film's composition. Dunne's theories are complex, but definitely hinge upon the notion of multiple "time states," which are numbered (Time 1, 2, etc.). "Time 1," Sterritt reminds us, "is the linear time of everyday, with the world experienced in succession. Time 2, which coexists with Time 1, is not linear but integrated in a kind of fourth dimension, where future, past and present merge together"—an analogon no doubt to the Bergsonian "Whole." "Time 2 is compared to 'the Everlasting Now' of Eastern philosophy (our dreams take place in Time 2), and can be accessed through trance, dreams, hypnosis. We recount dreams as if it were Time 1 (linear)" (Sterritt 2005: 189). By placing the semi-scientific, semi-mystical book in the hands of its unfortunate female protagonist, Noé is clearly giving the attentive viewer a clue, endowing the film with more weight or respectability—something the director must have felt would be needed considering the graphic and exploitative violence of his film.[6] In short, if we follow Dunne strictly, the future is unavoidable because it already exists in the present, as suggested in the film's "omens," which could be traced back to Chekhov's guns, establishing a sense of order in the chaos and violence of the film. The clearest indicator here is Alex's dream of tunnels branching into two directions. But this very dream (which announces the rape scene) complicates this assertion, hinting at the possibility of an alternate future, closer to Zugzwang or string theory than Dunne's conceptions. But it is of little importance in the end: as Kubrick's *Barry*

Lyndon narrator reminds us, "great or good or bad, handsome or ugly, rich or poor, *they are all equal now*."

Sterritt identifies, following the works of Wojcik, a fatalist and apocalyptic thought in Noé's films. While modern drama—a version of tragedy reworked through the lens of individualism—gives slightly more freedom to the subject, Noé's films reminds us, at the very least, of the predetermined nature of most fiction films, in line with Martin Buber's conviction that "everything is pre-determined, all human decisions are only sham struggles" (1957: 201).[7] For Sterritt, the film also takes on a political dimension through its denunciation of the hypocrisy of modernity: "It's this existential deadness that *Irreversible* assails" (193). But as Kubrick's interest in T-symmetry asserts, time is a dimension where entropy may occur, but also where life is born and evolves in a pattern of endless forking paths, of which *Irreversible* suggests only one instantiation. So, while the film plot and structure itself narrate a tale of irreversible doom, and thus can be aligned (as it is by Sterritt) with unconditional apocalyptical and fatalist thought, the very act of filmmaking is a way to channel, exorcise, and conquer the inevitability of fate, complicating the argument whereby "le temps détruit tout," closer indeed to Schopenhauer's "the world is Hell, and men are on the one hand the tormented souls and on the other the devils in it" (1979: 48). Perhaps the most distressing aspect of *Irreversible*, to some, is how it shows that there can still be beauty in this hell. In any case, Noé's meditation on time draws closer to Kubrick's than Nolan's ever could in that it is generative, questioning: it resists the "war on time" and instead forces us to grapple with both its horrifying and potentially liberating dimensions, which are given concrete form through the film itself.

With his 2009 magnum opus, *Enter the Void*, Noé exalts even the most sordid aspects of life, and elaborates upon this notion of coexisting temporalities. This time, he borrows from another book, whose popularity is largely connected with a revival of interest in certain hallucinogenic drugs. Taking the *Tibetan Book of the Dead* as his literary anchoring point and *2001*'s psychedelic trip as his chief audiovisual model, he illustrates the "ultimate trip" with even more formal radicalism than in *Irreversible*. The film opens with a subjective point-of-view shot from the perspective of Oscar (including eye-blinking), a petty Canadian drug dealer living in Tokyo with his sister Linda, who makes a living as a stripper. Orphaned at an early age, Oscar and Linda are close and love each other, but they are clearly scarred and seemingly destined to doom and misery. Smoking DMT, Oscar hallucinates before being roused by an artist friend, Alex, who tells him about the sequence of a soul's journey after death, as described in the *Tibetan Book of the Dead*. Shortly thereafter, Oscar, who is carrying a stash of illegal drugs, is shot dead by the police in the bathroom of a seedy bar. His soul then exits his body and floats around Tokyo, revisiting his past leading up to his death, and witnessing the reactions of his loved ones. In the third sequence of the film, his spirit experiences a bad trip in which the protagonist briefly returns from the dead as a mute zombie. In a final psychedelic sequence, the ghost sees a series of characters of the film engaging in a variety of sexual activities, and finally elects to be reincarnated as Linda's and Alex's spawn, only to be reborn as his own dead mother's baby, thus performing a form of time travel, as though he were trapped in a loop, destined to repeat the same story we just witnessed. The short summary can scarcely do justice to the formal complexity of the film, and to its temporal structure—in turn maddening and fascinating. Noé very self-consciously plays with temporal flow to provide a riveting first part in pseudo-real time (with the trip on DMT making chronological time relative), something underlined by the faux, digitally stitched together forty-five-minute sequence shot. Then, following his killing, the meandering of Oscar's ghost, floating around and entering all sorts of orifices and light sources, provides a fascinating, almost hypnotic second section. The third part of the film, corresponding to the bad trip, is deliberately ponderous, tedious, and repetitious, causing somatic discomfort in the viewer even as it elicits intellectual fascination. The final "love hotel" orgy scene manages the feat of ending both in climax and anticlimax: the promise of the eternal return of the same ("the void" and drabness of existence) through reincarnation, redoubling the irreversibility of Oscar's fate. It is, after all, all about the journey, not about the final destination, Noé tells us with his film.

Interestingly, *Enter the Void* can be read as a true post-mortem narrative, or as a drugged dream or vision right before death: Oscar, after all, is still under the influence of DMT when killed, and does little else but follow the narrative sequence told to him by Alex just a few minutes earlier. This means that, in a masterful move, Noé may have created the most protracted few seconds in the history of cinema: the last moments of consciousness of a dying body, overdosing on the chemical released in the brain and allowing one to revisit one's life in the final moments before death. This is the exact inverse of the million-year ellipsis of *2001: A Space Odyssey*, but in both cases, the radical relativity of time, and cinema's specific capacity to render it, are key.

Furthermore, the irreversibility of a cyclical time can be experienced by watching *Enter the Void* several times: despite knowing the journey, we also somehow forget it, or we deliberately decide to take the ride one more time, instead of embracing the Nirvana or higher planes of consciousness. This could be, as Alex tells Oscar, because "people fucking love this world so much" that they elect to return to it (or because people know nothing outside of their perception of the material world, with drugs proposing merely a warped or illusory expansion of this perception). This could be because of a fear of the unknown beyond death, or because of humans' troubling need to repeat the same experience over and over again, as part of our anthropological makeup, and the virtue of repetition. The film speaks equally to all these possible interpretations. At any rate, the journey into the limbo between vicarious death and reincarnation speaks less to Schopenhauer, and more to the philosophy of Martin Heidegger, with death (called an "exceptional event" by Noé in his most recent opus, *Climax* [2018]) conferring meaning upon life (even as it does so "post facto" here) and with Oscar's ghost experiencing literally "ek-stasis," the state of being outside of one's body and of time, in death. Noé's insistence on making the spectator confront repetition and death stands in stark contrast to a neoliberal society in which the attempted eradication of time through constant consumption (which finds its mirrored, inverted image in the consumption of drugs in his films) functions as a means to deny mortality while giving the false impression of constant progression (through new sensations, commodities, etc.). He reminds us that consumption can entail not only a self-negating kind of addiction, but also a potential means (even if it is often rejected) for the transcendence of the desiring self, perhaps much like cinema itself.

Despite being often criticized for his regressive and adolescent fantasies and the stupid characters who inhabit them, Gaspar Noé, like all auteurs dealt with in this chapter, is a very intelligent man no doubt. Intelligent enough, that is, to have yielded one of the few cogent and truly challenging filmographies among French filmmakers of the last thirty years, but also to be aware of where his strengths lie, and that his capacities fall short of allowing him to reach the master's Icaric heights (Kubrick's fabled IQ of 200), and the aspirations that some other Kubrickian epigones nurture in such brave or brazen manner. While formally he has been exceptionally ambitious and creative, from a narrative standpoint Noé has consistently opted for the "Dedalian" route: he flies, or crawls, low, wallowing in the miasma and stench of the gutter, recreating a miniature, reduced, base and yet cinematically invigorating version of Kubrick's world. In a filmography so clearly identified with an imagery of bodies—often defiled, crushed, or violated—and bodily secretions, Noé as a matter of fact belongs to the tradition of what Deleuze posits as the cinema of the brain: but of a brain that has been reduced, without a cerebral cortex, but still connected to the brain nexus (and "mini cortex") through the basic functions imparted to the most primitive part of the human brain, namely the reptilian brain. Containing the cerebellum and the brainstem (like that of a reptile), it controls the body's vital functions such as heart rate, breathing, body temperature, and balance. Noé's cinema would then qualify as a cinema of the reptilian brain—intimately correlated to the bodily, and liminal in that sense, but of the brain nonetheless. And while it cannot possibly conceive of it, a reptilian brain, governed by the strict rhythms of heartbeat, and so on, still experiences time, governed as it is by physiological cycles and rhythms. And rhythm, as Nietzsche argued, is the most primary sensation of time and, indeed, may be the form of time itself. Hence the deep correlation in Noé between a pursuit and representation of shapes of time, and regressive narratives.

In a second movement, originating with knee-jerk reflexes and the most basic plots, Noé's cinema surreptitiously elevates itself, reconnecting with the outer space of the inner space inside the brain—and its often stunning imagery, that of meditation, deep unconsciousness, and hallucination—when thought hasn't really formed yet, or, more precisely, when the waking body hasn't seized a semblance of control of the thought process. These narratives are all aborted, failed, or incomplete odysseys, marked by a fundamental contradiction in temporal terms, as Pramaggiore notes of Kubrick's 1968 opus, with its chronological, referential date ("2001") and its a-temporal, cyclical "odyssey," "a process that encompasses the circularity of unstructured voyage and return" (34). Such journeys, whether conceived of as failures or successes, descents into the subhuman or voyages beyond the limits of the human, perhaps hinge on a belief that something such as a non-spatialized time can exist, that to journey is not necessarily to travel; for Noé, such journeys can perhaps only exist inside the brain under the influence of psychotropic substances, insofar as their possibility is largely denied by the eternal present of the postmodern.

Even so, signs remain that such journeys can indeed lead to some kind of transcendence, ambivalent though it may be. The *2001*'s voyage to Jupiter and beyond the infinite, filled with psychedelic imagery, is clearly there in the final abstraction at *Irreversible*'s end, and the floating camera taking on the perspective of Oscar's ghost after his physical death in *Enter the Void* leads us through imagery of fetuses and children turned from the triumphant Star Child and Strauss's pomp at the end of *2001* to the stuff of abortion and obstetrics clinics alike: a hymn to life in spite of the drab depictions and characterizations, with the promise of a "return of the same" inscribed therein. The dance floor of *Climax*—and that film's sequence-shot dance number (which uses camera movements extremely similar to those in the Discovery sequences in *2001*), meanwhile, appears as a kind of brain in the process of transforming itself: the dancing bodies and individualities blend together, forming a collective, intelligent artificial organism (explicitly so when five male dancers combine into one moving entity), a functioning, harmonious brain (Figure 5.3). When the characters are drugged unbeknownst to them and the party unravels, their bodies become the allegory of a malfunctioning brain, literally enacting the nightmarish scenarios one can portray when experiencing a paranoid trip—ending in some of the dancers' death. From that point on, the film becomes a whodunit of sorts, although that narrative argument is only marginally relevant. More important, as in *Climax*'s opening dance number, is the multiplicity of coexisting individuals,[8] of coexisting presents, a beautiful image of intermingling singular temporalities in their complexity. A meditation on time, even in its most subjective form, thus carries deep political implications and gestures toward a positive transcendence of the unified time of the neoliberal present.

Figure 5.3 The dancers form a collective, brain-like organism in *Climax* (2018), copyright Wild Bunch et al.

In reinventing the cinema as brain, and recreating worlds that are epic journeys into the neocortex, and even into death, Noé becomes, against the odds perhaps, a philosopher of cinema. And this is where it is useful to recall Deleuze's bemused quip on Pauline Harvey's note that "the philosopher is he who thinks he is gone from the dead." Both Noé's and Kubrick's cinema, we might say, come to us "from beyond death." Hence the shell-shocked, ghostly demeanors of the protagonists, and hence, too, the prevalence of "cold" atmospheres and the fondness for icy spaces (outer space, the wintry hotel, the corpses of Vietcongs next to whom American GI's pose cheerfully—as good as dead—in *Full Metal Jacket*, but also the glacial interiors of *Barry Lyndon* and *Eyes Wide Shut*). These are what Deleuze calls "Lazarean" characters, who move through landscapes that are reflections of mental states, and whose mental states are cartographies. Hence the obsession with wandering urban spaces in Noé's Paris or Tokyo, and hence, of course, the unfolding of the post-mortem evocations in *Irreversible* (constructed backward so as to explore the unraveling of the premortem and look at it "from beyond" violence and death), the ghostly explorations of Oscar in *Enter the Void*, all the way to reincarnation, and the morbidly sweet reminiscences of Murphy in *Love* [2015]. This is further intimated to the viewer by the fascinating soundtrack of *Enter the Void*, where, barely audible, we hear dialogues from earlier scenes, like echoes, replayed and relived scenes from a past that has become relative in the time of the afterlife, in the antechamber between nirvana and reincarnation.

In *Love*, too, Noé evokes the Lazarean complex, the desire of the protagonist, through the consumption of opium, to forget about the present, to be re-immersed in a happier past, till human voices—and the body of the child—wake the hero, and he "drowns" from the foggy opium trip and the watery space of his bathtub, shedding tears of nostalgia and self-pity in the painful, present waking time, the time of harsh reality and loss. Yet another echo of Kubrick's Star Child and its brain-like membrane, this is an instance of rebirth, an anticlimactic resurrection, a rite of initiation from youth into the responsibilities of adulthood. The brain is again the site of it all: the crucible of memories, where all most precious sensations of physical bliss are stored (or produced, as though on a factory-line, as Deleuze and Guattari would put it), and where the need to move on seems inscribed. In this, Noé's cinema recognizes its limitations and failure to expand from cinema of the brain to truly cerebral (not to be mistaken with intellectual) cinema. But it also pierces the membrane, reaching out two ways: yearning toward the limbic system and neocortex on the one hand, and on the other toward the posture, the corporeal, the body, both lost, voicing the much-needed cry of contemporary digital cinema: *give us a body, give us a brain*. And give us time.

Jonathan Glazer: The Time of Missed Connections, Drift, Distraction, and Encounter with the Self

If indeed time is money, and good ideas are valuable, then the latter are a matter of time, too. Jonathan Glazer was candid in acknowledging as much, when he claimed that he "took [Kubrick's] wallet," and with that, its temporal tricks and concepts. Originally a music video artist, Glazer's work for Blur, "The Universal," references a spate of Kubrickian images (particularly *A Clockwork Orange*), while his debut feature, the dazzling *Sexy Beast* (2000), operates along the lines of the proper timing of a heist, echoing *The Killing*. His sophomore feature, *Birth* (2004), revives the notion of untimeliness, asynchrony and the Lazarean complex derived from the screen as brain and Kubrick's cinema, blending these with a satirical tone à la Buñuel, imported by screenwriter Jean-Claude Carrière. *Birth* opens with a man's voice, evidently giving some sort of talk, doubting the existence of the afterlife. In the following scene (a tracking shot quoting the jogging session of Frank Poole in *2001*), the man, Sean, jogs through Central Park, before dying from a stroke under a bridge. At the same moment, a child is born. Years later, Sean's beautiful Upper East Side widow, Anna, is about to remarry at last. This is where Glazer experiments with time, although he does so through a realistic frame: a lower middle-class child, also named Sean, and whom we presume to be the baby we saw being born, comes up to Anna and pretends to be her dead husband reincarnate. Anna's initial reaction of skepticism gives way to doubt as Sean seems to know facts about her intimate life. Her gradual will to believe that the boy is indeed the reincarnation of Sean, against all scientific evidence, yields on the one hand a psychologically compelling study of self-delusion, and on the other, proposes a "realistic" time paradox: this young boy is not only a would-be reincarnation or vessel for metempsychosis. He becomes a Bergsonian entity, an "aberration of movement," wherein past and present are collapsed, in a manner that is neither fantastic nor magical realist, but still uncanny. In this context, it is not surprising that the film should borrow from *The Shining*, not least in the Oedipal tension at its heart. But the effect here is of a soft, almost "homey" uncanny—a contradiction in terms if there ever was one—*Birth* always eschewing the gothic in favor of a slightly surrealist tone. In Kubrickian fashion, the film works most elegantly with ellipsis. Its muted and weird asynchronous romance apart, with its connotation of missed rendezvous (but also creepy hints of pedophilia) echoes the spirit of untimeliness that Pramaggiore extols in *Barry Lyndon*. Besides the upstart and impostor narrative and literal quote (the chamber concert scene during which Anna's fiancé, Joseph, attacks Sean), the spirit of 1970s cinema permeates *Birth*, from its eschewing of twenty-first century temporal markers to the hue of the cinematography and handheld framing in certain scenes, particularly in the way the driving scenes are shot, to vintage mise-en-scène effects, such as the moment when a black cat jumps, seemingly out of nowhere, from behind Anna, as though marking or attesting to a world in which the impossible and magical creeps upon one unawares. In the end, despite Joseph's love, Anna remains prisoner of the past, hence her constant melancholy: she may never recover from Sean's death, ignorant to the end of his infidelity, which prompted the sinister, and very real, event that gives, one wintry night, a creative and elaborate idea to a child of modest extraction genuinely smitten with the alluring and apparently unreachable bourgeois woman—and the temporal short-circuit generated by such mésalliance. *Birth* is thus marked by untimeliness both in its narrative and in the world it creates. Yet this untimeliness oscillates between a seemingly magical quality—as something that would let us overcome or even master time—and merely being a kind of ruse or fraud. As such, it can be seen as gesturing toward a dialectic that will certainly be present in any film seeking to evoke Kubrick, or past cinema more broadly, in the present.

Glazer's subsequent film, *Under the Skin* (2013), is full of Kubrickian citations: the opening (the creation of an artificial eye) strikingly resembles the spaceship Discovery One (with the round orb and elongated cylinder), while the dark doorway to the alien's home-like trap echoes the dark monolith of *2001*. The film is loosely based on Michel Faber's eco-critical and feminist science fiction novel, about a working-class female alien who is mutilated in order to look human, and sent to earth to abduct hitchhikers, bringing them to a farm where they are slowly turned into cattle-like fat, mindless slobs for alien meat consumption. Glazer strips most of the novel's explicit humanist and feminist discourse, just as it mutes the alien's inner voice (in free indirect discourse in the novel): the alien in the film is not mutilated, but dons an artificial skin that gives it the exact likeness of an attractive female earthling. She emotes so little that it is not far-fetched to see her as an artificial intelligence rather than a biological organism. The film experiments on a variety of levels with empathy (some scenes, like the one involving a crying, clearly distraught baby on a wintry beach, after his parents have both drowned, are particularly disturbing), leading the viewer to feel for the alien when she falls victim, in turn, to a sexual predator. But what is most interesting to this chapter's argument is the way in which the film engages with time.

Under the Skin hints at two distinct temporalities: that of the fiction film and that of the documentary. Indeed, several scenes involving the alien driving are shot documentary style, with a network of hidden cameras rigged inside the van. What goes on there is the stuff of fiction film (the actress, Scarlett Johansson, had a measure of autonomy in driving around town, but had to perform her role as the preying alien when interacting with random strangers encountered on the streets—shifting registers from a friendly, if inquisitive, "prowling" mode to a complete blank, deadpan expression when losing interest in the potential prey). The types of slightly wide angles of the cameras for these driving scenes evoke Kubrick's fictions in particular insofar as they make the van's interior resemble a spacecraft pilot cabin or pod from *2001*. Conversely, the documentary style used for the exteriors evokes instead a kind of liveness or contingency, a sense of seeing time as it unfolds rather than as a constructed artifice, as in fiction film. The fictional and familiar (inside of the van) is actually the alien's realm, while the outside (the real streets of a Scottish city) is "alien," defamiliarized—not least in the way in which real-life passersby move in front of the camera. The mismatch between these two temporalities leads to a kind of perceptual confusion that suggests the way in which even "real time" now feels mediated and constructed, perhaps even less real than fictional time: in short, the real becomes uncanny, and vice versa, through what Baudrillard tellingly describes as a kind of mediatization of the real, in which "the surrounding landscape unfold[s] like a televised screen (instead of a live-in projectile as it was before)" ([6] in Morse, 196). Television is also evoked in one of the film's darkly amusing scenes: after the alien has found temporary shelter at a man's house, the two sit and watch a comedy show. We see her inscrutable expression in front of the spectacle, mystified or befuddled, either by the humor unfolding on the screen, or by the senselessness of sitting in front of a televised set reproducing equally senseless images. (Figure 5.4) While the question of temporality is not as directly relevant here as in the previous example, we can certainly see the television broadcast itself as something bizarre and alienating due to its detachment from any clear temporal framework—yet another example of postmodern "timelessness."

Margaret Morse's critique of an alienated, televised, late capitalist society and observations on the ontology of everyday distraction (1990) are useful here. The three media that Morse engages with—the highway, the mall, and the television, spaces that are "non-places" because they are divorced from a time of actual, fully-engaged praxis, "partially derealized realm[s] from which a new quotidian fiction emanates" (196)—are all referenced in *Under the Skin*. The alien drives along city roads and on highways in search of prey but also in an attempt to escape her overseers. She visits a mall to buy some items of clothing, perfectly registering the absent and distracted way people walk around these timeless spaces from which the wear and tear of time is constantly erased. Finally, there is the TV comedy skit scene. The seemingly contradictory perceptual and emotional modes displayed in these scenes (attentive and focused, yet also absent/deadpan while driving; emotionally responsive yet uncomprehending; resigned yet panicking when attacked at the film's end) not only characterize the protagonist but also capture a new condition generated by neoliberal society, namely, as Morse puts it, one of distraction. This "in-between" state is, furthermore, characteristic of the film itself: unwittingly perhaps, Glazer creates, with *Under the Skin*, a film that seems to provide a narrative that is only semi-fictional, and engaged only partially with narration and cinema's temporality, akin to William Severini Kowinski's description of a shopping mall:

> It was its own world, pulled out of time and space, but not only by windowless walls and a roof, or by the neutral zone of the parking lot between it and the highway, the

Figure 5.4 The alien (Scarlett Johansson) watches a comedy skit on television, befuddled and mystified, in *Under the Skin* (2013), copyright Film 4 et al.

asphalt moat around the magic castle. It was *enclosed* in an even more profound sense—and certainly more than other mere buildings—because all these elements, and others, psychologically separated it from the outside and created the special domain within its embrace. It's *meant* to be its own special world with its own rules and reality. (1985: 60)

A simulacrum of a film, *Under the Skin* presents us with a simulacrum of human being, moving around in a simulacrum of human society. Yet this is a simulacrum that can be short-circuited, that is revealed in some way as contingent and thus perhaps escapable, at least in principle: such short circuits arise following the encounter with the man afflicted with neurofibromatosis, and following the alien's encountering of herself in a mirror reflection and, later, when the rapist tears her "human" skin, when she holds her own face in her hands, looking at it in a mixture of stunned contemplation and sad ravishment. This time of the encounter is suddenly charged, dense, not only with the dread of the alien's prowling, but with the sudden incursion of the face of another. Otherness, both ontological and temporal, breaks the unified world of the simulacrum. This moment echoes Kubrickian concerns in the reversibility of the gaze it instantiates, between prey and victim. The same occurs in *Birth*, between Sean and Anna. As a result of this temporality, made more complex by an inscrutability and multi-directionality of gazes that arise through new encounters, the characters are suddenly lost, but not so much out of place or displaced (although the alien is that too, of course) as out of time, "distimed." To be displaced or "distimed" in such a manner is, on one hand, terrifying and disorienting, yet at the sometime it nonetheless reveals the possibility of an outside, or an "out-of-time," that is nothing of the sort, but instead simply the result of the cracks that have formed in the seemingly unified time that is itself an illusion.

"For the Hungry Boy": Paul Thomas Anderson's Time Crystal

Once a wide-eyed visitor on the set of *Eyes Wide Shut*, Paul Thomas Anderson has also repeatedly (and very self-consciously) quoted Kubrick in attempts to infuse his generically polymorphous films with his own brand of an irony-infused yet heartfelt epic quality, be they romantic comedies, dramas, or period pieces. His referencing of Kubrick has only become increasingly conspicuous over the years: *There Will Be Blood* (2007) quotes *Full Metal Jacket* both literally, when Daniel berates Eli— echoing almost literally the insults of Sgt. Hartman at Private Gomer Pyle—and more subtly, as with the men silhouetted against the oil well on fire, very evocative of the surviving Marines singing the Mickey Mouse song. There are strong nods in Jonny Greenwood's score to Penderecki's music (drawn from an earlier, original string piece by Greenwood owing much to the Polish composer), and the barren landscape with which the film opens evokes that of the "Dawn of Man" segment in *2001*. Daniel Plainview, drooling, growling, and pin-wielding, certainly regresses to the state of man-ape when clubbing Eli to death, while also evoking the limping Jack

Torrance in a bowling room reminiscent of the Overlook Hotel's interiors. While it does not carry out million-year jumps, the film nonetheless resorts frequently to ellipses that are Kubrickian in spirit. Yet still, for all the epic feel and increased density of *There Will Be Blood*, it is the far more intimate *Phantom Thread* (2017) which seems to have accomplished the rare feat of summoning Kubrick more fully at last, and generated a rare instance of crystal image in the Deleuzean sense for twenty-first century cinema.

The film starts with a dandyish middle-aged Englishman, Reynolds Woodcock, getting ready for his day as an haute couture designer. Later, the man meets a far younger woman who, while not a nymphet, could clearly be his daughter. This is only a thinly veiled reference to Kubrick's *Lolita* (1962), even as the more direct visual quotes are from *Clockwork Orange* (the car ride) and *The Shining* (the slow, almost sinister cross-dissolves). The first scene where the two protagonists meet is a rare authentic instance of the time-image that is not merely cliché or "crystalline" in a flat, postmodern fashion. In this, Anderson comes close to Luchino Visconti's "crystal," as theorized by Deleuze: a crystal in decomposition, where aristocracy, decay, and history arrive all *too late*. Think of the rendezvous manqué of Prince Salina and Angelica, the lady of the people promised to Salina's nephew Tancredi in *The Leopard* (*Il gattopardo*, 1963), or the seal of doom over the mésalliance between the upstart Redmond Barry and Lady Lyndon yearning for a lover. But in Anderson, the fateful untimeliness is redeemed, the characters given a final chance. The mercurial Reynolds, on the verge of turning into a *vieux beau* (not so far removed from Visconti's Aschenbach in *Death in Venice* [1971]), takes a journey to the countryside to refresh his mind away from his workshop and his army of seamstresses and discarded flames. In the first defining scene of the film, Reynolds is sitting in the seaside hotel's restaurant when a maid, Alma, enters the room. Upon seeing Reynolds, Alma seems out of sorts: she stumbles and bumps into a table, causing a small ruckus. Reynolds notices her and she blushes. It is as though they sense the powerful chemistry between them from across the room. But what is happening here is also a seductive layering of temporalities, something like *The Shining*'s *déjà vu*, although of a less sinister kind (Reynolds does not, like Jack Torrance, think he is home and doomed to be frozen in the Overlook Hotel maze). Reynolds and Alma have somehow met before (although she seems to be more keenly aware of this), in a universe where linear chronology and circular temporalities coexist in a Bergsonian whole. The two characters do not merely flirt or sense each other across space: they recognize each other from across time, and we, with them, experience this subtly vertiginous event. A crystal image arises, not yet decaying like Visconti's, or sealed with doom like Kubrick's, but full of promise, of the necessary joining of the aging aristocratic genius and the youthful working-class and vital body. A fleeting glimpse of eternity appears, through the crystal of cinema. In such fragile, delicate moments, Anderson's film, but also those of the other filmmakers mentioned here, manage to summon the project of Kubrick's cinema, namely, to speak both to the brain and the senses, to the mind and to the emotions.

As its title suggests, *Phantom Thread* most definitely has to do with the untimely, the fleeting, the impermanent. And here again, the soundtrack of the film provides us with a clue. Composer Greenwood hardly contents himself with delivering mere musical pastiche, instead creating tunes and sounds which evoke a bygone era, yet stand alone as original compositions: the main theme from *Phantom Thread*, "House of Woodcock," for instance, is a remarkable improvement upon Bob Harris's maudlin theme for *Lolita* (which sounds like Liberace playing Saint-Saëns). Both tunes carry a strong Hollywood classic piano concerto-y feel, crescendo-ing mellifluously to their central melody, so that it seems fair to assume that Anderson used the Harris piece as inspiration, or even as a temp track, for this film. But Greenwood endows his composition with wit and whimsy that makes it very charming indeed, imbuing it with subtle irony. Likewise, *Phantom Thread* can be seen as an improved version of the relationship of an older man and younger woman, set against the backdrop of a bourgeois world hell-bent on decorum and obsessed with the question of impermanence and fading beauty. Through the possibility of a woman falling in love with a man such as Reynolds, Anderson sends a love letter to any admirable but capricious and unlovable master, opening onto existential and philosophical considerations that share the depth and poignancy—as well as the sheer simplicity—of *Barry Lyndon*'s ending. Both Anderson's and Kubrick's films demonstrate how a vast, immense expenditure of energy and human work is summoned in order to allow, as Alex Nemerov puts it, a single, singular "Moment of Truth" to emerge, while Anderson and Greenwood's nods to the master suggest that this moment also depends on both returning to and reworking, even transfiguring, a previous moment. Here, this truth has to do with the ineffable, but it is also connected to very specific and pedestrian elements in a way that allows the film to both engage in dialogue with Kubrick and carry out a meditation on time, desire, (anxiety of) obsolescence, and commodification. When Alma approaches Reynolds's table to take his order, the memorable dialogue is characterized by an enumeration of food items, metonyms for sexual and cinematic appetite and for base materialist concern in equal part:

Alma: What would you like to order?
    [pause]
Reynolds: A Welsh rarebit, with a poached egg on top please, not too runny. And
    bacon. Scones. Butter. Cream. Jam. Not strawberry.
Alma: No. Raspberry?
Reynolds: What else?
Alma: Coffee or tea?
Reynolds: Do you have Lapsang? A pot of Lapsang please.
Alma (as though to herself): Good choice.
Reynolds: And some sausages
Alma: And some sausages.
Reynolds: Show me. [He takes the stub] Will you remember?
Alma: Yes.
Reynolds: I am keeping this.

Alma then returns with the ordered food, and Reynolds asks her out to dinner. She says yes, and hands him a note she has already prepared: "For the hungry boy. My name is Alma." Here too we find echoes to *Lolita*, the novel:

> In the gay town of Lepingville I bought her four books of comics, a box of candy, a box of sanitary pads, two cokes, a manicure set, a travel clock with a luminous dial, a ring with a real topaz, a tennis racket, roller skates with white high shoes, field glasses, a portable radio set, chewing gum, a transparent raincoat, sunglasses, some more garments swooners, shorts, all kinds of summer frocks. At the hotel we had separate rooms, but in the middle of the night she came sobbing into mine, and we made it up very gently. You see, she had absolutely nowhere else to go. (Nabokov 1953: part 1, chapter 33)

Phantom Thread proposes a happier and slightly less pathological version of the Humbert Humbert–Dolores Haze rapport. Humbert, after "having made it up very nicely" with the "nymphet," showers her with commodities—and she of course is only a thinly veiled commodity in his hands, too, in a cycle of commodification that is grotesque yet devastating, and which will only end once Dolores, as Robert Kolker observes (2016), turns into a bland *hausfrau*, a crushing and devastating revelation of the impermanence of all things. Yet, as Nabokov and Anderson show better than Kubrick in this instance, there is an oddly touching beauty in the quixotic desire to freeze not a human being, but an emotion—to capture the ever evanescent. The whole novel, as well as Anderson's film, among the many other perspectives they can be analyzed from, thus become a critique of consumerism and alienation. They remind us at one and the same time that there are things money can't buy—and that, again, time very much is money. But it is also much more than that.

As its title *also* suggests, *Phantom Thread* most definitely has to do with something immaterial but eternal, deeply connecting human beings. While tied by the bonds of passion, the two protagonists remain uneven throughout (in age, in social status, and by virtue of their gender), and it is the project of the film to put them on an even footing. The climax of *Phantom Thread* uncannily echoes the free will question at the heart of *A Clockwork Orange*, and the sense of romantic doom of *Barry Lyndon*, but here too proposes a happier outcome. Alma has poisoned Reynolds once before, when she felt he was neglecting her and was about to discard her like all his previous muses. As Reynolds shows new signs of losing interest, Alma, in a quasi-ritualistic manner, prepares an omelet flavored with poisonous mushrooms. Reynolds somehow understands this. The two sit face to face. Whereas in the restaurant scene, when they first met, Alma knew something Reynolds only intuited, they are now equal. Reynolds now knows that Alma has poisoned him—not to kill him, but to make him weak, to bring him down from his egotistic pedestal, and to be able to take care of him and nurse him back to health. After a long pause, he obliges her, eating a spoonful of the omelet. Whereas the gesture of Redmond Barry to not shoot Lord Bullingdon went unrewarded in *Barry Lyndon*, with the characters all equal only in death, *Phantom Thread*'s strangely comforting finale suggests the possibility of an even footing, in the present, in life. This is all that cinema can do, to provide us with these visions of pure time as a kind of present in which all that can be has already been fulfilled, in which the ineffable moment crystalizes into a concrete form, which become our proxy to a glimpse of eternity. In this, the films fulfill at one and the same time a capitalist project and its opposite, giving concrete, even stable, form to ephemerality itself, as though satisfying our desire to hold it in our hands, while nonetheless refusing the static, one-dimensional temporality of the commodity—the kind of rich contradiction that Kubrick would have appreciated in more way than one.

Notes

1 Thanks go to Michael Cramer for his peerless and considerable assistance on this chapter—both in terms of editing and contributing his own ideas.
2 Kubrick's unrealized projects also closely dealt with time. Spanning millennia, *A.I.* questions time's relativity, and its perception by a non-human entity: after he has been comforted by his human mother that they will be together for "a long time" the robot boy asks the "supertoy" teddy bear, whether seventy years is a long time. "I don't think so," says the bear. Kubrick also joked (Ciment 2001: 197) that he considered making his Napoleon into a TV miniseries, shot over twenty years (an idea echoed years later by Richard Linklater's *Boyhood*).
3 Here, one may wonder if Kubrick ever saw Oldrich Lipsky's truculent *Happy End* (1967), a film unfolding in reverse motion, starting with the protagonist's execution following a crime of passion, and going through the events that led to it. The striking use of time aside—which yields its more than fair share of macabre humor, as death is equated with birth, and a coffin with an incubator—the film's Mitteleuropean setting summons echoes of Lubitsch and Ophüls, and Kubrick used the same Rossini pieces as Lipsky in *A Clockwork Orange*, including for the comical threesome in fast-forward motion, set to the tune of the *William Tell* Overture—Rossini's escalating musical structure, overlapping and relaying a variety of motifs a perfect fit for the ménage à trois imbroglio. (My thanks go to Professor Jakub Macha at Brno University for kindly and perceptively directing me to Lipsky's minor masterpiece; and to Kate McQuiston for deftly pointing to the congeniality of Rossini's music to the scenes depicted in Lipsky's and Kubrick's films).
4 The same criticism can be leveled against the TV show *Westworld*, written and produced by Christopher Nolan's brother and co-writer, Jonathan. The illogical and incomprehensible plot of *Westworld* does not for a minute hold water, using temporal paradoxes as sleight of hand rather than in any philosophical or intellectually persuasive or seductive way. As a result, the plot of the first two seasons is illogical and incomprehensible, but not in any artistic way, as say, David Lynch might have handled it.
5 "Time is that by virtue of which everything becomes nothingness in our hands, and loses all real value" (Schopenhauer 51, 1851).
6 Says Noé: "You experience things in a linear way, but when you reconstruct them with your mind, they're not linear any more. Your remembrance of your own past is not linear. It's just emotions, and moments, and they're in a chronological disorder. If you want to write a diary of what you did—say, three years ago—it will take you a long time to remember in which order the events took place. You just remember faces, moments, doors, rooms" (Noé, in Sterritt 190).

7   Sterritt also relates *Irreversible* to Wojcik's "unconditional apocalypticism," which would stem from the invention and use of the nuclear bomb. We find here oblique echoes to *Dr. Strangelove: or, How I Learned to Stop Worrying and Love the Bomb* (1964), and to Deleuze's correlation of the bomb with the time image.
8   Note also that several transgender actors/dancers perform not transgender people, but cis people. Transgenderism has clearly fascinated Noé, sometimes in unsavory ways, touching upon the "wrong man" trope and the question of time as gendered construct.

Works Cited

Buber, Martin. 1957. *Pointing the Way: Collected Essays*, trans. Maurice Freedman. Baltimore: The Johns Hopkins University Press.

Chodorov, Pip and Jeremi Szaniawski. 2018. "'The Absolute and Ultimate Manifestation of the Power of the Mind Over Technology': Gaspar Noé talks *2001: A Space Odyssey*." Senses of Cinema. Issue 87. June. http://sensesofcinema.com/2018/feature-articles/the-absolute-and-ultimate-manifestation-of-the-power-of-the-mind-over-technology-gaspar-noe-talks-2001-a-space-odyssey (accessed July 1, 2019).

Ciment, Michel. 2001. *Kubrick—The Definitive Edition*. Translated from the French by Gilbert Adair. New York: Faber and Faber.

Deleuze, Gilles. 1989. *Cinema 2: The Time-Image*, translated by Hugh Tomlinson and Robert Galeta, Minneapolis: University of Minnesota Press.

Dunne, J. W. 1927. *An Experiment with Time*. New York: The Macmillan Company.

Elsaesser, Thomas. 2004. "Evolutionary Imagineer," in *Stanley Kubrick*. Kinematograph 20. Frankfurt am Main. Deutsches filmmuseum, 136–47.

Herr, Michael. 2000. *Kubrick*. New York: Grove Press.

Hughes, David. 2000. *The Complete Kubrick*. London: Virgin Books; Virgin Complete Directors.

Kolker, Robert P. 2016. *The Extraordinary Image: Orson Welles, Alfred Hitchcock, Stanley Kubrick, and the Reimagining of Cinema*. Rutgers, NJ: Rutgers University Press.

Kowinski, William Severini. 1985. *The Malling of America: An Inside Look at the Great Consumer Paradise*. New York: William Morrow and co.

Nabokov, Vladimir. 1953. *Lolita*. New York: Penguin.

MacKay, John. 2014. "On Interstellar (2014)" https://www.academia.edu/9240536/On_INTERSTELLAR_2014 (accessed March 5, 2019).

Morse, Margaret. 1990. "An Ontology of Everyday Distraction—The Freeway, the Mall, and Television," in Patricia Mellencamp (ed.), *Logics of Television: Essays in Cultural Criticism*. Bloomington and London: BFI Books, Indiana University Press, 193–221.

Pramaggiore, Maria. 2015. *Making Time in Stanley Kubrick's Barry Lyndon: Art, History, and Empire*. New York, London: Bloomsbury.

Rodowick, David Norman. 1997. *Gilles Deleuze's Time Machine*. Durham: Duke University Press.

Schopenhauer, Arthur. 1979. *Essays and Aphorisms*, trans. R. J. Hollingdale. London: Penguin Books.

Stam, Robert. 2000. "Beyond Fidelity: the Dialogics of Adaptation," in James Naremore (ed.), *Film Adaptation*. New Brunswick, NJ: Rutgers University Press, 54–76.

Sterritt, David. 2005. "Noé Stands Alone—An Experiment with Time," in *Guiltless Pleasures: A David Sterritt Film Reader*. Jackson: University Press of Mississippi, 183–94.

6

Kubrickian Dread: Echoes of *2001: A Space Odyssey* and *The Shining* in Works by Jonathan Glazer, Paul Thomas Anderson, and David Lynch

Rick Warner

Stanley Kubrick, no less than Alfred Hitchcock, was a master of suspense. Indeed, one of Kubrick's most indelible contributions to film expression was an atmospheric form of suspense that unfolds slowly and resounds with dread. To grasp this key dimension of his work, however, one has to clear away some of the categorical baggage surrounding the term "suspense," whose very mention calls to mind a mass of clichés in horror films and thrillers: close-ups of rotating doorknobs, overhead views of coiling staircases, first-person framings that align the audience with the gaze of a not-yet-known stalker, last-second rescues conducted through crosscutting, and so forth. In film criticism and theory, when suspense isn't reductively handled as a genre unto itself, it tends to be demarcated in narrative terms that hinge on the spectator's vicarious attachment to, and psychological identification with, certain characters in the plot. But in our experiential encounter with Kubrick's spaces and textures, suspense often works chiefly as a matter of atmosphere. What moves us to feel suspense isn't just uncertainty about the fates of characters with whom we identify. In *2001: A Space Odyssey* (1968) and *The Shining* (1980), suspense develops through a slow, methodical escalation of disquiet and perplexity as we are confronted with cinematic environments that exude menace. We feel the visceral impact of this suspense even in repeat viewings of the same film, despite knowing the story's outcome, or as much of it as the film ever communicates.[1]

Kubrick's visceral use of suspense draws inspiration from Hitchcock's examples. Shelley Duvall, when recalling Kubrick's aims on the set of *The Shining*, notes that he was "crazy about Hitchcock" (Ciment 2001: 301). Hitchcock's influence strongly informs *The Shining*'s room 237 bathroom scene, which stages a volte-face of the shower murder in Hitchcock's *Psycho* (1960) by having the nude woman approach and assail the man (Cocks 2004: 219; Luckhurst 2013: 65–66). *The Shining* also reuses vocabulary from Hitchcock's *The Birds* (1963), from close-ups of mute, petrified faces to overhead views of humans miniaturized in the frame. But Kubrick's cinema invests even more energy in the *anticipatory prolongation* of suspense. Granted, both *Psycho* and *The Birds* feature extended passages of what Raymond Durgnat calls "low-key ominous suspense," rather than the "pursuit adrenaline" and "climactic nail-biting" varieties (2002: 169). However, Kubrickian suspense stretches out screen events and the spectator's unknowingness in even more profound and disconcerting ways.

Instructive on this score is Alanna Thain's theory of cinematic suspense, which focuses on the embodied role of the spectator (2017: 3–24). Dissecting Hitchcock's *Vertigo* (1958) and David Lynch's Hollywood trilogy, Thain contends that the affective thrust of suspense actually *undoes* psychological identification, revels in endless ambiguities, and thus flouts the formulaic kind of narrative suspense that promises future relief and clarity (138, 142, 255). For characters and viewers alike, this felt suspension of knowledge in the face of odd circumstances *unravels* subjectivity and opens experience onto circuits of "anotherness," thereby inciting "the body's own propensity to become other in time" (3). Much of what Thain writes in reference to these other directors applies to Kubrickian suspense as well. While drawing on her argument, I will sketch a more particular account of the affective sensations of dread that imbue our suspenseful engagements with *2001*, *The Shining*, and more recent films that strikingly reimagine Kubrick's aural and visual practices.[2]

Right away, a few elemental questions warrant attention. What constitutes our cinematic experience of dread? How does dread connect to suspense along atmospheric lines in Kubrick's work? Indeed, how can we attain a concrete understanding of so seemingly diffuse an aspect as atmosphere where his style and influence are concerned? Cynthia Freeland opens an inroad by differentiating dread and fear in the context of atmospheric horror films that are "more a matter of mood than monsters" (2004: 189). Fear, she maintains, arises in response to a definite object or agent, whereas dread lacks such bearings. Dread takes hold when one senses a threat that is "profound" yet "obscure." Both fear and dread build up through anticipation, but if fear entails punctuations of shock before an identifiable presence, dread is a more "ongoing" apprehension amid something vaguely evident and "abhorrent to reason" (191). Dread elicits "an exercise of imaginative conceptualization," a strained effort to surmise causal factors, as there is no clear basis for why the on-screen world unnerves us (195). Here, suspense follows from a dearth of rational explanation, a sort of silence that amplifies dread. For Freeland, dread has deeper and more enduring roots than either fear or anxiety, as it is nurtured by one's existential impression of an "unjust cosmos" (191–92). Though none of Kubrick's films appear in Freeland's essay, her concept of dread as a feeling brought on by obscurely menacing ambiences is germane, as is her linkage of dread to confusion in the face of some indefinite agency.[3]

If dread names the primary dramatic tone in *2001* and *The Shining*, Kubrick's suspenseful way of imparting dread isn't merely technical. Certain techniques are crucial—flowing camera movements; associative and abrupt cuts;[4] symmetrical, target-like images filmed by a clinical camera eye; oddly timed and delivered dialogue; and evocative mise-en-scène, noise, and music—but Kubrick's atmospheres are more than the sum of their devices. By atmosphere, I mean a qualitative circulation of force and affect that textures a film's world and extends that world to the audience by way of vibratory contact. A film's *atmos* (vapor) *sphaira* (globe) encompasses more than scenographic details on display. It is a "spatialised feeling" (Griffero 2014: 6) that marks the interface between screen and spectator, providing an envelope within which our viewing experience happens. Some films, of course, are more astutely atmospheric than others. Though many critics have griped about the cold, cerebral detachment of Kubrick's cinema, his command of atmosphere in fact plays on our immersive and embodied sensitivity to space, surface, light, color, sound, and motion.

What I am calling the suspenseful atmosphere of dread in Kubrick's work has often been accounted for under the category of the uncanny, particularly in readings of *The Shining*, a film that led Kubrick and co-screenwriter Diane Johnson to sift through Sigmund Freud's essay on the uncanny for inspiration (McAvoy 2015: 539). As several critics have shown, *The Shining* takes cues from Freud's inventory of uncanny things and events, adapting his investments in doublings, repetitions, doppelgängers, mirrors, and in/animate objects to the sensory needs of Gothic horror. Uncanny effects also bolster the theme of the buried, nightmarishly violent past resurfacing in the present, which transpires in the film along both patriarchal and colonial axes of meaning (Lutz 2010; Model 2012). It pays to recall that Freud describes the uncanny as an embodied response, as opposed to mere cognitive puzzlement. It is foremost a "feeling" triggered by the co-presence of the strange and familiar, the "unhomely" (*unheimlich*) and "homely" (*heimlich*). For Freud, who concentrates on aesthetic experience, the uncanny belongs to "the realm of the frightening, of what evokes fear and dread" (2003 [1919]: 123–25). Examinations of Kubrick's penchant for uncanniness tend to fixate on objects and themes while glossing over the viewer's dread-infused experience—the dizzy sensation of one's routine existence being "undercut by a subtle atmosphere of disquiet" (Trigg 2019). When speaking to what he learned from Freud, as well as from H. P. Lovecraft, Kubrick defined the uncanny as an "arena of feeling" conjured up where explanation fails (Foix 2016 [1980]: 678). As Kubrick's emulators well know, this "arena" is more atmospheric than narrative.

In what follows, my task will be to investigate how three filmmakers—Jonathan Glazer, Paul Thomas Anderson, and David Lynch—actualize Kubrickian dread in their own audacious experiments. Glazer's *Under the Skin* (2013), Anderson's *There Will Be Blood* (2007), and Lynch's *Twin Peaks: The Return* (2017) each reconfigure key elements from *2001* and *The Shining*, in essence regarding Kubrick's films as "prototypes" for intensive redevelopment (Elsaesser 2012). By studying their appropriations and tributes, I will demonstrate how these affiliates of Kubrickian dread enlarge upon Kubrick's use of atmosphere as an instrument to stage the viewer's confrontation with strange events and nonhuman agencies that exceed understanding. I will eventually maintain that Kubrickian dread occasions a form of the aesthetic sublime, combining exaltation with defeat, diminishment, and self-abdication where the film issues a hypnotic call of the void.

Glazer's *Under the Skin*

Thinly adapted from Michel Faber's 2000 novel of the same name, Glazer's slow and brooding science fiction/horror film *Under the Skin* bears a greater debt to Kubrick than to Faber at the levels of form, pace, and mood.[5] The film signals this affiliation in its first minutes, which invoke *2001* and, less overtly, *The Shining*. As with the overture of *2001*, the audience of Glazer's film must sit in total darkness for an unusually long period before the screen lights up. There is an ominous rise of music: layered and recursive tremolos in Mica Levi's score, which plays on György Ligeti's *Lontano* (used in *The Shining*) and *Atmosphères* (used in *2001*). From the middle of the black screen, a single white dot steadily grows larger, resembling an eye exam until it morphs into an ocular globe in its own right. We gather by degrees that we're seeing the manufacture of an eyeball, a black cylinder sliding into a pupil (there is a hint here of Kubrick's sexual spacecraft designs). Blurring the lines between biological, cosmic, and techno-industrial forms, this process echoes the alignment of celestial bodies in *2001* (at the outset and later, when the enigmatic monolith appears). This opening climaxes with an extreme close-up of the eye, fully constructed and endowed with life. All the while, the looping score fuses with a female voice (Scarlett Johansson's) speaking a series of words in English, implying the acquisition, or download, of a human language by an alien intelligence. A sudden cut transports us to a white title screen that counterbalances the earlier blackness (one thinks of the contrasts in *2001* between the gleaming white ship and pitch-dark outer space). This cut is audial as well, in that it sharply transitions, or as Michel Chion words it, "commutes," from one sonic ambience to another, this being a stylistic signature of *2001* (2001: 77–81).[6]

This introduction of the eye at once alludes to the villainous HAL and the metamorphic Dave Bowman (Keir Dullea)—the surveillance eye of a supercomputer and the bewildered eye of an astronaut. *2001* doesn't offer such extreme close-ups until late in the film, when Bowman travels through the stargate into another dimension of sight and bodily sensation over which, so it seems, a supernatural or alien force reigns. But Glazer—not unlike Ridley Scott's *Blade Runner* (1982) and Steven Soderbergh's reedit of *2001*, *The Return of W. De Rijk* (2015)—*begins* with this enormous eye, suggesting a recalibration of perception necessary for our engagement with the film to follow. This address of the eye indicates both that we are being watched and that we find our gaze uncannily doubled by and processed through that of the woman, or alien imitation of a woman, just produced. It's as if the nameless Johansson character and the viewer are created simultaneously in each other's image.

This spectatorial birth into the film's world continues after the title screen with surveys of the Scottish Highlands at night as a lone motorcycle winds through the hills. These shots invoke the opening of *The Shining*, albeit with static rather than serpentine aerial camerawork. Michael Haneke's *Funny Games* (1997, 2007) explicitly reenacts the start of Kubrick's horror film,[7] but *Under the Skin*, more in the vein of Philippe Grandrieux's homage in *Sombre* (1998), expresses its allusion in a lower key of dread, with art cinema ambiguity marking a less legible landscape and a still smaller human figure engulfed by it. The nod to *2001* is still in play, too. The countryside in effect stands in for the strange, electronically filtered landscapes over which Bowman glides when he passes through the stargate. Indeed, that sequence bears on Glazer's imagery when we cut to a frontal close-up of the speeding motorcyclist, whose glossy black helmet rhymes with the eyeball from the beginning and reflects colored streaks of light from passing vehicles. The scene is thus rendered abstract and made to resemble an interstellar flight. Whereas Kubrick's lightshow occasions a trip "beyond infinity" that leaves Bowman a shaken, awestruck cyborg, Glazer's variation begins to set forth a mysterious earthly world as studied through alien optics. We will soon learn that the cyclist is a supervisor who retrieves human bodies for our apparently extraterrestrial protagonist, but the plot has yet to declare itself. These first, alluring yet dreadful moments launch an atmosphere of suspense that reuses Kubrick's vocabulary to induct us into a curious mode of feeling and contemplation.[8]

Our intensifying dread owes both to the extreme reduction of narrative context and to our blocked capacity to know Johansson's alien. Unlike Kubrick's extraterrestrials, whose existence can only be deduced, she appears directly, but her body is a disguise, her behavior a surface that grants no access to her psychological motivations (Fisher 2016: 105). The Faber novel explains that a corporation on another planet has sent her to harvest humans for meat, but Glazer forgoes all exposition in this regard. This "woman," who spends the first half of the film driving around in a white van, stalking men whom she leads to their doom in a black liquid vault, is a hybrid of Bowman and HAL—a traveling spectator whose mechanized system of surveillance conspires with the formal system of the film itself. In Kubrick, the ambiguity that fuels dread stems partly from the suspenseful way in which he entwines his commanding style with an agential force at work in the fiction.[9] In *The Shining*, the mobile camera, montage, and sound are bound up with the ghostly agency of the Overlook Hotel and with the extrasensory potential to "shine." *2001* mingles its logic of display with both the panoptic eye of HAL and the atmospheric seductions and disturbances of the monolith. Glazer repeats this reflexive tactic by composing the driving scenes around the alien's point of view, her windshield functioning as a *mise en abyme* of our film screen. As she scans the human passersby, our attention overlaps with and is unnervingly mediated by hers. These drawn-out scenes humbly recall the majestic shots of the spaceship's flight deck in *2001*, where the window in front of the astronauts becomes a version of the film screen in front of us. Levi's score for the van scenes blends a Ligetian tone field with a cyclical noise that suggests breathing reminiscent of Bowman's oxygen tank when he vies with HAL. As in *2001*, this aural mix is "both assuring and disturbing, as if our head were in the maw of a lion" (Chion 2001: 99). We become ensnared within— or "vehicularized" by—a nonhuman perceptual system built around an unreadable impostor.[10] In contrast to traditional suspense, our attachment to a persona on-screen forms *in the absence of identification*, even as the alien serves as our focal point and perspectival filter.

In the far more communicative novel, the alien protagonist, who is named Isserley, serves as the constant locus of the third person limited narration. Where the film presents steely silence, the novel relates Isserley's thoughts and emotions, which include human-like bouts of empathy, anguish, and more. For the needs of the novel's satire (which allegorically remarks on how the proletarian body comes to see itself in the "meat" it harvests), Isserley is stripped of "alienness" as the distinction between humans and extraterrestrials is effaced (Fisher 2016: 104–5). But the film relishes eerie effects generated by the Johansson character's illegibility, even as we find ourselves

Figure 6.1 Possessed by an alien perceptual apparatus, we study the blank face of a woman (Scarlett Johannson) who is not in fact a woman, our impulse toward identification denied. Source: *Under the Skin* (Jonathan Glazer, 2013), copyright A24.

melded to her/its surveillance system. One of the perhaps unanswerable mysteries of *2001* is just what causes HAL's violent deviation. A technical breakdown? A contingency plan to which the crew are not privy? My take is that HAL's actions are inspired by his envy of the human body, its sensuous pursuits from eating and exercise to the manual activity of drawing. *Under the Skin* replays but reverses this dynamic by having the alien mysteriously shift *away from* her predatory mission, which leads her to test out (disastrously) gastronomic and sexual human pleasures. Is this turnabout brought on by her encounter with a disfigured man, which suggestively occurs at the film's exact midpoint but concludes with an ambiguous shot of him fleeing from her lair? Does she begin to empathize with her prey? Or does she undergo a glitch of the kind that possibly destabilizes HAL? These questions linger while our affective experience continues to be mediated by the alien's behavior and perception.

In varying ways and to different ends, both *2001* and *The Shining* expose their characters and their viewers to paranormal mediations. When indicating the possession of humans by such forces beyond comprehension, both films approach limits of expression, where images slip into abstraction, opacity, or ellipsis. Kubrick's two key dread-inducing emblems of the unknowable are the monolith in *2001* and the elevator of gushing blood in *The Shining*. Both are invoked in *Under the Skin*. Kubrick's blood has its echo in the alien tank where homo sapiens are liquefied into meat. In Elena Gorfinkel's description, a red "meat sludge" that looks like "molten lava" is transported "down a chute, turning over and converting into a depthless perspectival line of red at the center of the screen," along which the viewer is pulled in turn. With a cut, this fiery glow fills the screen, as if to plunge us into this process of bodily "transvaluation" (2016). Kubrick's image suggests the collective blood from past murders and abuses to which the Overlook Hotel has borne witness.[11] Further, in testifying to Danny

Torrance's (Danny Lloyd) capacity to shine, the elevator puts human consciousness in touch with the supernatural. The red ooze in Glazer's film leads to a more radical enmeshment of human and nonhuman perception that registers only as graphic abstraction. A starburst, dislodged from spatial and temporal markers, emits light and seems to return us to the genesis of an eye, intimating rebirth.

Under the Skin replicates Kubrick's monolith during one of the scenes in which the alien lures a man into her vault, which is tucked away within a decrepit house on the town's outskirts. Her doorway is impossibly black against the daylight. Unable to resist, the man walks inside and the camera follows, pushing into the rectangular entrance as its darkness expands to overtake the screen. This camera gesture replays Kubrick's middle-of-the-frame track *into* the monolith at the foot of Bowman's bed near the end of *2001*. Glazer also adapts Kubrick's reflexive alignment of the monolith with periodic black screens. In both films, this rectangular field of darkness arouses dread and curiosity in equal measure. It suggests both an obstacle and a portal to another realm, perhaps a superior plane of thought and perception. Glazer's abstract passages through darkness are liminal zones of transformation for both humans and the alien who, midway through the film, drastically veers from protocol.

In the wake of her interaction with the man with facial disfigurement, whom she appears to set free, the alien embarks on an improvised path of becoming human, or more specifically, becoming female. This turn proves ill-fated. The physicality (not only her beauty but also her costume as a working-class woman "on the prowl") that aided her seductions now makes her a target in a world where misogynistic violence is endemic (Osterweil 2014: 46–47). In the last section of the film, she takes refuge in a misty forest, passing through a blacked-out doorway to a shelter where she sleeps. On waking, she is hunted and attacked by a woodsman who, while trying to rape her,

Figure 6.2 The alien (Scarlett Johansson) enchantingly crosses a dark threshold, her male prey and the camera soon to follow. Source: *Under the Skin* (Jonathan Glazer, 2013), copyright A24.

tears her skin to reveal blackness underneath.[12] When the camera wraps around his stunned gaze to show her back-turned figure, her posterior wound duplicates that of the putrefied old woman Jack Torrance (Jack Nicholson) sees in the bathroom mirror of room 237. This connection is reinforced by similar music, the score now channeling Kubrick's use of Krzysztof Penderecki's *The Awakening of Jacob*. Glazer in this way reenacts the foiling of male fantasy in *The Shining* but recasts the "monstrous" woman as a victim in an all-too-human world of entrenched violence: the focus falls not on a scary hag but on a defenseless Other in retreat as she is doused in gasoline and set on fire. In the quiet ending, where smoke and ash from her corpse drift up into the snowy sky, the fantastic elements of horror and science fiction direct attention back onto cyclical murder and abuse at the core of human civilization—the immanent province of Kubrickian dread.

As we watch the decomposed matter of the alien dissipate into the winter landscape, the dreary cast of this ending takes on notes of wonder. Cueing the audience for this contemplative turn is an extreme long shot, moments earlier, of the alien's cyclist supervisor looking into the white void of the surroundings. This shot mimics Caspar David Friedrich's paintings of such figures who are pictured from behind and sublimely swallowed up by the scenes they study as spectators inscribed within the painting. Wonder and dread interlace in the film's final seconds as the smoke from the alien's body vanishes and the falling snow zips past the upturned camera in another minimalist echo of *2001*'s stargate sequence. The image spells death and evanescence but draws us into its blankness enticingly.

Anderson's *There Will Be Blood*

The influence of *2001* and *The Shining* reaches beyond the traditional precincts of horror and science fiction. As a number of critics have noted, Paul Thomas Anderson's *There Will Be Blood*, an epic portrait of the oil baron Daniel Plainview (Daniel Day-Lewis), is shot through with Kubrickian touches, from its meticulous but sparse formalism to its pervasive mood of dread. When asked about these resonances, Anderson replied, "We're all children of Kubrick, aren't we? Is there anything you can do that he hasn't done?" (quoted in Romney 2008: 24). Anderson's previous films display the influences of Robert Altman, Martin Scorsese, and Sidney Lumet, but *There Will Be Blood* shifts into a more austere style in the tonal and aesthetic vein of Kubrick, whom Anderson met in person on the set of *Eyes Wide Shut* (1999) when pursuing Tom Cruise for the ensemble cast of *Magnolia* (1999) (Sperb 2013: 204).

In *There Will Be Blood*, Kubrickian dread owes largely to the unconventional orchestral score by Jonny Greenwood. In each of the films under analysis in this chapter, music enhances and modulates our sense of dread in key ways. Levi's score for *Under the Skin* creates physical discomfort via its teeming microtones, which enclose the viewer-listener within a "beehive" of frenetic sound (Levi, quoted in Fitzmaurice 2014). Even more insistently, Greenwood's music goes beyond its role as support for the images by dominating our affective experience in certain stretches. This music limits itself to instruments particular to the film's 1890s–1920s setting and undergoes occasional distortions and "hesitations" to evoke, as Greenwood words it, "something dark happening among what is ordinarily a comforting sound" (quoted in Bell 2008: 34). This score is a prime example of "foreground music," as K. J. Donnelly rightly considers the musical aggressions of *The Shining* (2005: 36). Greenwood and Anderson in fact discussed *The Shining* as a reference point during the production of *There Will Be Blood* (Bell 2008: 34). What makes the Greenwood score Kubrickian—that is, similar to Kubrick's atmospheric use of Penderecki's, Ligeti's, and Béla Bartók's concert hall music—is its visceral power, as well as its function as a mediator between visual style, physical environment, and the increasingly grotesque and horrific characterization of Plainview.[13]

Roughly based on Upton Sinclair's 1926 novel *Oil!*, Anderson's *There Will Be Blood* is a Western parable about capitalistic greed and competitive individualism. The film takes additional cues from Kubrick's *2001*. Our prolonged, unspoken introduction to Plainview mining for silver in the desert carries echoes of *2001*'s "Dawn of Man" section. Dissonant strings, akin to Ligeti's *Atmosphères*, fade in against a lengthy black screen and introduce the image track with piercing "contrary-motion" glissandos, changes in pitch sliding both "toward and away from F#" (Mera 2016: 163). This initial shot is of barren mountains, as in *2001* after the prologue. Greenwood's music (lifted from his preexistent string orchestra suite *Popcorn Superhet Receiver*) underpins Plainview's grueling and hazardous conversion into an oilman. It pairs with tracking shots and slow, Kubrick-like cross-dissolves to bestow agitation and mystery. As George Toles points out, this score fills wordless scenes with sonorities that both connote the protest of the rocky terrain against human invasion *and* describe our neurotic protagonist, whose stony demeanor is just as unyielding as the landscape. The music, Toles argues, feels like a "contagion" that passes from Plainview to his coworkers as they refrain from conversing: its "rasping undertow seems attuned to the persistence of masculine apartness in the midst of collective endeavor. The sound works to suppress sociability" (2016: 75).

In contrast to *The Shining* and *2001*, nothing otherworldly inhabits the plot of *There Will Be Blood*, and yet the discovery of oil by Plainview and his crew comes across as an encounter with an alien substance. Creeping up from the ground as though from a stab wound, the black liquid—due in large part to the score—appears to exert a spellbinding influence over humans. Thematically and musically, the scene is reminiscent of the monolith's appearance before the clan of hominids in *2001*, which likewise occurs in a pit. The hominids' lively caresses of the alien artifact have as their equivalent Plainview's gesture of wiping oil from a metal shaft and raising his hand high in the air as the music undercuts his celebration with sentiments of doom. Greenwood's score synchronizes its nerve-fraying glissandos with workers pouring buckets of oil into a reservoir that recalls the waterhole over which rival hominids fight. Kubrick famously charts an evolution of violence from primeval to advanced technology, from bone to spaceship. Within a more condensed timeline, *There Will Be Blood* goads awareness of wars and disasters regarding this fossil fuel and resource capitalism. Dread gathers in the gap between Plainview's exhilaration and our knowledge of grave consequences ahead.

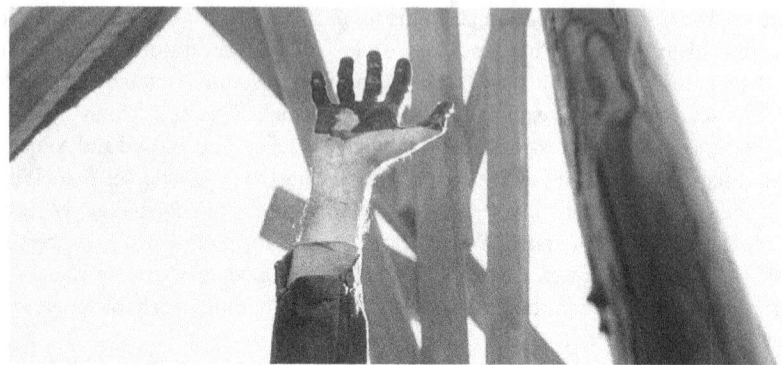

Figure 6.3 Daniel Plainview (Daniel Day-Lewis) lifts his oil-marked hand into the air as the Jonny Greenwood musical score lends this gesture an ominous tone. Source: *There Will Be Blood* (Paul Thomas Anderson, 2007), copyright Paramount.

This relation between a grotesque male protagonist and avant-garde music that dispenses a "tactile," bodily jolting atmospheric force (Mera 2016: 159–67) is where *There Will Be Blood* most resonantly approaches *The Shining*. James Naremore shows how an affinity for grotesque aesthetics, including performance style, lies at the crux of Kubrick's enterprise. By "grotesque," Naremore (who associates this term with the uncanny) means a mode of expression that sharply exaggerates physical and emotional traits, mixes conflicting tones, partakes of cynicism, brings the fantastic into play while keeping a foot in realism, and revels in unresolved ambiguity, irony, and paradox (2007: 24–41). Day-Lewis's Daniel Plainview and Nicholson's Jack Torrance (both actors share the first names of their roles) are grotesque incarnations through and through, from their overplayed performances by the criteria of naturalism to their agile conjunctions of horror and comedy. Despite the absence of the supernatural in *There Will Be Blood*, Plainview, much like Torrance, is introduced to us as a man already given over to a destructive impetus that will inevitably decide his course and threaten his family. Anderson establishes this parallel between characters early on by having a shot of Plainview swinging his pickax repeat, in both scale and direction, the shot of Torrance axing the bathroom door behind which his wife has taken cover (Plainview's ax will resurface, along with the same music, when he buries the man he kills for posing as his brother) (McDonald 2012: 218–19). Torrance seems slightly more mindful of his propensities at the start, but a reduction of narrative suspense marks both figures. *Atmospheric* suspense, however, thickens insofar as the precise relations between music, character behavior, and environment evade us. In *The Shining*, dread mounts through obscurity surrounding Jack's transition into homicidal rage: the line between hallucinatory psychosis and the spectral activity of the hotel is continually blurred, as is the line between his personal history of violence and the previous crimes carried out in the hotel. Music, especially Kubrick's use of multiple Penderecki pieces, keeps this confusion alive (Code 2010: 144–47). Greenwood's score, for its part, accents Plainview's misanthropic angst with

Pendereckian screeches and knots to suggest his possession by nebulous, infectious forces greater than himself.[14]

The finale of *There Will Be Blood*—in which Plainview murders one of his nemeses, the equally grotesque preacher Eli (Paul Dano)—again nods to *The Shining* through mise-en-scène. The site of this killing, Plainview's private bowling alley in his remote mansion, resembles the architecture and coloration of the corridor leading to the elevators in Kubrick's film (witness in particular the last, symmetrical shot of Anderson's film). Plainview, by this point a scraggly and drunken shell of a person despite his wealth, echoes the wolf-like appearance and antics of Jack, who likewise suffers from alcoholism. As Matthew McDonald suggests, the low-angle shot of Planview bludgeoning Eli with a bowling pin recreates Kubrick's low-angle shot in *2001* of the hominid discovering the lethal potential of the bone (2012: 216). Anderson's ending thus distills Plainview's competitive bent through a Kubrickian thematics of power, privilege, and deranged masculinity with an appetite for murder. "I told you I would eat you up!" Plainview growls at Eli while incorporating this assault into a butler-served meal. The grotesque ending replaces Greenwood's score with a cheerful violin concerto by Brahms. But we feel this music's incongruity with the action just staged—an event that ties Plainview's "victory" to primal violence and again stirs up our dread-filled knowledge of horrors to come in actual history. The Kubrickian blend of tones is such that we consider, alongside the dark comedy, our incapacity to reverse the inexorable capitalistic future that Plainview's arc foretells. He remains something of a cipher, a source of suspense at the level of interiority, but we know *too well* what the progress of his enterprise leads to in the context of global ecological destruction.

Lynch's *Twin Peaks: The Return*

No stranger to grotesque forms and malicious male figures, David Lynch is less typically discussed as Kubrick's disciple than either Glazer or Anderson, but his work shares a number of the atmospheric qualities I have previously stressed.[15] His practice of environmental dread and suspense is Kubrickian, not so much because of obsessive nods to certain Kubrick films (though allusions to *The Shining* and *Lolita* [1962] intermittently appear in *Twin Peaks* episodes and the feature film *Twin Peaks: Fire Walk With Me* [1992]), but because of elective affinities between artists whose styles overlap. In interviews, Lynch cites Kubrick as a formative influence alongside Hitchcock, Federico Fellini, Ingmar Bergman, and Jacques Tati (Ciment and Niogret 2009 [1990]: 114). He also recalls the "euphoria" he felt upon hearing through mutual contacts that his own *Eraserhead* (1977) was Kubrick's "favorite film" (quoted in Rodley 2015: 77).

The comparison between Lynch and Kubrick, which has been only sparingly taken up by critics,[16] could be explored on the basis of multiple links that concern atmospheric suspense and dread: camera movement (slow tracks and vertiginous aerials); audial murmurs; fascination with surface texture; uses of color; deadpan and dreamlike tones; a ubiquitous feeling of mystery that compels attention but defies solutions; and parallel interests in Hitchcock's cinema. What I will provide here, with an eye to sparking a fuller comparative study, is an analysis of the celebrated sequence in Part Eight ("Gotta Light?") of the Showtime series *Twin Peaks: The Return* (2017), in which the camera enters a cloud from an atomic explosion, pulling the viewer into a shifting vortex that distinctly reworks the stargate set piece in *2001*.

Lynch's sequence opens a portal from the fictional present to the nonfictional, cataclysmic past. The episode begins with a scene in which the evil version of Dale Cooper (Kyle MacLachlan) is double-crossed by a crime associate; we then cut to the roadhouse, where Trent Reznor and Nine Inch Nails perform a brooding song. Cut to the sinister Cooper raising up from the ground after having been revived by a gang of soot-covered woodsmen who maneuver at the border between worlds and conspiratorial networks. After a black screen, titles announce a grayscale landscape, "July 16, 1945 / White Sands, New Mexico / 5:29AM"—the site and date of the US Army's test of a thermonuclear weapon as part of the Manhattan Project. Synchronized with a burst of light, screechy orchestral strings—the music is Penderecki's *Threnody to the Victims of Hiroshima*—materialize. The camera glides toward and eventually into the mushroom cloud, passing through a manifestly digital series of abstract forms and textures that seem at once molecular and cosmic (not unlike the recreation of the Big Bang in Terrence Malick's *The Tree of Life* [2011], which uses immersive effects engineered by Douglas Trumbull, who also oversaw Kubrick's stargate imagery). The movie *2001* becomes an even more overt reference for Lynch when this forward propulsion of the synthetic camera slips through another membrane—a golden seed—and throws us into a black hole lined with red particles. After crossing a purple sea, the camera charges into the black window of a building atop a rock spire. This camera gesture—similar to Glazer's in *Under the Skin*—mimics Kubrick's self-reflexive track into the monolith.[17] We are led through a black screen to the plush interior of a 1930s-era movie theater where a rather tall character known as The Fireman (Carel Struycken) plays a projection of the same images we have just witnessed. Reacting to the bomb's genesis of the maniacal BOB (Frank Silva), The Fireman levitates in front of the theater's screen, which now teems with swirling stars. The harsh music has given way to a lilting, ethereal composition by Angelo Badalamenti. With the assistance of a female companion, The Fireman releases from his mouth a golden orb that seems to carry the seed for Laura Palmer's (Sheryl Lee) birth, this object miraculously trespassing the barrier of the screen and sailing toward Earth like a small meteorite. Connoting as it does fertilization and birth in a planetary register, this event in the movie theater reconfigures both the finale of *2001* (the fetal Starchild) and the opening of *Eraserhead* (the protagonist who orally emits a spermatozoon-like creature while suspended horizontally in outer—or inner?—space).

Lynch's atomic odyssey moves us through an array of speeds and affective tenors. Dread shades into frustration, melancholy, tenderness, and astonishment amid nonnarrative suspense. Although we lack a Dave Bowman-like escort—a surrogate viewer within the sequence whose body and brain undergo a metamorphosis—we are still made to feel as if we are injected into a chaotic process that uproots our very sense of self and redefines our relation to the screen. *Twin Peaks: The Return*, like Lynch's other creations, abounds with the motif of bodies in perpetual flux, whether through

Figure 6.4 The recreated test blast from 1945 into which the camera plunges. Source: *Twin Peaks: The Return* (David Lynch, 2017), copyright Showtime Entertainment.

doublings, repetitions, or journeys between parallel worlds. As Alanna Thain has shown, suspense in Lynch's oeuvre springs from uncertain trajectories of becoming-other-than-oneself—pathways that open up outside of linear time and precipitate the bodily transformation of characters and spectators alike (2017: 119–75). In *Twin Peaks: The Return*, figures pass back and forth through all manner of transductive portals that tie in thematically with a self-reflexive play on technological mediation and energy: wall plugs, screens, record players, power lines, gas stations, radio waves, and, of course, thermonuclear radiation all bear on the elaborate transferal and transmutation of bodies within and between different realms. Part Eight implicitly describes the embodied spectator's interface with the screen as an extension of this core trope. The screen itself, like theater curtains in Lynch's work (Fisher 2016: 53–59), figures as a weirdly permeable membrane, a threshold where convulsive energies wrench us out of our habitual conceptions and modes of individual subjectivity.[18]

With both Lynch's and Kubrick's immersive lightshows, dread involves—on top of acute uneasiness and disorientation—a sense of awe. This tonal complexity revives an archaic meaning of "dread," wherein fear of something powerful inspires reverence and surrender. Taking up this affective combination as it concerns both *The Shining* and *Eraserhead*, Cynthia Freeland writes that Kubrick's and Lynch's horror films partner dread with the sublime, or rather with what she calls the "antisublime" (2000: 236). She contends that Kubrick and Lynch provoke responses in rough accordance with the sublime, as Immanuel Kant defines it: faced with grand, mystifying events and forces, we feel overwhelmed, unable to comprehend and master our environment as our faculties of sense and imagination are pushed to their absolute limits.[19] For Kant, this initial disturbance and defeat lead to a stabilizing return of the reasoning faculty. We recover through the realization of our unlimited human capacity for *reflection upon* our limits (Kant 2000 [1790]: 142–43). And this recovery testifies to the superiority of our moral and reflective being over our mere sensible being (151). Kant ultimately locates the sublime not in the external world and its stimuli, but rather within an internalized, supersensible cognitive experience. "Sublimity resides in us," explains Eva Schaper, "in the powers of the human mind to rise above what threatens to engulf or annihilate us" (1992: 382). Freeland, however, argues that no such restoration of reason marks our confrontation with *The Shining* and *Eraserhead*. Elsewhere (1999: 70–83) she accepts that a Kantian aesthetics of sublimity, which leads from discomfort to the pleasurable and moral exercise of cognition, underpins films such as Carl-Theodor Dreyer's *The Passion of Joan of Arc* (1928) and Werner Herzog's *Aguirre, the Wrath of God* (1972); but when dealing with Kubrick's and Lynch's work, she meets with resolute uncanniness that heralds an all-out "dissolution of the self, meaning, and morality." We continue to feel overpowered "in relation to a force with which we cannot identify because it is too strange, vague, alien, or evil" (2000: 237).

In short, the aesthetics of Kubrickian dread partake in the first movement of the sublime without giving us the subsequent uplift of regained superiority over our environment. This very situation is economically compressed into the opening credits of each *Twin Peaks: The Return* episode. Operating within the iconography of the sublime and its stress on natural phenomena, the shots hover through vaporous air over mountains and then a waterfall filmed from directly overhead. Our vertigo is heightened as cross-dissolves turn the falling water into billowing red curtains and then into the rotating, zigzagged floor of the Black Lodge. These textures seem to open a recess in the image, drawing us inward, our sense of direction confounded as the music by Badalamenti lulls us into submission. It feels as though we have fallen outside of ourselves into the image and its dizzying play of forms, our experience altered by an uncanny disruption we cannot rationally surmount.

The experiential "dissolution of self" that plays out in the spectator's immersive relation to the work is accompanied by the more catastrophic theme of annihilation on a planetary scale. Hence the atomic explosion in Lynch's episode, which, like much of Kubrick's work, layers in the traumatic historical past, making it genetically of a piece with the fictional universe and its characters. Kubrick, of course, gave much attention to the probability of a nuclear apocalypse. Allowing for tonal differences, Lynch's Part Eight makes one think of the ending of Kubrick's *Dr. Strangelove* (1964) and its montage of mushroom clouds. For the finale of *2001*, Kubrick originally planned to have the Star Child observe the Earth's destruction in a fireworks show of nuclear detonations across its surface (Naremore 2007: 152). Once again, then, our exploration of Kubrickian dread leads us to take stock of humanity's foundational inclination toward brutal violence and conquest. This isn't just a theme upon which we reflect at a distance, but a force, a powerful atmospheric contagion, to which we are viscerally exposed. Kubrickian dread comes with interminable suspense that keeps us from sufficiently grasping how such forces work, but we are assured of their repeated destructive outcomes in the future. One dreads *the certainty of additional disasters*, particularly those of our own making—not least the extinction of our own species whether by militaristic, technological, or ecological means. Consider the open, but not entirely open, ending of another film that deftly orchestrates Kubrickian dread, Alex Garland's *Annihilation* (2018), which also evokes the atmospheres of Andrei Tarkovsky's *Stalker* (1979) and John Carpenter's *The Thing* (1982).[20] Garland's artful science fiction/horror film leaves us with the vague yet undeniable impression of an alien contaminant having unleashed itself upon human life as an undetectable impostor. Our abiding dread is twofold: we question the integrity of our selfhood, distrustful of our perhaps overconfident sense of self-possession; and second, our thoughts turn to human causal factors with which the alien intrusion is obliquely associated. Garland's film—much like our other examples of Kubrickian dread in this chapter—insists that we starkly confront the inexorability of our annihilation as a species, viewing it as a result, in no small part, of human folly dressed up as progress.

The Call of the Void

There remains the question as to why dread—a sensation we hope to be spared of in our daily lives—should be so enthralling in its Kubrickian forms. Why do we seek out this mix of prolonged distress, bewilderment, awe, and defeat? Why do we suffer these experiences gladly and *repeatedly*? After all, *The Shining* and *2001* are nothing if not labyrinthine films that invite our recurrent and obsessive engagement—hence their cult followings. I will put aside primarily psychological explanations that have to do with the spectator's vicarious enjoyment of dreadful experiences at a safe remove. To understand the appeal of Kubrickian dread, I want to continue my discussion of the sublime.

Kubrick's cinema activates not the antisublime so much as what I want to call *sublime dread*. Pleasure curiously marks our encounter where the film holds us in unrelieved states of confoundment. Never quite gaining mastery over the film, we feel a dreadful yet pleasurable reduction to nothingness that is isn't obviated by reason's reinstitution, be it in the form of an explanatory plot twist of the M. Night Shyamalan variety or, philosophically speaking, of a Kantian reinstatement of a subject position from which we can rationally manage, and contain, what has outstripped us. As I illustrated earlier, the sublime encounter, for Kant, is in the end an opportunity for the moral fortification of the individual subject, but this view necessitates on the part of Kant's method a debasement of exteriority, so that the mind's inner mechanisms might felicitously triumph over sense perception. Further, it is telling for our purposes that in Kant's earlier account of the sublime, the "grotesque" names a kind of false, downgraded version of sublime experience that Kant associates with the "unnatural," "the fantastic," and feelings of repugnance in response to either physical deformity or moral shortcomings of character (2001 [1764]: 21–22, 29). Given Kubrick's grotesque portraits of humanity, journeys into the fantastic, and skepticism toward triumphant rational order, his cinema of sublime dread plays up what the Kantian sublime ultimately screens out.[21]

The uses of sublime dread in the works I have examined are closer in mood to Edmund Burke's earlier treatise, with its embrace of the irrational and its heavier accent on pain, terror, confusion, obscurity, and quasi-physical danger, which are not fully overcome and which mix with pleasure to incite "delightful horror, a sort of tranquility tinged with terror" (1757 [1889]: 101). Like Kant, Burke repeatedly suggests that sublimity can only seize hold if the perceiving subject is removed from harm's way. Yet Burke's rhetoric all but belies his insistence on safety and self-preservation when he excitedly discusses limit points where one's sense of security is revoked, as in his account of the sublime effects of darkness (107–12). Kubrickian dread, as we have seen, develops amid atmospheric conditions that lend the spectator a feeling of exposure to destructive forces on-screen. Although the sound-images are virtual and not literally injurious, at certain points, they radiate a visceral atmosphere that counteracts our distance and establishes a kind of mediated immediacy keyed to our potential obliteration. When *Under the Skin* confronts us with a churning volcanic meat pit, our "safety" is tempered, modulated. Kubrickian dread thus embodies something of Arthur Schopenhauer's concept of the sublime, which entails an embrace of one's own *nullity* through an immersive aesthetic relation with the world.[22] In Schopenhauer's description, "we feel ourselves reduced to nothing . . . as transient phenomena of will, like drops in the ocean, dwindling and dissolving" (1966 [1818]: 205).

In the bounty of critical writings on the sublime, more recent theories of course consider technological modernity and the experiential impact of cinema. But as regards the films under discussion here, what still resonates with ideas of sublimity formulated before the arrival of the film medium is a hypnotic call of the void—a pull to engagement that combines exaltation with self-loss, contemplation with dizziness, and fear with astonishment. Kant registers this call in order to exorcise it. Schopenhauer molds it into a fusion of self and a "superhuman" environment raised to a potentially redemptive purpose (Vandenabeele 2015: 164–76). The Kubrickian sublime, for its part, fosters an abiding fascination whereby we relish, yet also dread, having our thoughts and perceptions run up against unconquerable limits.[23]

Across my main examples, sublime dread crystallizes in scenes that enact its partly attractive, partly repulsive force—scenes that also riff on *2001*, *The Shining*, or both: the cosmic eyeball, igneous meat, and blackened doorways in *Under the Skin*; the viscous oil reservoir shot from overhead in *There Will Be Blood*; the atomic cloud in *Twin Peaks: The Return*; and let us add the encroaching, electromagnetic "Shimmer" field in *Annihilation*.[24] Beyond their narrative functions, these visual and aural environments suspend us in the consideration of grave themes. The loss of identifiably human subjectivity shades into the looming extinction of humanity as a whole. Human grotesqueries figure as culprits, and yet the spectator, especially with *Under the Skin*, *Twin Peaks: The Return*, and *Annihilation*, is handed over to nonhuman agencies that are radically unknowable and insuperable. These Kubrickian works renounce closure not simply to saddle us with quandaries of theme, plot, or authorial intent. The lack of finality lets atmospheric dread and suspense grip us more lastingly, leaving us addled and reduced, but also energized for a future replay of this very experience.

Notes

1. The question of cinematic and literary influences on Kubrick, where his use of atmospheric suspense is concerned, deserves its own study. *The Shining*, in addition to its Hitchcockian touches, borrows inventively from Henri-Georges Clouzot's *Diabolique* (1955), Richard Donner's *The Omen* (1976), John Carpenter's *Halloween* (1978), and, more conspicuously, Stuart Rosenberg's *The Amityville Horror* (1979). It is understandable how initial reviews of *The Shining* saw it as a parody of the recently reinvigorated horror genre.
2. My argument could be expanded to include additional Kubrick films. One certainly thinks of atmospheric dread and suspense in *Full Metal Jacket* (1987) and *Eyes Wide Shut* (1999)—the Gothic accents of the former; the oneiric menace of the latter. For the sake of concision, I will limit my comparative analysis to *2001* and *The Shining*.
3. In the history of philosophy, dread and anxiety are intimately associated and often taken to be synonymous. Freeland, with reference to Søren Kierkegaard, claims that dread and anxiety are similar in that both have an indistinct object, but that "dread, unlike anxiety, involves an anticipated encounter with something 'profound'—something particularly powerful, grave, and inexorable." (Freeland 2000: 192).
4. Consider how *The Shining* intensifies its atmosphere of dread with both slow, associative cross-dissolves and hard cuts that happen a breath too soon at the end of longish takes.
5. Here is Jonathan Glazer on his debt to Kubrick: "People politely say 'homage,' but I probably stole his wallet." Glazer, quoted in Giroux 2014. Glazer's music videos (e.g., Massive Attack's "Karmacoma" and Blur's "The Universal") directly reference Kubrick films. And Glazer's film *Birth* (2004) lifts themes and expressive tactics from *The Shining* (1980) and *Eyes Wide Shut* (1999).
6. Among films indebted to Kubrick's *2001*, none exploits the atmospheric power of audial cuts more unnervingly than Ridley Scott's *Alien* (1979). Its changes of scene shift back and forth between loud and relatively quiet hums, whooshes, beeps, rattles, and hisses, the effect of which is to make the viewer feel a constant on-edgeness.
7. The beginning of Jordan Peele's *Get Out* (2017), with its road imagery, aquamarine titles, and music (Pendereckian choral whispers crossed with African-American blues), also pulls from the opening of *The Shining*. *Get Out* more overtly replays *A Clockwork Orange* (1971) in the scenes of its protagonist bound and forced to stare at a television.
8. While Glazer's borrowings from Kubrick are ample in *Under the Skin*, I want to acknowledge that his images, in particular his landscapes, are often texturally different: mistier, softer, more muted. Some of the fog-shrouded compositions are Antonioni-like, with *Red Desert* (1964) and *Identification of a Woman* (1982) figuring as references.
9. Kubrick's reflexivity is such that his directorial style frequently articulates itself in relation to a system of control embedded within the fictional world. In *The Killing* (1956), his formal system is bound up with the fastidiously planned heist. In *2001*, his style is linked with the mysterious agencies of HAL and the monolith. In *The Shining*, his style mixes with the Overlook's ghostly machinations. In *Full Metal Jacket* (1987), his style, specifically the rigid and neatly symmetrical framing, is entangled with the disciplinary institution of the US military.

10 On Kubrick's "vehicularization" of the spectator in *A Clockwork Orange* (1971), see Flaxman (2016: 181–86).
11 Geoffrey Cocks, who reads *The Shining* as Kubrick's pronouncement on the Holocaust, writes that this "ocean of blood flowing from the elevator . . . is the blood of centuries, the blood of millions, and, in particular, the blood of war and genocide in Kubrick's own century." Cocks 2004, 246.
12 For a study of the film's racial overtones, see Lucas Hilderbrand, "On the Matter of Blackness in *Under the Skin*," *Jump Cut* 57 (Fall 2016): https://www.ejumpcut.org/archive/jc57.2016/-HilderbrandUnderSkin/index.html (accessed November 16, 2018).
13 Anderson enlists another Kubrickian device that I don't have the space to consider: long, slow cross-dissolves that reinforce dread and blend atmospheres in ways that, like the music, soften boundaries between inner and outer registers, particularly when facial close-ups and landscapes are portentously overlaid.
14 Greenwood—who routinely names Penderecki as an influence not just on his film scores and other orchestral works but also on his music with Radiohead—has in fact collaborated with the Polish composer in a concert hall performance and a joint 2012 album from Nonesuch Records.
15 Common DNA exists between Lynch and P.T. Anderson as well. *Eraserhead* (1977) shares a filming location with *There Will Be Blood*, namely the Greystone Mansion in Beverly Hills. Jack Fisk, who served as Production Designer for Anderson's *There Will Be Blood* and *The Master* (2012), plays a small, if important, role as The Man in the Planet in *Eraserhead*, and has also worked as Production Designer for Lynch's *The Straight Story* (1999) and *Mulholland Drive* (2001). If the eerie oil reservoir, filmed from directly overhead in *There Will Be Blood*, reworks imagery from Kubrick's *2001*, it also bears a striking textural resemblance to the liquid crater in *Eraserhead* where the spermatozoon "baby" falls near the beginning.
16 Cinephile discourse has been quicker to probe connections between Kubrick and Lynch. See for example Richard Vezina's video mashup *Blue Shining* (2015): https://vimeo.com/129938191 (accessed December 16, 2018).
17 This comparable use of black screens combined with camera movements is one of a handful of similarities between this episode of *Twin Peaks: The Return* and *Under the Skin*. The anonymous digital body that vomits an egg containing BOB is strikingly similar to the dematerialized bodies stored in the alien's crypt in Glazer's film. Also, the first sequence in *Under the Skin*, after its creation of an eyeball, presents a waterfall and stream before cutting to the road surrounded by mountains. This allusively repeats steps from the opening credits sequence of the original *Twin Peaks* show.
18 It is not for nothing that Part Eight of *Twin Peaks: The Return* revisits the location Lynch used for the intensely reflexive, bodily convulsive "Club Silencio" scene in *Mulholland Drive* (2001), Los Angeles's Tower Theatre.
19 Freeland neglects to mention that Kant, in *Critique of the Power of Judgment*, delineates two types of the sublime—the mathematical sublime (brought on by our attempt to measure infinity) and the dynamical sublime (brought on by our encounter with physically imposing natural events). Both arguably apply to the respective works of Lynch and Kubrick, from their infinite repetitions to their landscapes that overwhelm and dwarf human beings. For an analytic survey of sublime moments in Kubrick's oeuvre, see Elisa Pezzotta, *Stanley Kubrick: Adapting the Sublime* (Jackson: University Press of Mississippi, 2013). My account resembles

hers in that she observes how Kubrick's authorial agency, through reflexive manifestations at the level of style, combines in uncanny ways with agential systems at work in the narrative (142–82).

20 Although it is nominally a remake of Christian Nyby and Howard Hawks's *The Thing from Another World* (1951), Carpenter's *The Thing* contains numerous allusions to *2001*. Kubrick's science fiction film had previously exerted a strong influence on Carpenter's *Dark Star* (1974). The dread-suffused, yet occasionally comical, atmosphere of Carpenter's *The Thing* overtly salutes *2001* when the research crew visit the site of the monstrous creature's exhumation: the music and imagery resemble Kubrick's scene of scientists gathered around the monolith before it emits a deafening high-pitch noise.

21 Is it simply a coincidence that seminal theories of the sublime (Edmund Burke's and Kant's) arose in an epoch and corner of the world that Kubrick, most overtly in *Barry Lyndon* (1975), reveals as harboring fierce aggression under its pose of civility and aristocratic splendor? I believe there is a link to be unearthed here. Many have discussed how eighteenth-century western Europe gives Kubrick a milieu riddled with political tensions between calm, rational order and teetering chaos either thinly or unsuccessfully held in check. Kubrick finds in this so-called age of Enlightenment the seeds for Cold War-era conflicts that preoccupy his thought (Ciment 2001: 59–123; Naremore 2007: 186–87). *Barry Lyndon* shows how despite this tempestuous state of things, the public semblance of reason and propriety must be rigidly maintained through institutionalized measures that inflict a repressive violence of their own.

22 Three graphically similar images from the Kubrickian films I have inspected come to mind as illustrations of this sense of the sublime in which catastrophe mixes with hypnotic fascination: the shot of ash and smoke ascending from the alien's lifeless body into the atmosphere in *Under the Skin*; the nocturnal shot of the column of fire shooting up from an oil derrick in *There Will Be Blood*; and the shot of the atomic cloud in Part Eight of *Twin Peaks: The Return*. All three events are centered in the frame, echoing the visual style of Kubrick.

23 Given this situation of thought and perception encountering an absolute limit, Gilles Deleuze could be brought in to elucidate further the sublime dread generated by Kubrick's work. In his cinema books, Deleuze rewrites the Kantian sublime partly by abandoning its assuring recourse to a model of stable, sovereign individual subjectivity. See Lambert (2000: 260–67). Deleuze takes up Kubrick's films in brief but remarkably dense passages. Kubrick doesn't figure directly within Deleuze's discussions of the sublime. My arguments here, however, could lend themselves to a consideration of Deleuze, Kubrick, and sublimity in modern cinema.

24 *Annihilation* creates a threatening/alluring atmosphere not only through its digital imagery but also through its musical use of the waterphone, the wobbly, distortional sounds of which serve as an amplification of the DNA-altering Shimmer.

Works Cited

Bell, James. 2004. "Jonny Greenwood." *Sight & Sound* 18(2) (February 2008): 34.

Burke, Edmund. 1757 (1889). *A Philosophical Enquiry into the Origin of Our Ideas of the Sublime and Beautiful*. London: George Bell and Sons.

Chion, Michel. 2001. *Kubrick's Cinema Odyssey*, trans. Claudia Gorbman. London: BFI.
Ciment, Michel. 2001. *Kubrick: The Definitive Edition*, trans. Gilbert Adair and Robert Bononno. New York: Faber and Faber.
Ciment, Michel, and Hubert Niogret. 2009 (1990). "Interview with David Lynch," in Richard A. Barney (ed.), *David Lynch: Interviews*. Jackson: University Press of Mississippi, 106–24.
Cocks, Geoffrey. 2004. *The Wolf at the Door: Stanley Kubrick, History, and the Holocaust*. New York: Peter Lang.
Durgnat, Raymond. 2002. *A Long Hard Look at "Psycho."* London: British Film Institute.
Elsaesser, Thomas. 2012. "Stanley Kubrick's Prototypes: The Author as World-Maker," in *The Persistence of Hollywood*. New York: Routledge, 213–22.
Fisher, Mark. 2016. *The Weird and the Eerie*. London: Repeater.
Fitzmaurice, Larry. 2014. "Jonathan Glazer and Mica Levi." *Pitchfork*, March 31. Available online: https://pitchfork.com/features/interview/9366-under-the-skins-jonathan-glazer-and-mica- levi (accessed November 14, 2018).
Freeland, Cynthia A. 1999. "The Sublime in Cinema," in Carl Plantinga and Greg M. Smith (eds.), *Passionate Views: Film, Cognition, and Emotion*. Baltimore: Johns Hopkins University Press, 65–83.
Freeland, Cynthia A. 2000. *The Naked and the Undead: Evil and the Appeal of Horror*. Boulder, CO: Westview.
Freeland, Cynthia A. 2004. "Horror and Art-Dread," in Stephen Prince (ed.), *The Horror Film*. New Brunswick, NJ: Rutgers University Press, 189–205.
Freud, Sigmund. 2003 (1919). *The Uncanny*, trans. David McClintock. London: Penguin.
Giroux, Jack. 2014. "Jonathan Glazer on 'Under the Skin,' Kubrick's Influence and How the Easiest Part of It Was Getting the Money." *Film School Rejects*, April 4. Available online: https://filmschoolrejects.com/jonathan-glazer-on-under-the-skin-kubrick-s-influence-and-how-the-easiest-part-of-it-was-getting-c7a3383e78e3 (accessed November 20, 2018).
Flaxman, Gregory. 2016. "Once More, with Feeling: Cinema and Cinesthesia," *SubStance* 45(3) (2016): 181–86.
Gorfinkel, Elena. 2016. "Sex, Sensation and Nonhuman Interiority in *Under the Skin*." *Jump Cut* 57 (Fall 2016). Available online: https://www.ejumpcut.org/archive/jc57.2016/-GorfinkelSkin/index.html (accessed November 16, 2018).
Griffero, Tonino. 2014. *Atmospheres: Aesthetics of Emotional Spaces*, trans. Sarah De Sanctis. Burlington, VT: Ashgate.
Hilderbrand, Lucas. 2016. "On the Matter of Blackness in *Under the Skin*." *Jump Cut* 57 (Fall 2016). Available online: https://www.ejumpcut.org/archive/jc57.2016/-HilderbrandUnderSkin/index.html (accessed November 16, 2018).
Kant, Immanuel. 2011 (1764). *Observations on the Feeling of the Beautiful and Sublime*, in Patrick Frierson and Paul Guyer (eds.), *Observations on the Feeling of the Beautiful and Sublime and Other Writings*. Cambridge: Cambridge University Press, 65–204.
Kant, Immanuel. 2000 (1790). *Critique of the Power of Judgment*, trans. Paul Guyer and Eric Matthews. Cambridge: Cambridge University Press.
Lambert, Gregg. 2000. "Cinema and the Outside," in *The Brain is the Screen: Deleuze and the Philosophy of Cinema*, ed. Gregory Flaxman (Minneapolis: University of Minnesota Press), 260–67.
Luckhurst, Roger. 2013. *The Shining*. London: British Film Institute.

Lutz, John. 2010. "From Domestic Nightmares to the Nightmare of History: Uncanny Eruptions of Violence in King's and Kubrick's Versions of the Shining," in Thomas Fahy (ed.), *The Philosophy of Horror*. Lexington: University Press of Kentucky, 161–78.
McAvoy, Catriona. 2015. "Diane Johnson," in Danel Olson (ed.), *The Shining: Studies in the Horror Film*. Lakewood: Centipede, 533–66.
McDonald, Matthew. 2012. "Mountains, Music, and Murder: Scoring the American West in *There Will Be Blood* and *No Country for Old Men*," in Kathryn Kalinak (ed.), *Music in the Western: Notes from the Frontier*. New York: Routledge, 214–27.
Mera, Miguel. 2016. "Materializing Film Music," in Mervyn Cooke and Fiona Ford (eds.), *The Cambridge Companion to Film Music*. Cambridge: Cambridge University Press, 157–72.
Model, Katie. 2012. "Gender Hyperbole and the Uncanny in the Horror Film," in Christine Gledhill (ed.), *Gender Meets Genre in Postwar Cinemas*. Urbana: University of Illinois Press, 146–58.
Molina Foix, Vicente. 2016 (1980). "An Interview with Stanley Kubrick," in Alison Castle (ed.), *The Stanley Kubrick Archives*. Köln: Taschen, 670–83.
Naremore, James. 2007. *On Kubrick*. London: British Film Institute.
Osterweil, Ara. 2014. "Under the Skin: The Perils of Becoming Female." *Film Quarterly* 67(4) (Summer 2014): 44–51.
Pezzotta, Elisa. 2013. *Stanley Kubrick: Adapting the Sublime*. Jackson: University Press of Mississippi.
Rodley, Chris. 2005. *Lynch on Lynch*. Rev. ed. London: Faber and Faber.
Romney, Jonathan. 2008. "The Boy From the Black Stuff." *The Independent on Sunday*, February 3. 24.
Schaper, Eva. 1992. "Taste, Sublimity, and Genius," in Paul Guyer (ed.), *The Cambridge Companion to Kant*. Cambridge: Cambridge University Press, 367–93.
Schopenhauer, Arthur. 1966 (1818). *The World as Will and Representation*, vol. 1, trans. E. F. J. Payne. New York: Dover.
Sperb, Jason. 2013. *Blossoms and Blood: Postmodern Media Culture and the Films of Paul Thomas Anderson*. Austin: University of Texas Press.
Thain, Alanna. 2017. *Bodies in Suspense: Time and Affect in Cinema*. Minneapolis: University of Minnesota Press.
Toles, George. 2016. *Paul Thomas Anderson*. Urbana: University of Illinois Press.
Trigg, Dylan. Forthcoming 2019. "The Uncanny," in Thomas Szanto and Hilge Landweer (eds.), *The Routledge Handbook of Phenomenology of Emotions*. New York: Routledge.
Vandenabeele, Bart. 2015. *The Sublime in Schophenhauer's Philosophy*. Basingstoke, Hampshire: Palgrave Macmillan.

7

Excessive and Incomplete: Kubrick's Turing

Marta Figlerowicz

Workable supercomputers appeared on both sides of the Iron Curtain just as Stanley Kubrick began directing. By the time he was making landmark films such as *Lolita*, the public knew these computers existed. Since 1945, the United States had the ENIAC, held at the University of Pennsylvania. Soon thereafter, the Soviets came up with the MESM at a facility in Feofaniya, Ukraine. The ENIAC and the MESM served immediate as well as long-term military ends. They calculated missile trajectories and developed formulas for nuclear weapons.[1]

These inventions inspired Norbert Wiener, John von Neumann, and others to more abstract generalizations. Wiener called the discipline they founded cybernetics. It studied goal-oriented thinking and information gathering in machines, humans, and animals. Soon, cybernetics came to focus on similarities between artificial and organic cognition. Both we and the machines we create are preprogrammed creatures, these scientists argued. Humans come into the world with biologically inscribed motivations akin to computer software. They then seek to pass on this programming to children.[2] Like computers, our bodies and minds self-regulate in ways we often cannot consciously access. The machines onto which we offload our thinking might differ from us physically, but our cognitive procedures resemble each other.

Kubrick's interest in AI is commonly known. But for the most part, critics have tended to highlight this interest's pessimistic expressions. Kubrick does often criticize twentieth-century technology for enabling human stupidity and aggression. He does so, for example, in his depiction of the Cold War's infamous equilibrium strategy in *Dr. Strangelove, or, How I Learned to Stop Worrying and Love the Bomb* (1964). Likening our inner programming to a relentless death drive, films like *Dr. Strangelove*—or *A Clockwork Orange* (1971)—depict us blindly bent on our own destruction, in ways we merely reinforce through what Alexander Walker calls "our enduring myths and fables" (Walker 2000: 15). Within this framework, more utopian films such as *2001: A Space Odyssey* (1968) can seem similarly anti-technological. They appear to fantasize about freeing our species from tools that have come to limit and subjugate us.[3]

Interviewed in *The New York Times* about *Dr. Strangelove*, Kubrick does argue that technology alone cannot secure our future. In the end, only "moral change" will save us:

> There is an almost total preoccupation with a technical solution to the problem of the bomb. Our theme is that there is no technical solution. The arms race is not likely to produce an everlasting peace and, on the other hand, even a perfectly inspected disarmament program, if not accompanied by a profound moral change in nations and men, would lead to quick rearmament and war. The only solution and defense lies in the minds and hearts of men. (Weiler 1962)

Philip Kuberski and Grant Stillman (who also quotes this passage) argue that such statements convey a generally techno-pessimistic stance. "For Kubrick," proposes Kuberski, "technology begins as a tool of violence, mutates into militarized cultures, and . . . then becomes mechanized, artificial, and bureaucratic" (Kuberski 2008: 66).[4] Kubrick's opinion about "human nature," Stillman adds, is "very bleak" (Nolan 2011: 181).

I argue against these views, following Aaron Taylor's hunch about Kubrick's deep interest in "the other minds problem" (Taylor 2016: 6).[5] Taylor shows how this interest informs Kubrick's depictions of human beings; I propose that it also extends to the cognitive networks humans form among each other and with intelligent machines. Even while denouncing mechanized abstractions, Kubrick's films express hopes for a human-computer symbiosis that embraces and affirms our embodiment. He finds in computers a tool for illustrating why embodiment is a crucial aspect of thinking and awareness. He also uses them to model a more relational, materialist approach to our world in which insight emerges not from an autonomous, detached intelligence, but through biomorphic interactions among embodied beings.

In these more positive depictions of thinking machines, Kubrick follows an alternative strain of cybernetic thinking that Wiener voiced in *The Human Use of Human Beings*, and which was popularized by the MIT scientist Vannevar Bush.[6] In a 1945 essay in the *Atlantic*, Bush introduces his readers to a symbiotic model of computers as tools for enhancing humans' cognitive capacities. He dreams up a device that, decades later, will inspire the first personal computer. It is a desk-sized storage unit that stores individual and collective memories, equal parts personal record and world encyclopedia. "Consider," Bush proposes,

> a future device for individual use, which is a sort of mechanized private file and library. It needs a name, and, to coin one at random, "memex" will do. A memex is a device in which an individual stores all his books, records, and communications, and which is mechanized so that it may be consulted with exceeding speed and flexibility. It is an enlarged intimate supplement to his memory. (Bush 1945)

In response to a notion of ourselves as preprogrammed, like computers, to fulfill tasks we did not choose for ourselves and that frequently place us in antagonistic relationships toward each other, Bush offers a vision of technology as a means of synthesizing and collecting our social and individual self-knowledge much better than our bodies themselves. He wants it to expand our capacities for self-awareness and memory in a way that remains firmly tied to our human needs and activities.[7]

In Kubrick's work and in the work of later directors influenced by him, such as Steven Spielberg, Jonathan Glazer, and Alex Garland, thinking machines are challenged to deepen their immersion in the human sensory field. Such embodied computers are used to critique naïve views of thinking and awareness as associated with disembodied autonomy and a release from social ties or inborn wants. Indeed, these directors suggest that a great part of our alienation from ourselves comes not simply from the machines we create, but from the misguided hopes of detachment we place in them. Already present in films such as *2001: A Space Odyssey*, this view is elaborated by Spielberg in his rendition of Kubrick's *A.I.* (2001), as well as by Garland in *Ex Machina* (2014) and by Glazer in *Under the Skin* (2013).

To appreciate the effect Kubrick has had on later depictions of artificial intelligence, it is best to begin with the obvious example: HAL 9000's conflict with the crew of the Discovery One in *2001: A Space Odyssey*. Kuberski describes *2001* as an exception to Kubrick's otherwise deeply satirical tone in this period. "It alone maintains a largely un-ironic vision of the human enterprise"; indeed it "is an awe-inspiring expression of the sublime reaches and potential of human imagination and achievement" (Kuberski 2008: 51). He and others have noted Kubrick's fascination with anthropologist Joseph Campbell and his theories of the mythical hero narrative. Within this framework, HAL functions as Bowman's unexpected, climactic antagonist. HAL catalyzes the film's climax by turning out to be "all too human": "suspicious, emotional, vengeful"—in contrast to the human being who, after defeating him, passes into a contrary, transcendent state of detachment and abstraction (Kuberski 2008: 52).[8] I would suggest an alternative reading of these scenes in which HAL functions not only as Bowman's antagonist but also as his *double*. This double propels Kubrick's plot by prolepsis, foreshadowing Bowman's climactic guided return to his material and temporal origins.[9]

As many critics before me have observed, HAL's artificial subjectivity and the cognitive challenges that undo him closely resemble those of his human co-passengers. In parallel, *2001* also makes the human beings around him, especially Bowman, seem machine-like (Naremore 2007: 145). Shortly after we meet him, HAL professes his superior cognitive skills in a televised interview. He then defeats one of his human crewmembers in a game of chess—a skill that computers were already being taught in 1968, but in which they would not achieve mastery until the late 1990s. The game represents HAL's extreme intelligence and rationality; it also prefigures the strategic confrontation that will soon happen between HAL and Bowman in real life.[10] In addition, chess creates a parallel between the astronauts and HAL as similarly capable of goal-oriented thinking—and as similarly constrained in this thinking by certain rules and expectations that they might not be able to modify on their own.

These parallels are drawn out in bodily terms. As HAL's voice becomes emotional and close-ups onto his electronic "eye" make him seem angry, Keir Dullea de-emphasizes Bowman's expression of emotion or affect. Soon, Bowman's feelings are signaled merely by the pace of his breathing. He and HAL are given analogous perspective shots and counter-shots that align our subjectivity now with Bowman's eyes, and now with the cyclops-eye of the supercomputer. In both cases, their mechanical and organic pupils are shielded by reflexive glass and framed in metal. Even in simplest visual terms, the red color of Bowman's spacesuit matches HAL's redness—both that of his eye and that of his mechanical brain, which Bowman slowly deconstructs with gestures analogous to the ones with which he and the other space travelers in the film insert and eject cards and discs to communicate with their loved ones on Earth. (Figures 7.1 and 7.2)

The last song HAL plays before he falls silent—"Daisy Bell"—constitutes, in this regard, both a moment of hyper-focus on HAL's artificiality, and a moment of alignment between HAL's experience with the one Bowman is about to undergo. "Daisy Bell" is one of the earliest tunes IBM supercomputers were programmed to "sing" in the sixties. It takes HAL back to the programming of these computers in a way that suggests that his own preprogrammed consciousness somehow includes, and takes its origins from,

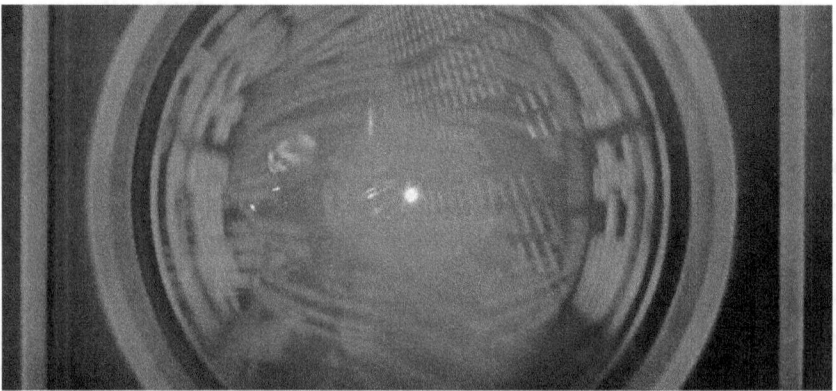

Figure 7.1 *2001: A Space Odyssey* (Stanley Kubrick, 1968), copyright Warner Brothers.

Figure 7.2 *2001: A Space Odyssey* (Stanley Kubrick, 1968), copyright Warner Brothers.

his mechanical predecessors.[11] For a viewer who knows this computing inside joke, the scene is something of an Easter egg. It is also quite poignant. Like a human being, the computer reverts back to its species' earliest memories. The film guided us through a similar species-evolution in its prehistoric segment; in the segment that follows, Bowman is going to repeat this backward journey himself.

It has attracted little critical notice that Bowman and HAL's mutual resemblances point to their surprisingly shared cognitive need for intersubjectivity. HAL cannot handle keeping secrets from his human co-passengers. An awkward attempt at open, collaborative communication—along with a preprogrammed prohibition against it— appear to trigger his initial malfunction. The malfunction begins when he clumsily tries to gesture toward the mission goals he has to keep secret from Bowman. His insistence that the radio is broken seems to be both a deflection and a projection of this secret—and the intensity of his aggression at the astronauts' subsequent mistrust of him speaks not only, as critics have observed, to his potential emotional investment in Bowman, but also to the degree to which he appears to have depended on this mutual trust and communication for his proper functioning.[12] As HAL warmly suggested in his opening interview—which, at that point, seemed merely perfunctory— he does, in the end, have a deep investment in his relations to his human makers. Indeed, his seemingly autonomous omniscience crucially depends on these relations' stability.

Bowman's subsequent interplanetary adventure—represented through images reminiscent of computer wiring—is a much more sublime and successful, but otherwise quite analogous, attempt to imagine a state of consciousness that is both immediate and intersubjective; it is a state in which intimate and shared knowledge, anthropomorphic sensory experience, and outwardly produced information reinforce and support each other in a smooth, continuous way.[13] What many critics have interpreted as a dream of transcendence—or what Brigitte Peucker calls "atemporality"—is also a dream of co-evolution and synergy. It derives individual self-awareness from a parallax view created by different kinds of human and nonhuman memories (Peucker 2001: 665). The parallel between this successful synergy and HAL's unsuccessful one is all the more striking since Bowman's self-discovery is not triggered by an organic process—a Freudian or Jungian psychoanalysis of a kind suggested by Kubrick's evocations of Campbell—but by his encounter with a metallic monolith suggestive of an alien technology with which he gradually learns to commune. The erotic undertones of queer interspecies love between HAL and Bowman that Dominic Janes finds in this film are thus, I would suggest, indicative of more than a commitment to socially and aesthetically subversive gender-bending (James 2011: 57–78). In a way that is developed even more explicitly in the half-Kubrickian and half-Spielbergian *A.I.*, as well as in *Under the Skin* and *Ex Machina*, such scenes represent an ideal of sensorially driven intellectual intimacy and elevate this interdependent perspective as a source of insight both into one's environments and into one's own self.

Kubrick returned to computers as models for such embodied, affectively charged cognitive interdependence as he prepared to adapt Brian Aldiss's "Supertoys Last All Summer Long" (1969): a sci-fi short story about a mechanical boy who is programmed to love a human woman as his mother and is then abandoned by her. Kubrick worked on this storyline for over a decade, before handing it over to Spielberg as his own death approached. An unresolved critical debate exists over the extent to which the resultant film, *A.I. Artificial Intelligence*, can still be attributed to or reflect on Kubrick. Many critics, including Ty Burr, dismiss the film as an unfortunate hybrid that fails convincingly to marry "Kubrickian irony and Spielbergian ick" (Burr 2002). The film certainly bears Spielberg's personal imprint, although Carl Freedman exaggerates somewhat when he describes as "bizarre" that the film would be counted within Kubrick's corpus at all (Freedman 2008: 137). In terms of plot and staging, Spielberg follows Kubrick's treatment for the film and its attendant visuals with considerable faithfulness (see Castle 2005: 504–08). Vivian Sobchack, James Narenmore, Rodney Hill, and others, see the film as successfully developing many Kubrickian visuals and themes in conversation with Spielberg's (Naremore 2007; Hill 2017; Sobchack 2008). Hill praises the film's "clear mythological dimension" (Hill 2017: 122). Sobchack admires its confrontation of Kubrick's and Spielberg's "quite opposed cultural visions of our displaced technological existence," which ultimately comes out on the side of Kubrickian irony and pessimism (Sobchack 2008: 2).

Spielberg's film does retain the basic structure of Kubrick's character construction. Along with this structure, it retains a notion of both artificial and human intelligence as deeply reliant on immediate, physical as well as cognitive relations to other intelligent beings. The unexpected optimism *A.I.* voices, saccharine as it may seem as shot by Spielberg, is ultimately analogous to the fantastical, hallucinatory optimism found in *2001*. It also similarly depends on computers' ambiguous reflective and codependent relation to ourselves. As in Kubrick's depiction of HAL, *A.I.* gradually shows that the blind spots and fixations that make its protagonist most machine-like are in fact the features that make him most like the men and women around him. In the end, it is in a collaborative, genealogical view of the shared history of humans and machines—filtered through a deeply subjective, anthropomorphic perspective—that the film places its hopes of the kind of sublime experiences of awareness that Bowman reaches in *2001*.

Like *2001*, *A.I.* takes its narrative impetus from an artificially intelligent being embroiled in an internal contradiction that his programming cannot resolve. The child-sized android David (Haley Joel Osment) is programmed unconditionally to love a parent figure. A couple mourning their human son Martin—placed in indefinite hibernation because present-day medicine cannot cure his illness—take him in as an emotional substitute and program him to become attached to the mother, Monica (Frances O'Connor). But unexpectedly, Martin is reanimated and healed; Monica then abandons David in a forest. Having heard the story of Pinocchio from her, the bereft David dreams up a fantastical solution. In order to rejoin his human mother, he needs to find a fairy that will turn him into a real boy Monica might love.

Even before Monica "imprints" herself on David, his relationship to her is uncomfortably invasive: he follows her around the house, even into the bathroom.[14] Once the attachment is activated, and especially after Monica's biological son comes back, David is consumed by insecurity and envy. His monomania makes him seem not only childish but also, as Sobchack has put it, "downright frightening" (Sobchack 2008: 7). Like a guided missile, he cannot unlearn his love for his adopted mother, or transform it into something like resentment or anger toward her, however many outward proofs he gets of her unfaithfulness and the mechanical nature of his attachment to her. Meeting his doppelgangers and the robot Gigolo Joe (Jude Law), who is programmed to have sex with any human being indiscriminately, makes him aware of his own artificiality in an abstract sense; however, it does not allow him to incorporate this self-knowledge into a version of himself that would want something else than the mother he lost.

Played by a child actor and intended to be treated as a child by his surroundings, David at first seems comparatively immature in his unwavering wants. But the adults around David soon become at least as remarkable for their cruelty toward mechanical beings, as for the childlike naiveté of the impulses that make them surround themselves with such beings in the first place. David's intensity matches the fixatedness of the desires and needs of the human adults around him. David's maker creates him, and other robots like him, as substitutes for his deceased son. His mother acquires him as an outlet for motherly feelings she cannot otherwise redirect or relinquish. As Tony E. Jackson observes, the fact that this film's humans never created humanoid robots whose major function was *not* to love and care for them, speaks to the predictability of their makers most poignantly of all (Jackson 2017: 58): these robots highlight the knee-jerk monomania of human psychology. Even the futuristic robots who dig up David show interest in him mostly as a vehicle of contact with their human makers, whom they are still designed to long for even though these human beings themselves are long extinct.

At the same time, as David ascends to his successive realms of robot-heaven—finally fulfilling his wishes before something like death—a transformation does take place in the way Spielberg's film depicts him. One might say that he comes to be represented ever less like the unfortunate, abandoned HAL or one of Kubrick's human psychopaths, and ever more like *2001*'s Bowman, in a way that is even reinforced by some visual and narrative echoes. David freezes behind futuristic glass as he extends his arms toward the figurehead he takes for the Blue Fairy. He then enacts a spectacular feat of time travel, as ice preserves him for millennia until he is rediscovered by dark, looming, geometrically featureless robots far more advanced than himself—and is finally allowed to effectively go back in time, to one perfect day in which he and Monica are alone once more. David's freezing repeats what Peucker has described as a fundamental feature of Kubrick's allegories: it shifts from a filmic to a quasi-photographic image, from rhythmic temporal movements to something like their transcendence (Peucker 2001: 665). When futuristic robots allow David to spend one day with a revived version of his mother, he spends this day going back to his apparent origins in human feelings, needs, and behaviors: lying in bed, having a real birthday, making art about his prior life history, and finally hearing from his mother the affectionate words he had been programmed to assume she would direct toward him.

In a way that is much more sentimental than Bowman's visions at the end of *2001*, but arguably no less utopian, David appears to live out within this day—an "eternal moment," as the narrator calls it—the entire life cycle he was made for. As he falls asleep at the end of this day, he goes back to the state of quiet potentiality from which his mother awakened him in the first place—a state in which, moreover, in another echo of Bowman's hallucination, he supposedly has his first real dream. As in *2001*, David does not go on to address us from his new point of consciousness. Also as in *2001*, this final, fantastical idyll relies on the notion of cyclicality: of being able to live out your past again, and reimmerse yourself in it more fully, as in a memory more exhaustive and precise than the ones our bodies can conjure up on our own. This idyll here again is the fruit of a technology created to embrace and enhance the embodiment of human consciousness rather than to supplant it.[15] This utopian awareness exists, as it did in *2001*, in a state of limbo between the human and the mechanical—a state in which the two appear to shift from competition to something like collaboration, freed from a human timescale but lived out in a way that remains deeply, hallucinatorily dependent on anthropomorphic sense perception.

Glazer and Garland, both of whom have been described—and self-described—as inspired by Kubrick, echo his preoccupation with expanded, intersubjective forms of consciousness.[16] Bringing computing technologies into the present, they persist in turning their viewers' attention away from a Turing-style, antagonistic relationship between AIs and humans, and toward a vision of them as similarly trapped in blinkering, linear desires and aims that they can only transcend through moments of mutual attunement or care. Like *A.I.*, these films choose robots, rather than human beings, as the centers of consciousness whose attempts at self-awareness and mutual awareness they follow. Glazer's robotic being does not achieve anything close to cognitive communion; Garland's achieves it in a way that exceeds its surrounding human beings' capacity to do so. But in both *Under the Skin* and *Ex Machina*, the focus of attention is not merely intelligence in itself, but relation and interdependence—a kind of cognition that arises out of intimate, embodied collaboration between several beings, embracing rather than transcending human or human-like subjectivity.

In *Ex Machina* and *Under the Skin*, this robotic or alien intelligence is played by a woman. This choice echoes the original Turing test, which famously models examining an artificial mind after the process of trying to tell apart the personalities and intelligences of women and men. The emphasis on gender difference also signals the films' particular preoccupation with sexuality as both a hindrance to our mental functioning and a foundation for many of our wants and needs. Human desire is depicted, in these films, as oddly mechanical but also inscrutable, cognitively limiting as well as surprisingly hard to fall in step with from an outside, nonhuman perspective. It is as difficult, Garland and Glazer both suggest, to imagine a transcendent intelligence fettered by such bodily wants, as it is to imagine any kind of autonomous intelligence that did not have a deep and immediate understanding of them.

Glazer's *Under the Skin* (loosely based on a sci-fi novel by Michel Faber) explores a scenario of intersubjective failure: the lack of human desires makes a nonhuman intelligence impossible to sustain and nurture in a human world. Critics have often remarked on this film's Kubrickian influences, pointing especially to Glazer's surreal landscapes and to the clean, withdrawn superficiality of the film's represented human interactions. One major resonance between Glazer's and Kubrick's work that has remained comparatively underexplored, however, lies in their parallel attempts to imagine a kind of consciousness that is in some parts human and in others, inhuman. This intelligence exceeds our lived spatiotemporal frameworks while remaining tethered to our bodily cycles and needs.

Glazer's Kubrickian inspirations are most striking, in this regard, when the plot and tenor of his film depart from the novel it adapts. Faber's book is told from the first-person perspective of an alien whose name, motivations, and reasoning are explained to the reader in careful introspective detail. This alien, Isserley, has been surgically altered to look like a human being, in a way that is described to us as painful and invasive; she captures human hitchhikers and takes them back to her home planet to be killed for food. Isserley begins to have second thoughts about her job after some of the humans beg her for mercy and especially once she sees how they are brutally castrated and butchered by her alien coworkers. Just as she is on the brink of quitting her job, her car crashes and she is forced to commit suicide. In its narration, Faber's book emphasizes processes of empathy and quasi-philosophical reflection as they occur from the alien's perspective. The discoveries Isserley makes in the course of the book are less about her and more about the human world she visits and her alien society's exploitation of it.[17]

Few of these formal qualities, and even fewer of the novel's principal plot twists, make their way into Glazer's film. Played by Scarlett Johansson, the alien is depicted entirely from the outside and in schematic conversations with human beings; we never get a sense of her introspective voice, and even her fellow aliens appear to treat her like a passively mechanical, automatized entity.[18] From the start, the harvesting of human bodies happens within Isserley's purview, and neither these harvests nor the process by which she prepares to orchestrate them seem particularly gruesome. They consist merely in the donning or shedding of human skins, which envelop the humans and the alien herself like costumes or like the film of a balloon. The opening shots, which depict Isserley's pupil in extreme close-up, obviously echo Kubrick's close-ups on HAL's cyclops-eye. From the start, they draw attention away from the alien's extraterrestrial provenance and toward the sheer artificiality of her existence on Earth.

Within this sterile, psychologically muted environment, Isserley confronts the humans around her as cognitive mysteries. In Glazer's film, her turn toward empathy begins when she encounters a man with neurofibromatosis and decides to set him free, presumably because of the earnest vulnerability with which he responds to her standardized effort at seduction. Before this conversion, she appeared to perceive human beings merely as physical entities in whose trajectories she intervened. The film reinforced this impression by frequently depicting them as small objects caught in water or fluidly moving in large crowds.[19] With this encounter, which culminates in the man's escape into the wilderness, stark naked, the film begins to adopt a quasi-romantic quality—as is also highlighted by a series of visual quotations from Caspar David Friedrich.[20] Moving away from perceiving the people around her as mere prey, the alien starts to relate to her earthly environment as something with a life, and a set of principles, of its own. In order to escape from her alien employers, she eventually attempts to align herself with the life rhythms she perceives around herself. The transition to this second part of the film is signaled by a shift in Glazer's camerawork. In the car, we see a series of improvised shots made with hidden cameras and nonactors.[21] As Isserley leaves the car and goes deeper into individual human interactions, the camera becomes more directed and purposeful, composing the film into almost allegorical natural landscapes.

But this emotional breakthrough also inaugurates a more complicated set of questions that Glazer then makes his primary focus: when the alien tries to act like a human being, both humans and her own, partly humanoid body leave her perpetually puzzled and out of sync. Isserley seems capable of registering human-like drives within her body, but not of following through on or satisfying them; of playing along with human beings' behaviors, but not of actually communicating with them.

In a first instance of this confusion, Isserley falls in the middle of a busy street to be picked up by strangers, and only then appears to realize that her body is hungry. When she tries to feed herself with a piece of cake at a restaurant, she instantly spits it out: she may have the capacity to want it, but not the capacity to swallow it. (Figure 7.3; Figure 7.4) There follows a series of increasingly dramatic misapprehensions. The hungry alien is found slouching in the corner of a bus by a stranger who takes her home and gives her a place to sleep. The two go on what the man, but not the alien, appears to perceive as a date: he carries her over a river in chivalric fashion and they scale a nearby historical tower. Back at his place, he tries to have sex with her—and she initially consents before jumping out of the bed in sudden surprise and horror, and shining a lamp on her vagina.[22] Eventually, she runs away into a forest, where another man tries to rape her. He tears her skin off to reveal a stone- or rubber-like pitch-black alien body and sets this body on fire in disgust and panic.

There is a sense in which, like Faber's novel, Glazer's is a feminist film about the ways in which women are abused and exploited by men (Osterweil 2014: 44–51). But

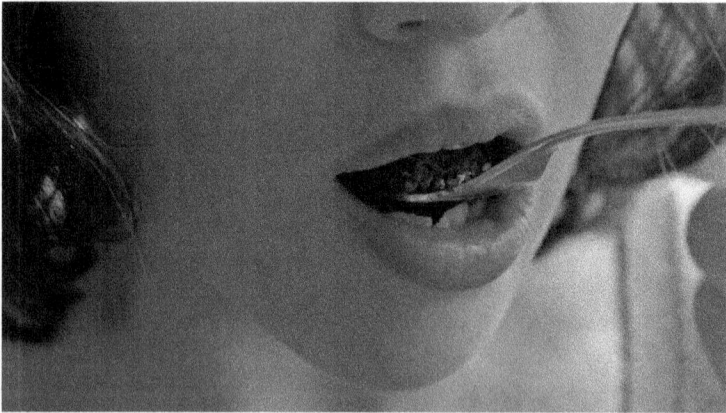

Figure 7.3 *Under the Skin* (Jonathan Glazer, 2013), copyright Copyright Film 4 et al.

Figure 7.4 *Under the Skin* (Jonathan Glazer, 2013), copyright Copyright Film 4 et al.

such an interpretation sells short its surreality, as well as its increasing preoccupation with the potential incomprehensibility of our biological urges. The point is not merely that the men whom the alien meets objectify and dehumanize her. The human rituals of mutual sustenance and courtship are alienated in an even more fundamental way: they are presented to us from the perspective of a being for whom these rituals seem completely unrelatable and unaffecting. Her inability to be nurtured by even some of them is highlighted by the increasing purposiveness with which Glazer's camera begins to represent these behaviors, in romantic terms, as biologically ingrained and culturally nonspecific—as behaviors to which, as human beings, we can hardly imagine not having a strong affective response. The lushly forested environment almost allegorically embodies the reproductive life on which she has been feeding, and into which she has tried to incorporate herself without quite being sure how to do so.

Endowed with knowledge that seems both excessive and incomplete, the alien is tantalized by her unsuccessful attempts to relate to humans in a way that impairs her not just emotionally and physically but also cognitively. Her incapacity to accurately interpret or predict human desires, beyond the narrow function they played in her gruesome harvests, makes her unable to survive in a human landscape. The apparently totalizing outside view she has of humans as prey does not contain within itself, and cannot substitute for, an understanding of what it would be like to think and act with them. The alien's tragedy is, in this regard, much like the tragedy of HAL: the supposedly detached, omniscient being that could not cope with, or insert itself into, a human network of needs and cares even though it had overseen and dominated this network with confidence and attentiveness. Through Isserley's dramatic demise, *Under the Skin* depicts such more immersed, interactive perspectives as both impossible to derive from a supposed state of objectivity, and vitally necessary. In the film's final scene, when she is set ablaze and runs through a forest, the alien is transformed into a light source. This time, however, instead of dominating the screen as it did in the opening, this light source is a single, increasingly tiny dot lost within it.

Ex Machina continues these considerations of intelligence and embodiment in a more meta-textual key. In the film, a programmer named Caleb Smith (Domhnall Gleeson) is invited by his techno-billionaire boss Nathan Bateman (Oscar Isaac), the founder of a Google-like web search company, to stay in his remote villa and give the Turing test to the AI Caleb has secretly manufactured and powered through the human knowledge filling the internet. The AI, Ava (Alicia Vikander) is a half-metallic, half-humanoid presence. She seduces Caleb into helping her escape Nathan's home, killing Nathan and imprisoning Caleb in the process.

As with *Under the Skin*, most critical discussion around *Ex Machina* has centered on its representations of gender relations: on the degree to which the film does, or does not, continue a line of Pygmalion-style representations of women as inferior and objectified beings pitted against their male creators. For some, such as Nick Jones, *Ex Machina* is feminist and "takes aim at a kind of masculinized digital narcissism" (Jones 2016: 300). Others have noted that the film's objectification of the female robot perpetuates stereotypes about the kinds of intelligence women must perform—and the very limited, heteronormative aims with which they need to perform it— in order to survive in a world ruled by men (Watercutter 2015).[23] Undoubtedly, Garland's film opens such feminist questions (like so many of Kubrick's films, whose gender politics are also often ambiguous and unresolved). But alongside these considerations, *Ex Machina* also pursues more abstract questions: can human beings recognize a form of intelligence that does not have such human, or human-like, desires and motivations? And can this intelligence outsmart us without becoming like us on a basic affective level?

When asked by Caleb why Ava was gendered in the first place, Nathan provides a double answer. Intelligence, he claims, is necessarily relational; it has to have a goal to gravitate toward, of a kind that sexuality readily provides. Then he adds, with a shrug of his shoulders, that he gave her the capacity to experience sexual pleasure "because it was fun." On the surface, this seems like the kind of egotistical response Nathan has for most of Caleb's questions: he aggrandizes and elevates into sublime achievements, inventions that also make him a lot of money and satisfy his animal needs. But the point also goes deeper. Garland's film uses such scenes to show how difficult it often is to separate from each other our lofty and carnal, sublimated and unsublimated mental aims. When we try to imagine an intelligence superior to ours, would that intelligence be free from our baser wants or merely able to satisfy them better? *Ex Machina* suggests that what we dream of as superior minds are always also superior and superiorly satisfied bodies—that what we would truly respect an autonomous machine for is not detachment from our experiences, but a relation to them that was somehow deeper and more rewarding.

Most of the femme fatale films with which *Ex Machina* tends to be compared are concerned with AIs as harbingers of a human or nonhuman future: as forces with which we have to reckon to secure the fulfillment and perpetuation of our human aspirations and dreams.[24] *Ex Machina*, by contrast, stresses the degree to which intelligences are shaped by their past and present. In the process of interacting with Ava, Caleb becomes preoccupied with his physical makeup as a human being, trying to get at the ultimate preexisting proof of his humanity by cutting into his own veins and watching himself bleed. These exercises are, in the end, unable to reveal to him or help him transcend the ways in which his behavior toward Ava and Nathan has been "imprinted" onto him both by Nathan's manipulation and by his upbringing. Locked in Nathan's great mansion, in the end he seems to have been duped by them both. Indeed, as he realizes, he had never been truly separate from his intelligent environments in the first place.

Intelligence and bodily pleasure are thus inextricably bound in *Ex Machina*; most of the film's plot twists consist merely in further revelations of this inextricability. We gradually find out that Nathan's other AIs are former or current sex slaves; it also turns out that the actual Turing test Nathan placed before Ava was whether or not she would be able to seduce Caleb for the purpose of escaping. When we first meet him, Nathan seems health-conscious and ascetic; but it soon becomes clear that his lifestyle is, instead, a careful balance between maximizing his pleasures and enhancing his body's capacity to take them in. Synergies between the film's camerawork and the high modernist aesthetics of Nathan's household reinforce this impression. Often shot like an ad for Nathan's refined, luxurious simplicity, the film makes his lifestyle seem beautifully seamless. Contrasted both against Caleb's more awkward intrusions into these frames—and against Ava's imprisonment within a small subset of them—the film ambiguously equates computer intelligence with both a large, synchronized artificial environment and a sensing human body at its center by whom the rewards of this distributed intelligence can be reaped. The house as such functions as Nathan's extended memex, to use Bush's term, to which the rest of his environment is subordinated. The perfectly synchronized way in which Nathan and his sex robot dance together in an often-reproduced scene from the film provides a near-allegorical image of this paradox: a studied choreography of hedonism. In this sense, Nathan is a very Kubrickian character, perhaps most directly akin to *Lolita*'s Clare Quilty; he also harks back to the controlling male psychopaths scattered throughout Kubrick's oeuvre.

It might appear that Ava's goal and her eventual achievement is to be free from the human needs and urges that surround her. Comparing this film to *A.I.*, Jones remarks on its idealization of robots who can somehow "break their programming." "Ava shows ... a calculating desire for self-determination, a ferocious will to define the parameters of one's own programming" (Jones 2016: 301). By destroying her maker, Ava proves herself to be not a copy of but an improvement on him; by escaping into the real world beyond his mansion, she becomes free of the purposes to which he tried to put her. In this regard, the film would appear to follow the pattern of other recent science fiction films such as *Lucy* (2014), *Transcendence* (2014), or *Her* (2013). But such a reading sells short the scenes of self-discovery that precede the film's denouement—and whose wordlessness often makes them seem as ambiguous and sublime as the birth sequences of *2001* or the more maudlin but equally mysterious final sequences of *A.I.* In these scenes, Ava appears to discover her origins: she moves back in robotic evolutionary time, all the way back to the human beings out of whose interactions she was programmed, in order to escape.

Before this finale, the film frequently raises the question of whether, and how, Ava could become truly aware of the data she has absorbed from internet search engines and networks. Caleb at one point illustrates this conundrum, in his own mind, by imagining her as Mary from the famous philosophical thought exercise: a woman who has spent all her life exposed to knowledge about red but not the color itself, finally confronted with this sensory data she previously knew only abstractly. Ava herself looks for answers to this question by testing out on Caleb the many kinds of interaction she has previously only found out about in lines of code. Her self-knowledge deepens further when she realizes how many previous versions of herself used to exist, and are still hidden in Nathan's closets; she also appears to recognize in Kyoko (Sonoya Mizuno) a parallel self. When Ava discovers her hyper-sexualized predecessors and kills Nathan with the help of one of them, she kills the person who created and tried to control her; however, she also fulfills a revenge fantasy that re-emphasizes, rather than erases, the affective link between them. Incorporating into herself parts of Kyoko, and immediately flying away, in a sexy outfit, to be among human beings, she then re-immerses herself into the complicated, networked relationality out of which Nathan made her in the first place. (Figure 7.5)

These scenes of Ava's self-discovery are especially striking given how preoccupied Garland's film otherwise is—in visual as well as narrative fashion—with Bluebeard-style motifs of locked doors, walls, and eavesdropping. To escape Nathan's castle, Ava and Caleb both need to immerse themselves in it as deeply as possible. But Caleb's notion of embodiment is too narrow; it singles out sexualized female bodies while overlooking, or locally instrumentalizing, the intelligence of doors, walls, and security cameras. By contrast, Ava manages to escape by attuning herself as broadly as possible to the human and the electric circuits around her, replacing Caleb as their most sensitive, live center—and finally becoming an eerily transcendent, Bowman-like figure. She breaks free from Nathan and fulfills what she claimed to Caleb had been her deepest wishes by leaning

Figure 7.5 *Ex Machina* (Alex Garland, 2014), copyright Film 4, DNA pictures.

into her relations to the humans out of whose thoughts and affects she was constructed, as well as into the material affordances that led her to them.

In philosophical treatments of artificial intelligence, Turing's antagonistic notions of AI were only replaced with more relational, embodied, and distributed ones at the turn of the twenty-first century.[25] Examining Kubrick's films reveals him to have held a more intersubjective view of artificial thinking considerably earlier. Taking seriously a notion of our minds as embodied and governed by not fully controllable biological motivations, he shows how difficult it is to imagine a conscious being without similar hard-wired impulses and a particular bodily presence associated with them—and how much of what we conceive of as transcendence or even just as intelligence, has to do with inhabiting these impulses and using them as paths toward broader material and personal relations. Interpreting *A.I., Under the Skin,* and *Ex Machina* as continuations of this view allows us better to discern their own philosophical depth and aesthetic choices. It also helps us appreciate Kubrick's prescience about the new ways AI connects us back to supposedly "mechanical" parts of ourselves.

Notes

1 See Peters (2016). These early computers were partly modeled on the Turing machine that the British intelligence used to crack the Enigma code, which itself took much of its inspiration from the Analytical Engine dreamed up a hundred years earlier by Ada Lovelace and Charles Babbage. For a general overview of this history, see Gleick (2012) or Dyson (2012).
2 See Wiener (1961); Shannon (1971), and others.
3 As in, for instance, Nelson (1982: 15; 114–17).
4 For other restatements of this view, see Cook (2004: 120) and Kagan (1972: 160–61).
5 For a Lacanian phrasing of an analogous point, see Todd McGowan's chapter on Kubrick (2008).
6 See Wiener (1988).
7 In a way that eerily echoes Bush's description of the memex, Alexander Walker speculates that Kubrick's fascination with artificial intelligence stems from his own gradual adoption of it as a directing and organizing tool. See Walker (1972: 37). All the same, Walker describes "intelligence," as Kubrick's preoccupation, in ways that echo some of the abstractions that I would argue Kubrick starkly opposes; see Walker 1972: 244–45 and especially 265, where Walker describes intelligence, on Kubrick's view, as "a sort of God."
8 See also Walker 1972: 254–55.
9 This is among the few of *2001*'s doublings—perhaps the only one—that Naremore doesn't remark on in *On Kubrick* (London, UK: British Film Institute, 2007), 145.
10 Note that Kubrick introduced a glitch in the chess playing scene deliberately, a hint that HAL was already malfunctioning, which only a few members of the audience could pick up on right off the bat.
11 See Kaye (2012).
12 This, in spite of HAL's apparent omnipresence around the ship, as described by Gary D. Rhodes—one might say that, in the end, Kubrick depicts the ship as HAL's body

in a way that is much more vulnerable than its towering size might make it seem. (Rhodes 2008: 96).

13. As Geoffrey Cooks has observed, the total absence of dialogue in this last section of the film (as in the first one), and its replacement by music, heightens this immediate, emotive effect. "[*2001*] allow[s] the emotive force of music to break the boundaries often set to meaning by words." (Cocks 2004: 116). See also Kubrick's comments on his aims in imagining and editing these sequences quoted in Kagan (1972: 146–47).
14. Significantly and comically, Monica is found reading a book titled *Freud and Women* (Naremore 2007: 249).
15. As Naremore puts it, this persistent emphasis artificiality also forestalls an easier reading of the scene as an actual, Disney-style, happy ending (259).
16. See Taylor, 9; Jones (2016: 302), Watercutter (2015), Patches (2015); and many others.
17. See Faber (2001).
18. "Glazer: I think the explanation of things like her cohorts, these alien entities as bikers—they're performing a function. We see him clearing up after her, inspecting her at one point. There's a sense in that scene that there's something not quite right with her that he's detecting, like a hairline fracture or a crack in the wing of an airplane. He's satisfied that there isn't and carries on with his day." Sam Adams, "Space Oddity: Jonathan Glazer on *Under the Skin*," *Rolling Stone*, April 4, 2014, www.rollingstone.com/movies/news/space-oddity-jonathan-glazer-on-under-the-skin-20140404.
19. "Glazer: I think routine is what we wanted to show. Her job, her at work. Really the first half of the film is that. It's watching her go about her job if you like. If you make her presence equivalent to ours, it's like she's in a routine and a job she hates and she begins to lose her focus and leaves her job." Hank Sartin, "Jonathan Glazer Talks about His New Film *Under the Skin*," *RogerEbert.com*, April 10, 2014, www.rogerebert.com/interviews/jonathan-glazer-talks-about-under-the-skin.
20. I analyze these parallels in more detail in "Inanimism: *Nymphomaniac*, *Under the Skin*, and Capitalist Late Style," *Camera Obscura* 33(3) (2018): 40–67.
21. See Herzog (2016).
22. See Gorfinkel (2016).
23. See also Lane (2015).
24. See especially Lane, online.
25. See Clark (2001), and Noe (2010).

Works Cited

Burr, Ty. 2002. "*A.I. Artificial Intelligence*." *Entertainment Weekly*. https://ew.com/article/2002/03/05/ai-artificial-intelligence (accessed August 8, 2018).

Bush, Vannevar. 1945. "As We May Think." *The Atlantic*. https://www.theatlantic.com/magazine/archive/1945/07/as-we-may-think/303881 (accessed August 8, 2018)

Castle, Alison. 2005. "Stanley Kubrick's A.I." *The Stanley Kubrick Archives*, ed. Alison Castle. London: Taschen, 504–08.

Clark, Andy. 2010. *Supersizing the Mind*. New York, NY: Oxford University Press.

Cocks, Geoffrey. 2004. *The Wolf at the Door: Stanley Kubrick, History, and the Holocaust*. New York, NY: Peter Lang.

Faber, Michel. 2001. *Under the Skin*. New York, NY: Harvest.

Figlerowicz, Marta. 2018. "Inanimism: *Nymphomaniac*, *Under the Skin*, and Capitalist Late Style," *Camera Obscura* 33(3): 40–67.

Freedman, Carl. 2008. "James Narenmore's *On Kubrick*: A Review," *Science Fiction Film and Television* 1(1): 133–38.

Gleick, James. 2012. *The Information*. New York, NY: Vintage.

Gorfinkel, Elena. 2016. "Sex, Sensation, and Nonhuman Interiority in *Under the Skin*," *Jump Cut*, no. 57 (2016), www.ejumpcut.org/currentissue/-GorfinkelSkin/index.html.

Herzog, Amy. 2016. "Star Vehicle: Labor and Corporeal Traffic in *Under the Skin*," *Jump Cut*, no. 57 (2016), www.ejumpcut.org/currentissue/-HerzogSkin/index.html.

Hill, Rodney. 2017. "*A.I. Artificial Intelligence*, dir. by Steven Spielberg." *Film & History: An Interdisciplinary Journal* 47(1): 121–24.

Jackson, Tony E. 2017. "Imitative Identity, Imitative Art, and *AI: Artificial Intelligence*." *Mosaic: An Interdisciplinary Journal* 50(2): 47–64.

James, Dominic. 2011. "Clarke and Kubrick's *2001*: A Queer Odyssey." *Science Fiction Film and Television* 4(1): 57–78.

Jones, Nick. 2016. "Ex Machina (review)." *Science Fiction Film and Television* 9(2): 299–303.

Kaye, Don. 2012. "Little-Known Sci-Fi Fact: Why HAL 9000 sang 'Daisy' in *2001*," *Syfy Wire*, December 14, 2012, accessed online on 9/1/18 at https://www.syfy.com/syfywire/littleknown_sci_fi_fact.

Kagan, Norman. 1972. *The Cinema of Stanley Kubrick*. New York, NY: Holt, Rinehart, and Winston, 160–61.

Kuberski, Philip. 2008. "Kubrick's *Odyssey*: Myth, Technology, Gnosis." *Arizona Quarterly* 63(3): 51–73.

Lane, Anthony. "Feelings," *The New Yorker*, April 13, 2015, https://www.newyorker.com/magazine/2015/04/13/feelings-cinema-anthony-lane.

Naremore, James. 2007. *On Kubrick*. London: British Film Institute.

McGowan, Todd. 2008. *The Real Gaze: Film Theory after Lacan*. New York, NY: SUNY Press.

Nelson, Thomas Allen, 1982. *Kubrick: Inside a Film Artist's Maze*. Bloomington, IN: Indiana University Press, 15.

Noe, Alva. 2010. *Out of Our Heads*. New York, NY: Hill and Wang.

Nolan, Amy. 2011. "Seeing is Digesting: Labyrinths of Historical Ruin in Stanley Kubrick's *The Shining*." *Cultural Critique* 77: 180–204.

Osterweil, Ara. 2014. "The Perils of Becoming Female." *Film Quarterly* 67.4: 44–51.

Patches, Matt. 2015. "*Ex Machina* A.I. Inspirations," April 25, 2015, https://www.esquire.com/entertainment/movies/interviews/a34599/ex-machina-artificial-intelligence-google-theories.

Peucker, Brigitte. 2001. "Kubrick and Kafka: The Corporeal Uncanny." *Modernism/modernity* 8(4): 663–74.

Peters, Benjamin. 2016. *How Not to Network a Nation: The Uneasy History of the Soviet Internet*. Cambridge, MA: The MIT Press.

Rhodes, Gary D. "Believing is Seeing: Surveillance and *2001: A Space Odyssey*," in *Stanley Kubrick: Essays on His Films and Legacy*, ed. Gary D. Rhodes (London, UK: McFarland & Co., 2008).

Shannon, Claude. 1971. *The Mathematical Theory of Communication*. Springfield, IL: University of Illinois Press.
Sobchack, Vivian. 2008. "Love Machines: Boy Toys, Toy Boys, and the Oxymorons of *A.I.: Artificial Intelligence*." *Science Fiction Film and Television* 1(1): 1–13.
Taylor, Aaron. 2016. "Blind Spots and Mind Games: Performance, Motivation, and Emotion in the Films of Stanley Kubrick." *The Velvet Light Trap* 77: https://doi.org/10.7560/VLT7702.
Walker, Alexander. 1972. *Stanley Kubrick Directs*. New York, NY: Harcourt.
Walker, Alexander. 2000. *Stanley Kubrick, Director*, expanded edition. New York: W. W. Norton.
Watercutter, Angela. 2015. "*Ex Machina* Has a Serious Fembot Problem." Wired. https://www.wired.com/2015/04/ex-machina-turing-bechdel-test (accessed August 8, 2018).
Weiler, A.H. 1962. , "The East: Kubrick's and Sellers' New Film." *The New York Times*, May 6. Quoted in Stillman, Grant. 2008. "Two of the MADdest Scientists." *Film History* 20(4).
Wiener, Norbert. 1961. *Cybernetics: Or the Control and Communication in the Animal and the Machine*. New York, NY: Martino Books, reprinted in 2013).
Wiener, Norbert. 1988. *The Human Use of Human Beings: Cybernetics and Society*. New York, NY: Da Capo Press.

8

Thus Spoke Kubrick: "Guide Pieces," Modes of Citation and the Rise of the Temp Track

Adrian Daub

When it came to how movies sounded, Stanley Kubrick was of a particular moment, but he seized that moment in a unique way. The moment—one might designate it as 1968, though it extends beyond the calendar year—was one that Kubrick shared with other innovative young filmmakers who sought to renegotiate how films were scored. The end of the Golden Age studio system brought with it an end to one kind of smoothed-over Hollywood sound. And the rise of the Hollywood auteur presented new opportunities to incorporate unusual types of music in mainstream cinema. From rock songs, jazz, avant-garde music, or plain absence of non-diegetic music, the films that shared cinemas with *2001: A Space Odyssey*, or that came shortly after it, went in new directions when it came to how a hit film sounded.

At the same time, Kubrick's response to this opportunity was particular in how it highlighted and foregrounded certain features of the process by which film is made to sound. And that process, unlike some of the sonic gestures that defined films like *Bonnie & Clyde* (1967), *Easy Rider* (1969), or *Harold and Maude* (1971), was itself deeply traditional. The classical music that, rather unusually, formed the basis for *2001*'s eventual soundtrack originated as "guide pieces" during the film's prolonged editing process. The use of "guide pieces" or "temp tracks" was a long-established practice both in Hollywood and outside it—and given that it tended to function as a guarantor of a certain continuity of sound and dynamism in film sound, the practice represented the film industry at its most industrial, its most anti-auteurist.

This is something that Kubrick's filmic odyssey utilizes to great effect. Unlike the smoothness with which, say, *The Graduate* (1967) maintains its dialogue with the Simon & Garfunkel songs that provide almost all its soundtrack, *2001* drew its sounds into an awkward, often ironic, *pas-de-deux* with its images. Kate McQuiston (2013: 43) has spoken of Kubrick's creation of "musical atmospheres" (43), the atmospheres of *2001* defined by a "bare salinity" (129), brought about by the isolation of individual visual and sonic signals. Staging close encounters between image and music, Kubrick forced the viewer to interrogate how soundtracks make meaning—a technique he would remain faithful to for the rest of his oeuvre, and that in recent years filmmakers like Terrence Malick, Paul Thomas Anderson, and Lars von Trier have put to effective use.

The Path to *Zarathustra*

Perhaps the most surprising fact about the soundtrack of *2001: A Space Odyssey* is that for long stretches the film remains quite sparing in its use of extra-diegetic music. The film is justly famous for its use of classical music, and some of its most indelible scenes are forever associated with their musical accompaniment. But in fact at the very center of the film is a lack of music—from the moment astronaut Frank Poole stops his morning jog to the title card announcing the film's final chapter, the extradiegetic soundtrack falls almost entirely silent. Even when *2001* was to have a far more conventional score, the only material written for it was intended for about the first hour—Alex North, the original score composer, never got to write much more than that. The music of *2001* as we have it today if anything reduces what North composed—about forty minutes of music distributed in the first forty and final thirty minutes of the film (Shaw-Miller 2017: 47).

The process of arriving at the soundtrack that would make *2001* iconic was an unusually labyrinthine and protracted one. And it was one that led, in a circuitous way, back to the beginning. The soundtracks that became famous alongside the film had originally constituted the temp track of so-called Guide Pieces, which Kubrick had used to help in the editing of the film. Initially these had been supposed to guide the hired composer in creating an original score.

While Kubrick's decision to jettison North's score in favor of the erstwhile temp track has often been interpreted as evidence of his uncompromising, and perhaps somewhat eccentric, vision, North's role in the little drama bespeaks a viewpoint just as strong. When North arrived in London to write and record his score, he claims, "I realized that [Kubrick] liked these tracks, but I couldn't accept the idea of composing part of the score interpolated with other composers." This was not as uncommon an attitude then as it is now, but even in 1968 soundtrack composers often had to share the orchestra pit with Old Masters or modish pop songs. North, however, claims to have balked at this.

The reasons he adduced for this refusal in hindsight offer some hints about Kubrick's thinking as well. "I felt," North said afterward, "I could compose music that had the ingredients and essence of what Kubrick wanted and give it a consistency and homogeneity and contemporary feel." That description—"consistency," "homogeneity," "contemporary feel"—seems uncanny in the way it anticipates the exact opposite of what "our" *2001: A Space Odyssey* ended up sounding like. And it may well have been those three aesthetic lodestars—offered by North as somehow the obvious point of a film soundtrack—that may have driven Kubrick back into the embrace of what would become his permanent temp track.

The pieces gathered in this temp track have shaped audience response to *2001* ever since its release. The most famous is of course the opening of Richard Strauss's *Thus Spoke Zarathustra*, a piece probably better known among the lay public as the "*2001* theme" than as part of a symphonic poem. Almost as deeply identified with the sonic universe of Kubrick's film is Johann Strauss's *Blue Danube* waltz, which Kubrick repeatedly turns to when man-made objects navigate outer space. So apropos is this choice in hindsight that Kubrick's soundlessly spinning spaceships and the whirling, repetitive waltz-melodies have fused into one single audiovisual icon. Something similar is true for the three pieces by György Ligeti included in the film—the *Requiem, Lux Aeterna,* and *Atmosphères*. Less well-remembered is the adagio from Aram Khachaturian's *Gayane* Suite (1942), which falls somewhere in between the two musical worlds of this temp track, fin-de-siècle Vienna and atonal avant-garde, and which, perhaps not insignificantly appears at the mid-point of the narrative.

Compared to these pieces, North's opening is a far clearer fanfare, with a very non-Nietzschean dash of Aaron Copland. Until the closing organ chords, it feels like something that could open *Spartacus* (1960) or *Ben Hur* (William Wyler, 1959). This is borne out throughout the twelve cues of North's that have been preserved: the overall style is neoclassical, with just enough atonality to avoid a retro sound. And above all, North's soundtrack avoids any of the bizarre juxtapositions that characterized the film's temp track. North fully understood that this was in fact part of the job of a film composer, but he did not intuit that in this instance Kubrick didn't want him to do it. In contrast with the smoothing work North clearly attempted to perform in his rejected score, *2001: A Space Odyssey* as we see it today is riven by oppositions—light waltzes and avant-garde music, tonal and atonal, classical and modern (see Patterson 2004: 444–71)—its sound serves to parcel out the film's sequences rather than rendering them "consistent" or "homogeneous."

Many discussions of the genesis of *2001*'s music restrict themselves to these two polarities: temp track and soundtrack, Kubrick and North, auteur director and Hollywood machine. But historical research attests to the fact that Kubrick's thinking about the music for his film went through several more stages (see Benson 2018). Composer Bernard Herrmann claimed he was approached to score *2001*, but never wrote any music for it; Merkley suggests that, given that Herrmann was even more allergic than North to sharing screen time with preexisting pieces, this was likely why the proposed collaboration never took off.

Merkley further points out that Kubrick was deeply impressed with the work of Carl Orff and may have considered bringing him on to write a soundtrack. This would not have been altogether unheard of—Ralph Vaughan Williams's score for *Scott of the Antarctic* (in the composer's adaptation as his 1952 Symphony No. 7) became one of the pieces Kubrick would play for his actors on set. But it would indicate that Kubrick looked toward art music, rather than the studio system, when he imagined the sound for his science fiction epic. Kubrick seems to have seriously considered replacing the temp track with more classical music—specifically Gustav Mahler's Symphony No. 3, which, like Strauss's *Zarathustra* is partly a commentary on texts by Friedrich Nietzsche, and which, again like *Zarathustra*, contains a powerful musical depiction of a sunrise. Kubrick approached Frank Cordell to record adapted sections of the symphony, likely in order to bring Mahler's titanic symphony into closer alignment with the film taking shape in the editing room.

Whether Mahler's music would have replaced all of the guide pieces (at nearly ninety minutes the Third is certainly capable of furnishing all of the music Kubrick ended up using the film), whether it would have replaced only specific guide pieces (it would have made a good period fit for *Zarathustra*, and its concluding adagio might have been a serviceable substitute for Khachaturian's *Gayane* Suite), we do not know. Whatever shape this inclusion of Mahler would have taken, it is certainly worth commenting on the idea of substituting one preexisting classical piece for another.

Substituting one temp track for another would have been a self-application of a technique Kubrick seems to have otherwise reserved for his actors. As Michel Chion has pointed out, Kubrick often played music on the set, but almost exclusively music that was out of sync with the music he intended to use (or at any rate ended up using) in the scene in question. For instance, in the jogging scene in the centrifuge, Kubrick had his actors move to a waltz, but the piece that ends up accompanying the scene in the film is Khachaturian's adagio—"carefully chosen and edited," as Chion puts it, "so as not to give the sense that the character is moving to the music or that he hears it" (2001: 19). Khachaturian's ballet is music meant to be moved to, but the characters move as though they were hearing a very different kind of music. And it is, perhaps not insignificantly, music that shares its time signature with a piece heard earlier in the film: the characters move to inaudible echoes of earlier scenes.

Whatever Kubrick's precise intentions in considering Mahler's Symphony No. 3, his interest in it certainly argues against the view that Kubrick had a hard time freeing his imagination from what Kathryn Kalinak called the "tyranny of the temp track" (2010: 105). As much as Kubrick "liked these tracks," as North had observed, Mahler was not part of the temp track—although assistant film editor David de Wilde provided a tape of Mahler's symphony for Kubrick early in the production, the piece was only in the air, not on any sort of temp track. Rather than being wedded to the preexisting compositions because he had gotten used to them in the editing process, Kubrick seems to have gotten attached to the idea of using preexisting compositions.

A (Very) Brief History of the Temp Track

In a magisterial investigation of the genesis of *2001*'s music, Paul Merkeley suggests that "in his goal to make a landmark science-fiction film, perhaps the director was also aiming for a score in a new musical style."(8) This may well have been how Kubrick saw it, at least when it came to the inclusion of atonal avant-garde music like Ligeti's *Requiem*. However, the overall mode of assembly of *2001*'s soundtrack seems if anything like a pronounced backward nod: many of the compositions Kubrick used or considered (above all the *Zarathustra*-fanfare) hail from the period that perhaps did more than any other to shape the musical idiom of the classic Hollywood soundtrack. And as alien as the idea of using only preexisting pieces to score a film would have been to the generation of Herrmann and North, the practice is of course older than actual dedicated film scores.

Until the 1930s, an assortment of preexisting melodies was the rule, not the exception: throughout the silent film era, films arrived in theaters to well-known arrangements of well-known tunes. And even a film with a score as iconic as *Gone With the Wind* could go out for sneak previews still partly tracked to the score for 1937's *The Prisoner of Zenda*. If anything, the rise of the temp score is an index of the relative rise in stature of the soundtrack composer: seasoned professionals working in postproduction to shape the film at eye-level with the director. For that reason, some of the most sought-after composers of the 1950s and 1960s resisted temp tracks as film directors' attempts to take away hard-won autonomy.

Ronald H. Sadoff (166) has pointed out that the introduction of "guide pieces" changed the relationship between sound and visuals. Unlike the early "compilation tracks" that accompanied silent features, the temp track consists of prerecorded sound, and maps onto the finished film "block by block," rather than "moment by moment" (Sadoff 2006: 166–67). Unlike the ululations of a Wurlitzer, the temp track cannot dynamically respond to the film's images, but rather functions as the semirigid scaffold around which those images are organized and assembled. As we shall see, this rigidity is something that Kubrick seems to have been actively in when making his temp track permanent: the soundtrack of *2001* can feel deliberately static and unresponsive.

The guide pieces of a temp track also tend to cluster around sequences and set pieces, thus influencing how individual building blocks of the film are organized. They are not meant to create a greater cohesion, the way themes and instrumentation in a soundtrack composed specifically for a film would. At the same time, guide pieces not only guide the editor, but also the composer. In terms of both economy and economy of prestige, the temp track constitutes a reaction to the elevation of the role of the film composer—an anxious effort to rein in a semiautonomous source of signification in the process of assembling a film. It gives an outsize role to a sound editor, a position that, as Sadoff points out, isn't usually included in a film's credits, and one that usually does not go to a composer.

But when it comes to the audience's relationship to film music, the temp track has been largely judged as leading to the solidification and indeed ossification of compositional styles. Temping, critics of the practice insist, leads to bland interchangeability and to a citationality that can border on plagiarism. It also ossifies a film audience's relationship to the soundtrack—if the same *types* of pieces get recycled again and again, the compass of meanings one is meant to look for by holding up the soundtrack against the image dwindles starkly. This is a risk that by the 1960s was already more than evident—and Kubrick's way of not only assembling his soundtrack, but letting the audience notice the assemblage was intended to subvert rote modes of sound-image combination.

The Permanent Temp

It is worth drawing out in detail just how Kubrick uses his preexisting tracks in *2001: A Space Odyssey*. Where North had offered Kubrick "consistency and homogeneity and contemporary feel," music that had "the ingredients and essence" of the music he had liked as guide pieces, the finished film uses music in much the opposite way. For one thing, it moves its constituent pieces around without any variation. The iconic *Thus Spoke Zarathustra* that opens the film is a literal icon: the same snippet of the same recording of it reoccurs twice in the first twenty minutes; first over the opening sunrise-earthrise sequence, and second over early man's discovery of tools. A third repetition closes the film. And these are repetitions, not reprises. As is customary in a temp track, this is the same recorded sound laid over different images. Similarly, as McQuiston points out, the Blue Danube reenters the soundtrack "resuming from an earlier point compared to where it left off"—it too behaves not like a melody of motif, but a track on a record (McQuiston 2013: 48).

Both moments suggest, in other words, a matter of editing rather than of composition. This is of course something that can be true even of soundtracks composed specifically for the screen, but the way in which the piece is edited unaltered into the soundtrack seems to emphasize the fact that the film encounters here a found sonic object. The images have to huddle around it as though it were a sonic monolith, and they have to do so three times. Precisely by emphasizing how unresponsive the musical material is to the on-screen visuals, the iconic use of the sonorous emblem stages *2001*'s encounters and re-encounters with its soundtrack as technological feats, quite analogous to humanity's encounters and re-encounters with the monoliths.

Another remarkable facet of Kubrick's use of music has to do with what the director does not do: alongside perhaps T. E. Lawrence blowing out his match, the match cut from the bone thrown in the air by an early hominid to the spaceplane approaching the Space Station 5 is perhaps the most iconic transition in cinema history. It is noticeable that this transition, and all the other big jumps the films allows itself, are unmusical. The movie *2001* tells its story across vast gulfs of space, time and logic, and music can help powerfully in bridging those gulfs. But the famous musical pieces—*Thus Spoke Zarathustra*, the *Blue Danube*, Ligeti's *Requiem* and *Lux Aeterna*—are invariably self-contained within the scenes they accompany. In Kubrick's space opera they are numbers rather than a *Zwischenspiel*.

The effect, especially when contrasted with what the film would have felt like with North's score, is to parcel out *2001*, to break down its action into discrete tableaux. This constitutes something of a deliberate withdrawal from a power its music could easily have had. "Compared with seeing," Theodor W. Adorno claimed, "hearing is 'archaic' and has lagged behind technology" (2005: 88). For that very reason music can guide us through moments of visual absence or transformation—whether they are intermezzi in the *opera seria*, or incidental music in the theater, such pieces jump in to hold our attention at moments when visually we might register discontinuity. *2001*'s use of its music only within its individual sequences leaves us alone with the film's massive leaps when they occur.

The only moment at which this does not hold true is the final repetition of Strauss's *Zarathustra*, in which the music indeed seems to aid the image in telescoping space and time. We see the Star Child hovering over the bed in which Bowman has lain just seconds ago, as the hushed opening double low C of *Thus Spoke Zarathustra* play. By the time the trumpets cut in with their C-G-C (Strauss's "dawn" motif), Kubrick's camera has begun pulling into the monolith at the foot of the bed. The film's final match cut, as the blackness of the monolith becomes the blackness of space, accompanies the G-G flat half-step. Each shot seems to respond carefully to Strauss's music. But this only makes more noticeable that this is something the film has not allowed itself to do up until these final moments.

Just as noticeable is that the film's music is entirely non-diegetic: in Arthur C. Clarke's novel (written concurrently with the screenplay), classical music is a constant companion to the astronauts on their long mission to Jupiter—Clarke provides an entire list of pieces. In the 1951 short story "The Sentinel," on which *2001* is based, the narrator finds himself laughing hysterically when he imagines the monolith singing "I'm A Stranger Here Myself" from Kurt Weill's and Ogden Nash's 1943 musical *One Touch of Venus*. In an early draft of the screenplay, Kubrick and Clarke thought they might send one astronaut (who is in hibernation in the final film) hurtling off into space due to a malfunction—beyond rescue by his shipmates, he would request a musical send-off: Beethoven's *Pastoral* symphony (see Gengaro 2013).

With the exception of "Daisy Bell," the song that accompanies HAL's final shutdown, the characters of Kubrick's *2001* never themselves produce music or cause it to be played (Merkley 2007: 3). Music seizes hold of their world from without, it is something that seems to exist only for us spectators. As something that has to be contemplated as a commentary on the images on-screen, as in no way native to them. While the musical pieces Kubrick uses do not necessarily displace diegetic sound—we can hear the piercing signal emitted by the monolith during the *Lux Aeterna* sequence on the moon, Bowman's and Poole's footsteps tap throughout Aram Khachaturian's adagio—no character ever speaks over the music. The pieces that North had wanted to assimilate into a unitary idiom instead litter the film like monoliths. They are made to be noticed, made to stand unintegrated, made to raise questions by their very placement. They colonize the space around them, but the shadow they cast is diffuse, question-begging rather than reassuring.

What, then, is the overall effect of Kubrick's central aesthetic choice? As Merkley has pointed out, for *2001* "Kubrick chose music that had been written not for film but for the concert hall, some of it widely renowned, all of it for large orchestra" or large chorus. This, he argues, results in a thickness of sound far beyond what a traditional studio orchestra would provide. Taken together with the iconic nature of most of the pieces, then, the effect was to stymie the kind of unobtrusiveness a film soundtrack like North's would have provided. We register the music as a presence on-screen, we understand it is being deployed to particular ends. And it comes to us in a shape that signals to the concertgoer in all of us that it needs to be paid attention to. In a cinema, we are allowed to let the music slip in almost semi-consciously, in the concert hall the point is attentiveness.

Of course recognizably distinct musical pieces allow for another level of musical signification. In a film that spans millennia, having the musical soundtrack open up noticeable temporal relationships between its constituent units, whether these manifest as continuity and consonance, or else as discontinuity and counterpoint, can add to the points a film is making about time, history and consciousness. As Merkley puts it, "These 'future archaisms' help to link together the different eras of man; the preserved musical elements lend a continuity to the evolution of the species that would otherwise appear to be disjunct." (11) Precisely because the temp track brings together disconnected pieces, it can prepare us for the task of making connections.

Listening for *2001* in the Twenty-first Century

2001 was to remain formative for Kubrick's relationship to his soundtracks. *A Clockwork Orange* mixed classical cues with synthesizer music by Wendy Carlos, a strategy Kubrick would return to for *The Shining*. For *Full Metal Jacket*, the synth score was by Kubrick's daughter Vivian (under the pseudonym Abigail Mead) and the preexisting music was largely period-appropriate pop. *Barry Lyndon* used Handel's Sarabande from the D minor Suite as an icon in much the same vein as *2001* uses Strauss and Ligeti. At the same time, Kubrick renegotiated the relationship between soundtrack and image in significant ways.

In this respect it is instructive to look at the opening of *The Shining* (1980). This was another film for which Kubrick turned to classical music cues, including more avant-garde and atonal music. But Kubrick draws on two other musical universes—popular song and a soundtrack composed specifically for the film. The piece that accompanies Jack Torrance's first drive to the Overlook Hotel is one such original composition by Wendy Carlos and Rachel Elkind entitled "Rocky Mountains," one of only three cues of the soundtrack to actually be retained in the final film. Its placement in the film suggests that it will function as an overture, and in a sense it does. But unlike what we might expect in a traditional score, the thematic material it introduces will not resurface in the rest of the film. Instead, the piece consists of amelodic underscore with a slow motif that manages to sound foreboding and possibly ironic all at once.

But even this piece engages in a sustained dialogue with identifiable elements of the classical repertoire. The ominous motif carried in the track by some rather synthetic-sounding horns is a direct quotation from the final movement of Hector Berlioz's *Symphonie fantastique*. But the way Carlos and Elkind present the melody, divested of all the burlesque phantasmagoria of Berlioz's "songe d'un nuit de sabbat," serves in a way as an emblem for the way the film that follows will literally chill down King's horror tale—right down to a finale that, in the book, involves a topiary coming to life and in the film revolves around slowly freezing to death in a hedge maze. The music thus foregrounds not just a concern with how *The Shining* will absorb other music, but how it will absorb its own source text.

The recognizable citation peeling out of the amelodic underscore also sets the tone for the way music will function in *The Shining* more broadly. As Christine Lee Gengaro has pointed out, music in *The Shining* comes in two shapes: "avant-garde, possibly atonal, amelodic cues that are extra diegetic" and the "tonal, tuneful and pleasant" (190) music heard by the characters in the film themselves. Berlioz's *Symphonie fantastique* is famously structured around a musical *idée fixe* that is varied throughout its five movements—its inclusion in Carlos and Elkind's score draws attention to the fact that this is a gesture the film never permits its score. If this piece functions as something of an overture, it does so in ways that have nothing to do with thematic material.

It was this mode, rather than the stark side by side of *2001: A Space Odyssey* that would, in the late twentieth and early twenty-first centuries, emerge as a calling card of a certain kind of self-conscious auteurism. In it, dependence on the classical canon paradoxically comes to connote independence from Hollywood studios. It functions as a ready-made index of directorial micro-managing, the director very audibly not handing over the reins to another professional. But it also tends to smooth over the stark contrasts Kubrick was quite deliberately allowing to appear in turning *2001*'s temp track into its soundtrack. Terrence Malick, Lars von Trier and Paul Thomas Anderson are all frank in their indebtedness to the musical soundscape Kubrick created for *2001*. But on close listen the results of this debt wind up functioning and sounding quite different from what Kubrick's distinctive approach.

Terrence Malick is an inveterate plunderer of the classical canon. The "Aquarium" vignette of Saint-Saëns *Carnaval des animaux* becomes a kind of dreamy leitmotif for *Days of Heaven* (1979), *The Thin Red Line* (1998) features a well-known soundtrack by Hans Zimmer, but also finds room for music by Charles Ives, Gabriel Fauré and Arvo Pärt. *The New World* (2005) turns to Wagner's *Das Rheingold* for its opening and later includes Mozart on the soundtrack, even though most of the music is either by composer James Horner or by Francesco Lupica performing on his "Cosmic Beam." *The Tree of Life* (2011), in which Brad Pitt's character dreams of being a musician and in which his record collection functions as a Greek chorus of sorts, features music by Smetana, Schumann, Brahms, and Holst.

But while, as Gengaro points out, Malick's instincts "echo Kubrick's modus operandi" (Gengaro 2019: 48), his practice is in many places very distinct from Kubrick's, at least when it comes to *2001: A Space Odyssey*. For one thing, Malick's cuts come from the more tonal, accessible end of contemporary classical music. Arvo Pärt, Einojuhani Rautavaara, Henryk Gorecki, and John Tavener all tend toward recognizable harmonies and a pseudo-sacral meditativeness. And while Malick like Kubrick delights in cuts and sequences that transcend traditional logics of filmic narrative, Malick tends to use recognizable musical material to connect his disparate tableaux, where, especially in *2001*, Kubrick uses music to further heighten the space between them.

In 2012's *To the Wonder*, Malick turns to Wagner, in a gesture that may both serve as an interesting example and as almost a thesis statement of how Malick sees himself managing and utilizing preexisting musical material. The sequence opens with Marina (Olga Kurylenko) and Neil (Ben Affleck) in Paris, deciding to move to the United States. As Ottorini Respighi's "Ancient Air and Dances" suite enters the soundtrack, the camera pulls into the small replica of the Statue of Liberty that until 2014 stood in the Jardin du Luxembourg, then tracks over a body of water, then the undulating crabgrass of Oklahoma. The viewer will recognize the body of water as the tidal flats around Mont St. Michel where Marina and Neil head toward the beginning of the film, to the strains of Wagner's prelude to *Parsifal*.

In the film's final minute, the film crosses the Atlantic again in the opposite direction: Marina pictures herself walking through the Oklahoma prairie and, as the *Parsifal* prelude plays, suddenly finds herself bathed in the light of "the wonder"—Mont St. Michel. The classical pieces thus work to stitch together the different locations that the film's main characters seek to reconcile. Rather than discrete tableaux, each piece performs and re-performs the leap across the Atlantic, across time, from the beginning of a relationship to its dissolution. And they are pieces one and all chosen to highlight this bridging function: Respighi "Ancient Airs" are semi-transcriptions of sixteenth-century lute pieces, an attempt to capture ancient sounds by means of a modern orchestra. And Wagner's opera opens on the grail castle where, as its steward Gurnemanz puts it to young Parsifal, "time becomes space."

Malick's classical music almost invariably functions in this way: it allows this meditative filmmaker to fold time and space, to unite incompatible perspectives and memories. This is how *The New World* stages the moment where English settlers and Native Americans show up on each other's horizon to Wagner's prelude to *Das Rheingold*, a piece that literally assembles a new world out of a simple E flat major chord. That is how *The Tree of Life* can edit together rapid, momentary impressions of a Texas childhood to the surges of Smetana's *Vltava*. In this the music functions similarly to Malick's characteristic monologues: in the bravura sequence halfway through *The Tree of Life* in which the film leaves Waco, Texas for a self-consciously Kubrickian fast-forward through creation, it remains connected to the story of the O'Brien family by dint of two elements of the soundtrack: Zbigniew Preisner's "Lacrimosa 2" and Jessica Chastain's voice-over, both of which echo the aftershocks of grief over the death of one of the O'Briens' sons.

A more innovative use of Kubrickian temp track techniques comes from Lars von Trier. Von Trier's *Melancholia* (2011) uses Wagner's prelude to *Tristan und Isolde* to mark the titular yearning. It reoccurs as the film's only soundtrack at certain intervals, and while at first it irrupts into the scenes in Kubrickian isolation (i.e., drowning out any diegetic sound the soundtrack might wish to include), in the film's final seconds it finds itself overwhelmed by diegetic noise. The film is not shy in invoking Kubrick's legacy: the half dozen sequences Wagner's prelude underpins involve heavenly bodies, outer space and cosmic connections, frank in their Kubrickian ambitions. As the film's sole musical soundtrack, repeated several times throughout the film, it becomes a musical icon very much in the vein of *2001*'s use of Strauss. Von Trier has described this effect as deliberately "vulgar."

The prelude's constant straining and desirous striving nevertheless ushers in in each iteration death, nonexistence, annihilation. As Ahmed Elbehlawy has put it, "Wagner's music gains more importance precisely when it stops; in other words, when it returns to where it came from" (2017: 163). And that place is not necessarily silence: in several instances (including the final seconds of the film) what drowns out Wagner is the deafening grumble of the titular planet slamming into the earth, according to von Trier "the loudest thing I've ever mixed" (von Trier quoted in Coulthard 2013: 123).

Lisa Coulthard has referred to von Trier's way of having the sound design disrupt and put pressure on the non-diegetic music as "dirty sound" (123). Where *2001* generates meaning out of leaving its classical music pure and largely uncorrupted by in-scene sound, let alone dialogue, von Trier means to distress his music. In the opening half of *Melancholia*, the titular planet is a distant blip in the sky, noticed only by Kirsten Dunst's Justine—and Wagner's prelude plays over and in fact drowns out the quotidian squabbles and domestic scenes into which he interrupts unbidden. But in the final minutes, this changes. A low-frequency growl eventually swallows up Wagner, constituting something of a reply to the pristine silence in which Kubrick encases his classical cues.

But it also points to a fact of physics: Kubrick's music tends to enter, as a kind of music of the spheres, when the vacuum of space would allow no plausible diegetic sound. In *Melancholia*, the music grows distressed when outer space enters into a distinctly human cosmos: when the giant planet melancholia looms like a pale sun behind Justine, Claire and her son Leo holding hands on their front lawn, the strains of *Tristan* seem to pull it toward the camera, but its roar also slowly drowns out Wagner. Both Malick and von Trier pose a question that Kubrick doesn't: what happens when cosmic forces enter into a recognizably human, private, familial space. And both filmmakers seem more interested in the reverberations of the cosmic within the private than the dissipation of the human within the cosmic. They can signal this shift in focus by the way they treat their classical tracks.

Paul Thomas Anderson's films frequently rely on a mix of pastiche and interpolation for their soundtracks, in a way that builds on Kubrick's approach, but distends it as well. The soundtrack for *There Will Be Blood* (2007) includes music by Johannes Brahms and Arvo Pärt, but Jonny Greenwood's score also utilizes preexisting material—the Academy of Motion Picture Arts and Sciences ruled the soundtrack ineligible for the Best Soundtrack Oscar on account of it. To the *New York Times*, Greenwood, bassist of the band Radiohead, describes his composing process as "a really ugly cross-pollination"—his soundtracks consist of Greenwood-penned material that nevertheless sounds like other composer's, and works by classical composers that feel integrated into the sound world he has established. In *There Will Be Blood*, Greenwood's role is halfway between a composer and a curator.

Consider a scene in which Eli (Paul Dano) confronts Daniel Plainview (Daniel Day-Lewis), which ends with them wrestling in oily mud. It is a nervy scene, one of the intense scenes of violence and humiliation that punctuate the often ponderous film. The soundtrack is Arvo Pärt's *Fratres*, a well-known and recognizable piece. And yet it probably isn't right to say that the scene is edited to fit it. *Fratres* exists in more than a dozen different written and recorded versions, all of which differ with respect to instrumentation and tempo. To pick *Fratres* for your soundtrack is thus to really *pick*: the version for cello and piano that Anderson turns to here is by far the most tense. It dissolves the piece's constitutive eight chord sequences into arpeggios, and in place of the percussion most versions of the piece rely on this version relies on *pizzicato*, a common trope in soundtracks for generating suspense. In other words, while picking Pärt as his soundtrack, Anderson seems to submit to someone else's rhythms and meanings; but by integrating a specific version into the soundtrack, he actually has Pärt do the scene's bidding in a way that resembles a traditional film score.

The most frequent use of Kubrick's technique has been parodic in nature. The ostentatious use of preexisting musical icons, especially of the musical icons Kubrick made famous, is of course welcome fodder for pastiche. But even when their turn to Kubrick seems at best semi-serious, films have to give serious thought to how preexisting music can be deployed vis-à-vis a film's visuals. In Michael Winterbottom's 2014 film *The Trip to Italy*, the music of Richard Strauss makes a distinctly Kubrickian appearance in a mode that feels half like parody and half like something else entirely. The film, a sequel to the miniseries/film *The Trip* from 2010, finds the comedians Steve Coogan and Rob Brydon (playing fictionalized versions of themselves) traveling through Italy on assignment to review a series of restaurants. Along the way they bicker, debate the work of Alanis Morissette, follow in the footsteps of Shelley and Byron, and confront their own mortality.

As they set out on a boat into the Gulf of Spezia (where Shelley's *Don Juan* sank on July 8, 1822), the soundtrack turns to the achingly sincere opening bars of Strauss's setting of Eichendorff's "Im Abendrot." It's a gesture of finality—the song cycle is known as Strauss's "Four Last Songs," "Im Abendrot" is traditionally played last in the cycle (although it was composed first), and ends by asking "Is this perhaps death?" Winterbottom, however, restricts himself to the twenty-bar orchestral opening—and he ends up repeating the exact same musical icon throughout the film. There is a sly joke in using this specific piece in this specific way: *The Trip to Italy* is the second iteration of fictional Coogan and Brydon traveling and confronting their own mortality (the previous *Trip* took them into the north of England and the gravesites of another set of romantic poets).

The piece thus raises the question of what happens to finality repeated. While the effect in each instance is ravishing, the repetition has the effect of giving the film's melancholy something ready-made. Strauss's anguished, meditative reconciliation with life's final mysteries turns into a sonic traffic signal: midlife crisis this way. And the way it builds toward, but never quite reaches the vocal portion of the *Lied*, too, registers as a sort of joke. "You and I have gone through trouble and joy together hand in hand," the singer intones at the beginning of "Im Abendrot." Cutting off the song before it ever gets to the line, the film seems to be doing its protagonists' bidding. "Coogan" and "Brydon" in each iteration of their trip seem deeply concerned about being misperceived as a couple; by cutting out the couple-y bits from "Im Abendrot," the soundtrack obliges even their most childish anxieties.

And in so doing, it becomes in its own way moving. Strauss's song, in Winterbottom's hands, becomes both a signifier for the process of growing old and a signifier for all the absurd things we reach for during that process. By making the temp his soundtrack, Winterbottom makes explicit something that Kubrick could still plausibly deny: Strauss becomes accoutrement, gesture, legerdemain. He turns an index of directorial narcissism into a monument to his characters' self-involvement. Where Malick and Anderson seem to regard Kubrickian interpolation as a way of suggesting seamlessness and unity, von Trier and Winterbottom turn to him as a guide for how to double or even triple up on irony in a scene. The fact that neither side is wrong about Kubrick's use of music is perhaps the greatest testament to the enduring power of the music of *2001*.

Stanley Kubrick's use of temp tracks has to be seen against the backdrop of the dominance of the coherent, through-composed orchestral soundtrack. As they became something close to the norm (and only *where* they become something close to the norm), his use of musical icons could charge with meaning an aspect of film that the through-composed soundtrack had subsumed under the dictate of what we might call brand identity. It allowed filmmakers to signal auteurism, to make points about film sound that even viewers not well versed in the history of film soundtracks could pick up on. By seemingly putting on a record from their own collection, the director could center their decisions as *the* central meaning of a particular scene or film.

The use of iconic preexisting musical pieces co-evolves with the rise of the soundtrack album as commodity. And in many respects it functions as its other. While those soundtracks perform uniqueness, while being secretly iterable (from the factory-like production of a predictable sound among Hans Zimmer's stable of composers, via the self-citation of James Horner or mid-period John Williams), the temp track technique projects an auteurist uniqueness by foregrounding the iterability (indeed canonicity) of what we hear. And it rewards recognition and association in ways that through-composed soundtracks do not.

There is, in other words, nothing that recognizing the muffled drums from the late James Horner's *Braveheart* (1995) as a rather naked import from his earlier soundtrack to *Legends of the Fall* (1994) does for our understanding of either film. Understanding how a director *uses* a recognizable piece, by contrast, rather showily highlights an entire level of signification that the studio soundtrack (ironically by means of using temp tracks) threatens to hand over to rote and unreflective audience response. This may account for the enduring appeal of Kubrick's use of the musical icon: Kubrick kept open a level of signification for commentary that elsewhere the collaborative process of film production threatened to close. And *2001*'s soundtrack is and remains the locus classicus of this level of signification for a simple reason: Kubrick's circuitous path back to *Zarathustra* constitutes its founding myth.

Works Cited

Adorno, Theodor W. 2005. *In Search of Wagner*. London: Verso.
Benson, Michael. 2018. *Space Odyssey: Stanley Kubrick, Arthur C. Clarke and the Making of a Masterpiece*. New York: Simon & Schuster.
Chion, Michel. 2001. *Kubrick's Cinema Odyssey*. London: British Film Institute.
Coulthard, Lisa. 2013. "Dirty Sound: Haptic Sound in New Extremism," in Carol Vernallis, Amy Herzog and John Richardson (eds.), *The Oxford Handbook of Sound and Image in Digital Media*. Oxford: Oxford University Press, 115–26.
Elbehlawy, Ahmed. 2017. *Woman in Lars von Trier's Cinema, 1996–2014*. Berlin: Springer.
Gengaro, Christine Lee. 2013. *Listening to Stanley Kubrick: The Music in his Films*. Toronto: Scarecrow Press.
Gengaro, Christine Lee. 2019. "Looking Back, Looking Ahead," in Michael Broderick (ed.), *The Kubrick Legacy*. London: Routledge, 37–51.

Kalinak, Kathryn. 2010. *Film Music: A Very Short Introduction*. Oxford: Oxford University Press.
McQuiston, Kate. 2013. *We'll Meet Again: Musical Design in the Films of Stanley Kubrick*. Oxford: Oxford University Press.
Merkley, Paul. 2007. "'Stanley Hates This but I Like It!': North vs. Kubrick on the Music for *2001: A Space Odyssey*," *Film Music* 2(1): 1–34.
Patterson, David W. 2004. "Music, Structure and Metaphor in Stanley Kubrick's *2001: A Space Odyssey*," *American Music* 22(3): 444–74.
Sadoff, Ronald H. 2006. "The Role of the Music Editor and the 'Temp Track' as Blueprint for the Scores, Source Music, and Source Music of Films," *Popular Music*, 25(2):165–83.
Shaw-Miller, Simon. 2017. *Eye hEar: The Visual in Music*. London: Routledge.

9

Fade to Crude:
Petro-Horror and Kubrick's *The Shining*

Pansy Duncan

Few horror films have enjoyed as much critical attention as *The Shining* (1980), Stanley Kubrick's first and only outing in the genre. Few scenes *within The Shining*, meanwhile, have enjoyed as much attention as the so-called "blood elevator" sequence—a nightmarish, twenty-two-second long hallucination on the part of the film's resident psychic child, Danny (Danny Lloyd). Appearing not once but four times in the course of the film, the hallucination makes its debut relatively early on, in a scene that opens with Danny in conversation with his imaginary friend, Tony ("he lives in my mouth"), in the bathroom mirror. Chancing upon this intimate exchange, the Steadicam-mounted camera pushes stealthily toward the boy, before drifting past Danny himself and "into" his reflection in the vanity mirror—a standard filmic convention for transitioning from the "real" world into an imagined or interior world. At this point, we cut to a static, symmetrical frontal shot of two fire-engine-red elevator doors in the vacant Art Deco foyer of what we now know to be the Overlook Hotel. Suddenly, through the join in the door of the left elevator, a torrent of blood surges into the lobby in fulsome slow motion, splashing up the walls and coursing across the granite floor to the backdrop of Krzysztof Penderecki's rumbling, ominous score. There are two quick cutaways, both of them flash-forward to later moments in the film: the first features the ghostly twin girls Danny will encounter in the corridors of the Overlook, while the second features Danny's face in close-up, pallid with terror before the expression of his father's homicidal rage. But these cutaways barely register for the viewer amid the horror of the blood itself, which ultimately envelops the camera, obliterating our view of the space and, in the process, our grip on what we've just seen. Widely recognized today as one of "the most effectively uncanny or frightening moments in cinema" history, this iconic scene has become a mainstay of critical accounts of the film, with few commentators passing up the opportunity to extol its visual effects, to recount its troubled production history, or to evoke the "horror" it engenders in the putative spectator (Luckhurst 2013: 9).

Yet while the first three-quarters of the scene have inspired considerable commentary, its final moments, in which a surge of blood engulfs the camera for a full six seconds of screen time, have passed almost entirely without mention. What is at

Figure 9.1 *The Shining* (Stanley Kubrick, 1980), copyright Warner Brothers.

Figure 9.2 *The Shining* (Stanley Kubrick, 1980), copyright Warner Brothers.

stake in this moment of Stygian blackness, a moment so prolonged that the diegetic black of blood mutates into the non-diegetic black of what Richard Misek (2017) calls "the black screen"? Representationally, of course, what we are presented with here is quite literally nothing—the absence, not just of an image, but of form and of the light that serves as the condition of form; of "black screen[s]" like these, in fact, Misek has contended quite confidently that "the black screen itself . . . communicates nothing beyond its own blackness" (120). Materially, however, what we see is undeniably something. If, as Misek also notes, the "white [screen] is . . . the light of a projector *before* a film is threaded through its gate," the black screen, conversely, flags the presence of the unexposed film stock itself—film stock in its raw, pre-representational state (120). And, by 1980, film stocks were increasingly constituted not of acetate or cellulose nitrate, but of polyester, a petroleum derivative. While polyester stock did not come into mainstream use for cinema exhibition until the 1990s, its early application to 8mm and 16mm film stocks meant that many of the low-budget hits of 1970s horror were shot on that format, from *Texas Chainsaw Massacre* (Tobe Hooper, 1974) to *Halloween* (Carpenter, 1978) (Enticknapp 2005: 40). If the liquid that dominates the first section of the sequence is blood, then, it is another kind of liquid—crude oil—that rises to the surface in the final few frames of the sequence. The effect of this revelation is twofold. On the one hand, *The Shining*'s striking visual furniture—from the garish mustards and pastels of ballroom to the raspberry red of this wave of blood—emerge as so much "eyewash" (Kittler 1999: 1), mere masks for a more foundational petrochemical base. On the other, the objects in the mise-en-scène are shown to be composed and constituted of oil (a substance long celebrated for its capacity to assume any form, texture or color—"lightweight, durable . . . chemically inert, endlessly remoldable" [Freinkel 2011: 61]—oil-based plastics like polyester have been pressed into all kinds of service in Western consumer cultures, from garbage bags to artificial hips, and from Tupperware to toys). As the wave of blood engulfs the camera, *The Shining* reveals film's dark, petroleum substrate, while gesturing more broadly to the petrocultural foundations of our vivid, Crayola-colorful universe.

Building on this re-inscription of the "blood elevator" scene, this chapter makes a simple but striking argument about *The Shining*, and about the "New Regime" horror (Clover 2015: 3) of which the film appeared to mark the generic apotheosis. It contends that, torrents of blood notwithstanding, the sense of dread famously induced by the film converges not around blood but crude oil. It further contends that, in this respect, *The Shining* moves beyond what Eugene Thacker (2011) calls "human fear in a human world" (8) to connect with what Patricia Yaeger (2017) has dubbed the "energy unconscious" (443), tapping into contemporary anxieties about Western petrocultures' radical dependence on this "animate, creeping ooze" (Thacker, 92)—a fossil fuel composed of buried geologic deposits of organic material. I will develop this argument as follows. Attending closely to the film's material register rather than to its representational register (Brown 1996: 4), I will identify moments of substitution in which petroleum or petroleum derivatives take the place of blood as the object of what Linda Williams (1991) refers to as horror's signature scenes of "gross display" (3) or what Steffen Hantke (2004) calls horror's "money shot[s]" (57). In these scenes, I will show, *The Shining* applies a set of spectacular techniques (the close-up, the swish-pan, slow motion, the musical burst) conventionally used to exhibit the "unseemly, gratuitous" presence of bloody violence to crude oil and its byproducts, with an eye to exacting an appropriate visceral response from the audience. In the process, I will contend, *The Shining* achieves two effects. On the one hand, it speaks to contemporary anxieties about Western petrocultures' reliance on a resource whose availability, by the late 1970s, was increasingly in question and whose environmental effects seemed increasingly nefarious. On the other, it retroactively reframes the 1970s "New Regime" horror as a genre awash in oil.

Certainly, to identify oil, not blood, as *The Shining*'s primary object of dread is to fly in the face of orthodox understandings both of the film itself and of the 1970s "New Regime" horror whose logics it condensed, pastiched and refracted. Blood is a staple of critical accounts of *The Shining*, with critics devoting outsize attention to the small handful of scenes in the film that involve or imply gore: the "REDRUM" sequence, the murder of the Overlook's chef, Dick Hallorann (Scatman Crothers), and, of course, Danny's hallucination of an "ocean of blood flowing from the elevator" (Cocks 1999: 2). And blood is also a staple of critical accounts of film horror more generally, accounts that have effectively installed blood as the genre's signature secretion. For Williams (1991), for example, whose seminal essay, "Film Bodies," developed an influential somatic taxonomy of the "body genres," blood is the horror film's most reliable visual talisman; just as melodrama's "ecstasy" (anguish or loss) is "shown by" tears, and pornography's (orgasm) is "shown by" ejaculate, so the horror genre's ecstasy, namely the emotion of horror, finds a physical substantiation on-screen in the form of blood (9). For Barbara Creed (2002)—cribbing heavily from Julia Kristeva's classic of psychoanalysis, *Powers of Horror* (1982)—it is blood (and only secondarily "urine, excrement, and bile") that expresses the horror genre's effort to "point [. . .] to the fragility of the symbolic order in the domain of the body" (74). And for Cosimo Urbano (2004), horror's "visual displays of gore" are one of the genre's universals, even as horror's generic "essence" is located elsewhere (25). While in general a disputatious bunch, horror scholars present a united front when it comes to the critical conjunction of horror (a genre, and thus a complex industrial and aesthetic assemblage) and blood (a bodily fluid that serves to deliver nutrients and oxygen to the cells).

This tight critical fit between blood and the horror film has had profound consequences for our understanding of the genre's broader purchase on what Robin Wood has famously and influentially called our "collective nightmare" (qtd. in Benshoff 2017: xiv). More specifically, it has helped sustain and propagate a very particular claim about the *contents* of that "nightmare." In general—the pig's gore that drenches the titular protagonist of *Carrie* (Brian De Palma, 1976) notwithstanding—the blood that saturates the "new regime" horror belongs to its characters, marking the violation of human bodies and the desecration of human flesh. Horror criticism's instatement of blood as horror's signature liquid, then, has gone hand in hand with its instatement of the specter of human psychic, social and physical harm at the heart of horror's "collective nightmare." To couple horror with blood, that is, is to sustain a model of horror, Thacker puts it, as a genre "about human in a human world" (8). This is certainly true of *The Shining*, where the blood that flushes through the elevator sequence has served as crucial evidence for claims that the "collective nightmare[s]" into which the film taps trade in the spectacle of harm done to *human* groups or individuals—whether the genocide of Native Americans (Cook 1984: 2), the oppression of the proletariat (Jameson 2013: 95), the genocidal trauma of the Holocaust (Cocks 1999: 17) or the violence boiling away in the conventional, bourgeois family unit. Across criticism of *The Shining*, then, references to blood have helped cement our sense that the film's primary concerns are human concerns, whether these are construed literally as the problem of violence within the family, or allegorically as the memory of the Holocaust.

To draw attention to the crude oil that underwrites the "blood elevator" sequence, then, is to call into question our foundational assumptions about both the specific fluids in which film horror is steeped and the specific anxieties it channels. First, it points up the sheer diversity of fluids that have suffused and that continue to suffuse this evolving generic formation, whether conspicuously or inconspicuously. Slime, ooze and mist, for example, have long been a visual mainstay of the gothic, sci-fi horror or psychological subgenres, from 1958's *The Blob* (Irvin S. Yeaworth), which saw strawberry-colored alien goo engulf a small town in America, to Frank Darabont's 2007 *The Mist*, in which a thick fog rolls in and engulfs a tiny seaside town. And while the "New Regime" horror that dominated the 1970s and 1980s— decisive decades in the history of horror scholarship—traded primarily in human plasma, the crude oil that underwrites the "blood elevator" sequence suggests that other liquids might also be coursing through these films' veins. Second, it points up the variety of forms of anxiety that have animated the genre. As Peter Hutchings has noted, the 1960s and 1970s were dominated by "the erosion of dominant social norms and authority," fuelling anxieties about social, sexual and bodily transgression (Hutchings 2017: 296).

Yet while accounts of these anxieties have to date shaped the way we understand horror, peak oil and human-induced climate change have foregrounded a different set of cultural anxieties—anxieties that Yaeger has captured under the banner of the "energy unconscious." At the heart of the "energy unconscious" is the repressed but powerful knowledge that, as Imre Szeman and Dominic Boyer (2017) have put it, "our everyday practices and activities have been shaped by energy" (8) in ways that far exceed our control or knowledge. And if awareness of our originary dependence on fossil fuels, or any other one of Earth's finite resources, can be said to form a "collective nightmare," it is a nightmare organized not around the threat of human (psychic, social or physical) harm, but rather, as Thacker has put it, around "the *limits* of the human as it confronts a world that is . . . also a Planet (the world-without-us)" (8).[1]

Both oil itself, and the alternative anxieties it channels, are on full display in a number of recent releases with debts to the "horror" genre, from Paul Thomas Anderson's 2007 masterpiece *There Will Be Blood*, which uses the spectacle of peak oil in the early twenty-first century as a pretext for revisiting the oil industry's early-twentieth-century origins, to the less widely acclaimed *Deepwater Horizon* (Peter Berg, 2016) and *The Last Winter* (Larry Fessenden, 2006). A filmic remediation of Upton Sinclair's notorious muckraking classic *Oil!* (1927), *There Will Be Blood* repeatedly applies to the visualization of crude oil a set of generic techniques more typically applied to the visualization of blood. Indeed, this substitution is clearly signaled by the film's title, which invites us to read the oil on which the film's narrative manifestly turns as a kind of proxy for the crimson body fluid that won't appear in any great quantity until the final grisly showdown between its two central players. The scene in which protagonist Daniel Plainview (Daniel Day-Lewis) and an unnamed collaborator first discover oil is exemplary of this substitution.[2] Like many climactic scenes in the film horror canon, the scene opens with a studied banality, showing Daniel and his partner winding up the drill on their derrick and dropping it over the side. Suddenly, however, Daniel's partner lets the rope slip from his grip, sending it slicing through the shaft as the drill-bit races to the bottom of the well. After a brief cut to an up-shot of the two men leaning over the lip of the well, we are back at its bottom, circling the almost fully submerged drill-bit as the lustrous, satiny oil bubbles around it in a spectacle reminiscent of scenes depicting what Philip Simpson (2004) calls "graphic gore" (85). Even more notable for our purposes than *There Will Be Blood*'s attention to oil-as-blood is the fact that this substitution is articulated through a set of characterological and formal cues that are strongly reminiscent of *The Shining*. There is Jonny Greenwood's Penderecki-esque score; Robert Elswit's unsettling, Kubrick-esque wide shots; and Daniel Day-Lewis's exaggerated, Jack Nicholson-esque performance as Plainview. In this sense, *There Will Be Blood*'s substitution of oil for blood against the backdrop of the early twentieth-century oilfield may be understood as an attempt to at once draw attention to and provide prehistory of a similar dynamic in *The Shining*.

Yet while *There Will Be Blood*'s affinity with oil is self-evident, the argument that *The Shining* inscribes petroleum products as the horrific object of its scenes of "gross display" is less immediately obvious. In the twenty-first century our dependence on oil has become a matter of profound public concern; inevitabilities, but were these concerns as pressing across the late 1970s when *The Shining* was in pre-production? Historical accounts of the period suggest that they were. Indeed, by the late 1970s oil was more deeply woven into the fabric of American life than ever before: decades of cheap gasoline had seen US car registrations increase fourfold between 1945 and 1973, from 25 million to over 100 million, and per capita oil consumption had more than doubled, meaning that, by 1972, oil accounted for 45.6 percent of US energy consumption (Painter 2012: 25).

Indeed, oil's saturation of everyday life in the 1970s routinely exceeded, quite literally, the nation's ability to contain it, as the increasingly ubiquitous cultural figure of the "oil spill" became the focus of an embryonic environmental movement (LeMenager 2012: 63). And *The Shining* itself does not let us forget for a moment the petrocultural foundations on which the Torrance family's troubled domestic life depends. The film initiates us into its unsettling landscapes by inviting us to follow Jack Torrance's yellow VW as it snakes through the snowy peaks of Glacier National Park; several crucial scenes in the film (the family's drive to the hotel, Hallorann's rescue effort in the snowcat) take place not in the semi-domestic confines of the hotel, but across the network of transportation and communication networks that feed and sustain it; while Danny's relentless circuits of the hotel corridors on his "big wheel" sound a tattoo across the second half of the film. Yet if the 1970s was a decade marked by a sense of oil's (over-)abundance, it was also a decade marked by an emerging sense of its scarcity, due to a series of crises in the availability of oil that elevated petrol prices, lightened the wallets of car owners, and put a strain on the American economy. Precipitating this crisis was a series of geopolitical upheavals in the Middle East, from the 1973 Arab-Israeli War, which led to an embargo of oil shipments to the United States and a cutback in oil production in response to US aid to Israel, to the

Iranian Revolution (1978), which saw Iran fall to religious fundamentalism (Painter 2012: 34). In the 1970s, as today, America's shaky petrochemical foundations could not be ignored.

But how to begin tracing, through *The Shining*'s inscription of petroleum products as the horrific object of the scene of "gross display," the liquescent profile of this oil unconscious? The film's first moment of petro-horror, I suggest, occurs about two-thirds of the way into the narrative in a scene that affords Wendy her first glimpse into the extent of her husband's mental disorder. Already wary of Jack's increasingly volatile temper, Duvall's Wendy has been cowering in the caretaker's quarters along with her young son. At some point, eager to reassess the situation, she props Danny in front of an episode of *Road Runner* and descends into the central atrium of the hotel, the Colorado Lounge, where Jack has set up his office. All the filmic conventions in the scene serve to heighten the suspense as she approaches the writing desk calling Jack's name, her sitcom-sweet tones belied by the fact that she is carrying a baseball bat. The mobile, Steadicam-mounted camera that tracks her in long shot as she moves through the airy space is a slasher genre signature, designed, as Adam Rockoff (2013) puts it, to "mirror the stalker's gaze" (93). The Pendereckian strings rising on the soundtrack as she approaches the typewriter are an equally hackneyed device intended to mark the imminence of the horrific "money shot" (Lerner 2009: 21). And when Wendy reaches the typewriter, the shot of her face we are delivered is a case study in what Williams (2006) describes as "the woman's terrified look at the horrible body of the monster" (62). With the camera located behind and below the looming shadow of the typewriter itself, which takes on enormous proportions in the extreme foreground of the shot, we see Wendy's face rise slowly into the frame. We linger for several, prolonged seconds on Duvall's soft, doll-like features as she stands over the typewriter, her breath quickening, her pupils dilated, her eyes wide, and her expression a floppy mask of horror. As viewers, we are now desperate for the reverse shot, desperate to see what she sees.

It is therefore notable that when the "monster" is finally revealed, and we are afforded the reverse shot we have been waiting for, there is no monster at all. Rather, we are shown a page loaded up in the typewriter, bearing a single, famous phrase repeated ad infinitum: "All work and no play makes Jack a dull boy." We cut briefly back to Wendy's horrified face, before cutting again to what she sees, zooming in, this time, on the thick stack of pages sitting next to the typewriter. As Wendy's fingers leaf through the pile, the litany continues, the mind-boggling monotony of the repetition only heightened by occasional formatting variations and typographic errors. But what is the central object on which this scene's mobilization of classic horror conventions turns? It is easy enough, of course, to read the horror of this scene through a psychological lens, treating the pages of obsessive, obsidian typescript as a signifier, perhaps the *ultimate* signifier, of Jack's madness. As Shoshana Felman (2003) has observed, "madness appears in discourse as a passion for the signifier, as a *repetition of signs*—without regard for what is signified" (108), and the text is nothing if not repetitive. Yet when read through the lens of petroculture, this repetition points us not just to the "sign," as Felman puts it, but to the *materiality of the signifier*— in this case, the black ink

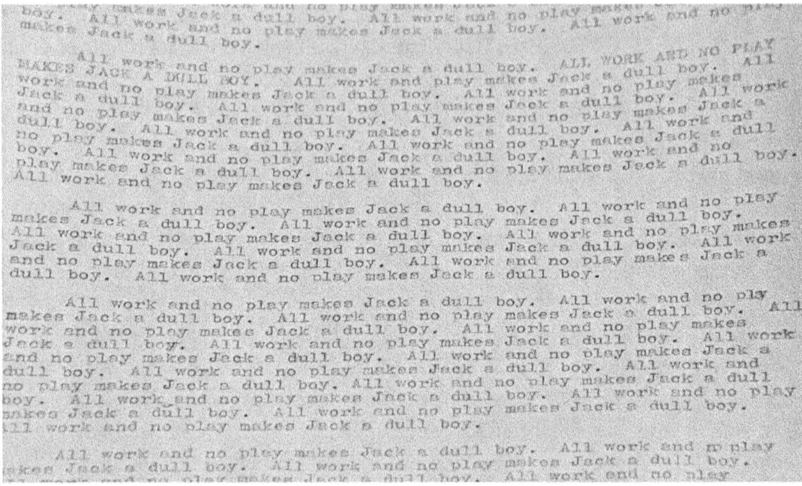

Figure 9.3 *The Shining* (Stanley Kubrick, 1980), copyright Warner Brothers.

that comprises it. And as Stephanie LeMenager (2014) reminds us, "the ink used in modern print media is essentially petroleum" (100). In this sense, the horror of the scene may lie not in the revelation of Jack's psychological state, but in the image of the oil-based ink that Jack is spilling on the page, exposing the dark petrochemical heart of mechanical inscription.

But the scene's establishment of petroleum as an object of horror does not end with the discovery of Jack's demented manuscript. After a final reverse shot of the breathless, trembling Wendy, we cut to another "black screen," a seemingly unbroken, un-illuminated field of darkness that serves, as our rereading of the blood elevator sequence suggests, as a nod to polyester film stock's petrochemical origins. As our eyes slowly adjust to the change in the quantity of light, we are able to make out the shape of an image in the blackness, and to pick out a wall adorned by a series of framed pictures, although beyond this our whereabouts are unclear. As if in answer to this implicit question, the camera glides to the left, reaches the edge of the near-black wall, and reveals the brightly lit Colorado Lounge beyond. There—the right half of the frame masked by the wall in the foreground and the deep space of the left half of the frame flooded with snowy daylight—we glimpse Wendy. Still poring over the typewriter, she is shown this time from afar and from behind, underscoring her vulnerability and suggesting the point of view of a concealed and/or predatory observer. At this point, a silhouetted head and shoulders—unmistakably Jack's—detach themselves from the wall masking the right half of the frame, as if issuing directly from the primordial geologic ooze. This near-perfect elision of Jack's perspective with the reservoir of petrochemical blackness from which he emerges serves to confer on that oily trace some of the horror that already accrues to Jack himself.

Petroleum's status as the horrific object of *The Shining*'s central scenes of "gross display" is reinforced in a later sequence, which shows Danny, sleepwalking, inscribe

Figure 9.4 *The Shining* (Stanley Kubrick, 1980), copyright Warner Brothers.

the word REDRUM on the door of his parents' bedroom in lipstick. For most critics, of course, the scene is the apogee of the film's aesthetics of blood. As Amy Nolan (2011) confidently announces, "REDRUM is the blood that signifies mass slaughter" (190), while for David A. Cook (1984), "'Redrum,' as Danny first discovers it, [is] the anagram for 'Murder'" (2). In this reading, the word "redrum" is merely "murder" in mirror script, and the instrument used to inscribe it, namely lipstick, is merely a vehicle for the color red (a color that, connoting blood, complements the connotations of bloody death that attach to the term "murder"). By these lights, that is, the material tool used (lipstick) and the literal word spelled out (REDRUM) are simply ciphers—codes that, properly translated, return us to the familiar visual paraphernalia of the horror film. What would it mean, then, to read the horror of this scene of "gross display" with an eye not to its encoded meaning, but to the material objects used in its production— to trace, as Brown (1996) has put it, "the pressure that such materiality . . . exerts on . . . texts" (4)? To do so, I suggest, would be to note that, while at an iconic level, the red mirror script recalls blood, and at a symbolic level, it evokes a criminal act of murder, at the indexical or material level, it has a very different set of affinities. As Cecily Devereaux has shown, lipstick was the cornerstone of an emerging commerce in cosmetics that had a foundational relationship with the oil industries, with petroleum a central ingredient of mascara, lipstick, and foundation, which in turn made up what Devereaux (2017) calls "the petrocultural feminine" (167). It is not just that, as Teresa Riordan (2004) has put it, the 1950s and 1960s saw petroleum turning into a kind of "motherlode of new wonder synthetics" (30–31). Rather, so tight was the connection between mid-century North American cosmetic companies and the petroleum industry that the fuel industry itself began to produce cosmetics, with the oil and gas company Esso, for example, "patent[ing] a new mascara made with hydrocarbon solvents" (Riordan, 31).

Indeed, lipstick's own debts to the oil industry and to petroleum-based ingredients point up the similar debts of the substance for which it substituted, namely theatrical or "fake" blood. This reddest of liquids—like any number of *The Shining*'s garishly hued props and furnishings—has its roots in oil. Consider, for example, the fact that the primary ingredient of "fake blood" was corn-syrup mixed with one cup of water, along with maize flour, a dose of red food coloring and ten drops of blue food. (In producing *The Shining*, Kubrick himself used "Kensington gore," a brand of fake blood used in films and in theater during the 1960s and 1970s, and made to exactly this formula.) For corn production's connection to America's fuel economy cannot be overstated. On the one hand, there is the fuel use associated with raising corn as a crop. On the other, there is the fact that, when fermented to produce ethyl alcohol (ethanol), corn actually has fuel-burning properties, and can itself be used as a motor fuel or motor fuel additive. Indeed, in 1978, in the wake of the oil crises of the 1970s, the US Congress was beginning to promote the use of ethanol in motor fuel by providing tax credits to those who blended ethanol with gasoline, and by setting in place tariffs to block the import of cheaper sugar-based ethanol from Brazil and the Caribbean (Paarlberg 2013: 103). By the end of the 1970s, then, corn was beginning to acquire a substitutive relationship with petroleum in the American imagination.

But in seeking to grasp the relationship between lipstick and petroleum established in the REDRUM scenario, it is worth remembering the broader filmic context in which the word appears—that is, at the very end of a sequence bristling with far more powerful signifiers of blood. As the scene opens, we see Danny approaching the bed; he picks up the butcher's knife from his mother's bedside, holds it aloft over her sleeping body, and, in mid-shot, runs his hands down its point, as a series of intense, anguished strings scrape on the soundtrack. As a tableau, the scenario directly telegraphs homicidal intent. Danny himself is a dead ringer for any number of other demonic, psychic or otherwise supernatural children that had populated the 1970s horror, from William Friedkin's *The Exorcist* (1973), to Richard Donner's *The Omen* (1976) and Cronenberg's *The Brood* (1979). The knife, meanwhile, is not just a signifier of murder but a literal weapon of murder, an index (like the fabled fingerprint, mold, or death mask) of the act that Danny strives to evoke or channel. Yet after holding the pose in tableau-like fashion for just a few seconds, Danny turns abruptly away from the bed and toward the camera in the direction of something that lurks slightly behind us—the dressing table, which a slow pan reveals to be loaded with a plethora of feminine beauty products, from hand-creams and perfumes to lipstick. It is only at this point, then, that Danny—having grabbed the lipstick—proceeds, still sleepwalking, to inscribe the word REDRUM on the back of the door. And when set in this broader context, the REDRUM moment's relationship to blood is weak. While a butcher's knife held over a sleeping woman clearly telegraphs murder, a word scrawled on a door in lipstick is far less explicit in its connotations. A different set of affinities, then, must be evoked to account for this scene. If, as I have explained above, lipsticks have their basis in oil, then the "MURDER" at the heart of the scene may be the less the murder of the family via the spilling of blood, than the destruction of the Earth via the reliance on crude oil, whether through the emission of carbon dioxide, or through tank vessel spills in rivers and oceans.

To suggest that oil forms the true focus of *The Shining*'s horrific "money shots"—from the typewriter scene, to the blood elevator image to the REDRUM sequence—is not to deny the critical role played by blood in the film. Much of the film's narrative is driven by Jack's professed desire to "bash [his wife's] brains in," and while surprisingly thin on the ground for such a supposedly gory film, blood *is* spilled, and more than once, in the film's diegetic universe. A spectral reveler who greets Wendy in the hallway with the words "great party" has a bloody fissure running through his skull; Jack acquires a minor head wound after toppling backward down the stairs of the Colorado Lounge—and as Wendy drags his prostrate body downstairs to lock him in the pantry, the camera floats in low mode alongside Jack's head, revealing a corn-syrup trickle at his temple that will harden, scab and then freeze across the course of the final few hours of story-time. Later, in the final bathroom scene, Wendy will slash the back of her husband's hand as it reaches through the broken door to twist the handle; while Hallorann—the Torrance family's putative savior—will be stabbed to death by Jack's ax, and a gratuitous close-up of the carnage shows the ax-head wedged in his chest, as claret-colored stage-blood cascades down his khaki windbreaker. Yet not one of these moments of (actual) bloodshed have garnered anywhere near as much critical attention, nor seem to excite as much spectatorial trepidation, as those scenes that turn, as we have seen, on petroleum products.

In Jack's case, in fact, the appearance of blood is coded in comic rather than horrific terms, thanks in part to what Sharon Marie Carnicke politely calls Nicholson's "nonrealistic . . . exaggerated performance" style as Jack (2006: 22). And the very different textual and spectatorial valuations of the two liquids may not be an accident. If, as we have seen, genre scholarship identifying blood as horror's liquid mainspring relies heavily on Kristeva's account of blood as the ultimate object of abjection, to return to that seminal work is to notice that even as "urine, blood, sperm, excrement" horrify, they also, according to Kristeva (1982), "show up *in order to reassure* a subject that is lacking its 'own and clean self'" (53). In this reading, blood emerges precisely as that which shores up the boundaries of the subject, a reassuringly anthropogenic liquid set over and against an oil that repeatedly reminds us of our terrifying dependence on broader, nonhuman assemblages. As LeMenager (2014) assesses the situation: "We *hope* that there will be blood in this literature [of oil] . . . if only blood from an errant thumb subjected to a hammer, so that we might see ourselves again in the world we make" (99). The spectacle of blood, in other words, may be a welcome, anthropomorphic respite from the more profound systemic threat posed by crude oil. In fact, it may provide such relief that, according to LeMenager, where it doesn't appear of its own accord, we are likely to usher it into being by (figuratively) subjecting our "errant thumbs" to a hammer.

The Shining is careful to situate this desire for blood, of course, in the context of a postindustrial society then transitioning into a service and information economy—an economy that, while predicated on oil, increasingly delegated the *pursuit* of oil offshore. On the one hand, that is, oil is everywhere in the film—the high-spec Alpine luxury of the Overlook Hotel intersecting, at every point, and in the most explicit ways, with well-established petrocultural systems, perhaps most notably the network of highways that service it. On the other hand, however, America's intensifying reliance on imported oil, combined with an automation of basic petroleum exploration, extraction and processes, has made the model of the "oil man," embodied by Daniel Day-Lewis's Daniel Plainview, unfeasible. As the film opens, then, Jack—like many men in America's emerging petrocultural economy—is in a double bind. Trained to revere the figure of the heroic extractor of oil, he has found himself a mere functionary of the society to which oil extraction has given rise, adrift among pencil-pushers, hotel clerks, ad men and other auxiliaries of the automobile. As Jack screams at Wendy, when, concerned for Danny's well-being, she begs her husband to let them return to Boulder:

> It is *so fucking typical* of you to create a problem like this when I finally have a chance to accomplish something, when I'm really *in* the writing.... I could really write my own ticket if I went back to Boulder now, couldn't I? ... Shovelling out driveways, working at a carwash, would any of that appeal to you?!

Jack is reluctant to leave his position at the Overlook, it seems, for the same reason that he was excited to take it up in the first place. Resisting the prospect of serving, essentially, as a kind of accessory to the motor-car, Jack aims to write the Great American novel, searching, like *There Will Be Blood*'s Daniel Plainview, to "strike it lucky" by stumbling across a buried trove of geological riches. Jack Torrance's "torrents," of course, are internal: instead of striking oil in the desert, he must look within. Yet the work of artistic "extraction" has gone the same way as the work of literal extraction in the wake of the dried-up Texan oil wells that, tapped out by decades of industrial-scale corporate profiteering, no longer yield the product they once did. The crisis of work, that is, is also the crisis of *the* work. If Jack seeks blood, that is, it is in some sense precisely because he cannot, either literally or figuratively, seek "oil."

Given oil's critical role in some of *The Shining*'s better-known scenes of horror, it should come as no surprise that it also serves as the central horrific object of a scene that, while little-noted by critics, amounts to the film's climactic moment of dread. The lead-up to the scene features Wendy cowering outside the pantry into which she has dragged and locked her violent husband after the episode in the Colorado Lounge. Tearful and hesitant, she announces her intent to escape: "I'm gonna go now ... I'm gonna try and get Danny down the sidewinder in the snowcat today.... I'm gonna go now ..." Shots from the interior of the pantry show Jack from below, grinning malignantly, his head against the door. "Wendy," he announces, "You got a big surprise coming to you. You're not going anywhere. Go check out the snowcat radio and you'll see what I mean." As Penderecki's spidery strings creep up and down the scales, we track Wendy as she flees, knife in hand, through the clinically lit corridors of the hotel and into the desolate blue snowfield outside. The climax of the sequence takes place in the interior of the garage, in a single shot that deploys a host of horror film conventions traditionally applied to moments involving the discovery of a body or the encounter with a monster. To the left of the screen, we see Wendy, in long shot, stopping in her tracks in horror before the spectacle that greets her. To the right of the screen is the blood-red snowcat, its bonnet open to show an intestinal tangle of wires and mechanical parts. Jack, it seems, has anticipated Wendy's escape-attempt, and his mutilation of the vehicle registers with the same force as a mutilation of her own body. The camera tracks in slowly in on Wendy as she takes the scene in, moving from the long shot of the initial encounter; to mid-shot, as she advances toward the vehicle and retrieves the battery; to a close up showing her staring at the broken machinery; and finally to a tight close up of her face, her chest heaving.

Identifying oil, not blood, as the primary object of dread in *The Shining*, this essay has pegged the iconic Kubrick classic as a pioneering "petro-horror" that redirects the sensational energies of the "New Regime" horror genre from the spectacle of human harm to the spectacle of our broader imbrication in global petrocultural regimes. Clearly, this chapter marks a re-inscription of Kubrick's *The Shining*, a film whose varied interpretations have been united by a shared investment, first, in the notion that blood is the film's signature liquid, and second in the notion that human harm forms the film's psychic mainspring. Yet this chapter also marks a re-inscription of the horror film more generally. While critical accounts of the horror genre have been overdetermined by the blood-soaked slasher flicks that dominated the 1970s, this analysis of Kubrick's *The Shining* has drawn attention both to the other liquids that suffuse it and to the more diverse kinds of fear—many of them resonating beyond the human—that animate it. Indeed, in identifying *The Shining* as a pioneering "petro-horror," this chapter provides a generic rubric that may be useful both for drawing a series of recent films that turn on oil into the remit of the horror genre and for identifying the role of oil in a set of films that *don't* explicitly turn on oil—most notably examples of the "new regime" horror. While this chapter's primary resonances, however, are for studies of film genre, its argument also ramifies beyond film studies, through what has become known as

Figure 9.5 *The Shining* (Stanley Kubrick, 1980) copyright Warner Brothers.

the "energy humanities." Much of this body of work emerges as a reckoning with and response to critic Amitav Ghosh's (1992) now-notorious claim that "there isn't a Great American Oil Novel," let alone a great "epic poem," because "the history of oil is a matter of embarrassment verging on the unspeakable, the pornographic" (29). For what has been overlooked in the rush either to bear out or to counter Ghosh's assertion is the fact that, while pointing to oil's absence from high cultural modes like the novel or the epic poem, Ghosh doesn't in fact point to its absence *per se*. Rather, he identifies oil as "unspeakable" and "pornographic," modes that form the stock-in-trade of two exceptionally popular mass cultural forms: pornography ("the pornographic") and horror ("the unspeakable"). This chapter, then, turns to a classic of the latter form—*The Shining*—to help recover part of an under-acknowledged oil canon, showing how, precisely *as* the "unspeakable," the "history of oil" may have animated a film genre that makes the unspeakable its metier.

Notes

1. To assimilate oil to the "energy unconscious," and to yoke it to a new set of anxieties about what Thacker calls the "world outside" the human (Thacker, *In the Dust of This Planet*, 4) is not to negate the host of more familiar allegorical meanings that have attached to the liquid, which, historically, has signified everything from biological indeterminacy ("neither living nor dead, but . . . an uncanny and utterly inhuman afterlife of ancestral animals"), to dead labour (that which is exploited, consumed or burned up in the production of surplus). Oxana Timofeeva, "Ultra-Black: Towards a Materialist Theory of Oil," in *e-flux*, 83 https://www.e-flux.com/journal/84/149335/ultra-black-towards-a- materialist-theory-of-oil (accessed September 6, 2018).Yet it is to say that in the early twenty-first century this second set of anxieties may have gained ascendance in our understanding of oil.
2. While the screenplay identifies the character as H. B. Ailman (Barry Del Sherman), in the film he remains nameless and voiceless.

Works Cited

Benshoff, Harry M. 2017. "Preface," in Harry M. Benshoff (ed.), *A Companion to the Horror Film*. Hoboken, NJ: John Wiley & Sons, xiii–xix.

Brown, Bill. 1996. *The Material Unconscious: American Amusement, Stephen Crane & the Economies of Play*. Cambridge, MA: Harvard University Press.

Carnicke, Sharon Marie. 2006. "The Material Poetry of Acting: 'Objects of Attention,' Performance Style, and Gender in *The Shining* and *Eyes Wide Shut*." *Journal of Film and Video* 58(1/2): 21–30.

Clover, Carol J. 2015. *Men, Women, and Chain Saws: Gender in the Modern Horror Film—Updated Edition*. Princeton, NJ: Princeton University Press.

Cocks, Geoffrey. 1999. *The Wolf at the Door: Stanley Kubrick, History and the Holocaust*. New York: Peter Lang.

Cook, David A. 1984. "American Horror: The Shining." *Literature/Film Quarterly* 12(1): 2–4.
Creed, Barbara. 2002. "Horror and the Monstrous-Feminine," in Mark Jancovich (ed.), *Horror, the Film Reader*. New York: Psychology Press, 67–79.
Devereux, Cecily. 2017. " 'Made For Mankind': Cars, Cosmetics, and the Petrocultural Feminine," in Sheena Wilson, Adam Carlson, and Imre Szeman (eds.), *Petrocultures: Oil, Politics, Culture*. Montreal: McGill-Queen's Press, 162–85.
Enticknap, Leo. 2005. *Moving Image Technology: From Zoetrope to Digital*. New York: Wallflower Press.
Felman, Shoshana, and Martha Noel Evans. 2003. *Writing and Madness: Literature/ Philosophy/ Psychoanalysis*. Stanford: Stanford University Press.
Freinkel, Susan. 2011. *Plastic: A Toxic Love Story*. Boston: Houghton Mifflin Harcourt.
Ghosh, Amitav. 1992. "Petrofiction: The Oil Encounter and the Novel." *New Republic* 206(9, 29): 29–34.
Hantke, Steffen. 2004. *Horror Film: Creating and Marketing Fear*. Jackson: University Press of Mississippi.
Hutchings, Peter. 2017. "International Horror in the 1970s," in Harry M. Benshoff (ed.), *A Companion to the Horror Film*. London: John Wiley & Sons, 292–309.
Jameson, Fredric. 2013. *Signatures of the Visible*. New York: Routledge.
Kittler, Friedrich A. 1999. *Gramophone*, Film, *Typewriter*. Stanford: Stanford University Press.
Kristeva, Julia. 1982. *Powers of Horror*. New York: Columbia University Press.
LeMenager, Stephanie. 2012. "The Aesthetics of Petroleum, after *Oil!*" *American Literary History* 24(1): 59–86.
LeMenager, Stephanie. 2014. *Living Oil: Petroleum Culture in the American Century*. New York: Oxford University Press USA.
Lerner, Neil. 2009. *Music in the Horror Film: Listening to Fear*. London: Routledge.
Luckhurst, Roger. 2013. *The Shining*. London: Bloomsbury Academic.
Misek, Richard. 2017. "The Black Screen," in Martine Beugnet, Allan Cameron, and Arild Fetveit (eds.), *Indefinite Visions: Cinema and the Attractions of Uncertainty*. Edinburgh: Edinburgh University Press, 38–52.
Nolan, Amy. 2011. "Seeing is Digesting: Labyrinths of Historical Ruin in Stanley Kubrick's *The Shining*." *Cultural Critique* 77: 180–204.
Paarlberg, Robert. 2013. *Food Politics: What Everyone Needs to Know*® Oxford: Oxford University Press.
Painter, David S. 2012. "Oil and the American Century." *The Journal of American History* 99(1): 24–39.
Riordan, Teresa. 2004. *Inventing Beauty: A History of the Innovations that have Made Us Beautiful*. New York: Broadway Books.
Rockoff, Adam. 2013. *Going to Pieces: The Rise and Fall of the Slasher Film, 1978–1986*. Jefferson: McFarland, 2016.
Simpson, Philip. 2004. "The Horror Event Movie: *The Mummy, Hannibal* and *Signs*," in Steffen Hantke (ed.) *Horror Film: Creating and Marketing Fear*. Oxford, MS: University Press of Mississippi, 85–98.
Szeman, Imre and Dominic Boyer. 2017. "Introduction," in Imre Szeman and Dominic Boyer (eds.), *Energy Humanities: An Anthology*. Baltimore, MA: Johns Hopkins University Press, 1–14.

Thacker, Eugene. 2011. *In the Dust of This Planet: Horror of Philosophy*. Winchester: Zero Books.

Timofeeva, Oxana. 2018. "Ultra-Black: Towards a Materialist Theory of Oil." In *e-flux*, 83 https://www.e-flux.com/journal/84/149335/ultra-black-towards-a-materialist-theory-of-oil (accessed September 6, 2018).

Urbano, Cosimo. 2004. "What's the Matter with Melanie?" in Steven Jay Schneider (ed.), *Horror Film and Psychoanalysis: Freud's Worst Nightmare*. Cambridge: Cambridge University Press, 17–34.

Williams, Linda. 1991. "Film Bodies: Gender, Genre and Excess." *Film Quarterly* 44(4): 2–13.

Williams, Linda. 2006. "When the Woman Looks," in Mark Jancovich (ed.), *Horror, the Film Reader*. New York: Psychology Press, 60–66.

Yaeger, Patricia. 2017. "Literature in the Ages of Wood, Tallow, Coal, Whale Oil, Gasoline, Atomic Power, and Other Energy Sources," in Imre Szeman and Dominic Boyer (eds.), *Energy Humanities: An Anthology*. Baltimore, MA: Johns Hopkins University Press, 440–45.

10

The Anxiety of Interpretation: *The Shining, Room 237* and Film Criticism

Daniel Fairfax

Rodney Ascher's essayistic documentary *Room 237* (2012) is structured around interpretations of Stanley Kubrick's *The Shining* (1980) by five of the film's legion of obsessives. Midway through the film, one of them, Jay Weidner, lays his cards on the table. Likening the film to a game of "3D chess," in which the director is able to simultaneously relate multiple stories across different narrative vectors, Weidner claims to have discerned a hidden meaning to the film, a coded message from a director wracked with guilt at his role in a colossal act of deception. The footage of the Apollo XI moon landing, it turns out, was faked, and Kubrick himself had assisted NASA with producing the fraudulent film, his cinematic genius enabling the space agency to convincingly confect the requisite images. Indeed, the production of Kubrick's 1968 release *2001: A Space Odyssey* was actually a research project for simulating the moon landing footage, which involved a sophisticated use of front-projection photography.

Weidner is quick to prevent the spectator of *Room 237* from jumping to any extreme conclusions about his views: he does not believe the moon landing itself was faked. NASA *did*, Weidner yields, send a man to the moon. He insists, however, that the footage we associate with this event was filmed, not on the lunar surface, but on a studio backlot in the United States, with Kubrick himself in the director's chair. *The Shining*, therefore, was made as a kind of confession, from Kubrick to his own wife, demonstrating the filmmaker's sense of remorse in misleading the population of the world in so spectacular a manner. As Weidner phrases it, addressing Kubrick in the second person: "What was it like when your wife found out what you were doing?"

Weidner's hypothesis is indisputably outlandish, and he has little concrete evidence to support it outside of the revelations ostensibly contained "within the mise-en-scène of *The Shining*". He himself admits to being initially uncertain of its veracity as he rewatched Kubrick's 1980 film, which had earlier left a lukewarm impression on him, far less potent than the impact *2001* had made a decade earlier. Indeed, the proof Weidner gives for his theory is, for the most part, rather insubstantial: a pattern in the hallway carpet that bears a purported resemblance to the Apollo XI launch pad; a room key with the words "Room No." on it, which could (almost) be anagrammatically rearranged to spell "Moon Room," the number of the room itself (237), changed from

217 in the book, which is said to be the then best estimate, in thousands of miles, of the distance of the Earth from the moon; the uncanny physiognomic similarity between Stuart Ullman (Barry Nelson), responsible for hiring Jack Torrance (Jack Nicholson) as caretaker of the Overlook Hotel, and John F. Kennedy, who famously instigated the program to send a manned mission to the moon by the end of the 1960s; and a tirade delivered by Jack to his wife Wendy (Shelley Duvall), in which he blusters about the "obligations" that he is beholden to as a result of the contract he signed with his employers, seen here as a veiled profession of guilt from Kubrick.

The viewer can be forgiven for remaining unconvinced by this flimsy, circumstantial evidence, and dubious as to the actual existence of the improbable conspiracy Weidner has outlined. But then Weidner, aided in the careful unfolding of his analysis by Ascher's editing, reveals his trump card: fifty-eight minutes into *The Shining*, as Jack and Wendy's son Danny is playing on the floor of the hotel corridor, the child sits up, and is revealed to be wearing a woolen sweater with a hand-stitched Apollo XI design clearly visible on the front. For a moment, the viewer is thrown off-kilter, and Weidner's theory about the true meaning of *The Shining* does not actually seem all that demented. After all, what *is* that Apollo XI sweater doing there? Why would Kubrick include it in the film, by unless... unless...

For a moment, then, we believe in the conspiracy. We share Weidner's delusion.

Of course, this moment of credulity is fleeting, transitory, so short-lived as to almost immediately be expunged from our minds. Having succumbed, however briefly, to the twisted logic of the conspiracy theorist, our critical faculties quickly take over once more. The sweater's appearance in *The Shining* is a curious one, but it is no more than that. To postulate, on the basis of this cinematic non sequitur, the existence of a momentous act of deception is preposterous. Having been momentarily unnerved, the viewer once again mentally composes himself. The world returns to order.

But for the viewer of *Room 237* who happens to be a film critic, or film studies academic (or both), the sense of unease produced by the film will linger far longer, and the questions it poses are far more difficult to provide easy answers to. Of course, we can easily dismiss Weidner's bizarre exegesis of *The Shining*. But this and the other theories that Ascher's film presents to us are not so easy to conclusively divorce from our own practice. What is it, in the end, that separates "reputable" film analysis from the far-fetched fabulations concocted by Jay Weidner and his ilk? Is the dividing-line really so clear-cut? How can a critic—especially in the present day, now that we have largely been unshackled from the limitations of authorial intentionality—avoid yielding to the same fate as the conspiracy theorist? When it comes to the close reading of a film, how close is too close? Even the most self-assured of film analysts is dogged by such questions surrounding the methods, functioning and social role of what they do. We can call this perpetual auto-interrogation, this irreconcilable uncertainty about the validity of the act of critically receiving a film, the "anxiety of interpretation."

That it is *The Shining* that is the object of theories such as Weidner's is, assuredly, not a coincidence. Kubrick's film has given rise to both a rich seam of academic film scholarship *and* an outpouring of more esoteric or paranoiac forms of film writing. Not only does Kubrick's reputation as a filmmaker—the uncompromising, all-seeing auteur, controlling the visual content of his films with a maniacal single-mindedness— have a tendency to foster such output, with respect to which he is only rivaled by figures such as Orson Welles and Alfred Hitchcock, but, more specifically, *The Shining* is a film that is centrally concerned with the writing process itself, and that hovers along the porous boundary between artistic production and madness. In this sense, the theme of the film effectively programs its own reception, in a feedback loop between the work and its analysis from which, for those unlucky enough to become trapped inside of it, there is no escape.

* * *

In much of the reception to the film, *Room 237* has frequently been mischaracterized as presenting the views held by five "conspiracy theorists" on *The Shining*. In fact, only Weidner's take on the film, with its supposition of Kubrick's involvement in a vast, governmental operation to hoodwink the world's population, fits the category of conspiracy theory. The other four Kubrick enthusiasts partake, in various ways, in what could be called obsessive close readings of *The Shining*, in which Kubrick's film is treated as a complex puzzle to be deciphered, one in which every detail, no matter how minute or seemingly insignificant, is suitable material for their particular hermeneutic undertaking. Two of Ascher's interviewees offer analyses of the film which, if at times strained, are nonetheless perfectly within the range of reputable, "mainstream" film scholarship, and it is also notable that these two figures have respectable professional positions, whether in journalism or academia, which broadly conform to their mode of interpretation. Bill Blakemore, a broadcaster who reveals that he first encountered *The Shining* while he was the Rome bureau chief of NBC News, insists that the real theme of the film is the centuries-long genocide of Native Americans by white European settlers, a theory which he first laid out in a 1987 article for the *San Francisco Chronicle Syndicate*. Geoffrey Cocks, meanwhile, a professor of history at Albion College in Michigan and author of the 2004 monograph *The Wolf at the Door: Stanley Kubrick, History, and the Holocaust*, links *The Shining* to another act of genocide: that of European Jews by the Nazis during the Second World War.

Both interpretations have an undeniably legitimate basis, and are even overtly signaled in the film: most noticeably, Ullman explains to Jack and Wendy that the Overlook Hotel was built on the site of an ancient Indian burial ground, adding, "I believe they actually had to repel a few Indian attacks as they were building it," and the interiors of the building are festooned with Native American iconography, while the film's iconic image of blood gushing out of an elevator, and other scenes such as the meat freezer that Chef Halloran shows to Danny and Wendy, seem to incite overt connections with the death camps. But the focus of Blakemore's and Cocks' discussions tends to lie elsewhere, in smaller details and hidden clues peppered throughout the film. Blakemore, for instance, avows that his interest was initially piqued by the slogan on the film's promotional poster for its European release ("The wave of terror that swept across America," a clear allusion, in his view, to the mass murder of American Indians), as well as the presence of tins of Calumet baking powder in two scenes in the store room—the Calumet peace pipe signaling the treaties with Indian tribes that were unceremoniously broken by European settlers during their westward expansion, as well as the "honest treaty" between Halloran and Danny, on the one hand (both of whom have been gifted with ability to "shine"), and the "dishonest treaty" between Jack and the ghosts inhabiting the Overlook. The film's opening theme, meanwhile, with its haunting reworking of the "Dies Irae" hymn, gives the viewer "thousands of voices of the past," thereby enabling us to see through the manifold layers of history, and the horrors sedimented within them.

Likewise, Cocks unearths seemingly inconsequential features in the film's mise-en-scène to defend his hypothesis on *The Shining*'s coded references to the Holocaust, arguing that his training as a historian has taught him that "objects have intentional meaning" and that "nothing is arbitrary" when it comes to the presence of details in a work of art. Eagles—a symbol of both German and American imperial power—appear frequently in the film: whether as a statue on Ullman's desk, an image on the T-shirt Jack wears to bed, or on the brand of typewriter he uses when writing: Adler is the German word for eagle.

Cocks' attention to the typewriter was no doubt piqued by its enigmatic change of color from white to dark blue midway through the film—something, he phlegmatically notes, that "typewriters don't generally do." Indeed, this is not the only supposed continuity error to which Cocks ascribes meaning: he also highlights the mysterious disappearance of a sticker of Dopey from the Disney film *Snow White and the Seven Dwarves* on the door of Danny's bedroom from one scene to the next. Given that the boy had, in an intervening scene, experienced a "Shining" episode where he sees the murdered Grady daughters, thereby gaining a glimpse into the horrors that await his family in the Overlook Hotel, Cocks, in a marvelously extreme act of hermeneutic excess, argues that the newly missing dwarf signifies that "Danny is no longer a dope about things." Even more strained is Cocks' recourse to numerology: the historian ascribes great importance to the role of the number 42 in the film, as signifying the year that the Final Solution was adopted as official Nazi policy, and he highlights its seemingly ubiquitous presence: a long-sleeved top Danny wears prominently displays the number, *The Summer of '42* plays on a TV set, there are precisely forty-two cars in the Overlook's parking lot when the Torrances arrive there, even the numbers 2, 3 and 7 multiply to form forty-two (although at this point a self-aware Cocks acknowledges, "I must admit I'm grasping at straws here").

The other two interviewees in *Room 237* have more marginal positions in the media/academic world, and, concomitantly, their interpretations of the film veer in a more nontraditional direction. Juli Kearns—an artist and writer who also maintains a website offering a detailed, near-forensic analysis of *The Shining*[1]—focuses on the spatial abnormalities and inconsistencies of Kubrick's scenography: her attempts to map the interiors of the hotel lead only to frustration. Corridors go in misleading directions, doorways are in impossible locations, and many of the hotel's rooms are too large for the spaces that are supposed to contain them. Most palpably, Kearns highlights the window in Ullman's office, which backs onto a glaring exterior, despite the fact that the rest of the film shows this space to be surrounded on all sides by other parts of the hotel. Likewise, she homes in on one of *The Shining*'s most arcane discrepancies: the fact that the carpet pattern in the hallway outside the fateful Room 237 appears to switch direction from one shot to the next. For Kearns, these considerations provide an entry point to her central claim about *The Shining*: that the entire film is structured around the ancient Greek myth of the Minotaur. If the presence of the hedge maze in the film (an invention of Kubrick's, as it did not feature in King's original novel), and the labyrinthine layout of the Overlook, not to mention Jack Nicholson's unmistakably taurine appearance at certain moments, offer clear enough nods to this fable, Kearns' interest is focused on far more recondite minutiae in support of her argument: a barely visible poster of a skier on the wall of the hotel's games room contains, she is convinced, a striking resemblance to the iconography of the Minotaur, and is intriguingly positioned opposite a picture of a cowboy riding a bucking bronco (creating a symmetrical opposition between "Bull Man" and "Cow Boy," as Kearns puts it).

John Fell Ryan, an archivist who has also kept a long-standing Tumblr account dedicated to *The Shining*,[2] similarly trains his eye on Kubrick's cinematic peccadilloes as a means of divining the film's meaning. The fact that Wendy and Danny watch a television that has no power cord, or the inordinate amount of luggage the Torrances bring when they arrive at the Overlook, are, Ryan argues, ways in which Kubrick plays on the spectator's "ignorance of visual information." Ryan also pinpoints Jack's reading material while waiting for Ullman in the hotel lobby as a hidden key to interpreting *The Shining*: although it is barely visible in the film, the magazine Jack is flicking through is the January 1979 edition of *Playgirl*, whose cover features telltale headlines such as "The Selling of (*Starsky and Hutch*'s) David Soul" and "Incest: Why Parents Sleep with their Children." Ryan's most original hermeneutic gambit, however, is inspired by the long cross-fades heralding transitions between scenes, and a comment he read from an online Kubrick exegete (who goes by the moniker of Mstrmnd) to the effect that *The Shining* was intended to be watched in reverse. Ryan took this idea literally and organized a screening in The Spectacle Theater in Brooklyn which projected the film backward and forward simultaneously, the two images superimposed onto one another. While this mode of viewing could not have been part of Kubrick's intentions with the film, Ryan revels in the curious parallels created by his experimental projection: paired with the closing image of Jack photographed in the Overlook Hotel in 1921, the opening helicopter shot comes to resemble a twisted postcard, while at another moment, a close-up of Jack combines with blood-spattered walls to make it appear as if the blood is dripping from his eyes. Frequent combinations of Wendy and the Grady twins are also visible, suggesting a broad parallel between the characters.

Ryan admits that such juxtapositions can be viewed merely as "fun jokes," but he also insists that there are serious discoveries to be made about the film through this speculative screening technique. Far from a gimmicky curiosity, then, along the lines of the pairing of *The Wizard of Oz* (Victor Fleming et al., 1939) with Pink Floyd's 1973 album "The Dark Side of the Moon," Ryan conceives of his method as a tool that enables otherwise unnoticed elements of the film to emerge.

Across the five interviews, therefore, *Room 237* not only provides us with a smorgasbord of specific analyses of *The Shining*, it also displays a broad gamut of interpretive methodologies and modes of film criticism, the social legitimation of which varies markedly. But these distinctions are significantly nullified by the sobriety of Ascher's filming technique. We see none of the interviewees on-screen, and, aside from their names and the occasional piece of information they divulge about themselves, are given very little sense of their biographical details. Instead, the interviewees remain invisible, present only as disembodied voiceovers, whose words are accompanied by extracts from *The Shining* (as well as various other archival footage). The images deployed by Ascher serve to confirm—or, occasionally, call into question—the interpretations enunciated on the soundtrack, and they are often played in slow motion, or reversed and replayed, in a filmic technique redolent of the act of obsessive watching that has given rise to such close readings. Aside from his subtle use of found footage, Ascher gives no commentary on these interpretations, and within the film we are never privy to his own stance on the views articulated—although he has been more open in the extra-filmic interviews he gave upon *Room 237*'s 2012 release.[3] Curiously, Ascher even, at times, retains the interviewees' verbal fumbles and meandering digressions in the final cut of the film. In the most poignant instance of this practice, John Fell Ryan's explication of the allusions to Jack's ostensible sexual abuse of Danny in the headlines of the *Playgirl* magazine is interrupted by his own young child crying in the background.

The director also frequently alternates between the interviewees, such that, with the exception of Juli Kearns, whose voice is clearly distinguished by her gender, they often merge together in the mind of the spectator, particularly on an initial viewing, transforming their disparate standpoints into a pleonastic stew of film interpretation.

* * *

The five readings contained in *Room 237*, however, are far from constituting an exhaustive array of *The Shining*'s critical reception. While Kubrick's film has given rise to a multitude of academic scholarship, it has also yielded copious amounts of more informal writing (disseminated, for the most part, online), which has a tendency to combine the method of obsessive close reading with a paranoiac mindset. Kevin McLeod, writing under the pseudonym Mstrmnd, for instance, who, as noted above, inspired John Fell Ryan's dual screening (and who, a title-card in the film informs us, declined to be interviewed by Ascher for *Room 237*), has set forth his views on the film in a multipart analysis published on the website www.mstrmnd.com, which, he notes, will be included in a forthcoming book dubbed "Physical Cosmologies of the Blockbuster."[4] Mstrmnd's claims for the films are grandiose: not only is *The Shining* "the most complex film ever made," but, when considered in reverse, it is "the most visually unifying motion-art ever conceived" and "operates beyond the scale of any built, ideal, or imagined form existing inside fantasy, philosophy or reality."[5] In a vertiginous discussion of the film, Mstrmnd adopts multiple interpretative prisms through which to understand it, but a recurring motif, inspired—in the writer's account, by the oversized "T" shape in the poster for the film's initial US release—is its deep relationship with Mayan symbolism, with which, Mstrmnd is convinced, Kubrick was profoundly familiar.

On his website www.collativelearning.com, Rob Ager offers an overview of *The Shining* that, in like fashion, veers between painstaking formal analysis and cryptic paranoia. Like Mstrmnd, the Liverpool-based Ager refused to be interviewed by Ascher, although after viewing *Room 237* he wrote a sympathetic-yet-critical response to the film. Ager has gained wider fame, however, through his numerous YouTube video essays on *The Shining*, which have received hundreds of thousands of views, and which invariably make bold claims about uncovering the "hidden depths" of Kubrick's filmmaking. While happy to debunk Weidner's moon landing theory, Ager espouses his own pet conspiracy theory—that *The Shining* actually communicates Kubrick's dismay at the abandonment of the gold standard in international currency exchange by Richard Nixon in 1973.[6] Moreover, Ager's efforts at film analysis are often imbued with his own far-right, pro-Brexit politics—he even dubiously marshals Kubrick to the anti-EU cause in one YouTube clip[7]—and the deleterious effects of his unusually popular video essays, incommensurable with the reach of more reputable scholarly publications on the film, have led at least one academic to write an acerbic takedown of his work.[8]

In terms of pure prolixity, however, neither McLeod nor Ager can match the blogpost composed by an anonymous internet user who simply goes by the name of Jonny53. Running to more than 70,000 words, "What You May (or may not) Have Seen Hidden in The Shining" (*sic*) was first posted in June 2007, but has been revised multiple times since. Deploying numerological reasoning so convoluted it would doubtless make even the interviewees of *Room 237* blush, Jonny53 is convinced that the July 4, 1921, date appearing in *The Shining* enigmatic final shot of a photograph of Jack Torrance in fact points to 12/24/2011, which at the time of filming was thought to be the date predicted by the Mayans for the apocalypse. Amid his near book-length response to the film, the blogger also contends that *The Shining*'s continuity errors are in fact caused by characters using telekinesis (both Jack and Wendy can, in this interpretation, "shine" without knowing it), and that the number 3 on the Torrance's apartment door is a reference to a looming third world war between the United States and the Soviet Union.

Other theories about *The Shining* variously suggest that it confesses to Kubrick's involvement in the Illuminati or CIA mind control experiments, or that Jack is signaled in the film as being the Devil incarnate—the last prompted chiefly by a resemblance of Jack Nicholson in the closing photograph to the Baphomet Tarot card. Perhaps most whimsically, one blogger has even suggested that the Disney animation film *Frozen* is a twisted remake of *The Shining*, using screenshots to point out the visual similarities between parallel scenes in the two films.[9]

Even with the widely disparate nature of these interpretations of *The Shining*, such examples of this obsessive mode of analysis share certain traits in common. Firstly, the ability to dissect a film with painstaking precision, focusing on almost-unnoticeable details or continuity errors, mapping out its spaces or logging its recurring idiosyncrasies (numbers, motifs, visual patterns, etc.), was enabled, or at least greatly facilitated, by the advent of home video (first VHS, and then DVD and online streaming). Indeed, many of the interviewees of *Room 237* openly avow that it was this form of viewing which opened their eyes to the film. Weidner, having been underwhelmed by *The Shining* during its initial theatrical release, only took to the film upon subsequent viewings on home video, years later. Kearns confesses to watching the film "over and over again as a rental" before later purchasing it on DVD, while Ryan's dual projection screening was carried out with a DVD copy of the film (a necessity given that an analog 35mm print would be too aleatory to produce definitive combinations of images). Indeed, it is perhaps not too much of an exaggeration to assert that *The Shining*, released in 1980, just as the VCR was becoming a common presence in First World households, is the first film made specifically for the video age, that it was a conscious strategy on the part of Kubrick to make a work whose full appreciation could only be gained through the analytic tools granted to the consumer by home video technology: pausing, rewinding, slow motion, and so on. This is, in fact, the conclusion reached by *Cahiers du cinéma* writer Jean-Pierre Oudart in his own semi-delirious review of the film. For Oudart, *The Shining* is, "a kind of video-film, a television broadcast that had escaped from the TV, a giant video that would be a horror film programming the story of a family escaping from social delirium" (4).[10] In representing a break with an aesthetics based on the hegemony of the cinematic *dispositif*, toward one in which films become readily accessible in multiple formats, in the home or in public spaces, *The Shining*, for Oudart, thus represents both a nostalgic "adieu to the old cinema" and a "flight towards a giant video-cinema" that would, from the standpoint of 1980, inexorably form the future of the medium (11).

The second unifying factor in so many of these analyses of *The Shining* is the rise of the internet, and the concomitant ability for film enthusiasts without any recognized credentials to freely disseminate their views to a global readership. The open-access nature of the internet allows these writers to bypass the previously hegemonic custodians of media content: the editors, peer-reviewers and other authority figures who commission, accept or refuse material for publication on the basis of their self-asserted expert judgment. Vaunted as a democratization of not only film criticism, but the circulation of ideas more generally, beyond the circles of those granted social legitimacy or possessing what French sociologist Pierre Bourdieu calls "cultural capital," the obliteration of these gatekeepers through online media also leads to an increased indeterminacy in what constitutes legitimate film criticism. With the online self-publishing of film analysis, there is no more filter between a potential writer's ideas—no matter how unsubstantiated, bizarre or factually inaccurate—and their popular reception. Processes of critical thinking, reasoned debate and verification are replaced by a free-marketization of ideas: the viewpoint that garners the most hits, views or likes, or which happens to gain the favor of the algorithms that Google, YouTube, and Facebook use to control online behavior, inexorably becomes the generally accepted attitude toward a given subject, even when the issue at hand—for instance, the meaning of the final photograph in *The Shining*—is obviously enigmatic and open to a plurality of interpretations.

* * *

Faced with the rise of these new, internet-enabled modes of film criticism and analysis, the response of "traditional" writers on the cinema has taken varied forms, and this is reflected in the reception that *Room 237* gained from members of what might be called—if doing so did not serve to further cultivate the conspiratorial mindset of so many *Shining* devotees—the "critical establishment." Watching Ascher's film at the 2012 Toronto film festival, prominent Chicago-based critic Jonathan Rosenbaum reacted to *Room 237* in a stridently negative manner, calling it "at once entertaining and reprehensible," and arguing that because the director "refuses to make any distinctions between interpretations that are semi-plausible or psychotic, conceivable or ridiculous, implying that they're all just 'film criticism,'" the result is an "undermining [of] criticism itself by making it all seem like a disreputable, absurd activity."[11] Rosenbaum's concerns were shared by the critic Girish Shambu, who attended the same screening. For Shambu, *Room 237* offered a "disturbing representation of the practice of film criticism" which reduces analysis to "little more than a clever puzzle-solving exercise" that is fundamentally "apolitical" and "hermetic" in nature.[12] This debased form of criticism, which comes across as "outré, freakish or crackpot," can be distinguished from "good" film analysis, in Shambu's view, chiefly by the presence of a politicized conception of aesthetics that would draw its methodology, however indirectly, from the tradition of critical theory (or "Theory"). As the critic concludes: "In *Room 237*, we have several 'theories' to account for the film but what I miss is any whiff of 'Theory,' in however casual or informal or un-academic a form." Shambu is justified in highlighting the evident superficiality of many of the "puzzle-solving" approaches to film analysis, which seem content with divining a secret meaning to a film, or mapping the impossibilities of its spatial architecture, without probing the deeper political and aesthetic implications that these would entail. But his invocation of "Theory" as the determining factor differentiating "good" from "bad" film criticism is unconvincing. Even those of us who are aligned with this tradition must accept that other methodologies—such as formalist, empiricist, or cognitivist approaches—may well come from a different political/theoretical lineage, but can still claim a place amid the firmament of legitimate film criticism and analysis.

Other responses to *Room 237* have been more favorable toward Ascher's endeavor. Covering the film for the website *Indiewire*, Robert Greene, whose status as a critic *and* filmmaker gives him experience on both sides of the camera, described *Room 237* as "the first great comedy about film criticism," featuring obsessive readings that, while "painfully hilarious," can nonetheless be seen as "a metaphor for all film analysis" due to the fact that they "open up the hidden wounds and secret tensions between filmmaking and film reviewing." If the film was rejected by critics such as Rosenbaum and Shambu (Greene mentions them by name), then this was because they refused to recognize that the "*id critic* movie monster" represented by the analysts of *The Shining* to whom the film gives voice also lurks within their own critical practice. Indeed, Greene interviews a host of critics who are more amenable to "recogniz[ing] the monster within." While these critics are hesitant to adopt the kind of "grand unifying themes" showcased in *Room 237*, they acknowledge that the critical analysis of a film can with all legitimacy go well beyond the preconceptions of the filmmaker, and in doing so align themselves with post-structuralist tendencies in the reception of art works. As Scott Tobias, quoted in the article, states: "Once a film is released, I believe firmly that it belongs to the viewer and that not all meanings are intentional."

A similar, albeit more conceptually rigorous, defense of *Room 237* was mounted by one of the major figures in North American academic film studies. Shortly after the film's release, David Bordwell wrote a post on the film for his and Kristin Thompson's personal website. After detailing the analyses found in *Room 237*, Bordwell rejoins: "Are these interpretations silly? Having spent forty-some years teaching film in a university, I found much of them pretty familiar. Some of the specifics were startling, but I've encountered interpretations in student papers, scholarly journals, and conference panels that had a lot of similarities." If the interpretations of *The Shining* do come across as "strained and forced, even loopy," then this is in fact one of the great virtues of *Room 237*, since Ascher's film impels us to ask: "What do we do when we interpret movies? What makes one film interpretation plausible and another not? Who gets to say? What historical factors lead ordinary viewers to launch this sort of scrutiny?" Indeed, Bordwell links such interpretation to venerable hermeneutic traditions commenting on sacred books (the Bible, the Torah, the Koran) or canonical works of literature (Homer, Dante, Shakespeare), which use techniques such as numerology, iconology or secret codes to ostensibly decipher hidden meanings in these texts. Even Ferdinand de Saussure, the founder of semiology, sought to detect anagrams in Latin poetry, Bordwell points out. And yet the "reasoning routines" of the readings in *Room 237* do, for Bordwell, distinguish themselves from "mainstream" film interpretation in a number of ways: the cues they focus on are typically minor, almost undetectable anomalies and disparities in narrative or mise-en-scène, and their efforts tend to culminate more in "implicit" rather than "referential" meanings. Finally, whereas film scholars are usually trained to be wary of what the "New Criticism" literary theorists dubbed the "intentional fallacy" (the notion that every element of a work of art can be ascribed to the artist's express will), the *Room 237* critics exhibit this interpretive tendency to an excessive degree, to the point of granting Kubrick almost supernatural powers of insight and control. But here, again, the boundaries between professional film analysis and what Bordwell calls "folk interpretation" are more fluid than we might assume: journalistic film reviewers "commonly make assumptions about what the filmmaker is up to," while even the most experienced of academics has been known to "indulge in hypotheses about directorial purpose."

* * *

All the above debates—whether around *The Shining* itself, or, in the second-degree, around *Room 237*—are haunted by a single, all-pervasive question: why is it that *this* film in particular should incite such a multitude of interpretation, whose perpetual accumulation shows no signs of abating, even now, nearly four decades after its initial release? What is it about Kubrick, what is it about his film, that leads scholars, critics, enthusiasts and conspiracy theorists alike to produce such a voluminous outpouring of analysis?

To a certain extent, this can be ascribed to Kubrick's authorial reputation, his esteem among his most devoted fans as not only a gifted filmmaker, but a genius with unparalleled insight into the human condition, as well as a seemingly omnipotent demiurge with absolute control over the filmmaking process. This status was certainly cultivated by Kubrick himself, through judicious use of film publicity, as well as through his idiosyncratic working methods, intended to convey, through the excessive repetition of takes or the meticulous attention to set details, a superhuman drive toward technical perfectionism. But his fanbase has developed it into a near-mystical aura, in which Kubrick becomes akin to what Gilles Deleuze, when writing on his films, described as a "world-brain" (206), capable of a kind of cosmic awareness of the universe beyond the bounds of everyday comprehension. The awestruck reverence with which the *Room 237* critics—along with the likes of Rob Ager, Mstrmnd and Jonny53—tend to speak of Kubrick is evidence of this attitude. In Ascher's film, for instance, Jay Weidner not only confesses to his "religious experience" while watching *2001: A Space Odyssey*, he also claims, without evidence, that Kubrick had an IQ of 200. In an unconscious echo of Deleuze, the otherwise more restrained Bill Blakemore even describes the filmmaker as a "mega-brain of the planet" who is concerned with the "implications of everything that exists."

While Kubrick's genius is hyperbolized in *Room 237*, his cultural omnivorousness was undeniable. In Ascher's film, numerous books that were (ostensibly, at least) read and absorbed by Kubrick are namechecked to bolster a given interpretation of *The Shining*—these include *The Destruction of the European Jews* by Raul Hilberg, *The Uses of Enchantment* by Bruno Bettelheim, and even *Subliminal Seduction* by Wilson Bryan Key. Kubrick's autodidactic thirst for knowledge, sprouting out in multiple directions, also determines another aspect of his films, perhaps most exemplified by *The Shining*: namely, their highly polysemic nature. Indeed, it is this disregarding of the potential for multiple readings of the film to be equally valid that invariably distinguishes the conspiracy theorist, prone to declaring that they have "unlocked the key" to a given film, or "discovered" its "hidden secrets," from more reputable film commentators, who are generally more modest in their claims. In the case of *The Shining*, there evidently are elements of the film that support an allegorical reading related to the genocide of Native Americans, the Holocaust of European Jews by the Nazis, the myth of Theseus and the Minotaur, Mayan doomsday scenarios, or the abandonment of the gold standard. Kubrick's mise-en-scène, laden with a plethora of otherwise extraneous details, expressly enables all of these interpretations to be possible. In this sense, then, many of the amateur analyses of the film do indeed have legitimacy. It is only the act of bestowing a single exclusive meaning upon the film to the exclusion of all others that represents an untenable hermeneutic step.

This said, it may be interesting to note that, while theories about *The Shining* have mostly proliferated after Kubrick's death, when he has been unable to correct the record, other individuals closely involved with the film have been willing to repudiate certain claims. Most notably, in 2016 Vivian Kubrick, the director's daughter, who was on the set of the film and responsible for a documentary about its shoot, felt the need to address the persistent rumors about his involvement in filming an ostensible faking of the moon landing—which have gone well beyond Weidner's claims, and which can likely find their origins in the French mockumentary *Dark Side of the Moon* (*Opération Lune*, William Karel, 2002). The younger Kubrick tweeted a statement reading: "the so called 'truth' these malicious cranks persist in forwarding—that my father conspired with the US Government to 'fake the moon landings'—is manifestly A GROTESQUE LIE."[13] Likewise, in a 2017 interview for *Entertainment Weekly*, Jan Harlan, an executive producer for *The Shining* and other Kubrick titles, forthrightly rejected a reading of the 1980 film that would link it to the Holocaust. Whereas other theories about *The Shining* are "much more harmless, where continuity mistakes are attributed with deep meaning," the idea that it is a film about the Holocaust is, according to Harlan, "outrageous. That's an insult to Kubrick, that he would deal with the most serious crime in human history in such a light way, and also an insult to victims of the Holocaust."[14]

It is not merely, however, the film's potential for a multiplicity of meanings that has resulted in *The Shining* being fertile terrain for acts of interpretation that tend toward critical delirium. Throughout the film, Kubrick appears to be consciously straining to produce a sense of cognitive dissonance within the viewer, leaving one prone to receive the film in ways that strain the bounds of rationality, especially when subjecting oneself to multiple viewings within a short space of time. Perhaps the most notable literary antecedent for this artistic strategy can be found in the writings of Kafka, whose work has similarly yielded a vast and conceptually heterogeneous critical reception.[15] As such, the prevalence of glaring continuity errors in the film, combined with the cast-iron knowledge that Kubrick, as a "master filmmaker" with a perfectionist's eye, would be incapable of innocently making them in the first place, let alone leaving them in the final cut, inexorably leads the susceptible viewer to inquire about their presence, and to probe into a possible deeper meaning to them. A similar effect is produced by what Thomas Allen Nelson calls the "visual schizophrenia" (1982: 215) of the film, with its jarring discordances of architectural and design styles: the bathroom of the Belle Époque-decorated Gold Ballroom, for instance, is decked out in starkly modernist reds and whites. This is further compounded by the spatial incongruities of the Overlook Hotel, with its impossible external windows, improbably large rooms, nonsensically situated doorways, illogically laid out corridors and shapeshifting exteriors (even the model of the hedge maze is perceptibly different from the maze itself), the ensemble of which leaves us disoriented and confused, incapable of successfully creating a mental map of the film's diegetic world. Other details of the mise-en-scène, many of which are highlighted by the *Room 237* interviewees, add to the spectatorial sense of disarray: the functioning television set bereft of a power cable, the excessive amount of luggage brought by the Torrances when they arrive at the hotel, or the unsettling presence of the taciturn Bill Watson at Jack's initial interview with Ullman. The film's narrative, too, is riddled with discrepancies. Jack's predecessor as caretaker at the Overlook Hotel is variously called Charles Grady or Delbert Grady. Ullman notes that the daughters he murdered were "eight and ten years old," but the ghosts seen by Danny, their iconography inspired by a renowned Diane Arbus photograph, are evidently twins.

Time itself seems to break down: the respective accounts provided by Jack and Wendy of the former's violent abuse of Danny differ markedly in the timeframes given, while the chronological markers furnished by the film's title cards produce a sense of ever-quickening acceleration, until, by the end, we inhabit a realm outside of human temporality, such that the Jack of 1980 can be visible in a photograph from 1921.

Of course, this pervasive sense of disorientation culminates in the overarching question posed by the film: are the supernatural entities spawned by the Overlook Hotel merely to be understood as products of Jack's psychological derangement, or do they have a "real" existence in the diegesis of *The Shining*? As with the ghost of Hamlet's father, an incontestable answer to this question is impossible to deliver, since different parts of the film lead to different conclusions. For James Naremore, this "is-this-happening-or-is-he-crazy" aspect of the film aligns closely with what the Russian literary theorist Tzvetan Todorov described as the "fantastic," a zone in which the reader hovers between two hypotheses concerning inexplicable events in a narrative: "either to reduce this phenomenon to known causes, to the natural order, describing the unwonted events as imaginary, or else to admit the existence of the supernatural and thereby to effect a modification in all the representations which form his image of the world" (188–89).[16] Moreover, the cognitive dissonance inculcated by Kubrick not only allows for a suspension of our critical faculties, enabling interpretations of the film that abolish the boundaries between commonsense reasoning and the ravings of a madman, it also places us, against our wills, into a close identification with Jack as he slides into violent insanity. For the viewer (and, by extension, the critic), Kubrick plays a role similar to that of Delbert Grady in relation to Jack, prodding and manipulating us into a state of full-blown paranoia. Here, the confluence between the spectator and the film's protagonist is bolstered by Jack Nicholson's inimitable performative style, which, like the film more generally, skirts between the serious and the parodic, between psychological realism and a grotesque pastiche of both the horror film genre and Nicholson's own extrafilmic persona. As Naremore writes: "The result is a killer clown and a particularly evil Lord of Misrule, but also a somewhat pathetic bum-madman-bully, an inept actor who leers with Nicholson's trademark nasty grin.... In other words, Jack is a bad version of Nicholson, played cleverly by Nicholson" (202).

Finally, we can posit that the surfeit of writing *on* the film is also a product of the fact that, on a fundamental level, *The Shining* is *about* the writing process itself, and about the angst and paranoia that this process generates—from the terror of the blank page to the ineluctable indeterminacy between lucidity and lunacy—as well as the human sacrifices that literary production so often entails, which are literalized in the film as Jack passes from the detached neglect of his wife and child to actively seeking to murder them. In order to devote himself to his art, Jack essentially entombs his family in a sealed-off mausoleum, but even then is crippled by writer's block, which only finds release in the hundreds of pages covered by the typewritten phrase "All work and no play make Jack a dull boy," an act of writing which comes to resemble concrete poetry. As Fredric Jameson notes, however, Jack is "not a writer, not someone who has something to say or likes doing things with words, but rather someone who would like to be a writer, who lives a fantasy about what the American writer is, along the lines of James Jones or Jack Kerouac" (93). Although Jack certainly engages in the physical act of writing, maniacally bashing the keys of typewriter, the sounds of which echo across the cavernous spaces of the Overlook Hotel, he merely produces what post-structuralist literary criticism has dubbed *du texte*: Jack's scriptural effusion is, according to Jameson, "very explicitly a text about work: it is a kind of zero point around which the film organizes itself, a kind of ultimate and empty auto-referential statement about the impossibility of cultural or literary production" (128).

Moreover, it is noteworthy that the infinite repetition of Jack's *du texte* is uncannily echoed in so much of the writing on Kubrick's film. It is as if the internet pages dedicated to analyzing *The Shining*, with their boundless blocks of text, an unending logorrhea whose culminating resolution is endlessly deferred, are preemptively caricatured by Kubrick, hyperaware of the effects that his filmmaking can have on his more zealous devotees. Indeed, toward the end of *Room 237*, the individuals interviewed by Ascher are cognizant of the inexhaustible nature of their project: Kearns exasperatedly claims that "Everything is so whacked out. The more you look at it the less sense it has," while Ryan laments that he is trapped in a perpetual attempt to grapple with the film: "My life," he states, "has actually become *The Shining*." Most notably, Cocks, who insists that there are yet more elements to the film that nobody has seen, and that this is a reason for the film to continue to be watched, here makes an appeal to postmodernist theory, arguing: "We know from postmodern film criticism that author intent is only part of the story of any work, that meanings are there regardless of intent." Indeed, many of the analytical strategies used in *Room 237* are echoed in the work of film scholars taking inspiration from the deconstructionist approach: free association, punning, an uninhibited recourse to intertextual references.[17] Here we have a striking case where *les extrêmes se touchent*: those Kubrick enthusiasts who elevate the director to a quasi-divine status end up methodologically resembling those who reject the very concept of the author as void of any significance. In both approaches the question of authorial intentionality ("Did the filmmaker *really* mean that?") is entirely evacuated: in one case because everything can be attributed to him, in the other because nothing need be imputed to him. The all-powerful author and the death of the author are one and the same. Now that the rationality check that the authority of the author represented for traditional criticism has been annihilated, there is no longer anything to curb the anxiety of interpretation. Like Jack Torrance, the film critic, today, finds himself perpetually perched on the threshold of psychosis.

* * *

But this is altogether too nightmarish a note to end on. Maybe we would do better to step back from the precipice. If Kubrick has his film vacillate between the straight and the parodic, the serious and the ironic, the profound and the playful, then we should take this a sign that the critic, too, can adopt a ludic approach when grappling with the material of *The Shining*: following the leads offered by the filmmaker, but treating them in the manner of a game to be played rather than a key to be deciphered. The notion of textual play was, of course, an early strategic maneuver in the post-structuralist trend of literary criticism as it shrugged off the rigidities of authorial hermeneutics or structural analysis—we can see it at work in Derrida's *Writing and Difference*, or Barthes's *Pleasure of the Text*. Every work of fiction—even the weightiest—is, in essence, a game-like exchange between the creator and the viewer, and it is an awareness of this essential element of playfulness in their activity, this understanding that writing about cinema is *not* a life and death matter, which paradoxically separates "serious" film critics from their paranoid, conspiracy-theorist counterparts.

In 2018, one of the most famous of all Kubrick obsessives, Steven Spielberg, delivered an elaborate homage to his mentor. In the middle of *Ready Player One*, a prolonged scene takes place within a digital recreation of the set of *The Shining*. The characters of Spielberg's film are playing a virtual reality video game which takes them inside the film, allowing them to investigate its spaces and freely interact with its characters. It is with this same spirit of freedom and exploration that the critic can best confront the task of writing on *The Shining*, and avoid becoming trapped in its maddeningly endless exegetical corridors.

Notes

1 See www.idyllopuspress.com.
2 See http://kdk12.tumblr.com/.
3 See, for instance, Xan Brooks, "Shining a light inside *Room 237*," https://www.theguardian.com/film/2012/oct/18/inside-room-237-the-shining.
4 This book appears never to have materialized, although Mstrmnd was given a forum to articulate his views on *The Shining* in the form of an audio commentary on the DVD release of *Room 237*.
5 See http://www.mstrmnd.com/log/802.
6 See Rob Ager, "*The Shining*—Kubrick's Gold Story," https://www.youtube.com/watch?v=IoWZEwedPkc.
7 See Rob Ager, "Stanley Kubrick would have supported Brexit," https://www.youtube.com/watch?v=Szy15XdYngQ.
8 See Dan Leberg, "Fanboys in the Ivory Tower: An Attempted Reconciliation of Science Fiction Film Academia and Fan Culture," *Gnovis Journal* 2 (Spring 2011), http://www.gnovisjournal.org/2011/08/08/fanboys-in-the-ivory-tower-an-attempted-reconciliation-of-science-fiction-film-academia-and-fan-culture/.
9 See https://mkhammer.squarespace.com/blog/2014/10/27/frozen-is-just-disneys-the-shining The blogger in question, Mary Katharine Ham, is also a conservative pundit who has frequently appeared on Fox News.
10 Own translation from the original French.
11 Jonathan Rosenbaum, "*Room 237* (and a Few Other Encounters) at the Toronto International Film Festival, 2012," https://www.jonathanrosenbaum.net/2018/01/room-237-and-a-few-other-encounters-at-the-toronto-international-film-festival-2012/.
12 Shambu does make an exception for Ryan's backward-forward projection, admiring its gesture of leading the film into "a larger realm of accident, chance and poetry that radiates outward into the world."

13 See https://variety.com/2016/film/news/stanley-kubrick-moon-landing-conspiracy-theory-addressed-daughter-vivian-1201809270/.
14 See https://ew.com/movies/2017/03/30/shining-ending-explained/ Harlan's argument was preemptively refuted by Geoffrey Cocks in *Room 237*, who argued that it was precisely Kubrick's inability to tackle the subject of the Holocaust head-on (his project on *The Aryan Papers* was never realized), that led to him addressing it in a more subterranean fashion.
15 For the broader parallels between the work of Kubrick and Kafka, see Brigitte Peucker (2001).
16 The Todorov quote is originally from *The Poetics of Prose*, trans. Richard Howard (Ithaca, NY: Cornell University Press, 1977), 179.
17 Bordwell mentions Tom Conley and Robert B. Ray in this vein, and we could also add, among others, the French academics Jean-Louis Leutrat and Suzanne Liandrat-Guiges.

Works Cited

Ager, Rob. ca. 2014. "*The Shining*—Kubrick's Gold Story," https://www.youtube.com/watch?v=IoWZEwedPkc.
Ager, Rob. ca. 2016. "Stanley Kubrick would have supported Brexit," https://www.youtube.com/watch?v=Szy15XdYngQ.
Blakemore, Bill. 1987. "The Family of Man," *San Francisco Chronicle Syndicate*, July 29.
Bordwell, David. 2013. "All play and no work? *Room 237*," http://www.davidbordwell.net/blog/2013/04/07/all-play-and-no-work-room-237.
Cocks, Geoffrey. 2004. *The Wolf at the Door: Stanley Kubrick, History, and the Holocaust*. New York: Peter Lang.
Deleuze, Gilles. 1989. *Cinema 2: The Time-Image*, trans. Hugh Tomlinson and Robert Galeta. Minneapolis: University of Minnesota Press.
Green, Robert. 2013. "*Room 237* and the Attack of the Id Critic," https://www.indiewire.com/2013/04/room-237-and-the-attack-of-the-id-critic-133796.
Ham, Mary Katherine. 2014. "*Frozen* is just Disney's *The Shining*," https://mkhammer.squarespace.com/blog/2014/10/27/frozen-is-just-disneys-the-shining.
Jameson, Fredric. 1990. *Signatures of the Visible*. London: Routledge.
Leberg, Dan. 2011. "Fanboys in the Ivory Tower: An Attempted Reconciliation of Science Fiction Film Academia and Fan Culture," *Gnovis Journal* 2 (Spring), http://www.gnovisjournal.org/2011/08/08/fanboys-in-the-ivory-tower-an-attempted-reconciliation-of-science-fiction-film-academia-and-fan-culture.
Naremore, James. 2007. *On Kubrick*. London: BFI.
Nelson, Thomas Allen. 1982. *Kubrick: Inside a Film Artist's Maze*. Bloomington: Indiana University Press.
Oudart, Jean-Pierre. 1980. "Les inconnus dans la maison (*Shining*)," *Cahiers du cinéma* 317 (November): 4–11.
Peucker, Brigitte. 2001. "Kubrick and Kafka: The Corporeal Uncanny," *Modernism/Modernity* 8(4) (November): 663–67.

Rosenbaum, Jonathan. 2012. "*Room 237* (and a Few Other Encounters) at the Toronto International Film Festival, 2012," https://www.jonathanrosenbaum.net/2018/01/room-237-and-a-few-other-encounters-at-the-toronto-international-film-festival-2012/.
Shambu, Girish. 2012. "On 'Room 237,' Criticism and Theory," http://girishshambu.blogspot.com/2012/10/on-room-237-criticism-and-theory.html.
Todorov, Tzvetan. 1977. *The Poetics of Prose*, trans. Richard Howard. Ithaca, NY: Cornell University Press.

11

Political Opacity in the Films of Stanley Kubrick

John Pitseys

Los Angeles is a sunny city: all the more reason to be cautious there, distrustful even. Beautiful Sarah wears a wide-brimmed hat and flashes her irresistible blue eyes and bright smile. Sam is her neighbor. He would like to fall in love with Sarah, but their first date will also be their last: the next day, he finds her apartment empty. Breaking into her place, he finds a strange sign on the wall of her bedroom, as well as a shoebox in her closet, containing a polaroid picture of the young woman and few other trinkets. To Sam, this disappearance cannot be due to chance alone. Sarah has been kidnapped, or worse. David Robert Mitchell's *Under the Silver Lake* (2018) recounts Sam's investigation and what turns it into an existential and psychogeographic wandering—unless it is the other way around.

For Sam, the world is a strange place, but a patient interpretation of the clues it yields will end up giving him access to its hidden truths. Sam takes each encounter as a coincidence, each coincidence as a clue, and each clue as a logical step on his journey to discovery: a dancer covered in balloons that revelers at a party are invited to pop; obscure codes exchanged with loiterers, or found in a cereal box or in song lyrics listened to backward; a mysterious whale cult—all the situations Sam runs into seem as incongruous as they are enlightening. Sarah's vanishing cannot just be a mundane and sordid news item (ostensibly she has died in the company of a millionaire in a car crash): "deep under the surface of the silver lake," the young woman's disappearance must be the tail end of an all-encompassing conspiracy.

The strangeness of it all, the odd encounters, the musical cues, the inexplicable disappearance, occult parties for the elites taking place in lavish buildings, and a murderous "owl"—a sculptural naked woman wearing a feathered mask: were it not for the inescapable topography of Los Angeles, which it obsessively paces, *Under the Silver Lake* could be a verbose copycat of *Eyes Wide Shut* (1999), or, at least, a strange twin version of the memory that one keeps of Stanley Kubrick's final film. Accumulating nods and references to Hitchcock and film noir, but also, most importantly I want to argue, to Kubrick, Mitchell's film tells us that the visible world makes no sense and that one has to see through its chaotic veils to see it for what it really is—be it in the dark hallways of a remote gated manor house, for instance, or inside an abandoned underground nuclear bomb shelter under the hills of Griffith Park. This is the world, furthermore, of those in power—a power governing us. Naturally, Mitchell's protagonist will be revealed in the end as a delusional paranoid man, hounded by anxieties related to unpaid rent, and a growing *objet petit a* complex. This is where it is not, ultimately, only paying lip service to those who find absurd the many conspiracy theories surrounding the "codes" or messages to be found in Stanley Kubrick's films but also hinting at the fact that, as I want to argue, the latter, instead of enshrining fabled paranoid worldviews and yielding secret codes to the world or faked moon landings, are, indeed, doing almost the exact opposite.

What is power? What does speaking and carrying out actions in the name of other people entail? What meaning are we to give to political action, if the latter turns out to be merely a smokescreen, a mise-en-scène? While Kubrick's conception of politics and modes of representation have been commented upon widely and in a variety of venues, the study of the relationship between the two—his representation of politics—has been less scrutinized, be it the relationship of power to representation, or the specific relationship of power to the cinematic image. Ostensibly representing Kubrick's will to power, his cinema not only institutes a *rapport de force* with the audience: it also makes power visible. The question of political visibility has a central but also paradoxical place in Kubrick's work, since it is represented through what is usually considered to be the opposite of the visible: secrets (suppressed voices, underhanded or mysterious social codes, political conspiracies, and collective taboos). A looking glass to contemporary fascination for the ideal of transparency, the staging of secrecy interrogates our relationship to political truth, and to the relationship between power and political representation. I would like to show how power and politics are ubiquitous in Kubrick's films, while also arguing that secret itself, against the odds, is all but absent from them.

Secrets Everywhere?

"I can see clearly now." *Under the Silver Lake* is nearing its end, and Sam looks at the southern California skies, arms on his window ledge. He knows now that he will never find Sarah, and his voice speaks to the viewer: "You're living in a carnival, throwing little plastic rings at oversized pop bottles hoping to win a price. What are you gonna win? [...] It's all just a shitty sawdust filled rabbit."

A clear view of truth requires the understanding of the world around us as a bundle of illusions.

How is it possible, then, to see what must be seen? How can one escape the "carnival"? Secrecy, and political opacity, appear as important elements of at least four Kubrick films: *Dr. Strangelove, or, How I Learned to Stop Worrying and Love the Bomb* (1964), *Barry Lyndon* (1975), *The Shining* (1980), and *Eyes Wide Shut*. The secrets they feature need to be exposed in order to address the visibility of the political therein.

Dr. Strangelove's conceit relies on the will to make political opacity a vector of the spectacular. The parodic representation of political bureaucracy and the American military-industrial complex is made possible here by the very fact that they take place on an army base and inside the "war room"—a secret antinuclear bunker. These very locations of the secret are filmed like theater. Conversely, the theatricalization of secret itself and of places of power shed light on their endogamous codes and discursive logics. The staff palavers. The president consults his advisers. The Americans are negotiating with the Russians. But in any case, political institutions—the Parliament, the government, and the Judicial Courts—just like the public sphere itself, are absent from the plot, as they are from the images themselves: both invisible and silenced/suppressed. Political theory tends to agree that public deliberation seldom encounters the ideal conditions of a rational debate, among which the possibility given to each participant to freely express their views and preferences; a dynamic of mutual amendment; and, ideally, the formation of a rational consensus around the exchanged arguments. Through *Dr. Strangelove*, Kubrick ironically demonstrates that secret deliberations are not necessarily more rational than public ones. Refusing to take responsibility for its action, but not wanting to withhold it either, the gloved hand of Strangelove, alternately strangling him and performing a Nazi salute, reminds the public of the founding secret of liberal modernity. The modern state walks on two legs: the first one is the social contract, which legitimizes why individuals leave their weapons behind in favor of civil peace. The other one is the reason of state, namely, the putting into place of a set of means necessary to ensure the viability of the political community. The foundation of the community does not rely solely on its members' consent, but also on a violent founding act; and its existence relies on the exercise of coercion. Modernity may want to suppress the memory of this founding violence and relegate it to the margins of the political: it is precisely this philosophical tour de force that theories of the social contract have endeavored to perform, over and over again. Cinema itself can stage this violence as a civic act: it is of course a central motif of the western genre, of which *The Man Who Shot Liberty Valance* (John Ford, 1962) remains the theoretical masterpiece, and of which Stanley Cavell (1979) famously analyzed the stakes (the "valence of liberty"). However, reason of state is not a totalitarian "other" of modernity: it is one of its intrinsic dimensions indeed. The exercise of power is not necessarily occult: that it has as its essential object its own preservation, beyond any individual interest, or even beyond the collective good, however, is a scandalous fact that must not be spoken or uncovered.

Genuine power does not rest alone in the exercise of reason of state, but also in the survival of the fittest. Continuing the questions raised by *Dr. Strangelove*, *Barry Lyndon* follows the path of an adventurer, a cheat who tries to win at a metaphorical game of cards, the genuine rules of which are inaccessible to him—namely, the codes, both implicit and endogamous, of the English aristocracy, of which he will never be a part, for all his efforts. Be it in its ballet of gazes, its evocative silences, or its epigrammatic sentencing, *Barry Lyndon* associates with the social game the image of a dangerous board game. With the difference that any good player is supposed to know that this game's dice are loaded. Those in power, like the impostors, believe in their cheating, but to varying degrees and with diverse consequences. The former do not even know they are cheating, since they take for granted that the dice must and will favor them. The latter believe they can use the apparent rules of the game to their advantage, not however grasping the real stakes or nature of the game: wig-wearing and mastering the etiquette are but the garments of power, and what parades as a game is indeed a hunting preserve wherein only select members are admitted (Figure 11.1).

Contrary to *Dr. Strangelove*, *Barry Lyndon* does not stage a conspiracy, since no conspiring is required to perpetuate the structures of political domination, let alone to prevent the petty upstart from breaking through the glass ceiling of aristocracy. However, while these structures and said metaphorical ceiling are tangible, their mechanisms seem impenetrable. The film itself presents like a flagship out of the past, covered in dark and thick veneer—distant, useless. The images seem sapped of their vitality (think of Lady Lyndon in her bathtub). The actors, covered in makeup and powder, appear corpselike. In this context, the feeling of social impenetrability is reinforced by the distance between viewer and images. *Barry Lyndon* is staged itself as though it were not a period piece, but a historical simulation, a reconstruction—be it in the use of the zoom out and wide shots, of the meta-ironic function of the voice-over, and the reproduction of famous eighteenth-century paintings within the shots or, more generally, in the openly spectacular and artificial character of historical pastiche. Kubrick is a puppeteer who, unlike the protagonist of his film, wishes to remain aware of the fact that he too is merely a character in his own act. Unlike the director, Redmond Barry successfully embraces social decorum (see Miller), but without grasping its ideological dimension. However ambitious and opportunistic, Barry remains as naive in the final duel as he was at the outset. He believes that rules can merely have two possible functions: one, strategic, and the other, moral—the worth of these rules being determined by the existence (or lack thereof) of a preexisting *signified*. Barry believes

Figure 11.1 Rules of the (social) game: the card playing scene. *Barry Lyndon* (1975) copyright Warner Brothers.

that the strategic use of the norm will allow him to elevate himself socially, and that his moral interpretation and elevation will then allow him to be redeemed. He is wrong on both counts: in his final duel with Lord Bullingdon, Barry believes he has satisfied a certain idea of honor. But the rules of honor only apply among peers. When his turn comes to shoot the pistol, Lord Bullingdon does not for an instant think of sparing Barry's life, not because of the rules, not even because of the feelings of possessive tenderness he harbors for his mother whom Barry has married, but precisely in the name of social status.

The Shining probes the same questions further. Interpreted as a look at one of America's most glaring blind spots, namely, the genocide of Native Americans, it is Kubrick's most political film. Many elements reinforce this interpretation: the Native American rugs and motifs present throughout the hotel, the Calumet powder cans in the pantry (featuring a Chief), the reference to the Overlook Hotel being built on an "ancient Indian burial ground," and so on—together these allusions all conspire to summon an overlooked Native American identity and history. Whether one decides to follow this interpretation or not, the idea whereby the visual fabric of *The Shining* is loaded with political allusion and meaning is both instructive and problematic. It is instructive because of the way the epistemological *dispositif* of the film feeds off of it, and the conception of political visibility derives from it. But it is also problematic, because it misses the main points. The angst and uncanny emanating from *The Shining* do not come from the horror tropes or gore on display, be it surreptitiously, but from the fact that what the film shows conceals something far more horrible. *The Shining* captures the horror one feels upon realizing that one is doomed to remain closed off to oneself, in a state of unsolvable self-opacity. The film could be interpreted as an attempt by the mind to repress this feeling of horror. And it describes the horror one feels once one realizes that this repression is at the source of one's blindness. In this sense, the very name of the Overlook Hotel is of course meaningful (it both "looks over," sees all, and "overlooks," fails to see). Danny's telepathic powers are the scandalous reason behind the demonic maelstrom, as the child sees something that is meant to remain unseen, and must die for that reason. As for the infamous "All work and no play makes Jack a dull boy" moment, it is all the more profound because it marks the failure of the project that Richard Rorty (but also Stephen King!) assign to literature: to make visible to the mind what the mind wants to keep invisible. Kubrick's nightmarish vision joins and overtakes King's, and the act of writing in the film turns out to be incapable of piercing through the veil, and for a good reason, too: Jack Torrance goes berserk because what was to free him—namely, the conscious, furthermore self-conscious, exercise of literature—drives him insane. *The Shining* is a film about what cannot be spoken if one wants to remain soundly on one's feet, but which must be discussed and talked about, if one wants to remain human.

While *The Shining* is of course more than a political film, its political reach is most important. Henry Sidgwick (1893: 48)[1] indicates that to know the existence of a secret threatens its content.[2] The existence of the secret must thus itself be kept secret so that it may have its useful/desired effect. And so the efficiency of the double secret also risks increasing the toxicity already contained in the simple secret. The secret's secret can acquire a psychological dimension: the alienation of the individual designates precisely the non-awareness of the unconscious. It presents, too, a social and political dimension, which Sidgwick largely illustrates. *The Shining* plays with the secret's dual dimension: psychological and political. In *Dr. Strangelove*, the political secret is explicit: it is even used as gag fodder. In *Barry Lyndon*, the secret is allusive; one surmises that the official rules don't say all, but the officious, unspoken rules remain impenetrable. In *The Shining*, the secret itself is forgotten or kept under some dark oath. The ghosts don't know they are ghosts. They are not aware of the violence they constitute the repressed of, and for a good reason: the very nature of taboo is not that some subjects or topics must be avoided, but that their avoidance or sidelining itself must be obscured. A social phenomenon before it is an individual act of repression, the taboo questions, through its non-addressing, through its silence, and through its invisibility, the very foundation of our political societies: Can a political community be instituted without an original sacrifice, and, more broadly, without a foundational act of violence? Does the institution of political community not require the repression of this original sacrifice? *The Shining* does not only suggest that we are blind to what we are. It reminds us that the way individuals cohere in society happens largely through this blind spot. The American myth of Manifest Destiny is thus founded on the erasure of the country's indigenous peoples. Jack Torrance is in this sense a medium for American political false consciousness. To kill one's family is the logical conclusion of the scenario just as it is the original act of the foundation of the community.

Eyes Wide Shut proposes a synthesis of the three treatments of secrecy laid out here. The film does not speak of desire, but of the opacity of consciousness. And while it does feature a sentimental dimension, the question of power is central to the film—be it in the couple dynamic, social relations at large, or the capitalist market. The Harfords are shown as a couple in a constant state of negotiation, even as the terms of the negotiation remain unspoken. The interactions that Bill has with different people during his night of wandering are always conducted on an asymmetrical mode, be it because of social status (he is inferior to Ziegler, but has a higher status than the prostitutes, or even than his college old boy, Nick Nightingale) or the de facto position of superiority (Milic, the costume shop-keeper, although lower on the social scale, takes advantage of an urgent need to demand a prohibitive price for the rental of the cloak and mask), especially coming from the ones who see without being seen. The orgy, in this sense, summarizes all the fantasies associated with the "real" power of economic elites—cloaks, masks, rituals, and remote manor house—in this frame, the representation of power is tightly associated with the secrecy figures mentioned earlier: the obscene secret of power is revealed in its crudeness, the implicit secret of power whose access codes are also secret codes, and the double secret of a power whose very existence must be kept secret. Much as in *Barry Lyndon*, the spectacularization of power is an intrinsic dimension of its opacity: power hides all the better as it shows off. Just as in *Dr. Strangelove* an extravagant mise-en-scène of secrecy allows to turn the question of power into a real narrative stake of the film: again, power hides by displaying itself. No doubt secrecy is constantly made visible in *Eyes Wide Shut* (the tall manor gates, the ominous old man bringing Bill a threatening note, the burly bald man shadowing him on the streets at night, the mysterious death of the prostitute, and her mute corpse at the morgue, etc). At the center of this representation stands the avuncular Victor Ziegler, leaving no doubt—but providing little tangible evidence still—as to the sinister nature of the secret, and contributing to emphasize it just as he derides it as pure "mumbo jumbo." And as in *The Shining*, the repression of the secret paradoxically reveals its nature. Supposed to cover up for the murder of the prostitute following the orgy scene—by discouraging Harford from pursuing his own private investigation—threat, blackmail, and shadowing illustrate the relationship of social and political domination surrounding the characters. For Kubrick, the ostensible mise-en-scène of an occult power is no diversion or smokescreen, but, again, a clue: upon closer scrutiny, there is secret in power only to those who want to keep their eyes wide shut.

No Secret in Sight

The game between transparency and opacity renders the dialogue between the intimate and political dimensions of Kubrick's cinema more substantial: the secret is a powerful symbolic operator, allowing thus to show characters obsessed with the idea of hiding—or divulging—the true nature of things. However, the staging of the secret does not mean for all that that there is a secret to stage (and reveal) in the first place. The four Kubrick films (but also *Under the Silver Lake*) are not about what they hide, but what they show: even if the very existence of the secret is of little interest, its representation or intimation remains fundamental.

In *Dr. Strangelove*, the staging of secrecy is ubiquitous precisely because there is no secret in the plot itself to begin with. To be sure, the exchanges between the protagonists are meant to be kept secret—"classified information" as the war and espionage films lingo has it. But this allows them to express themselves in the most open and revealing manner. The film is founded upon a factitious separation between the outside world, of which the viewer/spectator is supposed to be part, and the place of actual power, which the viewer can at best observe through a peeping hole, as it were, or like a fly on the wall. This separation shows the political and military figures in a way in which they are never supposed to be seen publicly. However, the narrative use of the secret is little more but another way to light the scene. The war room is filmed like a stage, not like some claustrophobic space. Ripper, Strangelove, the president and his Russian homologue, the political and military figures that dwell in the war room, all behave exactly as they would at home. They conceal nothing and repress hardly anything at all. In this sense, it is telling that Peter Sellers plays three characters: the polite and stuck up Mandrake's British etiquette, set against Ripper's boorishness, serves as a mirror image of Strangelove's obsequious and fake courtesy in front of President Muffley. In short, humans are inside the way they appear outside, and vice versa. In this sense, the *huis clos* reveals no hidden side of politics—if, perhaps, the latter's everyday mundaneness. Strangelove is often shown as a sleazy manipulator, but he hides nothing of what he thinks: indeed, he voices it, his Nazi past is well known, and his arm does and shows the rest. What we find here is a well-known argument in political theory, that of "Frankness and Candor."[3] It stands by the idea whereby the secret presents us at once with the moral risk and the epistemic advantage of being able to present points of views that otherwise would be censored or outright rejected in the case of a public deliberation (see Pestiau 2001: 39). From the very first scene of the film all the way to Strangelove's final speech, the cinematic mise-en-scène of secrecy paradoxically allows for sincere exchanges on-screen: processes of political decision-making remain themselves rather transparent; stakes and political intentions are clearly laid out; protagonists don't lie to one another; and the dialogue between Russians and American is almost cordial. Finally, doomsday happens because of a computer, an algorithm acting without emotion, or subjectivity: its operation is not secret, but inscrutable, opaque, leaving the characters confronted with their cowardice rather than their secret intentions. Be it in its settings, characters, or decision-making processes portrayed, *Dr. Strangelove* contains no actual conspiracy: it tells us not of political secrets, but of political stupidity and incompetence. In view of this, the only mystery of the plot is the reason behind the Doomsday Machine's enigmatic mistake.

Machiavelli has kept reminding us for over four-and-a-half centuries now that the immanent reality of power is inseparable from its representation: refining what had already been stated in *Dr. Strangelove*, *Barry Lyndon* shows us this. Although the mysteries of power remain non-dissociable from what Turquet de Mayerne called the "splendor" of power, this relationship is also reversible. The splendor of power is not merely a facade.

In the introduction to his "Barry Lyndon Reconsidered," Mark Crispin Miller describes one of the film's famous scenes, during which Barry attempts to comment on a painting in front of Lord Hallam, using what he believes to be the aesthetic codes of the nobility, seeing them as access codes to the higher class. What he fails to see, however, is that these codes are both the decor of power, its backdrop, and one of its intrinsic dimensions. Be it in the class hierarchy, order of precedence, or etiquette, court manners fulfill a triple ideological dimension: they contribute to a cohesive regulation of political domination, mask its nature, and rationalize its justification. Seen thus, it is because the protagonist assumes the rules of the game are merely a backdrop that he remains ultimately powerless. Granted an interview with King George, Barry Lyndon reminds his financial support to the King's wars when the sovereign asks only for his military support (see Miller 1976). The king then dryly entreats the former military man to go with his men on the battlefield, like a real gentleman. And yet, it is precisely because Barry is no real gentleman that the king calls upon his newly acquired aristocratic obligations. Nobility compels only those who *pretend* to it, not those who *are* part of it. The scene during which Barry thrashes Lord Bullington in front of the high society underlines the asymmetry of social rapports between the two men. Barry remains uncomprehending of this, perhaps the only uncomprehending party in the room (next to his young son). Klein describes the final duel which ensues in those terms:

> As the duel begins Bullingdon's second asks, "Mr. Lyndon, do you know the rules?" Barry abides by the highest ideals of the code of the society he has aspired

to enter. He declines to fire at Bullingdon after his stepson's pistol accidentally discharges. Lord Bullingdon, a secure member of the dominant class, interprets the rules of the game from his own perspective, and declaring he has not "received satisfaction" refuses to waive his second shot and conclude the duel. (Klein 1981: 106)

Honor, in other words, remains first and foremost a socially regulatory technique of the aristocracy.

For Jean Baudrillard (2004: 43–8), *Barry Lyndon* was evidence of the fact that power is but a simulacrum. Strictly speaking (that power existed in fact only to conceal the absence of power), this would be true, if the representation of power remained its only tangible reality. But from the very first to the very last shot of the film, *Barry Lyndon* reminds us that there is no order of precedence between the map and the territory. For Kubrick, the image does not determine the reality of things, nor does reality determine the truth of the image—but their mutual, reciprocal determining through the sensitive filter of the image. Kubrick's cinematic image is neither the icon of a revealed truth nor the strategic artifice of a reality surging from its own spectacularization. It relies on the sensitive realm to produce signifiers whose determination depends on an individual or collective judgment and not on the correspondence (or non-correspondence) to a signified already there: in this way, Kubrick's cinema is conceptual in a most Kantian way. In any Kubrick film, and most clearly in *Barry Lyndon*, the indeterminate, undecipherable quality of the characters makes them subjects for thought proper. The lag between real past, represented past, and recounted past, as well as the affected virtuosity of historical reconstitution, all underline the discursive dimension of the narrative. The voice-over is not a description, but a commentary of the image—at times fallible, or sarcastic, often wise, and no less but no more reliable than the image itself (see Klein). Power is exposed here neither in its secrecy, nor in its transparency, but in its *publicity*.[4] A philosophical product of the times at which the film takes place (the eighteenth century), the principle of publicity covers the access both to speech and to information, and allows for discussion surrounding the facts and arguments it is derived from. Seen thus, a call for publicity is always a call for the public. What the film shows is thus similar to what it attempts to demonstrate: the deployment of a sensitive surface and the interpellation of the viewer, representing both the cinematic intention and the intellectual project of the film. More still than *Dr. Strangelove*, *Barry Lyndon* is a case-study film of Kubrick's cinema, and thus his masterpiece in the strict sense.

Conversely, it is because the theme of *The Shining* presents a central challenge to this conception of the visible that it remains perhaps the director's most affecting among the four films discussed here. As Mark Fenster points out, the desire for transparency tends to increase the collective distrust for political institutions, and to generate a growing fascination for what would be the hidden truth of power. The two phenomena are not contradictory: as soon as the discovery of the thing itself requires to not be fooled by the illusory veil that covers it, metaphysical dogmatism can perfectly feed a relativistic approach from an epistemological point of view. Seen thus, the Lovecraftian tonality of *The Shining* seems at first to feed this double and mutual rapport. A world thrown off-kilter and upside down is supposed to bear the paradoxical trace of a silenced but radical truth. It comes as no surprise, then, that *The Shining* has been the object of an over-abundant critical apparatus, centered around and amplified by the widespread idea that the film contains a hidden meaning, a code—the conceit behind *Under the Silver Lake*, and which the latter film ridicules while showing the idea's noxious power of seduction.[5] And yet, as I mentioned earlier, *The Shining* tells us that one should not mistake secret with what one does not want to talk about. Fredric Jameson (1990) reminds us that *The Shining* does not narrate the horrifying discovery of a hidden truth, but the encounter of man with one's ghosts. By contrast with the classical definition of the genre, the *fantastique* is not born out of the irruption of the occult in the real here, but of the reemergence, on the sensible surface of things, of a reality that one would rather remained buried or submerged, be it our own private mazes or the way in which the American political classless liberal imaginary represses the material reality of political and social domination.[6] Much like *Dr. Strangelove* and *Barry Lyndon*, *The Shining* intends to represent what is considered—wrongly—to be unspeakable, namely, the foundational violence of the social pact: the original spoliation/expropriation of the property of the land, the legitimizing of privileges resulting from this appropriation, and the institution and justification of the violence (and "reason") of the state. In this sense, the ball scene is the moment of political truth of the film, not because it reveals to the viewer a hidden supernatural truth, but because it stages the last moment of the American history, when the "totem" of hyper-wealth was not yet taboo. In those prodigal 1920s, Jameson tells us:

> A genuine American leisure class led an aggressive and ostentatious public existence, in which an American ruling class projected a class-conscious and unapologetic image of itself and enjoyed its privileges without guilt, openly and armed with its emblems of top-hat and champagne glass, on the social stage in full view of the other classes. (123)

The Shining ends not coincidentally with clapping and chattering following the song which accompanies the end credits, "Midnight, the Stars and You"—echoing the sound of the audience leaving the theater. It is the end of the show, and the film asks: in what way is the viewer in 1980 different from the ghosts encountered by Jack in the Gold Room? The staging of political opacity reminds us that it is impossible to apprehend political truth in any other way than through its own representation. That the words to describe it do not come to us make this representation all the more necessary.

Last but not least, the plot of *Eyes Wide Shut* does not only reprise, again the three narrative devices of *Dr. Strangelove*, *Barry Lyndon* and *The Shining*, namely the spectacularization of the secret, the distancing of the image, and the representation of the unspeakable. Kubrick's last film also synthesizes the three critical positions that were derived from these: the refusal of transparency, the ironic wager of publicity, and the recusing of political esotericism.

For Michel Chion, *Eyes Wide Shut* "tells us that motives do not matter and that we cannot know them" (2002: 84). This holds true for the protagonists, centered on their intimacy, but bereft of any interiority, as it does for the depiction of the political. In strict terms, *Eyes Wide Shut* narrates a string of events only loosely connected, with an uncertain, meandering narrative progression, the stakes of which remain all but unclear until the end. The story as a whole constitutes a case study of suspense without an object. The viewer is entreated to believe that Bill Harford is confronted with some sort of great secret, the unveiling of which will expose the intimate social, and political mechanism of the film. Alack! Much like Harford himself, the viewer will never know anything of the secret society whose orgy they witnessed. They will never be made privy to the subtle machinations that seem to animate the film. They don't even know if the events depicted actually take place at all or are, as Sperb suggests, simply the fruit of a solitary rumination, or the projection of an overactive, sexually repressed, and frustrated imagination.

Is there anything behind the mask at the party (or, in Einsensteinian fashion, do they hide another mask, as in *Que Viva Mexico!*)? Appearances and representations of power escape nevertheless the baudrillardian categories of representation. These appearances mask no deeper truth, nor do they ultimately reveal the absence thereof, for that matter. They do however have something to do with reality. The simulacrum is at once the mode of existence of the characters (was Tom Cruise indeed ever better cast than as a self-searching empty vessel?) and the mode of phenomenalization of the cinematic image itself (hence the lush palettes, the oversaturated hues that *Under the Silver Lake* cannily reprises and transports to LA). However, the simulacrum itself is exposed as an object of representation. *Eyes Wide Shut* does not show that reality is a simulacrum. It shows a social world for which the simulacrum constitutes the only possible mode of representation. Hence, perhaps, the morbid, frigid, stilted, un-erotic quality of the orgy itself, sexuality as a performative act and little else, not contained but displaced, and the naked masked girls looking like the mannequins in Milic's shop—properly uncanny, or unheimlich, in effect.

The term *heimlich*,[7] for Freud, belongs to two ensembles of representation that, without being opposed, are nonetheless far apart one from the other: one has to do with the home, the cozy ("homey" as Jack describes the little janitorial quarters in *The Shining*), and then that of the hidden, the dissimulated. Moving from an ultimately banal depiction of a couple of the NYC upper-middle class, to a tale of meandering, wandering, and perambulation through the city's streets and suburbs, *Eyes Wide Shut* is structured around this exchange between the two semantic sets of implications of the term *heimlich*. Naturally the secret plays a key role in this articulation, in the way in which it allows to reveal a part of strangeness to the everyday (reinforced by the eerie, studio-set reconstructed Greenwich village), while suggesting that this part of strangeness or uncanny sends us to social and political domination that are very real—all the more so as they are kept out of sight and implicit. The social power is indeed visible for those who accept to look it straight in the eyes. It is present in every shot, be it in the apparently luxurious lifestyle of the protagonists (an upper East side Manhattan condominium) to the upper-class lifestyle of the Zieglers that dwarfs it in comparison, the description of the many layers of existence in Manhattan, or the toy store of the final scene, whose commodities do little else but prolong the gendered fantasies of the protagonists. The teddy bear—once a monstrous fuzzy ghost in *The Shining*—becomes here a discreet multiplied reminder on a shelf. The human ghosts of the gold room become people of flesh and blood. However, their depiction does not only portray the ice-cold traits of the Empire. It lays out the ideological processes that are susceptible of obfuscating these cold traits of the Empire itself, in the eyes of the characters as well as in the eyes of the spectators. Kubrick presents an upper-middle-class couple parading as plain middle class. Bill's urban perambulations are presented in the guise of egalitarian transactions, while their fantasized tenor is based on a relationship of domination. As for the self-centered baring of the Harford couple's desire, it is consciously represented as an ideological mask meant to have us believe that alienation is but a psychological process, that a quest for the self is a matter of authenticity, and that the subject of the film is sentimental life and urban bourgeoisie. In this sense, the orgy scene is paradoxically the most descriptive moment in the film, not because it unveils the place of real power, but because it exposes its ideological dimension. The wearing of the mask is meant to suggest that each and everyone accepts the shedding of their social garments during the ceremony. However, the "equalizing" of the partakers is strictly limited in time and space. And the party is by invitation only. Finally, no mask can make one forget the reality of lived power: the orgy does not put equal individuals in presence, but rather masters and servants.

The men shadowing Bill in *Eyes Wide Shut* could have reappeared in *Under the Silver Lake*: ominous silhouettes in dark alleyways, pure Id-like menace and yet reminders of the superego's basic functions. These presences remain unaccounted for, be it in Kubrick or Mitchell's film. However, this is neither an esoteric signature nor the trace of a hidden power. Secret or public, explicit or implicit, power is both a vector and a product of representations.[8] Seeing the mask he was wearing at the party on the pillow next to his sleeping wife, Bill decides to confess to her all his nocturnal adventures, even as they never reached the stage of philandering. However, this surge toward consciousness isn't, with both characters "waking up," as has been pointed out elsewhere (see Marsa), a refusal of the smokescreen. What Kubrick shows is that once one awakens from the dream, only the mask remains. This does not mean that the reality of things can be reduced to their simulation. But that the conceptualization of the real is consubstantial with its sensitive apprehension, be it imaginary. *Eyes Wide Shut* does not narrate the plunge into the self, so much as the surge upward toward consciousness: consciousness of the self, of desire, of power.

From Mask to Obstacle

The central scene of *Under the Silver Lake* is unwittingly revealing. Meeting a mysterious songwriter-composer figure living and composing as a recluse in a vast mansion, Sam finds out that the old man wrote all the tunes that accompanied his teenage revolts: "Even when you rebelled, you rebelled to the sound of my music. . . . I am the voice of your generation. . . . All your dreams are the product of the ambition of others." A century after the *Mutual Film Corporation v. Industrial Commission of*

Ohio case, the film pokes fun (or does it?) at the fact that the cultural industry's nature, first and foremost, as a mercantile enterprise, should come as a shock and revelation to the otherwise all-doubting and inquisitive protagonist. In what type of world does Sam live, that the words of the old man can pass as revelation? Who can believe that capitalism is an occult system? We live, in Europe and the United States at least, on the contrary, in the most manifest political and economic regime that can be: so long, of course, as one accepts to see it for what it is.

Kubrick gave no more importance to the interiority of power than he did to the characters. If social and political life require shutting up or dissimulation, the act or the actor in hiding, are within the act or the actor who dissimulates. Only what can be seen can be conceptualized: if the real individual is inseparable from the public person, then real power is not distinct from sensitive/sensible power. Kubrick's oeuvre presents itself like a game of esoteric signatures, the clandestine decoding key which is kept by the spectator's unconscious. This is critical nonsense, and perhaps bait from Kubrick himself to the audience or critic.

Viewers will find no unveiling of reality of power in *Dr. Strangelove*, but merely its ordinary crudeness. They will find no conspiracy in the social cheating and trickery of which *Barry Lyndon* is in turn the subject, and the object. As for *The Shining*, it reminds us that there is nothing to explore in the human soul that isn't already at its surface. Power is never transparent, it can only be represented if it is thought out, and it can only be thought through its representation—be it allusive, indirect, tormented, or unspeakable. "Jesus wouldn't hide a message in a message" says Sam at one point in *Under the Silver Lake*. But the exercise of power has nothing in common with the language of saints or angels, which is a language without language, without signified mediation, without subtleties and shades of gray, and without equivocation or possible betrayal (see Chrétien 1990). Whether power is deployed in physical or symbolic spaces, the principle of publicity designates both the conditions of a dialectical shaping of the shown and the thought: in this sense, Kubrick is a cinematic thinker, not of secrecy and conspiracy, but of publicity indeed.

Secrecy is often opposed to transparency, and this is why it is often considered a perversion of political activity or, at best, a necessary evil. Kubrick's cinema reminds us that the practice of secret and the desire for transparency indeed share a similar relationship to political truth. Whether the war room of *Dr. Strangelove*, the backstage rulings of *Barry Lyndon*, the unspeakable gothic of *The Shining*, or the pseudo-estotericism of *Eyes Wide Shut*—or all four gathered in *Under the Silver Lake*—the secret must institute a place removed from the world, isolated from the public, within which immediate communication is however made possible. The secret is each time presented as a nonideal device aiming to approximate the conditions of authentic transparency within a narrow frame. Paradoxically, like transparency, the secret must allow in itself a perfect communication, stripped of any undesirable distortion. At last, it paves the way to candid interactions (*Strangelove*); to codes shared without any preliminary deliberation being necessary (*Barry Lyndon*); to a space where one can communicate without even having to talk (*Eyes Wide Shut*). Of course, masks are never entirely removed, even among the revelers. Besides, it is possible to conceive of this perfect transparency only in the silent monologue of one's inner self. And such monologue is either impossible, or self-destructing and maddening (*The Shining*). But in political terms, both transparency and secrecy rely on the idea that the justification of power is not something that can be built together, but which is discovered or rediscovered like a precious object, a lost moment. This ideal of communication without interference is founded on the conception of political rationality whereby political truth can be discovered independently of the practical circumstances of human interactions. As shown in another way in the "carceral-therapeutic" system of *A Clockwork Orange* (1971), it is the reason why the pursuit of so-called transparency is perfectly compatible with the practical restoration of secrecy in a nondemocratic regime. To believe in the secrecy of power is tantamount to believing in its possible transparency.

The Images to Say It, the Words to Show It

For Kubrick, political power is no silent truth to unearth, and the ideal of transparency is just one concept among other ones. The bunkers where it hides, the rites that legitimize it, the nightmares concealing its nature, and the masks it wears are not only what makes it visible. They are part of its very nature. Whether they are the codes of the *Ancien Régime* in *Barry Lyndon* or the taboo of infanticide in *The Shining*, the truth of power does not reside in its opacity, but in the staging of this opacity. Publicity and transparency are often associated in the public debate, insofar as ideas seem to call for more visibility of power. In truth, the publicity principle and the ideal of transparency are founded on different, even diverging, conceptions of public reason. Publicity is the art of political mediation; transparency leads on the contrary to an ideal of political immediacy. Transparency is to favor a candid relationship between the members of a political community; publicity, on the contrary, transforms public debate into a constant process of surveillance and contradiction. Transparency must contribute to the unifying of consciousness. Publicity has as its effect and function the nourishment of political conflict. Lastly, and most importantly, the ideal of transparency is based on the idea that immediate communication is desirable because it takes for granted that the common good is not built but unveiled. The principle of publicity is based on the idea whereby linguistic mediation is not a lesser evil, but a necessary tool. For a theorist like Carl Schmitt, the problem with the publicity principle is not that it makes political activity overly visible, but, on the contrary, that it is incapable of making the latter authentically transparent: political language must come as close as possible to divine silence. For Kubrick, on the contrary, transparency is a toxic illusion. Cinema is not a means to elucidate the real, but to think about the way man creates the real.

While the discovery of the political is inseparable from its representations, Kubrick takes cinema for a rhetorical device all the more dangerous that it is asymmetrical. To quote Simone Chambers, cinema constitutes the plebiscitary *dispositif* par excellence (Chambers 2009). Within this frame, the setting of a publicity-oriented cinema does not only reflect Kubrick's political conception. It also constitutes a full-blown ethical proposal. On the one hand, distance must allow one to defuse or undermine domination. Be it in the films discussed here or in *Fear and Desire* (1953), *The Killing* (1956), and *Paths of Glory* (1958)—the use of voice-over is a metonym of Kubrick's cinema as a whole: it marks a will to master the narrative,[9] creates a distance, vis-à-vis the filming subjectivity as well as vis-à-vis the filmed subjectivities. This distance does not mean that the voice speaks the truth or is candid,[10] but rather that reason has something to say. On the other hand, communication must prevent authoritarian or coercive dimension of the instilled distance. Be it the Harfords, the Lyndons, or the Torrances, it is the impossibility of talking to one another or to oneself that is the source of moral, social, and political alienation. Conversely, it is the acknowledgment of their limits that allows—or could have allowed—the characters to accept their humanity as well as the mundane reality of power.

The political proposal central to Kubrick's cinema is however more provocative altogether: while rescuing reason requires the promotion of a publicity conception of public reason, promoting a publicity conception of public reason is tantamount to admitting that lies are just an inevitable dimension of political activity. If we consider that the exercise of reason always revolves around shared significations, this means that the exercise of public reason revolves around publicly justifiable significations. Viewed thus, no doubt it is desirable that these significations correspond to exact enunciations (*énoncés*), to sincere opinions, or to deliberations conducted in good faith. However, the definition of these criteria is circumstantial, and their determination not easily verifiable. How can one verify the exactness of a statement before any contradictory debate? How can one determine what constitutes a sincere deliberation? Finally, how can one define what constitutes insincerity itself? May the Kubrickian character be characterized by the fact that they are (self) deceiving—despite what they reveal (to oneself), or the opposite? A lie does not consist univocally in passing for real a false statement. The empty eyes of Bill Harford tell of the character and his time, even perhaps without realizing it. And as is underlined in almost every scene of *Barry Lyndon*, the belief that the liars themselves hold true can turn out to be false, whereas the belief that they publicly hold for false can incidentally be true. On the one hand, a Kubrickian character's lies, and on the other hand, inauthenticity and alienation, do nonetheless cause real and genuine effects. A social simulacrum, a revealed fantasy or unearthed madness, may neither be real nor false, yet this doesn't mean they are without signification. As such, lying is much more revealing than the angelic muteness presiding over the pursuit of transparency. On the other hand, if access to the world does not require taking off the mask, but keeping it on and observing the uses and rules, the distinction between publicity and lies is practically indeterminate. The use of lies would not be intrinsically noxious to reflection if it were possible to clearly distinguish what turns out to be the autonomous exercise of imagination, and what constitutes an abusive language exercise. And yet, whatever the moral worth attributed to lies or to the ideal of publicity, the definition and justification of lies and publicity are themselves a matter of representation—even one of representation's representation.

The fascination for secrecy and the desire for transparency are fed on the same myths (Fenster 2017): they can only be solitary or unanimous. For Kubrick, what is thinkable is consubstantial to the visible. The political, like cinema, does not unveil itself: it displays itself. Kubrick's fabled skeptical rationalism thus leads to an apparent dilemma: to will transparency is to go mad; to defend publicity is to acquiesce to lies. In this frame, the difference between publicity and lies is very thin. It doesn't reside in the opposition between reason and passion, between facts and fiction, between benevolence and malevolence, nor even between candor and cunning. It resides in our ability to put words on an experience and to put an experience on the words we use. It is by failing in this enterprise that Redmond Barry exits the story, that Jack Torrance gets lost and freezes to death in the maze, and that the Harford couple thinks it can and should just fuck while awaiting death. Lies have as their object the rupture of the rapport that we have to the world, by presenting this world as obvious, intelligible. Publicity allows one to speak of the world as a problematic entity: in public life as in cinema, to not fall for the narrative/what is being shown requires, also, that one cannot leave it unscathed. The exercise of power remains secret only to those who don't dare to look, there, at the surface of things, thinking that some dark truth lies instead at the bottom of the silver lake.

Notes

1 See also Vincent, « Une histoire du secret » (1987).
2 To pick but one example, Axel Gosseries analyzes the "Glomar response" case in the American jurisprudence. The *Freedom of Information Act* guarantees the citizen general access to the public documents as well as to the reasons that would justify a possible refusal to divulge these documents (*Phillippi vs. C.I.A*, 546 F. 2d 1009, 1011 [D.C. Cir. 1976]). However, there are certain cases in which the reasons for this refusal also reveal the content of the document. In this context, the effectiveness of the unofficial standard requires secrecy. This is also the paradoxical reason why secrecy often accompanies the spectacularisation of the "official" norm.
3 The "candor and frankness" argument was used successively by the Nixon, Reagan, Clinton, and Bush administrations—and supported by the Supreme Court, which deems it to be plain commonsense (*US vs. Nixon*, 483 U.S. 683, 1974, pp. 705–06 et 708): it is time for somebody in the administration, somebody in the executive branch to stop the slide, where presidential authority, constitutionally vested, has been yielded to Congress, since Watergate and Vietnam. That's been a steady erosion of constitutional authority, granted to the President. The damage to a democracy that can get done, is if people—the next group of people, of ethicists and academicians who would get called on to give a President counsel, say, "I cannot give you counsel because a year from now, six months from now, one month from now, they may want to have everything I say to you be turned into a press release. And I think the nation is best served by me being able to speak to you candidly and from the heart." (Office of the Press Secretary, Press briefing conducted by White House spokesperson Ari Fleischer, 2002 [in Griffin 2003: 35]).
4 Lest it be misunderstood, publicity is meant here not as 'advertisement' or promotion (of which Kubrick was a great master, after all), but as the systematic making public

of a debate or deliberation, or any other form of political activity. It is, in this sense, opposed to the principle of secrecy or deliberation behind closed doors.
5   See for instance the documentary *Room 237* (Rodney Ascher, 2012), or Cocks (2004).
6   So "Jack Nicholson of *The Shining* is possessed neither by evil as such nor by the 'devil' or some analogous occult force, but rather simply by History, by the American past as it has left its sedimented traces in the corridors and dismembered suites of this monumental rabbit warren, which oddly projects its empty formal after-image in the maze outside (significantly, the maze is Kubrick's own addition)" (Jameson 123).
7   Freud (1998: 221).
8   "At the end of Stanley Kubrick's career, narrative authority seemed to be a failed pursuit in the face of the kind of ambiguity that pervades *Eyes Wide Shut* [...] Bill once again returns home. Shocked even further by the sight of his orgy mask lying next to Alice-painfully realizing the unavoidability of counternarratives he cannot control-Bill finally breaks down in tears and opens up to his wife. 'I'll tell you everything,' he confesses, something he should have been prepared to do the night they both got high and Alice told him about her secret sexual desires. This willingness to confess, meanwhile, perhaps points to the possibility of Bill finally emerging as a relatively successful narrator, recalling to his wife neither his foolish desires nor faulty assumptions but merely his own limited experiences," (Sperb 2004: 37). See also Marsa (2010).
9   See Sperb; Garcia Mainar (1999).
10 See Miller; Kozloff (1988: 119). As Bilge Ebiri observes, "Kubrick's characters have no recollection of the past, and no awareness of the future. It is the disembodied voice so prevalent in his films—the HAL 9000 computer or the narrator of *Barry Lyndon*—that see several moves ahead and see destiny at work. These voices, however, eventually become characters themselves, at the mercy of another being, another force, one that may be identified with Kubrick's camera, or simply the spectator."

Works Cited

Baudrillard, Jean. 2004. "History: A Retro Scenario," in *Simulacra and Simulation*, trans. Sheila Faria Glaser. Ann Arbor: University of Michigan.
Gosseries, Axel. 2005/2017. "Publicity," *Stanford Encyclopedia of Philosophy*, http://plato.stanford.edu/entries/publicity/A. Gosseries.
Chambers, Simone. 2009. "Rhetoric and the Public Sphere: Has Deliberative Democracy Abandoned Mass Democracy?," *Political Theory* 37(3 June): 323–50.
Chion, Michel. 2002. *Eyes Wide Shut*, trans. T. Selous. London: British Film Institute.
Chrétien, Jean-Louis. 1990. *La voix nue. Phénoménologie de la promesse*. Paris: Minuit.
Cocks, Geoffrey. 2004. *The Wolf at the Door: Stanley Kubrick, History and the Holocaust*. New York: Peter Lang.
Ebiri, Bilge (2006) "Barry Lyndon: the Shape of Things to Come." Blog entry. http://www.visual-memory.co.uk/amk/doc/0026.html.

Fenster, Mark. 2017. *The Transparency Fix: Secrets, Leaks, and Uncontrollable Government Information*. Stanford: Stanford University Press.
Freud, Sigmund. 1998. *L'Inquiétante Étrangeté et autres* essais [1919] (Paris: Gallimard, 1998), 221.
Griffin, Christopher G. 2003. "An *Egalitarian* Argument *Against Executive Privilege*," *Journal of Information Ethics* 12(1), 34–44.
Jameson, Fredric. 1990. "Historicism in *The Shining* (1981)," in *Signatures of the Visible*. New York and London: Routledge, 112–35.
Klein, Michael. 1981. "Narrative and Discourse in Kubrick's Modern Tragedy," in Michael Klein and Parker Gillian (ed.), *The English Novel and the Movies*. New York, Frederick Ungar Publishing, 95–107.
Kozloff, Sarah. 1988. *Invisible Storytellers: Voice-Over Narration in American Fiction Film*. Berkeley: University of California Press.
Garcia Mainar, Luis M. 1999. *Narrative and Stylistic Patterns in the Films of Stanley Kubrick* Rochester, NY: Camden House.
Marsa, Julien. 2010. "Du sommeil à l'état de veille," April 20. https://www.critikat.com/panorama/analyse/eyes-wide-shut.
Miller, Mark Crispin. 1976. "*Barry Lyndon* reconsidered," *The Georgia Review* 30(4): 827–53.
Pestiau, J. 2001. "Mondialisation et bricolage démocratique », *Mondialisation: perspectives philosophiques, Actes du colloque Philosophie et mondialisation tenu à l'Université du Québec à Trois-Rivières les 23 et 24 févr. 2001.*" Paris: L'Harmattan.
Sidgwick, Henry. 1893. *The Method of Ethics*, 5th ed. London: Macmillan.
Sperb, Jason. 2004. "The Country of the Mind in Kubrick's *Fear and Desire*," *Film Criticism* 29(1, Fall): 23–37.
Turquet de Mayerne, Loys. 1611. *La monarchie aristodémocratique, ou le Gouvernement composé et meslé des trois formes de lgitimes rpubliques*. Paris: Jean Berjon et Jean Le Bouc.
Vincent, Gérard. 1987. « Une histoire du secret », in Ariès, Philippe, Duby, Georges (eds.), *Histoire de la vie privée tome 5 : de la première guerre mondiale à nos jours*. Paris: Seuil, 155–90.

12

Coping with the Unknown in *2001: A Space Odyssey* and *Interstellar*

Mircea Valeriu Deaca

While many have marveled at the visual feats and special effects of *2001: A Space Odyssey* (Stanley Kubrick, 1968) and *Interstellar* (Christopher Nolan, 2014), the latter overtly paying homage to the former, I propose to analyze, in what follows, how, from a cognitive science perspective, the films operate on very different levels, despite constituting definite landmarks of the science fiction genre.

The Sci-Fi Template

2001: A Space Odyssey and *Interstellar* feature a strong resemblance, a kinship almost. A post hoc analysis can construe them as prototypes of the science fiction film: Nolan continues Kubrick's artistic legacy, and, at the same time, brings a different approach to the genre. In *2001*, the main components of the science fiction template are the *spaceship* and the *cosmic landscape*. Kubrick insistently uses descriptive shots that explore the interior of the ship. His camera foregrounds the austere futuristic interior design and the stylized shapes of screen monitors in preparation for the sequences that display mobility. Nolan prefers instead to integrate the more complex interior design of the spaceship in dramatic and dialogue sequences. The cockpit is for Nolan a hybrid between the static interior and the mobile exterior view. Both directors use extreme long shots and long takes that focus either on the cosmic landscape devoid of human artifacts or on the minuscule insertion of human artifacts in cosmic space.

Few elements are needed in order to evoke the sci-fi template; *monitor screens* and *telecommunication screens*, *robots* (HAL-9000, TARS, and CASE), *spaceships*, *space costumes*, *screens*, and *laboratories* suffice. The *cosmonaut* and *the scientific authority* (Professor Brand and Dr. Floyd) are equally represented in Kubrick's and Nolan's films. A common attitude of deception in the face of a crisis that cannot be epistemically mastered underlies the treatment of science and scientific artifacts in both films. For Kubrick, the crisis is generated by the apparition of incomprehensible objects and events, while for Nolan, crisis has a natural cause: Earth's depletion of natural resources and the coterminous increase of nitrogen in the atmosphere. In both films, the failure of the scientific procedures and instruments attract attention to the human factor. The fragility of the human body and mind is forced to confront the inhuman vastness of nature, unprotected by technological prosthetics.

For both directors, the failure of technology is a metaphor for the human condition before nature. For Kubrick, this metaphor is mapped in timelessness and rebirth (the final image of the Star Child floating near the Earth), while for Nolan, romantic love represents the essence of human nature that can surpass the ineluctability of the "arrow of time." Kubrick's metaphor is open; the viewer can freely choose a multitude of symbolic and even sacred interpretations. The movie *2001* is "endlessly suggestive," as Annette Michelson (1969) pointed out. In a sense, for Kubrick, the reversal of fate is self-referential, and illustrates "the grand theme and subject of learning as self recognition" (Michelson 1969). Kubrick doesn't elaborate on emotions and empathy. He depicts the encounter between the human element with a transcendental factor that can be experienced and apprehended in its benevolent facet (Bowman is the spectator of his own life) or malevolent aspect (HAL's inhuman logic). Transcendental reality can be experienced as wisdom or as madness. For Nolan, artificial intelligence is beneficial as long as it is infused with human qualities like friendship, humor, and love. Nolan depicts emotion and love as human elements that counterbalance nature's inhumanity. Surpassing the crisis means mastering the knowledge of the human self in romantic love and affective bonding.

The component elements that cue the sci-fi template can be understood as integrated *functional bundles*—a term used by Torben Grodal that designates "mental units that are invented, mind-grabbing, attention-grabbing, and widely communicated" (Grodal 2009: 31–35). Salient functional bundles—comparable to objects like spears, wheels, and bridges—perform an "easy-to-grasp function in relation to quasi-universal needs and mental models" (34). For example, shields or protective surfaces are imitations of natural elements—say, the shells of turtles—and can be transformed into force shields that protect against laser beams or rockets. In most sci-fi films we find a *functional bundle* in which one concept refers to something which is *familiar* and *known*, and the other features something that is *unfamiliar* and *strange*. For example, the *functional bundle* of the "mad scientist" incorporates the familiar figure of the "scientist" and the concept of "madness," an unfamiliar and alien mental state. The "robot" is also a mixture of the human and nonhuman. In other cases, both concepts can be familiar, but some aspect of the fictional world that they inhabit isn't. The presence of a hybrid composed of elements not normally expected to occur together in conventional instances, either as a "functional bundle" or as an entire new counterfactual situation, is a characteristic of the sci-fi template. The main role played by the familiar component of the hybrid is to focus the viewer's experience and reflection on social and moral grounds. In other words, the film invites the viewer to philosophical thinking.

The "What If" Scenario and the Unknown Factor

A main feature of the sci-fi template is understood as a thought experiment based on the "what if" speech act scenario. The conceptual description of the counterfactual proposition contains a comparison between an actual situation (the grounding natural world conception) and an alien one (the proposed new situation or event). Due to this discursive act, sci-fi presents a vision of the fictional world that is "in itself valuable as a pronouncement on everyday reality" (Tan 1996: 97). Sci-fi is often linked to allegorical reading and meta-cinematic interpretations (*La Jetée* [1963], *The Truman Show* [1998], or *Alphaville* [1965]). The viewer is invited to reconsider the fragile nature of the elements that compose his everyday environment and his inner self.

In addition, we can separate the "what if" scenario from the *unknown factor*. The unknown factor represents any experience where the object perceived cannot be classified; it has an expressive manifestation, but its conceptual content can be constructed as a very limited one (it is grasped only through metaphor). In the sci-fi template, the "what if" is the result of the emergence of a new configuration of known elements or the change of salience of one component. In contrast, the unknown is provided by an uncategorizable entity, object, or event. Sci-fi films are mixtures of these two aspects. Some films play up the "what if" scenario, and others foreground the *unknown factor*.

In *Interstellar*, the "what if" scenario is instantiated as the catastrophe of a dying Earth. The disturbing circumstance is a known one. The viewer knows the possible consequences of overpopulation and scarcity of resources. We find several other what if scenarios in the film. What if Earth exhausted its resources? What if a wormhole appeared near Earth? What if we could explore the inside of a black hole? What if we could explore space and time irrespective of the dimensional obstacle? In *Interstellar*, the "big" unknowns are the arrow of time, gravity, and space configuration in black hole conditions (singularities and wormholes), and extra dimensions of space, which can somehow be navigated by humans.

In *2001*, the monolith is the emblematic manifestation of the unknown and, at the same time, the expression of the "what if" scenario. The situation can be summarized as follows: What if one day in the course of (pre)human life, some unknown factor manifested itself? The unknown takes shape as uncontrollable elements. The unknown factor is represented by the monolith, time, and mental confusion. HAL 9000 as an artificial entity is also a manifestation of the unknown. Its madness is the hypostatization of the unknown.

The Reification of Qualities

For Kubrick, the unknown is represented as hyperbolic displays of audiovisual stimuli. Awe-inspiring sequences in long takes disclose the perceptual appearance of the unknown (Spielberg followed suit with *Close Encounters of the Third Kind* [1977]). These sequences are cinema-as-spectacle in its purest form, where all diegetic pretensions are left behind for the pure epiphany of the "undescribable." In *2001*, movement is extracted as an essential and reified feature of the unknown. For example, in the first chapter of the film, the movement of the bone is identical to the movement of the spaceship. The shared movement of two different objects alienates the objects in movement and makes perceptible movement *per se*, which acquires a transcendental essence.

We as humans sense the movement behind objects in motion, but we do not directly perceive movement as a substance. Kubrick invites the viewer to conceptualize that which grounds moving entities in an imperceptible way: a relationship that is fluid in time, and is a condensation of the quality of movement. The uneasiness experienced by the viewer is caused by the fact that once we subtract the object, we can't apprehend movement as an autonomous entity, independent of the bodies that instantiate it. Movement as qualia of the unknown is displayed or revealed by objects and, at the same time, it is hidden as an ever-unattainable entity.[1]

For Michelson, *2001*'s "formal statement" concerns the nature of movement. Viewing is, through the "acknowledgment of disorientation," the discovery of "what is to see, to learn, to know, and of what it is to be, seeing" (Michelson 1969: 58). Kubrick's film clarifies "something of the essential nature of motion itself" (58). In this sense, Kubrick's film is evocative of the discourse on the mimetic function of art. Thus, art becomes an exploration of the component elements of consciousness that, through the work of imagination, create reality.

The movement of the landscape in the "Jupiter and beyond the infinite" sequence is ambiguous in terms of its spatial frame of reference. During the long point-of-view sequence, the viewer can either interpret the abstract landscape as moving toward Bowman or the character himself as moving forward. This kinetic trope renders the unknown of time-movement in spatial terms. Is the arrow of time a flow in which the reference point is static, or is the forward motion engaging the reference point, thus rendering it fluid? Motion, and not the object in motion, is the profiled and alienating element of the film. It is one possible manifestation of the unknown.

For Michelson, the main theme of the film is the movement of bodies in space during the exploration of the Unknown in order to regain the familiar and the Real. In contrast, I stress here the presence of what we can qualify as the unknown in the perceptual experience itself. Kubrick deconstructs the familiarity of entities in order to isolate and render salient their component qualities. The unknown is thus what lies under the surface of the subjective perceptual experience and grounds experience and consciousness. The episode of "Jupiter and beyond the infinite" isolates the features that compose integrated perceptual experience, and displays them as autonomous abstract concepts: shape, color, texture, and movement.

In *2001*, Kubrick explores the interplay between equilibrium and disequilibrium, and the slow motion that infuses objects and entities. Several scenes insist on the choreographic effects of the lack of gravity (an estrangement of natural movement), and others highlight the technical devices used in order to create artificial gravity (an element of realism). Characters' bodies stand upright in gravity-controlled settings and—as a sign of the inhuman intervention—as the film progresses, bodies are turned upside down and made to float freely. Bodies gradually lose their material rigidity in order to make visible the ungraspable qualia of movement, its spiritual essence. *2001* insists over and over again on the aesthetics and mysticism of movement in order to make tangible the "unknown." The journey or the quest is one manifestation of this vital animation out of which one can apprehend the meaning of the world. In order to grasp essential human nature, we have to discard the body and discover movement as fundamental animation. Therefore, we can say that, for Kubrick, the perfect human body is the dead body of the astronaut drifting freely through the cosmic void.

Relevant here is Sheets-Johnstone's idea that qualitative kinetic dynamics are a way of coordination with the inherent movement created by the alternation between stable and unstable states of nature, and a way of understanding the world's impermanence. The patterns of movement represent the dynamics of thinking. As such, even stillness is a repository of virtual movement patterns. Stillness contains tension and is imbued with the expectancy of future movement. Aliveness is grounded in movement as the concept of self agency (*I can*). For Sheets-Johnstone "kinaesthetic awareness constitutes our basic 'perceptual organ' of space and time" (Sheets-Johnstone 1999: 113).

For Kubrick, the trajectories of floating bodies are mapped through seamless camera movement. Baroque object movement or sophisticated camera movements will dominate films that belong to this paradigm: *The Matrix* (1999–2003), *Gravity* (2012), *Transformers* (2003–2017), or the *Batman* or *Spiderman* films. Sci-fi films that belong to this category tend to privilege the awe-inspiring sequence. By having their expectations teased via baroque displays of light and movement, the audience is prepared for the sublime landscape of the unknown—which is the exacerbation of cinema's potential. These sequences are about cinema tricks revealed or cinema in its purest form (see for instance *Ready Player One* [2018]). Often camera movement is, from an explanatory standpoint, diegetically motivated: it describes and mirrors point-of-view shots of characters either endowed with superhuman abilities or inscribed in exceptional contexts. At first it seems the cosmic renderings of the intergalactic ships or the black hole visualization (*Interstellar*), the futuristic city landscape (*Metropolis*, *Blade Runner*, and *Star Wars*) or the natural landscapes of exoplanets (*Star Wars* and *Avatar*) are motivated by the fictional situation. But, upon second glance, complex and dizzying camera movements generate the feeling of the fluid ungraspable qualities detached from the stable substance of objects. Camera movement metaphorically maps the reality of the unknown; it is an illustration of the strangeness of the unknown, rendering salient the features of the unconceivable.

In order to render visible the estrangement of movement, *Interstellar* reiterates shots framed from the vantage point of a camera attached to the body of a rocket. The object in movement is firmly still and the landscape through which the viewer navigates is mobile. The frame of reference is unnaturally reversed. The viewer has to make a retro-perceptual effort in order to understand the dynamic of the object in movement.

In *2001*, Kubrick deconstructs human experience in component modalities that gain prominence as transcendental qualia by, for example, disembodying the human voice.[2] Like movement, voice is given focus and attentional enhancement in order to gain the status of autonomous qualia. HAL is a voice without a body, and the astronauts are bodies without voices. HAL's vision of humans is skewed and distorted. Human bodies and faces seen from the vantage point of the inhuman AI are distorted shapes. As abstract expressive features, they gain autonomy through reification. Just like movement, voice, shapes, and colors are extracted from their diegetic context and are enlarged as salient expressive features of the image. This estrangement generates an anxiety-rich experience that can be metaphorically construed as mapping the features of the concept of the spiritual.

Similarly, Kubrick renders perceptible the unknown dwelling under familiarity, and induces the viewer's uneasiness with extremely balanced and symmetrical shot designs. Michelson again explains that in this film form, "parameters of movement, scale, direction, intensity are examined, exploited," and "seeing itself" is profiled (61). Decoupling qualia from the objects they are fused with leads to their abstracting. Decoupling movement from the body in movement allows us to think about the concept of "movement," and subsequently to apply it to different conceptual domains. Features of experience such as spatial coordinates, time flow, movement, or shape thus provide us with patterns employed in the thinking process. Bodily experience of movement can in this way be conceived as a feature of symbolic thinking ("ideas come and go").

The historical jump from the "ape-like" epistemic condition to space technology is prompted by the use of such abstract concepts. The cognitive leap is achieved via the abstracting of the relationships between objects. The movie *2001* describes the progress of humankind in the famous juxtaposition of the shot displaying the airborne bone of the ape, and the one that shows the starship floating in space. Perceiving a new causal chain allows the hominid ape to instrumentalize the bone. The bone is thus conceived as an instrument of control over the terrestrial environment. The spaceship allows humanity to control the cosmic environment. But Kubrick's film also enacts the decoupling of abstract features from their original context.

Both *2001* and *Interstellar* dedicate a final sequence to the deconstructed representation of time. In *2001*, different slices of Bowman's life span coexist in a single spatial setting. The image of the space pod dwelling inside the Louis XVI interior design disrupts familiarity. The interior design is also an "unnatural" hybrid that blends two familiar domains, that is, starships and antique furniture, in order to make manifest the estrangement, the unknown, or the time frozen into a reified time bereft of any flow. Time is no more an impalpable continuous drift between slices, but is extracted from experience as a substantive quality consubstantial with its domain of manifestation. Kubrick's impossible hybrids reinvigorate the old literary tradition of images of chaos revealing the transcendental order. The motif of the *impossibilia* or *adynata* has a long history in medieval literature (Curtius 2013: 95). The "stringing together of impossibilities" represents exceptional moments where the world is out of joint or turned upside down in a crisis that reveals the sacred/divine, the transcendental, or the after-world.[3] The encounter between old Bowman and the fetus is also a revival of the ancient literary topos of the *puer senex* in which old and young coincide in the same hybrid entity (Curtius 2013: 99).

Nolan adopts a different strategy in *Interstellar*: separate instances of a lifetime coexist in a single tesseract maze that displays time in spatial terms, and where movement is hypostasized as emotion. Emotion is what moves us. For Kubrick, movement is abstract and rendered separate from the object engaged in movement. For Nolan, movement is grounded on the reference system of the starship. The spaceship is the stable element that allows the viewer to perceive motion in space. Movement is grounded in emotional experience. Whereas for Kubrick, the Renaissance moment is figured as an epistemic leap of humanity, for Nolan, the dawn of a new era is conceived as the recovery of romantic love (love between father and daughter, son and mother, and man and woman).

Taming the Beast

In sci-fi films, the viewer can be in a safe position of control, hidden behind the window of screens, safer even than the thick glasses separating spationauts from the cosmic void. These devices allow control of the seen but protect the viewer from any direct interference with the distant and potential harmful object. Technology is one representation of what is known as the *control cycle* at the diegetic level of films. The control cycle is a cognitive model that comprises elements in interaction as well as several phases unfolding in time dynamically; it can be applied to numerous instances of human experience: physical, perceptual, mental, and social. In the epistemic realm, the control cycle is manifest in the way that some knowledge is acquired by a conceptualizer (see Langacker 2009: 259; Nakashima 2016). The conceptual model of the sci-fi genre would be thus the appropriation of the unknown by use of the control cycle. This appropriation can be diegetic, formal-aesthetic, discursive, or epistemic.

Discursive control is often favored. Overt explanations given by different characters or by extradiegetic means (e.g., voice-over or graphic inserts) are also a manner of "taming the beast" that is the unknown, and making it conceivable for the audience. Quite often, sci-fi narratives create a strong expectation for the explanation that will rationalize an aberrant behavior, or the mysterious goals and motives of the alien "Other." Unsurprisingly, then, sci-fi narratives often unfold according to the template of the criminal investigation (the mystery plot) (e.g., *Blade Runner*—itself strongly influenced by Kubrick's films—or *Dark City* [Alex Proyas, 1998]).

Another frequent type of control of the unknown in sci-fi films is narrative control and closure. Suspense is based on the fear of losing control over the strange entity—the abstract concept that cannot be understood directly, but only in a metaphorical, oblique way. Immersed or engaged viewers have the satisfaction of being able to master their fear and experience a feeling of "mastering and competence" (Tan 1996: 28). For Tan, feature films create and offer a resolution of tension (35). Narratives induce tension— that is, a disturbance in an orderly state—that through a process of causal unfolding will be finally resolved, allowing order to be restored. Narrative closure contains an element of emotional tension reduction and creates a feeling of control: the enemy is defeated or the emotional suspense is resolved.

The viewer achieves satisfaction from disclosing the ordered patterns of plot and style as well as from resolution of narrative and diegetic conundrums. One can easily see how this is negotiated in a far more classical way in *Interstellar* than in *2001*.

Sometimes the unknown is rationalized on epistemic and emotional grounds. While for Kubrick aesthetic qualia and conceptual mappings are the concepts that gain the upper hand in front of a frightening unknown, for Nolan it is emotions—romantic and parental love—that are the qualia operating and regulating the control cycle. Cognitive and affective concerns are formulated, assessed, intensified, and finally, through some action, resolved. The aesthetic experience derived from awe-inspiring film sequences is an instance of the process of naturalizing the unknown. On this note, Tan makes a distinction between *film emotion* (emotion created by immersion in the diegesis through narrative flow and emotional simulation) and *artifact emotion* (the reaction of the viewer confronted with the cinematic construal: style or genre recognition) (55). Grasping a particular stylistic pattern is also a way of "tension reduction," and thus a manner of resolving the control cycle. Moreover, audiences watching films of this type are experiencing fear, but they nevertheless also experience the satisfaction of being able to master their fear. Exciting films, such as thrillers and, above all, suspenseful thrillers and horror films, give viewers the opportunity to experience a feeling of mastery or "competence" (28).

Awe-inspiring special effects sequences are frequent in sci-fi films, and constitute a modern version of what Tom Gunning has labeled a "cinema of attractions" (1990). The representation of the strangeness of the "unknown" and of the "Other" as aesthetic objects refurbished for contemplation is one manifestation of the epistemic control cycle. Strange objects are thus apprehended and controlled in an aesthetic mode becoming spectacle. As Johnston points out: "visual spectacle plays a psychological role for the audience, a release that allows them to fantasize about worldwide destruction, or the ability of special effects to tame the sublime and produce 'cognitive mastery' of the panoramic and visually spectacular" (Johnston 2011: 46).

Aesthetics of astonishment serve as catalyst for transcendental seduction in sci-fi dramas and conflicts. Angela Ndalianis defines sci-fi in her *Neo-Baroque Aesthetics and Contemporary Entertainment* (2004) as a contemporary manifestation of the baroque style and conception that, among other features, offers us the "sensual seduction" of transcendence. Ndalianis highlights the features of Neo-Baroque as excessive display of virtuosity, special effects, and intense design of perceptual wonders.[4] The exuberant display of a cinematic roller coaster of the senses created by enhanced cinematic illusionism provides the audiences with a sentiment of transcendence and "spiritual presence" (Ndalianis 2004: 209). Here both *2001* and *Interstellar* serve as prime examples: the spiritual encounter with the sacred is projected in spatial journeys and cyberspace (226). The narrative drama and confrontation with the evil played out in this film give characters mythical proportions. The sci-fi protagonist achieves the dimensions of a mythical hero of sorts.

The viewer's fascination and emotional engrossment in the abstract flow of aesthetically satisfying images produce a conversion of the fear of the unknown into the feeling of control and tension resolution. As Johnston highlighted, inserting the camera in the midst of a special effects sequence has become prevalent in sci-fi films, thus mirroring the enhanced effects of sound design and actors' bodily performance in 3D settings (Johnston 2011: 19). Kubrick stages the human control of the unknown as intensified aesthetic experience while Nolan stages the control drama as intensification of human bonding and empathy. We see that Nolan prefers framings that enhance the sublime *impossibilia* of landscape, for example, maelstroms of water, cosmic voids, the oxymoronic vortex of a blazing black hole, and solid frozen clouds.[5] Against this background, the melodramatic tension of emotion and action is foregrounded. The viewer is engaged in the empathic follow up of the character in order to have the experience of intense emotional involvement and absorption (See Tan 2008). Unlike Kubrick's, Nolan's drama stages the control cycle not as a pure aesthetic experience, but as emotional coping with the inhuman unknown.

The Sublime(s)

Kubrick favors the viewer's visual and aural pleasure, their contemplation of infinity, and the theme of the transcendental as a means of aesthetic control. During his journey to Jupiter and beyond, Dave Bowman is the passive spectator of the unfolding display of "formless," "monstrous," and purely "negative entities" that manifest the existence of the invisible unknown in the realm of the visible. Ineffable qualities (movement, shape, texture, and sound) that normally constitute just the building blocks of "integrated" conceptual entities are transposed as autonomous entities. Grodal remarks that Kubrick cultivates the "grandiose aesthetics of space" that are "mental models of phenomena beyond an enactive human control, and they evoke pure perception and contemplation" (1999: 276). Grodal highlights the passive position of the viewer that simulates the mental states of the character driven by major exterior forces. For him, "this produces a feeling of heteronomy, of being carried away by sublime exterior forces, inputs that can only be processed by non-motor simulating, affective reactions" (1999: 255). In the present analytical framework, the viewer is prompted by Kubrick to experience an active perceptual and aesthetic pleasurable control of the unknown revealed as raw expression and pure cinema.

David Rodowick states about Lyotard's figural and Kantian's version of the sublime: "When one represents the non-demonstrable, representation itself is martyred" (2001: 23). In this concept of the sublime, spiritual essence and art coalesce. Art is a simulacrum that makes present the non-representable. Kubrick's intensification and reification of the expressive and his intensification of conceptual and emotional capacity linked to the perception of aesthetic qualities promotes the transcendental as art in its purest form (See also Grodal 2009: 240). *2001: A Space Odyssey* is an experimental artwork whose "nondeterminable and nonteleological orientation" aims at the interrogation of the foundations of art. Arriving in the wake of Kant/Lyotard, Kubrick's art is, again quoting from Rodowick, a "'genre' without a specific end, a genre whose end is always in question and to be determined, never already determined" (29).

To sum up, for Kubrick, humanity is defined by a series of epistemic leaps. With each leap, humans can design better conceptual tools for solving existential problems, and can make better use of their imaginative capacities and metaphoric thinking. Kubrick embraces a disembodied approach to cognition, a faculty of the mind independent of the body that can shape the world *and* the body. From a philosophical perspective, then, Kubrick is a Cartesian.

Nolan, in contrast, favors the emotional involvement in the melodrama and sadness caused by loss and separation in a post-mortem journey.[6] Cooper, in the Dantesque tradition, impersonates the metaphor of "life is a journey." Awe-inspiring scenes and tragic moments induce helplessness and coerce surrender to something "bigger than life" (Grodal 2009: 128). But rituals of death, grief, and mourning are also a way of creating a bond between humans. Fear and pain caused by loss, separation and lack of control can be—in an ambivalent manner—reversed into intense exhilarating emotional moments (Grodal 2009: 134–39). In a cathartic twist, intense affective arousal appraised as dysphoric or unpleasant is converted into an intense affective arousal coded as euphoric or pleasant. A common human identity is constructed based on empathy in the face of adversity. The same awe-inspiring situation that sustains sadness and loss is thus recategorized as a pleasant emotion based on a reflection on social bonding and human values. The high arousal of distress becomes an overwhelming thrill. Empathic care and control reverse the fear provoked by the unknown, and reifies the affective bonding between the members of a community. The sublime cultivated by Nolan is the intensification of the transcendental, shared "we-emotions" (Grodal 2017). The lesson we can draw from Nolan's aesthetics is the following: Abstract thinking can be employed in the pursuit of knowledge devoid of affect. However, only when paired with abstracted emotions does abstract thinking rise to the task of defining our humanity. Nolan's approach, then, would be akin to that of a phenomenologist, adopting an embodied approach to cognition based on emotional concepts. Social interactions are based on emotional concepts, and social roles influence how one apprehends oneself and the world. By changing our emotions, we become different, and consequently the world with which we are coupled changes too.

Notes

1 I use the term "qualia" as a perceptual feature infused or blended with cognitive and emotional valence.
2 See a theoretical approach of the notion of "acousmêtre," and a rich illustration of the disembodied voices in film in Michel Chion's book, *La voix au cinéma* (1982).
3 For the use of impossible hybrids see the theme of the "world upside down" in carnival tradition and in Federico Fellini's films in Deaca (2009).
4 Similar predilections appear in contemporary theater (See Lehman 2006) or in Hollywood films as "intensified continuity" of the classical narrative style (See Bordwell 2006).
5 The image of the frozen clouds is also a revival of the oxymoronic of the "inanimate animate" (the automaton, the moving statue) that was a widespread topos in the carnivalesque tradition and baroque imaginary (Deaca 2009; Ndalianis 2004). It can be related to the image of the last circle of hell in Dante's *Divine comedy* quoted in the final images of a frozen Venice in Fellini's *Casanova*.
6 See, for example, Plantinga's (2009) analysis of melodrama in *Titanic*.

Works Cited

Bordwell, David. 2006. *The Way Hollywood Tells It. Story and Style in Modern Movies*. Berkeley, CA: University of California Press.
Chion, Michel. 1982. *La voix au cinéma*. Paris : Cahiers du cinéma. Editions de l'Etoile.
Curtius, Ernst Robert. 2013 [1948] *European Literature and the Latin Middle Ages*. Trad. Willard R. Trask. Princeton: Princeton University Press.
Deaca, Mircea. 2009. *Le Carnaval et le Film de Fellini*. Bucuresti: Editura Libra.
Grodal, Torben. 2009. *Embodied Visions: Evolution. Emotion, Culture, and Film*. Oxford University Press.
Grodal, Torben. 2017. Audience Bonding: Film Viewing as Rituals of Emotional Bonding among Viewers. Working Paper. June 2018 DOI: 10.13140/RG.2.2.23334.73281. 06/2018, Version: one, State: In Progress, DOI: 10.13140/RG.2.2.23334.73281. 2017.
Gunning, Tom. 1990 [1986]. "The Cinema of Attractions. Early Film, Its Spectator and the Avant-Garde," in Thomas Elsaesser (ed.), *Early Cinema: Space. Frame. Narrative*. London: British Film Institute, 56–62.
Johnston, Keith M. 2011. *Science Fiction Film: A Critical Introduction*. London: Berg.
Langacker, Ronald W. 2009. *Investigations in Cognitive Grammar*, Berlin and New York: Mouton de Gruyter.
Lehmann, Hans-Thies. 2006 [1999]. *Postdramatic Theatre*. London: Routledge.
Michelson, Annette. 1969. "Bodies in Space: Film as 'Carnal Knowledge,'" *Artforum*, February 54–63.
Nakashima, Chiharu. 2016. "Two Types of Negatives: In Light of Langacker's Models." *Kyushu University Papers in Linguistics* 36: 227–37.
Ndalianis, Angela. 2004. *Neo-Baroque Aesthetics and Contemporary Entertainment*. Cambridge., MA: The MIT Press.
Plantinga, Carl. 2009. "Trauma. Pleasure and Emotion in the Viewing of *Titanic*. A Cognitive Approach," in Warren Buckland (ed.), *Film Theory and Contemporary Hollywood Movies*. London: Routledge; Francis & Taylor, 237–56.
Rodowick, David. 2001. *Reading the Figural or Philosophy after the New Media*. Durham: Duke University Press.
Sheets-Johnstone, Maxine. 1999. *The Primacy of Movement*. Amsterdam: John Benjamins.
Suvin, Darko. 1979. *Metamorphoses of Science Fiction: On the Poetics and History of a Literary Genre*. New Haven: Yale University Press.
Tan, Ed S. 1996. *Emotion and the Structure of Narrative Film: Film as Emotional Machine*. Hillsdale, NJ: Lawrence Erlbaum.
Tan, Ed S. 2008. "Entertainment is Emotion: The Functional Architecture of the Entertainment Experience." *Media Psychology* 11(1): 28–51.

13

Biopolitical Abjection and Sexuation: Stanley Kubrick's Political Films

Seung-hoon Jeong

Paths of Glory: A Path from Existentialism to Biopolitics

Paths of Glory (1958) may be Stanley Kubrick's most ironically entitled film. It depicts the trench warfare situation of the First World War in which a French division is ordered to take an impregnable German position at the predicted cost of many lives. After the inevitable failure of this "mission impossible," three soldiers are court-martialed for having retreated out of "cowardice." War only pushes them into paths of irrational orders, meaningless struggles, and unavoidable death. "The absurd," in Albert Camus's existentialist terms, indicates this gaping void where no coherent order, clear reason, or valuable meaning of life is found. For Camus (1991: 3), "one truly serious philosophical question" is thus nothing but "suicide," that is, to judge whether or not life is worth living. In a sense, it is as if the command of the suicidal attack and the execution of randomly picked survivors gave this judgment on behalf of those who still cling to life without facing its absurdity.

Existentialism was indeed the postwar zeitgeist, and its influence on early Kubrick is palpable in his war films including his debut feature *Fear and Desire* (1953).[1] His Heideggerian view of existence as "being-toward-death" culminates in *Dr. Strangelove, or, How I Learned to Stop Worrying and Love the Bomb* (1964) in which the ultimate failure of stopping the atomic bombing even suggests the collective suicide of humankind. One might then answer the question posed in the film's subtitle as follows: "By expecting that the bomb will terminate an absurd humanity." This absurd may include

> our proximity to a state of nature, the corruptness of authority and human institutions, disillusionment with ideals such as progress, the banality of the good, the pull of immediate pleasures, the divergence of appearances from reality, the seepage of the nightmare world into daily existence, and the grasping for salvation from beyond the human condition through technology or alien life. (Murray and Schuler 2009, 136)

Of course, the film's ironic subtitle is a nod to a seemingly inescapable doomsday, to which Kubrick alerts with the backdrop of the Cold War crisis and 1960s nuclear angst.

And yet his anti-war humanism, if any, is no naïve pacifism, but rather something like the last bid for the unknown potential of humanity despite the director's deep skepticism about it. Likewise, existentialist heroes—from Oedipus and Sisyphus to Meursault and Roquentin—overcome nihilism by embracing their absurd fate as willingly chosen, thereby performing subjective freedom that enables them to be the master of their life and create its meaning or essence themselves without any objective support (say, a God). This *amor fati*, a Nietzschean "yes," underlies Camus's passion for life as well as Jean-Paul Sartre's existentialism as humanism.

However, it should be noted that war in *Paths of Glory* is not just absurd but highly indicative of the systematic way that power works over life. It turns out that the suicidal mission was plotted to use its foreseeable victims as a means to boost morale among the soldiers stuck in the stagnant front line and unite them in fear of death. This politics of fear also works through the execution of scapegoated "cowards" as "inferior" soldiers. The mission is thus not so much a desperate operation to defeat the enemy as a necessary "shock therapy" to revitalize "our" army by culling some of its members, even stigmatizing them as disloyal or unpatriotic. In other words, the army is a self-recycling system that discards some of its parts like refuse, maybe potentially by repetition, in order to sustain itself.

In this fascistic sacrifice of a part for the whole, sacrifice itself is paradoxically deprived of any sacredness (related to sublime patriotism, etc.) as is the case with Giorgio Agamben (1998)'s *homo sacer*: the "sacred man" who, according to the ancient Roman law, may be killed with the killer's impunity and cannot be sacrificed (to gods), and who is thus no different from animal-like "bare life" put outside both human law and divine law, with no rights and sanctity of life. And it is sovereign power that can suspend the rule of law and create the "state of exception" in which anyone can become *homo sacer*. The General of the division in *Paths of Glory* wields such sovereignty when ordering his artillery to fire on its own men to force them onto the battlefield, whereas the artillery commander refuses to follow this inhuman order without its written confirmation as a juridical procedure. The court-martial also embodies supralegal sovereignty. The accused are called "socially undesirable," but are chosen simply by lot, and their rights are violated as the trial farcically proceeds with no indictment read, no stenographer present, and no evidence of acquittal admitted. They are not adequately summoned "before the law" so much as excluded from it. Only in this mode of exclusion are they included in the sovereign mechanism of (supra)legality. But since war itself represents a state of emergency, all this nonsensical wartime jurisdiction is not wholly unrealistic. In the name of security and victory, the nation is always ready to transcend its law.

From this standpoint, what deserves more attention than the existentialist Kubrick is the biopolitical Kubrick. What he highlights more than the subjective experience of the absurd world is the objective structure of how power generates, controls, and abandons subjects under and beyond the law. Here, biopolitics concerns not only Foucauldian biopower that governs the regulation of populations and the subjugation of their bodies to the nation-state, but primarily Agambenian sovereignty that creates the boundary between subjectivized bodies in the state and mere bodies cast out of it.

It is on this biopolitical ground established and sustained by sovereignty that innerstate political games are played out.

This quasi-animal life can be called "abject." As is well known, in psychoanalysis the notion refers to something filthy, nauseous, hateful, or threatening that the subject cuts off from itself for ego-formation or self-protection (Kristeva 1982). From vomit to flowing blood to severed body parts, the abject no longer belongs to the subject, but has not yet turned into a thing, thus embodying the ambivalence of subject and object, life and death. By extension, a subject as an individual can be an abject cast out by its community just like those soldiers, killed or to be killed, deprived of legitimate rights and subjectivity as citizens. This "abjection" of the subject by sovereign power has been investigated in the biopolitical revision of the concept.[2] This biopolitical abjection occurs relatively in any (subnational) community, even in a group of the abject, and yet it also opens room for liberating effects. The ending of *Paths of Glory* is noteworthy in this sense. Following the execution of three of their peers, the remaining soldiers are reveling at an inn, debased enough by the savagery of war to raucously leer at a captive, terrified German girl. The collective abject now takes sovereign power over the foreign abject by forming the fascistic male bond of animalistic desires. However, as they recognize the melancholic melody of a German song she sings (about a soldier's lost love), they start to hum and share an ineffable feeling with her. Affective solidarity is thus formed among all the abjects across their sexual and national marks of subjectivity. This is perhaps the only scene in Kubrick's entire filmography that suggests some ethical redemption of abject humanity.

Kubrick's political films may thus be worth revisiting biopolitically beyond the existential critique of absurd war and individual alienation. Moreover, as I just noted and will examine further through *Dr. Strangelove*, *A Clockwork Orange* (1971), and *Full Metal Jacket* (1987), the director's biopolitics also reveals how power produces and unites subjects of desire, who are not merely subject to totalitarian sovereignty but also complicit in its pleasure. It is telling that the death-row convicts in *Paths of Glory* mention the loss of sexual desire. The implication is that abjection is abjection from desire as well, the desire that power injects and represses at once in the process of subjectivation. The existential issues of fear and freedom, the core of human subjectivity, can also be reviewed in their overdetermination by power and desire. Indeed, a universal structure of power and desire has historically developed, relentlessly upgrading military, physical, scientific, and psychological apparatuses of subjectivation. Kubrick's *trenchant* look into this biopolitical system is still compelling and inspiring today. His real legacy may thus not be limited to his cinematic influences on certain directors and films. I will take his work as a useful point of reference to explore the entanglements of war and sex, violence and enjoyment, as well as politics and psychoanalysis.[3]

Dr. Strangelove: Masturbatory Sovereignty in Power and Desire

What catches the eye above all in *Dr. Strangelove* are its metaphors about communism. Anti-communism is compared with "purifying" the American people's "bodily fluids" polluted by "commies' fluoridation of water." Such purification is precisely the primary function of abjection as sanitization, that is, keeping the subject's body clean and its identity pure by filtering out dirty, harmful, contagious elements. The entire Soviet Union thus appears as the ultimate object of biopolitical abjection. For its annihilation (as complete purification), the mad General commands a nuclear attack supralegally, without the Pentagon's order. Interestingly, the code for controlling the bombs is P.O.E., doubly standing for "Peace on Earth" and "Purity of Essence" as if the pursuit of the latter would lead to the former. However, the end of the film shows the end of the world while the song "We'll Meet Again" ironically plays over the apocalyptic imagery of detonations that result from the automatic operation of the USSR's "doomsday device" triggered by the US attack, leaving no hope for tomorrow. The extermination of the other leads to nothing but that of the self; killing is suicide. In other words, the other and the self, the abject and the subject, are inseparable.

Of course, *Dr. Strangelove* is a black comedy that satirizes the ridiculous failure of two superpowers' attempts to avoid the apocalypse. Their discussion on the "hot line," despite the seriousness of the topic, is interrupted by distracting music, silly jokes, and unnecessary interventions. The war room only reveals the malfunction of power at the highest level of the decision-making process, and the absurd gap between formal lingo, administrative rituals, and their insane, ludicrous logic. The Soviet Premier even turns out to be a drunken womanizer; a US officer objects to the idea of breaking a vending machine to get coins to urgently call the President because it is a private property of the Coca-Cola Company. While the set time of bombing is fast approaching, all efforts to cancel the irreversible deadline are delayed continuously. Peter Sellers's triple role—as the inept US president Muffley, the lowly officer Mandrake, and the strange scientist Dr. Strangelove—implies that their differences do not matter compared with their joint involvement in the system of massive co-destruction, the sovereign machinery that they created yet cannot control.

Dr. Strangelove appears here as a scenarist of a post-apocalyptic redemption plan which embodies ultimate sovereignty. He suggests that only the several finest hundred thousand people should be selected and live in a bomb shelter for a breeding program to repopulate the world after the radiation has gone. As an ex-Nazi adviser to the US government, he thus updates the eugenic dream of raising a supreme race purified from the rest of humanity, using the nuclear nightmare as a new Holocaust. This fascist fantasy is symbolized bodily when, hitherto wheelchair-bound, Strangelove miraculously stands up and shouts, "Mein *Führer*, I can walk!" It is as if Nazism were not dead—though abjected like his paralyzed body—but regained its sovereign power over most of humanity in the mutually nuked American-Soviet coalition, which once defeated the Nazis. Again, the law, as well as all institutional procedures, gives way to sovereignty and abjection in a state of emergency, with the war zone extending from the French/German frontline in *Paths of Glory* to the entire planet in *Dr. Strangelove*. Paths of totalitarian glory turn, to an even worse degree, into paths of total mutual annihilation.

The selection of the few to survive a catastrophe is a well-known motif tracing back to the biblical ark story. Sovereignty becomes divine when the angry God pushes the reset button to purge everything but the chosen few, instead of correcting the world's corruption, and starts from a clean ground zero. But if the ark is at least a zoo of diverse species, its sci-fi variations have represented a new caste system and racism, a neoliberal survival game in the law of the jungle. Furthermore, what is unique in Dr. Strangelove's project is the selection of sexy females and alpha males in a 10:1 ratio to maximize pleasure and proliferation. This polygamous machoism revives the fantasy of sovereignty in sexuality, the dream of being a sexual sovereign, like the Freudian "primal father" possessing all women, who transcends the law of castration, prohibition, and repression that he imposes upon the others—his sons—in order to sustain the social order as the control system of desire. In some sense, this mythical libido, like some undead fascism, dominates Dr. Strangelove despite himself and erupts from his unconscious. His right hand moves arbitrarily like the uncontrollable penis; its Hitler salute to "Mein *Führer*," extended from his whole body standing up, does not fail to evoke a powerful erection.[4] In the finale, nuclear bombs explode like orgasms with the eminently phallic mushroom clouds spurting vertically.

Sexual codes and puns are prevalent elsewhere, too. The title sequence shows two planes' aerial refueling, evoking mating, to the tune of "Try a Little Tenderness." A pilot named King Kong looks at *Playboy* (centerfold Tracey Reed) in a plane, like the Kafkaesque judges who hide pornography under legal documents. General Buck Turgidson receives an emergency call at 3 a.m., half-naked, in the room of his secretary-lover (played by real-life Tracey Reed). While General Jack Ripper's phallic cigar and machine-gun are visually explicit, many names carry sexual puns and connotations: not only those noted above, but also Premier Kissov, Ambassador de Sadesky, President Merkin (a pubic wig) Muffley, Officer Mandrake (an anthropomorphic and aphrodisiac plant), and so on (Macklin 1965). The crucial point is that these libidinal symptoms in the nuclear regime are not properly communicated or resolved through sexual intercourse, but repressed until they explode in a masturbatory fashion. General Turgidson quits a tryst with his secretary to join the war room and enact a bomber's action. General Ripper fantasizes about the Reds' fluoridation while feeling "a loss of essence," presumably experiencing impotence. And King Kong rides the bomb down, crying out ecstatically until the climactic explosion. Without connecting to women, men enjoy the self-gratifying power of abjection, of destructive violence unleashed on both their enemies and themselves as though this could compensate for their sexual failure, their abjection from sex.

Dr. Strangelove's sovereign desire also has its downside. He rises from his wheelchair (symbolizing impotency), quite erect, as if to penetrate the uterus-like cave shelter he is envisioning and where to impregnate the *Überfrauen* seraglio. And yet, far from having sex, he only enjoys this sexual fantasy in a masturbatory manner, comical and tragic. An unused shot of his wayward hand touching his penis for pleasure (Starr 1991, 100) thus does not just seem to make fun of his puerility. As this hand also chocks him lethally, the masturbatory erection implied in his exclamation, "I can walk!" (ergo "I can *come!*"), is immediately followed by the images of doomsday, the end of the film only leaving the clouds under which he must be found dead like everyone else. In view of this, the abundance of allegories for sex and/as masturbation may not support the view that the film reflects the 1960s slogan of "Make love, not war," which sexual liberals and pacifists presented against right-wing militarism (Boxen n.d.). The latter is represented by Strangelove's black-gloved right hand, but this symbol of sovereign power also embodies the sovereign desire that fantasizes its primordial satisfaction and yet leads to the impasse of masturbatory self-destruction. The sexual relationship is impossible, or possible only in the masculine fantasy of desire whose fulfillment may leave nothing but ashes.

A Clockwork Orange: The Masculine Mechanism of Subjectivation and Abjection

One might recall here Jacques Lacan (1999)'s famous dictum, "There is no sexual relation" according to his formulas of sexuation. Different from biological sexuality, sexuation designates the unconscious differentiation of the masculine and the feminine logic of desire. Let me briefly explore the masculine formula in Lacan's binomial: all men are submitted to the phallic function, the law of symbolic castration that, in the name of the father, states the prohibition of incest and the foundation of desire. The son-as-subject's desire is then destined to fill in the lack of the primordial object (mother) with its replacements (other women) while never reaching satisfaction in the symbolic order of reality. But there exists at least one exception to this phallic law, namely, the aforementioned "primal father" supposed to have the phallus and enjoy all women. The name of the father is this signifier of the phallus (Φ) that all the others lack and desire in vain, the signifier of primary repression for them and of supreme enjoyment for him. The phallic father thus embodies both the superego and the id, the symbolic and the real, the law and its beyond. In reality, this Father does not exist, since a father is just an incompetent man. It is the phallus that reifies this mere father into the exceptional Father, prohibited and unattainable, who can exceed limited pleasure and have *jouissance* beyond castration. Far from being a biological entity, the phallus is, therefore, a fantasized signifier of fullness, an empty signifier into which the satisfaction of desire is projected and toward which the subjects of desire are oriented. It turns the inherently inconsistent Other, the symbolic order of the patriarchal law, into something sublime, just as God is projected to fill the gaps in our knowledge as the invisible hand pulling the strings of reality, which often seems to us unpredictable or inexplicable.

Biopolitics and psychoanalysis can overlap at this point. There is a homological structure of social and sexual subjectivation here, that includes the analogy between the sovereign's divine power and the patriarch's unrestrained desire in terms of supralegal exceptionality.[5] Simply put, the Father-as-Sovereign, like God, takes the center of his community under his law, which he can transcend. This center sets an ideal goal or utopian destination, and the desire for it is internalized in subjects even if it can never be fulfilled. This process works as the ideological mechanism of shared subjectivation in the same structure of power and desire. A subject is a particular member in a universal community organized around its central exception, which transcendently delimits and totalizes the very community and all its particulars. The center of structuration is outside the closed structure. The democratic multitudes are subject to, and the subjects of, that big Other. A unified community then emerges, nurturing the sense of belonging, membership, or nationality among the subjects and also forming the boundaries between inside and outside, "us" and "others," friends and enemies—with the latter in each dyad becoming the potential object of collective abjection. In sum, a biopolitical hierarchy of the sovereign, the subject, and the abject is established.

I am tempted to locate this tripartite hierarchy schematically in the tripartite narrative of *A Clockwork Orange*. In the first part, Alex appears as a charismatic delinquent who leads his gang of thugs called "droogs" (meaning "friends" in Russian), a sovereign figure who oppresses his buddies' desire for more equality while driving them into physical and sexual "ultra-violence," far beyond the law. They fight with a rival gang in a palace-like dilapidated theater, as if to build a mini-empire. They attack the homeless as well as bourgeois homes and abject "any-body-whatever" by treating them like animals in an ecstatic state of exception. What is at stake is neither money to steal nor social discontent to shatter, but the pure self-enjoyment of transgressive power. Their use of drugs, slang, and pre-punk style does not reflect the rebellious, revolutionary counterculture of the late 1960s–early 1970s when the film was made. It rather partakes of some mythical autonomy that is anarchic yet also proto-totalitarian, with the center of authority transcending the rest.

No wonder it is always Alex the sovereign, and not his droog-subjects, who rapes and kills women and enjoys a threesome with two girls picked up at a record store, surrounded by erotic arts/items including a sculpted phallus he uses as a lethal weapon. Far from a subcultural punk, he is even a sophisticated dandy who choreographs sexual assaults with "Singin' in the Rain" and feels artistic *jouissance* while listening to his idol Beethoven's Symphony No. 9. This classical masterpiece, the sublime symbol of overcoming suffering and mediocrity for Alex, is played along a rhythmic montage of phallic/orgasmic/morbid images: a snake over a vagina, naked Christ figures with bloody nails and raised fists (like Dr. Strangelove's hand-erection), Dracula's fangs, execution by hanging, and volcanic eruption and destruction. Alex perhaps experiences violence in a perverted criminal version of Artaudian cruelty to break existing boundaries and bring the sacred fusion of Eros and Thanatos as well as some liminal sensation beyond the order of mere life—although violence is not Artaud's core. In this way, he becomes an extraordinary individual freed from the slave morality of ordinary people, a master of sovereign power and desire.

Nonetheless, Alex is not a real sovereign. Betrayed by his minions, he is arrested for murder and placed under the real law. The second part shows how his sovereignty is absorbed into the Althusserian-Foucauldian apparatuses of state power, such as the prison and the hospital, that operate rehabilitation programs for total resubjectivation. The problem is that this is not a proper process of normalization, but an extreme mechanism of totalitarian subjection. Strapped to a chair and injected with drugs, Alex is only exploited as a test sample for an experimental aversion therapy that makes him nauseated by sexual violence in snuff porn. He is forced to watch it from the position of immobile, brutalized victims, to the point where he automatically averts, that is, "abjects" sexual stimulation. This neuro-sensorial torture based on behavioral psychology reappropriates Artaudian cruelty in another perverted way, now on behalf of the state. It culminates in the screening of Nazi films: Alex sees the *Führer*'s army marching and bombing while to the sound of his favorite "Ode to Joy." Alex cries out, "It's a sin!" It must be a sin to make that heavenly art of humanity serve the imperial joy of global destruction, but let us recall that this paradox characterized the aforesaid montage of the symphony's second movement that reflected Alex's masturbatory sovereign psyche.

This therapy called the Ludovico technique—evoking Beethoven's first name Ludwig—thus re-abuses the Nazi's abuse of Beethoven for racial abjection by forcing Alex to abject his beloved Beethoven. It is worthy of note that Beethoven, despite his Dutch/Flemish roots, was co-opted by the Third Reich as a pure Germanic genius to prove German racial superiority. The Ninth was often performed at state events such as the 1936 Olympics and Hitler's birthday in 1942, in order to signal Germany's rebirth under the new political master after the defeat in the First World War and its resurrection sanctified by the old musical master who triumphed over adversity. Beethoven's heroic romanticism was instrumentalized by National Socialism just like Nietzsche's master morality, and his art was propagandized as the gift of the German *Volk* to the whole world (Buch 2003: 45–65). Nazism, then, racially reframed the spirit of universal brotherhood in "Ode to Joy," originating in Schiller's poem. "Elysium," the paradise after death where "all people become brothers," began to imply nothing but the new German empire of Aryan brothers who "fall in worship" for "a loving Father" above the stars. While subjects in this supreme community were equally subject to its divine sovereign, inferior beings outside it were exterminated as the abject, or at best colonized as imperial subjects grateful for the gift of Germany.

This fascist appropriation of art was undoubtedly a prime example of what Walter Benjamin calls the "aestheticization of politics" (1968: 241–42). Artistic transcendence was incarnated into absolute power under which a beautiful hymn to a utopian regime resounded for everyone while silencing the abject's cries. Universality was enabled through abjection, thus made relative and inconsistent. No wonder the "Ode to Joy" has been played as an anthem of each different ideal and ideological universality based on some exclusion (if hidden or inevitable) in many political regimes from Mao's China to the European Union—as Slavoj Žižek notes, commenting on *A Clockwork Orange* in *The Pervert's Guide to Ideology* (2012).

As Kubrick observes, supreme sovereignty is also internalized into governing institutions and their agents to various degrees. The evil General in *Paths of Glory* and the (ex)Nazi doctor in *Dr. Strangelove* are not the transcendent centers of the army/government so much as a sort of sovereign agents serving the regime. In *A Clockwork Orange*, this institutionalization of totalitarian biopower is updated in the form of a more techno-bureaucratic complex with no single individual monopolizing all exclusive power. Instead, a set of anonymous agents perform systematic psycho-corporeal bioengineering to produce "good" citizens of a liberal democratic nation. The Ludovico technique reinforces the same totalitarian effect. The product is a docile subject robotized to avoid violence and sex, who renounces the will to power and desire, and thus becomes a citizen of a crime-free society. Though God is worshipped as the sole sovereign in the prison church, this ideological apparatus plays the same role in the state as the bioengineering hospital. The chaplain preaches about the free will to choose "good" in order to gain supreme happiness, but his fearmongering depiction of Hell is another aversion therapy that brainwashes Alex into the abjection of evil and the choice of good, depriving him of his will as such. Subjectivation is therefore paradoxical in itself. Alex is trained not to pursue endless desire with limited pleasure but to lose desire/pleasure altogether. Symbolically castrated and rendered impotent, yet not cast out of the regime, he is reborn as an immanently abject subject.

Maybe this precarious subjectivity renders Alex vulnerable to abjection back in society in the film's third part. He is let out as a free man, only to find out that his parents have let out his room to a surrogate son-like stranger (and done away with his pet snake). Homeless, he is attacked by the homeless he once brutalized. Saved by two policemen, he is shocked to realize that they are his former droogs, who then drown, beat up, and nearly kill him. All this revenge from people around him shows that he is getting his comeuppance in the reversed power hierarchy, as micro-level sovereignty is shifted from him to them. The climax occurs when Alex is housed by a political dissident who, aware of Alex's aversion therapy, plans to present Alex in public as a victim of the state power he criticizes. Then, at the moment when Alex breaks into "Singin' in the Rain," the dissident recognizes in Alex his late wife's rapist and murderer. He drugs and locks Alex in a room and plays Beethoven's Ninth to torture his erstwhile torturer. Beethoven is abused again, now from the opposite political position but for the same effect of aversion, which makes Alex commit suicide—abject himself—by jumping out of the window. Rescued again, however, Alex is hospitalized. Then, the Minister approaches him, apologizes for the Ludovico technique (following a public outcry against it), and offers Alex a job while seeking to enlist his help in the upcoming election. In short, Alex is none other than an undead abject that is neither dead nor living of his will, but exploited over and over by diverse sovereign agents, just as Beethoven has been ever since his death.

Then how can we understand the film's final scene? The Minister plays Beethoven as a goodwill gesture, the press appears to take photos of the Minister and Alex hugging each other, and Alex indulges in a fantasy about having sex with a woman, surrounded by an applauding crowd dressed like the bourgeoisie in Beethoven's era. Alex says: "I was cured, all right!" But cured of impotence back to the very *jouissance* that had to be eliminated? Let's be reminded here that sovereignty lies in both biopolitical power and sexual desire, and that sovereign agents, though collectively institutionalized in the regime, do not relinquish enjoyment. The superego enjoys the id from which the subject is banned. A probation officer hits Alex's penis as if to confirm his phallic superiority; a doctor and a nurse are found in the middle of sex like the General-secretary liaison in *Dr. Strangelove*.

Also, the pursuit of desire is perversely transformed into the exercise of power. The Ludovico technicians, the droog-policemen, and even the dissident group derive more or less pleasure from torturing Alex. The chief correctional officer with his

Hitlerian mustache does not really believe in the corrective function of prison and wields sadistically his power to enforce little rituals against Alex under the pretext of reformation. His nearly comic military style of commending ("Shut your filthy hole, you scum!") prefigures the drill instructor's extreme foul language in *Full Metal Jacket*. The sovereign regime, while not dominated by a single Father, is thus pervaded with obscene superegos whose enjoyment is further distorted by a dehumanizing and absurd bureaucracy. Alex's final fantasy indicates his desired admission to this inner circle, a sort of Oedipal trajectory that guides him from abjection to redemption under the approving gaze of the regime. His naked body in ecstasy exhibits what the spectators secretly desire and enjoy under their bourgeois garments. This fantasy stages the only imaginable way in which one could be resubjectivized.

Full Metal Jacket: Discipline, Obscenity, and the Feminine Abject-Neighbor

Masculine biopolitical sexuation underlies the totalitarian operation of power systems in Kubrick's political films. Desire is seemingly repressed, yet symptomatically allowed with the illusion of *jouissance* under the hedonistic superego that orders "Enjoy!" The ego can have enjoyment insofar as it follows, desires, and internalizes the law of phallic sovereignty, thereby becoming a subject as a sovereign agent who can wield power over the abject. This framework manifests itself most realistically in *Full Metal Jacket*. New US Marine Corps recruits for the Vietnam War are trained to be soldiers (the subject) granted supralegal power to kill the Vietcong as *homo sacer* (the abject), while this subjectivation also involves the process of remasculinization. Young trainees become machos by undergoing the trainer (father)'s law and death, inheriting his phallic sovereignty, and enjoying libidinal culture in the fascistic brotherhood built upon sharing commodified women in Vietnam. The universal phallic function set up by the sovereign ego-ideal totalizes all men in the masculine logic of identity formation, again through violence and sex, power and desire, at once. Although the film highlights the violent operation of military biopower, sexuality flows under the surface no less critically. This double layer is comparable to, but more complicated than, the double-narrative convention of the main plot (action) and the subplot (romance).

Let us take a closer look at the film's structure. The army in the first half of the film apparently exemplifies a "disciplinary society" in its Foucauldian sense: bodies are confined in an isolated space for a long-term period and trained to become skilled members of the community under surveillance and punishment. However, becoming a soldier is not simply changing civilian subjectivity into a military one. The film opens with the collective shaving of recruits' heads, the initiation ritual of removing individual subjectivity and abjecting them into a horde of indiscernible bodies that are brutally treated like naked animals. In this biopolitical mechanism, the boot camp is not too far from the Nazi camp and its variations such as the Gulag and the prisons in Abu Ghraib and Guantanamo. Military subjectivation starts from this abject state, a temporary state of exception in which drill instructor Hartman takes the sovereign position and embodies the living law by his words. This exceptional condition is even normalized in a daily routine. The army barrack is thus a prototype of the "camp as nomos" where bare life (*zoe*) and qualified life (*bios*) are rendered indistinct, as Agamben says (1998, 166–80). But unlike other detention camps, the army also turns the abject into sovereign subjects superior to civilians at least in the bigger state of exception, that is, war. "Born to kill," the phrase written on Private Joker's helmet, means their rebirth as killing machines grants the privates a license to kill with impunity. Hartman mentions former Marine sharpshooters including Charles Whitman and Lee Harvey Oswald as models to follow, suspending any judgment on their infamous crimes—the mass murder at the University of Texas and the assassination of President Kennedy—and only emphasizing marksmanship by which to treat human targets as nothing but moving animals.

This collective subjectivation also involves internal abjection. Physically standardized, all the recruits are called by monikers such as Joker, Cowboy, and Snowball, but an exception is Private Pyle, whose real name indicates undesirable individuality, including his obesity and haplessness. This internal "other" within the totalitarian community of the same is ill-fated to be a "loser," causing Hartman's rage and a group punishment for his substandard performance; Pyle consequently gets a gang beating by his fellow recruits. While this group changes from the abjects to the subjects, Pyle undergoes double abjection. As everyone hates him, his rifle becomes his only friend. The process by which he masters shooting skills, impresses Hartman. But Pyle eventually kills this authority figure as well as himself without seeking social integration, typifying a lone wolf's radicalization into a suicidal terrorist. The unredeemable abject overturns the power ladder instead of climbing it up normally, only to become an untouchable pseudo-sovereign who has no desire but to destroy "a world of shit." This way of taking revenge on bullies at an existential impasse is also common to campus shooters including (the more complicated case of) Charles Whitman. Given Hartman's praise of Whitman, it is as if Whitman returned as Pyle to destroy his corps with the skills learned from it. An added nuance is that the totalitarian sovereign system can be terrorized by its own immanently produced abject.

However, this terror hardly shakes up the system. After the terrorist is self-removed, no memory of him seems to haunt his comrades who passed the harsh drill. They are successfully incorporated into the army, internalizing Hartman's Law. The instructor thus never dies, at least as the institutional sovereign "Other"—on his opposite side is, of course, the internal abject "other," Pyle. In this sense, Hartman's (re)generation of loyal soldiers is naturalized like the father's (re)production of oedipalized sons, again, with sovereign power and desire overlapping. His most powerful training tool is his hate speech and repertoire of insults that prohibit yet also provoke sexuality. He debases the recruits' manhood, calling them "babies/faggots/ladies" with their pants down; he orders them to give their rifle a girl's name and sleep with it as "the only pussy you people are going to get!" The gun is also the "sun" and "life," indispensable for "fighting" and "fun," definitely evoking and resembling the phallus. At one point, the recruits are shown making a ridiculous gesture of masturbation, marching in their underwear, with their rifle in one hand, and the other holding their crotch.

The marching songs could not be more sexually inflected. I, the Oedipal son, feel desire by witnessing the primal scene ("Mama and Papa were laying in bed/Mama rolled over this is what she said/A gimme some"), but I repress it and obey the phallic order ("I don't want no teenage queen/I just want my M14"). The enemy is inferior to me ("Ho Chi Minh is a son-of-bitch/Got the blue balls, crabs, and the seven-year-itch"), and I enjoy an exotic fantasy ("Eskimo pussy is mighty cold/Mmm good, feels good, is good, real good"). The masculine logic of sexuation pervades daily life from tough interpellation to rhythmical chants and comical rituals and molds the effeminate recruits into the soldiers-as-son who desire the phallus under the Father's guidance.

Rather than real discipline incarnate, Hartman-as-Sovereign is thus a post-Foucauldian obscene superego who does not just repress, but circulates and promotes phallic desire along with fantasized objects to enjoy. The symbolic and the real, the official and foul languages, even divine holiness and sexual secularity are intertwined. When he says, "God has a hard-on for Marines, because we kill everything we see!," doesn't this divine erection and ejaculation of bullets recall Dr. Strangelove's phallic orgasm as masturbatory annihilation? Far from showing "moral chaos" (Conard 2009, 39), what we notice is a flexible update of oedipalization. The son's resistance to the father is oppressed while permitted if it qualifies him for paternal leadership, just as Hartman beats Joker for his proclaimed unbelief in the Virgin Mary, then appreciates his spirit and has him lead the corps.

Likewise, the transgression of the phallic order is part of the order itself. The succession of sons-becoming-fathers transmits the law of castration as the path to enjoyment, albeit limited, in the fantasy of having the phallus. Hartman's rules and tests are set up to transform "maggots" into "indestructible men" like a qualification exam for manhood in general. For those who pass it, Vietnam then appears partly as an outlet for their repressed desire and desired power in the film's second half. While sovereign masturbation explodes in the weird "slaughter then jerk off" ritual, Vietnamese prostitutes are within easy reach (the promised "Eskimo pussy" in Hartman's song). The soldiers display macho bravado in a sort of rap battle, brag about shooting civilians, play rock in battle, and appear in a movie; wearing a peace symbol, Joker ironically says he came to Vietnam to taste exoticism and killing. The war, less hellish than boring in effect, unfolds as a somewhat fantasized field of spectacle in which sovereign masculinity, violent or sexual, is shared and vented here and there while blurring the lines between inhibition and liberation, public and private, and reality and pleasure principles.

Accordingly, the state of exception—libidinal as well as biopolitical—extends from the camp (the first half) to the battlefield (the second half), while enjoyment is normalized mundanely, even apathetically so. This laxity signals some detachment from a horrible yet absurd reality, as the soldiers feel that they fight and die for the alleged cause of Vietnam's freedom, which does not seem wanted by the Vietnamese people themselves. Here, we could see the soldiers' potential affinity with the Last Man who, for Nietzsche, indulges in small pleasures after losing a big cause or true meaning of life. The *Übermensch*-like sovereign agents are at risk of this "passive nihilism" pervading the permissive post-disciplinary society. They merely seek individual gratifications in the fantasized but meaningless war.

However, this narcotic state is shaken when a young Vietnamese female sniper kills several US soldiers and begs for death herself when lethally wounded. She is a sort of "active nihilist" whose secular life is stoically denied and sacrificed to the big cause of National Liberation.[6] She is a fundamentalist sovereign agent dedicated to a transcendental ideal, an aseptic disciplinary superego without an id. For the American subjects, she is the antagonistic external "Other" whose desire they cannot share, or enjoy, unlike the prostitutes. This impenetrable otherness causes dread all the more so since the female sniper is a ghostly being, unseen and unidentified (the revelation of her gender is meant to surprise the viewer), hidden in a dark, ruined, cave-like building—a womblike space evoking the abject maternal body. What happens then is biopolitical abjection. The soldiers singularize their abstract terror into the reified form of a terrorist enemy, to be killed like an animal. After injuring her, they call her "dead meat" which leaves them with two choices, "let her rot" or "waste her." After "wasting" her, Joker stands above her body, his face an inscrutable mask, the surviving members of his team stunned by his action. Then, marching at dusk, as if they erased this abject body likened to "ugly hardcore" from their memory, the soldiers happily return to their camp, singing the "Mickey Mouse March" song with a renewed sense of bonding and stronger team spirit, proud and without fear.

Nonetheless, the ending credit song "Paint it Black" mitigates their attitude, as implied in its lyrics: "I'll fade away and not have to face the facts." What the Marines avoid is the traumatic Thing that ruptures their sovereign reality of domination and pleasure; the unthinkable Real that intrudes into their symbolic order in the form of a woman totally outside their desire. Let me, then, address Lacan (1999)'s feminine formula of sexuation: there is no exception to the phallic function, but not all are submitted to it. That is, castration applies to all women, who thus all lack and desire the phallus, even without a primal "mother" to enjoy all men. The absence of any exception, however, implies the absence of any boundary that makes a closed set of women under the law. Each woman is radically singular, not a member or example of generalized essential femininity. Unlike Man, Woman as universal thus does not exist. It is not that the symbolic is foreclosed—the case of Kubrick's male psychopaths such as Jack Torrance in *The Shining* (1980)—but that the feminine "not-all" is discordant with the phallus when it comes to the real. The question is not any positive feminine content of some women or some part of a woman beyond the male gaze or desire, but a pure formal cut between the woman for the other (man)'s fantasy and the woman in herself as empty substance. This fissure underlies the subject in general, the immanently barred Subject ($). The sexual difference is that woman knows her fundamental void of content but veils this abyss, whereas man believes in some substance in himself, some phallic potential that he desires to realize while illusively reducing her to a partial object-cause of desire (*objet petit a*) and projecting this fantasy onto her veil without realizing that it hides nothing. The woman then partially enjoys the phallus that man mistakes as his own, though she keeps her "nothingness" out of his possessive desire's reach (Žižek 1995). She is free from the phallic function without relinquishing it.

This paradoxical freedom allows a woman to not entirely belong to a biopolitical community whose boundaries are built on masculine sovereignty between inside and outside, self and other, friend and enemy, and subject and abject. Though the Vietnamese sniper is treated as an external enemy to abject, it is crucial to note that abjection implies not only deprivation but also liberation from subjectivity rigidified within a community. "Abjecthood" is, therefore, the most universal and foundational mode of being, the degree zero of life unconditioned by any biopolitical subjectivation. The abject sniper, in theory if not in reality, may then have the feminine potential to be freed from her double identity: from being an "abject-able" enemy of the American army—she is not a prostitute they can enjoy—and even from being a sovereign agent of the Viet Cong. Therein lies the positive power of a pure abject. She takes on "intrusive foreignness" to the self/other dichotomy while transgressing subjectivity like an "internal stranger"—floating like an *objet a* detached from the subject. Or she might embody the unrecognizable yet intimate secret of any subject, the drive of self-abjection toward an asubjective state of free, equal relations. Neither friend nor enemy, this "Third" is none other than the "neighbor" in ethics,[7] with whom we make the relationship of "a beside yet alike, separation and identity" (Lacan 1997, 51). We could then imagine a move from the virtual hierarchy of the sovereign-subject-abject to the horizontal equality between the abject who meet each other as neighbors; a move from the closed totality of "all versus exception" bound in their metaphoric semblance to an infinite series of abject-neighbors in the "not-all" of metonymic "knotting"; a move from a utopian community unified for a transcendent ideal to an "atopian" connection that has no topos of identity, only based on the commonality of abjecthood without community.

Let us now return to our original existentialist viewpoint and conclude as follows. A pure abject is not a heroic humanist who creates a value of life out of nothingness-in-herself. Neither is she a passive nihilist who consumes secured pleasures without a cause or meaning; nor is she an active nihilist who pursues no enjoyment but self-sacrifices to a transcendent value. She is, so to speak, a "positive nihilist" who embodies the void of being and nothing else, but by doing so, steps away from the illusion of subjectivity in the sovereign regime of power and desire. Though creating no utopian alternative, this move could make for atopian relations in which one does not stand "for" another (as in the subject-sovereign community) but stands "by" another as a neighbor. What happens between the German girl and the French soldiers at the end of *Paths of Glory* is this precarious yet precious solidarity of abjects-becoming-neighbors through unexpected encounters. When the American army kills the Vietnamese sniper in *Full Metal Jacket*, they "waste" the very potential to become her neighbors instead of friends or enemies and to feel some solidarity with each other instead of power or desire for each other. Nevertheless, at least we the viewers sense that it is in such an unrealized "atopia" of neighbors and not any peaceful utopia that a precious anti-war message could be found—not a small part of Kubrick's legacy, and a tribute if any to the political nature of his cinema.

Post-Kubrick Global Cinema

As an epilogue of sorts, let me add a few notes on post-Kubrick global Hollywood in terms of biopolitical abjection and sovereign agency. I draw attention to new millennial sci-fi/thriller films that prefigure a (dystopian) future of the rapidly globalizing system of sovereign power and its new enemies or antinomies, which Kubrick would undoubtedly have addressed, updating his related motifs and concerns. For example, there have been many futuristic variations of the post-nuclear eugenic shelter mentioned in *Dr. Strangelove*, from the downsized communities of *Downsizing* (Alexander Payne, 2017) to a space program in *Gattaca* (Andrew Niccol, 1997) to a rotating earth-like habitat in outer space in *Interstellar* (Christopher Nolan, 2014). While the latter seemingly includes everyone saved from a global catastrophe, the abandoned shelter of *Terminator 3: Rise of the Machines* (Jonathan Mostow, 2003) is far more grim, and *Elysium* (Neill Blomkamp, 2013) provides a more realistic alternative to the "ark" or "sky castle," with the eponymous luxurious ring-shaped space station housing the elite, while the rest of mankind resides on a ruined Earth. This exclusive, artificial heaven shows another ideological distortion of Beethoven's "Elysium" in "Ode to Joy." The new Elysium indicates new apartheid combined with "disaster capitalism," allegorizing neocolonial neoliberalism as updated racism. The one percent super-elite profits from global crises, while dominating the rest of mankind with high-tech security measures and sovereign violence.

Such a utopia for the privileged is not far from the crime-free city in *Minority Report* (Steven Spielberg, 2002) that runs the apparatus of premediating and preventing crimes, an upgraded version of the Ludovico technique for social purification. No wonder many dystopian films present extreme disciplinary societies equipped with a totalizing system of biopower, hierarchy, surveillance, and punishment. Even change to this system is sutured back into the system—the point made about the army's operation in *Paths of Glory*—as seen in *The Matrix* series (Wachowskis, 1999–2003) and, more tragically, *Snowpiercer* (Bong Joon-ho, 2013). Here, "revolution(s)" means rotation: the periodic cleansing of the autopoietic matrix/train, the regular abjection of unnecessary or threatening populations. *Snowpiercer* shows the consequent double bind of either remaining in the status quo, or escaping it only toward the destruction of the world.[8]

This impossibility of a radical revolution characterizes our so-called "post-political" age. Politics is driven by the passion for a big cause, freedom or equality, and brings change dialectically through action and reaction. But while political progress brings more and more freedom and equality, the world system becomes ever more democratic (inclusive, flexible, and tolerant of the victimized and multicultural others) and yet all the more totalitarian (violent, hierarchical, and retaliatory toward the ineligible, fundamentalist, and terrorist others). Politics then turns into the self-protecting administration of welfare systems, security services, and disposal methods—including military action. In this double "policing" lies the post-political (yet more explicitly biopolitical) sovereign power, which, while permitting liberal hedonism like the obscene superego, brutalizes anyone stigmatized as *homo sacer* as we have examined via Kubrick. The latter case of violent abjection notably underlies the war against terrorism, the most common subject in today's action films. Though Kubrick's age was not fully post-political, he in a sense made post-9/11 films of sorts: just consider the second half of *Full Metal Jacket* as a counter-terror operation against the female terrorist, rather than a political-military battle. Likewise, the heavily Kubrick-inflected *Starship Troopers* (Paul Verhoeven, 1997) predates post-9/11 cinema not so much in its depiction of a "terrorist" attack eerily similar to the footage of the Twin Towers in flame, as in the inclusive (non-gendered biased and race/color-blind) yet hierarchical and violent system of the military in the film, and the distinction it sets between "citizens" and "civilians."

One thing is for sure, we could not imagine a Kubrick film ending with a collective political victory as paraded in *V for Vendetta* (James McTeigue, 2005). Such a utopian dream ends up being illusory in more realistic post-political films including, again, *Snowpiercer*. If there is any significant resistance to the increasingly powerful global system, it tends to occur on the existential and ethical level of contingent solidarity between individuals abjected from the system even without a promise of utopia. Here is a palpable tendency of post-Kubrick global cinema: if Kubrick was critically obsessed with the totalitarian (re)formation of sovereign agents by military, ideological, and psychological state apparatuses, we now often see the reverse case in which sovereign agents undergo abjection from their organization and then turn into what I call "abject agents." These agents fight back against their sovereign system along with, or on behalf of, the abject others they encounter and embrace through the commonality of abjecthood without aiming at an alternative (yet potentially sovereign/totalitarian) community. This "atopian" solidarity, which I noted is missing in *Full Metal Jacket*, is what happens to abject agents in many dystopian sci-fi films: *Children of Men* (Alfonso Cuarón, 2006), *District 9* (Neill Blomkamp, 2009), *Blade Runner 2049* (Denis Villeneuve, 2017), and *Alita: Battle Angel* (Robert Rodriguez, 2019), to name a few. Their fight for the other abject even costs them their life, but this sacrifice revives the sense of a social cause that is lost in the post-political age and imbues their otherwise nihilistic life with some sublimity.

By extension, however, there is a case in which such a meaningful cause is not the ultimate point. The Bourne series—from *The Bourne Identity* (Doug Liman, 2002) to *Jason Bourne* (Paul Greengrass, 2016)—unfolds an ongoing saga of an ex-CIA agent as an abject agent par excellence, whose mission is not self-sacrifice but self-recovery after he has lost his memory. While he discovers and reveals the dirty secrets of the CIA in pursuit of this self-oriented mission, the sovereign (institutional) agency does everything to eliminate him as a sort of internal terrorist. This abject agent effectively fights the sovereign agency with skills he acquired from the latter, but his desire to be freed from can never be fulfilled, under its relentless surveillance and global operation. The terror-counter-terror loop is endless, leaving no room for escape. In other words, the global sovereign system allows no outside. It expands even by reintegrating its abject agents in more conventional spy films. The recent Bond films including *Skyfall* (Sam Mendes, 2012) betrays the influence of the Bourne franchise by depicting the abjection of 007 from his agency MI6, but in the end, his sovereign identity is reclaimed, and the state agency is reinforced to continue the war on terror.[9]

Furthermore, some "mind-game" films present more powerful and complex sovereign systems by using sci-fi motifs such as time travel, parallel worlds, human cloning, and memory manipulation. In *Source Code* (Duncan Jones, 2011), an injured, comatose soldier is plugged into the eponymous device to re-live the last few minutes of a victim of a train explosion, over and over, until completing his mission to identify the bomber. An abject body is thus reshaped as a virtual sovereign agent who has to die repeatedly if virtually, which itself is experienced as traumatic abjection. Namely, he is an "abject-sovereign agent," whose memory is to be erased after the mission in order to be recycled for other counter-terror operations. He eventually resists this exploitative sovereign system by abjecting himself in the way of choosing to die, while opening up an alternative reality in which the initial terrorist attack was prevented thanks to his sacrifice. The final paradox is that in this new reality, his comatose body is still lying in the Source Code office, waiting as a potential sovereign agent for an initial mission that is yet to come. His sacrifice in the former reality is "undone" here. What is sacrificed is the meaning of sacrifice itself.

This sacrifice of sacrifice as well as the fusion of sovereign and abject agency, or rather the constant co-option of abject agents by sovereign systems, bring a problematic happy ending to dystopian films. *Oblivion* (Joseph Kosinski, 2013), *Edge of Tomorrow* (Doug Liman, 2014), and *Ghost in the Shell* (Rupert Sanders, 2017) also end with the appearance of a cloned or reformatted agent whose memory-based identity is not that of a sacrificed protagonist, but whose mission remains similar. Put differently, they look identical but are replaceable or reformattable. It is not "our memories" but "our actions that define us," says the female cyborg in *Ghost in the Shell*. Her body is reassembled whenever destroyed; her mind is rebooted to be undisrupted by past traumas. In some sense, she is trained to become a subject with free will, to willingly embrace her abject-sovereign agency and focus on actions for given tasks. This flexible control of subjectivity by a future sovereign system is not far from what now happens to neoliberal subjects, entrepreneurs of themselves and yet precarious laborers at once, who only live in the perpetual present of working 24/7 at the perpetual risk of abjection from today's global system. What those sci-fi films prefigure is the perpetual reformation of the abject as sovereign agents. But then again, is this not what Kubrick had already—and incisively—captured decades ago? Let us think back, in closing, to the cringe-inducing finales of *A Clockwork Orange* and *Full Metal Jacket*. Alex and Joker seem fearless, happy. Can we claim the same?

Notes

1 See *The Philosophy of Stanley Kubrick* (Abrams 2009), an anthology about existentialism in Kubrick. Also, an interview shows Kubrick's existentialist idea that the universe in *2001: A Space Odyssey* is indifferent to humans like the universe depicted in Camus's *The Myth of Sisyphus* (Nordern 2001).

2   The initial remark on abjection by Georges Bataille was about sociopolitical subalterns, and the psychoanalytic abjection theory has recently been critiqued and expanded in this direction (Tyler 2013).
3   Likewise, *2001: A Space Odyssey*, beyond its artistic achievement, remains a frame of reference in which to rethink time and space, technology and evolution, the screen and the brain beyond its artistic achievement.
4   Twisting Gille Deleuze's notion of the "body without organs," Slavoj Žižek (2004: 172–73) calls such an autonomized hand—which beats up the heroes in *Fight Club* and *Me, Myself and Irene*—an "organ without body." It is a partial object through which the truth of unconscious drives speaks itself.
5   More precisely, Lacanian psychoanalysis has an affinity with the Schmittian political theology that underlies the Agambenian biopolitics (Žižek, Santner, and Reinhard 2013). See Reinhard's part in particular (13, 40).
6   Originating in Nietzsche, passive nihilism reflects postmodern detachment and cynicism on progress while active nihilism embodies utopian radicalism and revolutionary vanguardism, risking terrorist destruction (Critchley 2013: 13). Nihilism underlies the existentialist approach to Kubrick (Shaw 2009).
7   The two quoted expressions above are taken from Kenneth Reinhard (Reinhard 2013: 31–46). I reinterpret and reshape the neighbor in terms of the abject.
8   I elsewhere analyze *Snowpiercer* in detail, including with respect to this double bind (Jeong 2019b).
9   For a detailed analysis of *Skyfall*, see my paper (Jeong 2019a), where I trace the evolution of the Bond series and compare its recent segments, starring Daniel Craig, with the Bourne films.

Works Cited

Abrams, Jerold J., ed. 2009. *The Philosophy of Stanley Kubrick*. Lexington: University Press of Kentucky.
Agamben, Giorgio. 1998. *Homo Sacer: Sovereign Power and Bare Life*, trans. Daniel Heller-Roazen. Stanford, CA: Stanford University Press.
Banks, Gordon. 1990. "Kubrick's Psychopaths." 1990. http://www.gordonbanks.com/gordon/pubs/kubricks.html.
Benjamin, Walter. 1968. *Illuminations: Essays and Reflections*, ed. Hannah Arendt, trans. Harry Zohn. New York: Schocken Books.
Boxen, Jeremy. n.d. "Just What the Doctor Ordered: Cold War Purging, Political Dissent, and the Right Hand of Dr. Strangelove." http://www.visual- memory.co.uk/amk/doc/0029.html (accessed February 9, 2018).
Buch, Esteban. 2003. *Beethoven's Ninth: A Political History*, trans. Richard Miller. Chicago: University of Chicago Press.
Camus, Albert. 1991. *The Myth of Sisyphus: And Other Essays*, trans. Justin O'Brien. New York: Vintage Books.
Conard, Mark T. 2009. "Chaos, Order, and Morality: Nietzsche's Influence on Full Metal Jacket," in Jerold J. Abrams (ed.), *The Philosophy of Stanley Kubrick*. Lexington: University Press of Kentucky, 33–48.

Critchley, Simon. 2013. *Infinitely Demanding: Ethics of Commitment, Politics of Resistance*. New York: Verso.

Jeong, Seung-hoon. 2019. "Snowpiercer (2013): The Post-Historical Catastrophe of a Biopolitical Ecosystem," in Sangjoon Lee (ed.), *Rediscovering Korean Cinema*. Ann Arbor: University of Michigan Press, 486–501.

Jeong, Seung-hoon. 2020. "Global Agency between Bond and Bourne: The 007 Series and Skyfall (2012) in Comparison with the Bourne Series," in Jaap Verheul (ed.), *Beyond 007: James Bond Reconsidered*. Amsterdam: Amsterdam University Press.

Kristeva, Julia. 1982. *Powers of Horror: An Essay on Abjection*, trans. Leon S. Roudiez. New York: Columbia University Press.

Lacan, Jacques. 1997. *The Ethics of Psychoanalysis: The Seminar of Jacques Lacan (Book VII)*, ed. Jacques-Alain Miller, trans. Dennis Porter. New York: W. W. Norton.

Lacan, Jacques. 1999. *On Feminine Sexuality, the Limits of Love and Knowledge: The Seminar of Jacques Lacan (Book XX)*, ed. Jacques-Alain Miller, trans. Bruce Fink. New York: W. W. Norton.

Macklin, Tony. 1965. "Sex and Dr. Strangelove." *Film Comment*, 55–57.

Murray, Patrick, and Jeanne Schuler. 2009. "Rebel without a Cause: Stanley Kubrick and the Banality of the Good," in Jerold J. Abrams (ed.), *The Philosophy of Stanley Kubrick*. Lexington: University Press of Kentucky, 149–66.

Nordern, Eric. 2001. "Playboy Interview: Stanley Kubrick," in Gene D. Phillips (ed.), *Stanley Kubrick: Interviews*. Jackson: University Press of Mississippi, 47–74.

Reinhard, Kenneth. 2013. "Toward a Political Theology of the Neighbor," in Slavoj Žižek, Eric L. Santner, and Kenneth Reinhard (eds.), *The Neighbor: Three Inquiries in Political Theology*. Chicago: University of Chicago Press, 11–75.

Shaw, Daniel. 2009. "Nihilism and Freedom in the Films of Stanley Kubrick," in Jerold J. Abrams (ed.), *The Philosophy of Stanley Kubrick*. Lexington: University Press of Kentucky, 221–34.

Starr, Michael. 1991. *Peter Sellers: A Film History by Michael Starr*. Jefferson, NC: McFarland & Company.

Tyler, Imogen. 2013. *Revolting Subjects: Social Abjection and Resistance in Neoliberal Britain*. London: Zed Books.

Žižek, Slavoj. 1995. "Woman Is One of the Names-of-the-Father: Or How Not to Misread Lacan's Formulas of Sexuation." *Lacanian Ink* 10: 24–39.

Žižek, Slavoj. 2004. *Organs Without Bodies: Deleuze and Consequences*. New York: Routledge.

Žižek, Slavoj, Eric L. Santner, and Kenneth Reinhard. 2013. *The Neighbor: Three Inquiries in Political Theology*. Chicago: University of Chicago Press.

14

Kubrick at the Museum: Post-Cinematic Conditions, Limitations, and Possibilities[1]

Jihoon Kim

Following Stanley Kubrick's passing, one of the projects to celebrate his oeuvre and legacy became the Stanley Kubrick Exhibition (hereafter abbreviated "Kubrick Exhibition"). Borrowing on the massive collection of Kubrick's Estate, the Exhibition opened on March 30, 2004, in Frankfurt. It consists of an interplay of material borrowed from the Estate (props, pictures, notes and written documents, and film equipment), walk-through installations evoking Kubrick's films, and clips from the latter, courtesy of the studios owning the rights to these. As curator Hans Peter Reichmann puts it in the introduction to the Kinematograph catalogue showcasing the opening of the Exhibit: "The interdisciplinary exhibition draws attention to Kubrick's visionary adaptations of influences from the fine arts, design, and architecture, and enables us to experience the film cosmos of one of the great artists of the 20th century in all three dimensions" (9).

The Exhibition has toured the world over the years since, with venues such as ACMI in Melbourne (2005–2006), the Palazzo delle Espozioni in Rome (2007–2008), the Cinémathèque in Paris (2010), LACMA in Los Angeles (2013), SEMA in Seoul (2015–2016), and, most recently, the Design Museum in London (2019), for the twentieth anniversary of the director's death.[2] Such a phenomenon puts the emphasis on the way in which film auteurs and cinema itself, perhaps, have moved increasingly from their traditional locus (the movie theater) to other places, including, of course, the exhibition space and art gallery. This chapter contextualizes the Kubrick Exhibition within such a "post-cinematic" context, an array of conditions through/by way of which the idea and apparatus of the cinema as it developed in the twentieth century has increasingly become, roughly since the mid-1990s, displaced from its original formation and foundation and been repositioned within new technological, institutional, and discursive platforms, one of which is the museum. I shall examine both the limitations and possibilities of that exhibition while considering it a representative example of the migration of cinema, aka "the black box," into the gallery space, aka the "white cube," one of the most salient phenomena of the post-cinematic condition.

"Where Is Cinema?": Post-Cinematic Conditions

"What is cinema?" has long been one of the most fundamental questions in film theory and criticism, even before it became the title of André Bazin's book. This question involves the following sub-questions: What is the most "essential" element of cinema (celluloid filmstrip, camera, montage, illusion of movement, projection system, or larger-than-life spectacle)? And in what ways is cinema distinct from other arts (painting, photography, architecture, and theater) and media (television and video)? Asked first in the cinema's nascent stages and in the early twentieth century when critics strived to establish it as the "seventh art," the question remains valid in our not-so-young twenty-first century. Another less ontological but no less crucial question has emerged and been asked since the 1990s in film criticism and cinema and media studies: "Where is cinema?" This question has been posed in multiple contexts related to the emergence and increasing impact of electronic and digital technologies. First, the "filmic" moving image, previously grounded in the celluloid and film camera (both of which sustained the materiality of the image) is no longer the dominant factor of cinema today, as the digital camera and projection system have swiftly replaced both material foundations, and as digital imaging intimately engages with the synthesis and manipulation of images. Besides these material, technical, and aesthetic changes in the filmic image, the traditional "cinematic experience," too, has increasingly been dismantled, when the movie theater, which guaranteed that experience, characterized by its larger-than-life screen, the fixity of the audience, and the audience's concentration on the screen, in unbroken time, has increasingly been replaced by the various small screens in digital devices (laptops, smartphones, and tablets), the screens' fragmented windows, their portability and mobility, and the viewer (or user)'s flexible management of viewing time. In these two contexts, "post-cinematic condition" refers to the situations into which the cinema has been thrown by the double movement of deterritorialization and reconstruction, a consequence of the growing influences of post-filmic technologies, and of the arts and media that have been excluded from the traditional medium-specific ideas of cinema. This has caused a number of film and media scholars and film critics to proclaim the "death of cinema" and to talk of "post-cinema," both of which imply that the cinema's media ecology in the digital age transcends both the film-based ontology of cinema as well as its placement and the experience it offers, both previously entrenched in the theater space.[3] In this post-cinematic moment, the museum and gallery have emerged as a site providing a clear answer to the question "where is cinema?"

Emblematizing the "exhibition of cinema" as one type of migratory movements carried out by cinema, the Kubrick Exhibition is part of a process whereby cinema as the art of the twentieth century finds its new "virtual life" in digital visual culture, and has simultaneously been transformed into a cultural object that deserves preservation. This migration of sorts necessarily brings about clashes between the cinema and the museum, two ontologically and historically distinctive *dispositifs*. But it also reveals a couple of limitations that occur when the museum attempts to assimilate cinema into its own institutional practices and mechanisms of curating and exhibition. Nevertheless,

I also argue that the Kubrick Exhibition presents new possibilities, in that it offers three ways of preserving and self-reflexively revivifying not simply Kubrick's idea and practice of cinema, but also cinema in the broader sense: that is, the Exhibition opens up productive relations between the cinema and the museum by recuperating and concretizing three ideas relating to cinema that Kubrick realized throughout his career and oeuvre, namely, the concepts of the film auteur, of cinematic apparatus, and of cinema's intermediality.

Exhibition of Cinema, Cinema of Exhibition, and Film's Virtual Life

It is important to place the Kubrick Exhibition within a larger context: that of film in the post-cinematic condition, going beyond the movie theater and finding a new place or home for itself in the museum. The major museums and galleries in North America and Europe have contributed to shaping this context since the 1990s with a series of the events that have showcased cinema in various ways. Those events can be called the "exhibition of cinema," insofar as they spotlight a particular moment of the history of cinema, film's relationships with the developments of twentieth-century contemporary art (encompassing painting and video art), the idea of cinema as art, or a retrospective of an individual film auteur. In 1996, a year symbolic for celebrating cinema's first century, two large-scale exhibitions took place in the United Kingdom and the United States: "Spellbound: Art and Film in Britain" (Hayward Gallery in collaboration with the British Film Institute) and "Art and Film since 1945: Hall of Mirrors" (LACMA). These historic landmarks signaled to cinema's move from theater-based mass media to being part of the world of "art" and "culture." These exhibitions took as their curatorial assumption the fact that cinema was and is a distinct art that rivals and has a strong influence upon its neighboring arts such as painting, sculpture, performance, and so on: that is, an idea of "cinema as art" that goes beyond that of "art cinema" in the standard institutional practice of cinema.

"Exhibitions of cinema" since the 2000s have bifurcated into two series. The first one is an array of exhibitions that shed new light on avant-garde filmmakers and their works, repositioning them within the contemporary proliferation of artists' film and video productions. For instance, the event "Into the Light: The Projected Images in American Art, 1964–1977 (Whitney Museum of American Art, 2001)" was a landmark exhibition that reevaluated the anti-illusionist impulse of film and video installations in the 1960s and 1970s, their exploration of film's materiality and process-based nature, and their desire to give viewers an experience of embodied spectatorship as an alternative to the passive spectatorship of mainstream cinema and television. Since then, the canonical works of structural and materialist films as well as those in the broader history of avant-garde cinema have been showcased in other similar large-scale exhibitions, such as "X-Screen: Film Installation and Actions in the 1960s and 70s (Museum Moderner Kunst Stiftung Ludwig Wien, 2003–2004)" and "Le

Mouvement des Images (Centre Georges Pompidou, 2006)." The latter is a series of retrospective exhibitions focusing on an individual film auteur. Undoubtedly, Alfred Hitchcock was the first mainstream, popular director to receive a major museum's accolade, with the exhibitions "Notorious—Alfred Hitchcock and Contemporary Art (Museum of Modern Art in Oxford, 1999)" and "Hitchcock et l'Art: Coïncidences fatales (Pompidou, 2000–2001)," both of which predated the international boom of similar exhibitions, showcasing both the documents and objects related to Hitchcock's oeuvre and the works of the artists inspired by him. Hitchcock's entrance into the museum was followed by Jean Cocteau (Pompidou, 2003), Jean-Luc Godard ("Godard: Voyage(s) en utopie, JLG, 1946–2006," Pompidou, 2006), Ingmar Bergman ("Ingmar Bergman: Truths and Lies," Deutsch Kinematek, 2010), Martin Scorsese (Cinémathèque Française, 2014–2015), and Chris Marker (Paris, Brussels, 2018). Meanwhile, exhibitions about David Lynch and Tim Burton, which drew huge crowds, attempted to validate the two directors as more than film auteurs, that is, as multimedia artists who have extended their creative energy into painting or fairy-tale illustrations.

The Kubrick Exhibition is another example of "exhibition of cinema." The exhibition's space, wherever it is held, is filled with a multiplicity of projectors and monitors that play key scenes and soundtrack fragments compiled from Kubrick's oeuvre as well as short and feature-length documentaries about his films and life. While the Exhibition has varied in museography depending on the space hosting it, it usually greets its visitors with material concerning Kubrick's early career as photographer, while it bids farewell to them with a mass of books, sketches, and notes related to his unfinished projects including *Napoleon*, *The Aryan Papers*, and *A.I.* The Exhibition's major attractions are the original draft and completed scripts that Kubrick repeatedly rewrote and revised; research materials such as books, magazines, and location photographs; detailed storyboards; production documents such as call sheets, shooting schedules and continuity reports; letters that he sent not only to his supporters but also to censorship organizations; publicity materials; drawings; lenses that he continually upgraded film by film; and the details of the visual effects that he innovatively employed for *2001: A Space Odyssey* (1968), including the frontal projection used in the "Dawn of Man" sequence.

Another tendency of the migration of cinema into the gallery along with the "exhibition of cinema" is the burgeoning of film installations and video installations foregrounding cinematic elements. These moving image artworks, which have been termed "remaking cinema," "*cinéma d'exposition* [cinema of exhibition]," and "*autre cinéma* [other cinema],"[4] appropriate and at the same time transform various components of cinema, such as mise-en-scène, cinematography, montage, narrative, star image, particular sequences of a film, or particular film genres. These operations lead to either moving images that go beyond the confines of the traditional cinematic medium and enable it to coexist with video art and plastic arts, or meta-cinematic works that reflect upon the social, cultural, and ideological memory of cinema as we have known it as well as its destiny in the present and into the future. The leading figures of the "cinema of exhibition" or "other cinema" include both artists working in the context of the museum (Douglas Gordon, Pierre Huyghe, Stan Douglas, Steve

McQueen, etc.) and filmmakers such as Isaac Julien, Abbas Kiarostami, Harun Farocki, and Chantal Akerman, to name just a few, who are primarily known as practitioners of art cinema, experimental cinema, alternative documentary, or essay film.

Like Hitchcock, Bergman, or Andrei Tarkovsky, Kubrick has been a source for the work of several artists working within the "cinema of exhibition." In her interactive digital installation *Stiffs* (1999), Jennifer Steinkamp, for instance, uses six projectors to recreate the monolith in *2001* in the forms of 3D animation and ambient sound effects, thereby positioning its symbolic meanings, including its allusion to obelisks from Europe, South America, North Africa, and the Middle East, within the tension between visual illusion and the viewer's corporeal movement that breaks the illusion. Based upon the artists' research into the overwhelming amount of documents and photographs at the Kubrick Archive that Kubrick amassed for his unfinished film about the Holocaust, Jane and Louise Wilson's *Unfolding the Aryan Papers* (2009, single-channel video with three mirrors) reconfigures the archive as open-ended, marked by a dialogue between the documents and photographs, Kubrick's unrealized ideas about the film, and the artists' imaginary reconstruction of it. Finally, *Body Double 22* (2010), by French artist Brice Dellsperger, performs a remake of *Eyes Wide Shut*, featuring heavily tattooed actor Jean-Luc Verna playing every character in various scenes from the film. Not only do male actors frequently play female characters, they also occasionally switch back to male characters while still wearing the wigs and fake breasts they donned for the female roles. In some instances, multiple male and female actors play the same character in succession. By seeking to undermine the resemblance of these characters to their sources through inversions of gender, Dellsperger deconstructs the scenes and takes away the viewer's ability to observe passively.

The two post-cinematic phenomena that signal the museum's embrace of cinema, namely, the "exhibition of cinema" and the "cinema of exhibition," echo an awareness of the demise of a cinema that enjoyed its heyday in the twentieth century as a supreme art and form of mass culture. That is, they trigger us to recognize the crisis of the cinema that was grounded in the materiality of celluloid and the image as the "world viewed" (to borrow Stanley Cavell's formula), of the cinema led by the great auteurs of the last century, and of the cinema experienced collectively on the larger-than-life screen. The monumental moment of the centennial anniversary of cinema paradoxically was accompanied by the lamentation that the century of cinema had come to an end, which was expressed by both film scholars and by critics such as Susan Sontag, who declared the end of the "age of cinephilia," which had been replaced by "the reduction of cinema to assaultive images."[5] It was at that time that the museum began to emerge as the place to preserve the filmic image and medium, which were increasingly recognized as obsolete among the sweeping influx of bravura CGIs and stimulating digital entertainment. As D.N. Rodowick (2007) aptly remarks, "As digital capture, with its own particular capacities for creation and communication, makes photography more and more like information, and as our experience of filmic duration disappears from theatrical movie houses, film reappears in the art gallery and museum, seeking out a new virtual life" (163).

If we focus on the "exhibition of cinema," what Rodowick calls film's "virtual life" in the museum refers to the fact that the awareness of the death of cinema and the nostalgia-driven revival of cinephilia are developed in relation to the cinema's new relation to the art world. To put it another way, this situation is that the cinema, which was hitherto considered to be part of a world distinct from the art world, is given a new value as the heritage and culture of the past that the museum now is able to embrace with little hesitation. Dominique Païni (2002) has brilliantly written about this new status of cinema in the post-cinematic conditions: "Since the 1990s, after having been the curiosity of the century, the leisure of the century, the art of the century, the culture of the century, cinema becomes the patrimony of the century. Each film is now also a document, testimony, trace, memory" (78, translation mine). What the visitors of the Kubrick Exhibition experience—Kubrick's films as the culmination of the cinematic art—becomes the "document, testimony, trace, and [memory]" that the museum is capable of preserving and supporting, beyond the confines of the movie theater.

Cinema and the Museum: Far Away, Yet So Close

The migration of cinema into the gallery as a post-cinematic phenomenon, represented by the "exhibition of cinema," constitutes one case/example of what Francesco Casetti (2015, 2013) labels the "relocation of cinema." For Casetti, this concept refers to the double movement of cinema in the post-media condition, wherein cinema maintains some elements of the traditional filmic experience while simultaneously involving a variety of new formal and experiential elements. The relocation of cinema employs new places, platforms, and interfaces to extend the form of traditional cinema into a new experience. Like other experiences, the cinematic experience is reactivated in other sites and screens than the traditional film theater's larger-than-life single screen. In these cases, the "relocated" cinematic experiences allow traditional cinema to retain its communicative value, for although they are certainly not the same as the traditional cinematic experience, Casetti (2013) suggests these experiences maintain many of the film's characteristic traits.

By applying the interpretation of double movement to the "exhibitions of cinema," including those composed of a film director's documents and artifacts like the Kubrick Exhibition, we can see them as an encounter between the movie theater and the gallery as two spatiotemporally distinct places. The double movement migrates between cinema as a black box and the museum as a white cube, two different, if overlapping, institutional apparatuses. The "exhibition of cinema" maintains some elements of the traditional film and the filmic experience, while simultaneously inviting curatorial principles and an array of experiences unique to the white cube. In this encounter, other elements of cinema are necessarily omitted, demonstrating the conflicts between two ontologically distinct apparatuses.

The first conflict between cinema and the museum is that film does not consent to the objecthood of the artifact or artwork traditional to the white cube. The most conspicuous of museum elements that contribute to reconstructing the world of Kubrick in the Kubrick Exhibition are the range of artifacts associated with his work, including documents, cameras, lenses, wardrobes, props, and so on, rather than a focus on film clips as such (Figure 14.1). The white cube as the Kubrick Exhibition's locus of display construes the artifacts as stable objects worthy of preservation, and thereby endows them with both tangibility and distance (O'Doherty 2000). This objecthood of the museum is not cinema as it was previously experienced. Film as medium and cinema as experience are not precisely reduced to artifacts (filmstrips, film, stills, etc.). Their original existence can only be known when the film is projected on the screen for an audience sitting in a specially designed environment such as the movie theater, in an arrangement inspired by the traditional proscenium shape, with the screen now replacing the stage. The inherent impossibility of reducing film to an object or a limited set of objects is the reason Raymond Bellour (1975) called film an "unattainable text." For this reason, the museum should go beyond the objecthood of artifacts and should construct the condition for filmic experience, or film as a working system, to preserve film as an "unattainable text." In a similar vein to Bellour's, Horwath (2008) argues that if a museum is expected to make film fully appear to its viewers, it needs to investigate and realize the concept of its "system" rather than that of "the artifact-as-object (filmstrip)" (86). Following Horwath's assertion, we may conclude that the "exhibition of cinema" that showcases a film director's artifacts as its main object of display cannot fully capture the idea of "cinema as system," and the Kubrick Exhibition is no exception.

Figure 14.1 Wardrobes used for Kubrick's *Barry Lyndon* (1975), The Stanley Kubrick Exhibition. Photo: Seoul Museum of Arts.

Another conflict between cinema and the museum can be found in the viewing experience. Cinema and the museum operate differently based on their unique temporal economies. The temporal frame of filmic experience in cinema is screen time: spectators concentrate upon the duration of images on the screen when viewing a film, and screen time is a prerequisite for that concentration. In contrast, there is no *a priori* criterion in the gallery for determining how much time a visitor should spend viewing each individual artwork, a set of entire artworks, or an exhibition. An exhibition cannot impose a standardized time that replicates how a film is viewed upon its visitors. According to Osborne (2013: 184–90), it is for these reasons that the gallery visitors' spectatorship is a "distraction in perception" characterized by their pace and the freedom to choose where to go and how much time to invest in an artwork or object. This self-direction is in direct contrast with the attentive mode of spectatorship in the movie theater. While this spectatorship as distraction might relieve contemporary audiences of the anxiety required by concentration, it necessarily contradicts film spectatorship as concentration, a spectatorship that the avant-garde cinema since the 1960s has sought to preserve by cultivating its forms and its own culture of screening and viewing. Seen in this light, Pantenburg's (2014) insight into the limitations of film installation in an art gallery recognizes the viewers' difficulty of maintaining their engagement with the installation's duration in the same way as they do in the movie theater. Drawing on some exhibitions of the early 2010s that included projections of DVD copies of experimental films by Len Lye, Stan Brakhage, and Harry Smith, he contends that these examples validate limitations to a now prevalent ideology that the museum's incorporation of black boxes in its exhibition design can host every form of moving images regardless of their different materials and technical formats (2014: 49). Pantenburg's hypothesis is evidenced in the Kubrick Exhibition where clips are extracted and presented in several projection spaces in a fragmented manner to support a curatorial point about production and auteur mastery.

Film Auteur, Cinematic Apparatus, and Intermediality

Despite the two conflicts outlined in the preceding section, objecthood and temporal economy, as two contradictions between the experience of cinema and the museum experience, I argue that the Kubrick Exhibition succeeds in realizing possibilities for revivifying three ideas of cinema: film auteur, cinematic apparatus, and intermediality. Through these three ideas, it is possible to envision productive intersections between the two institutional apparatuses in post-cinematic conditions.

The Film Auteur as Museum Artist

The entrance of Kubrick's oeuvre from institutional cinema into the museum, like Bergman's and Scorsese's, developed without a foundation in work that might be considered to be part of the "cinema of exhibition." Kubrick has generally been "author-ized" as a distinctive film auteur in film criticism and the culture of cinephilia. By presenting his work as the product of a film auteur, the curatorial approach is able to satisfy the need to present an identity of the artist that aligns with traditional museum's discursive practices. To demonstrate this point, it is necessary to briefly summarize the ideas of "film auteur" and of "auteurist film criticism" that were initially proposed and developed in postwar French film criticism and cinephile culture. Auteurism, or "auteur theory" in film theory and criticism, held three assumptions:

1. A film director is the primary creative source of the film as art, despite the collaborative nature of its production;
2. The director's films express his/her creative vision of film and the world;
3. The films, then, are seen as consistent in style and themes, although there may be deviations, innovations, or changes among and between them.

To borrow the axiom of Andrew Sarris (1962 [1999]), film directors are authorized as auteurs when their films meet all three criteria: the directors' "technical competence," "distinguished personality," and "internal meanings" derive from the tension between their personality and the constraints that surround them.

Kubrick is generally considered to fulfill all these criteria of auteurist film criticism. Like Hitchcock, John Ford, Howard Hawks, and Vincente Minnelli, he enjoyed a high level of artistic control throughout his career within Hollywood's system of production and genre. As a result of this control, his films were capable of satisfying a novel project of auteurist film criticism: to challenge the dichotomy between art and commerce by evaluating the genre films directed by the studio filmmakers as expressing their technical competence and distinguished personality, and thereby elevating the films, previously recognized as mass entertainment, to the status of artworks.[6]

The examination of scholarly studies of Kubrick's films (Walker, Ruchti, and Taylor 1999; Ciment 2001; Naremore 2007) illustrates a series of their thematic and stylistic consistencies that auteurist film criticism generally demonstrates. These include the technical innovations he was lauded for, variations of camera movements and one-point perspective that appear in many of his films, conflicts between the controlling system and the human being's free will as subject matter used for character development, lead character's psychological complexity, and the use of an aesthetic of the grotesque. All these thematic and stylistic consistencies seem to be maintained throughout Kubrick's work, despite the difference in genre represented by each film.

The idea of Kubrick as auteur is also supported by an array of popular views on his personality and production process. He produced only thirteen feature-length films, from his debut feature *Fear and Desire* (1953) through his death in 1999. During that time, he was known for exercising meticulous control over all aspects of the filmmaking process (Philips 2001; Castle 2016). He was also described in the popular press and in scholarly reviews of his work for being reclusive (Philips 2001; D'Alessandro and Ulivieri 2016). His colleagues described him as a perfectionist, as attested to by an oft-repeated anecdote that he could commonly shoot as many as a hundred takes of a single shot (Philips 2001; D'Alessandro and Ulivieri 2016).

Lastly, he was known for undertaking wide-ranging research as he developed his films, including the legacy he left for his unfinished film projects *Napoleon, A.I. Artificial Intelligence*, and *Aryan Papers* (Figure 14.2). Taken together, these reports on his work process support auteur criticism's characterization of Kubrick as a transcendental genius closely related to the romantic idea of the artist.

Once he has been defined and enshrined as an auteur, the film director provides the museum with a notable point of attraction that reaches beyond the value of any film. The term designates, for the museum curator, an artist working in a unique art form that emerged in the twentieth century. Based on this definition of film auteur, the 1,000-square-meter or so space occupied by the Kubrick Exhibition becomes a discourse on an artistic process, an examination of the idea of film auteur.

The exhibition, however, also appears to be driven by another late twentieth century curatorial trend. Since the 1990s, art museums have embraced film auteurs in much the same way they mounted exhibitions on seminal artists of the modern movement, from van Gogh or Kandinsky to Warhol. In the same way, curators can apply the same scholarly process to the film auteur, surrounding their work with the aura of a romantic artist authorized by the public institution as worthy of curatorial inquiry and public presentation. Thus, the film auteur is transformed into a museum artist.

Once the status of a museum artist is conferred upon the auteur, the artifacts that the latter amassed become elevated by the curatorial presentation, endowing them with a sense of added value and authenticity. The exhibition displays selections from his

Figure 14.2 Section with the books and documents that Kubrick amassed and studied for his unfinished project *Napoleon*, The Stanley Kubrick Exhibition. Photo: Seoul Museum of Arts.

archives in the same manner as it would relics or artworks of the past. In the museum setting, the value attributed to these artifacts could be considered both as homage and, simultaneously, as ironic. As Benjamin (1938 [2003]) argues, film emblematized the "destruction of aura"—a new mechanical mode of perception and collective reception in the audience's experience of art.

In the late twentieth century, film—the medium that, for Benjamin had destroyed the aura of the traditional arts—is now transformed back into an "auratic" object itself, after its heyday has ended. The prominent mass media of the past is now relocated into the museum and recontextualized.

The museum's focus on the film auteur may thus be viewed as demonstrating how museums are now assimilating film into traditional practices. The curators have done so by constructing a new definition for originality and authenticity, and an aura of artwork created through deconstruction of the artist's output. In this case, the transformation of Kubrick's artifacts and documents into auratic objects validates its cultural status in what Païni (2002) calls cinema's "patrimonial value" in the post-cinematic condition.

Cinematic Apparatus: Aggregate Condition and Differential Specificity

The Kubrick Exhibition also presents visitors with a valuable opportunity for viewing and examining the idea of the cinematic apparatus through considerations of the director's production process, as evidenced by his films. Krauss (1999) argues that film is distinct from the mediums of traditional arts such as painting or sculpture because it cannot be reduced to a physical substance or a limited set of techniques. For Krauss, film's particular medium specificity derives from its "aggregate condition" grounded in the layering of materials, technologies, and conventions regarding these components' use. She states that the medium of film cannot be reduced to a single component, whether the celluloid strip, the camera, the projector, the beam of light, or the screen. Rather, Krauss argues that the medium of film is the model for producing a single, sustained experience of viewing predicated on "the utter interdependence of all these things" (1999: 25).

Krauss' description of the "aggregate" condition of the cinematic apparatus was dominant in 1970s film theory. Heath (1981) conceptualized the specificity of cinema as internal heterogeneity of its components and their particular arrangement (223), a condition consistent with Wollen's (1978) explanation of the cinematic apparatus as the interlocking of the camera, its recording process, projection, and the position of the spectator (21). Taken together as emblematic of the prevailing approach to film criticism at the time, Heath's and Wollen's accounts suggest that the cinematic apparatus is composed of the internal layering of its materials (camera, filmstrip, projector, and screen) and the immaterial form and patterns of production and consumption (cultural norms associated with the theater setting, viewing, rules of cinematography, editing, and narrative conventions). Despite the internal complexity of its apparatus, film maintains the idea of medium specificity by assimilating the differences between the components into "a single, indivisible, experiential unit" or, as Krauss states, "differential specificity" (1999: 30).

The Kubrick Exhibition examines the cinematic apparatus as "aggregate" and takes on its "differential specificity" in a self-reflexive manner. The exhibition highlights cameras and lenses that Kubrick used or updated during his life as well as his experience as a photographer before his filmmaking career. These give visitors a sense of Kubrick's mastery of the technical means of the production of images. Visitors are also able to experience an array of literary conventions underlying the mainstream cinema from the original novels adapted by Kubrick as well as see his original scripts; witness elements of mise-en-scène from still photos, set designs, and costumes; and explore how he achieved the aesthetic and technical details of his innovative visual effects in the production of *2001: A Space Odyssey* (Figure 14.3), including the slit-scan photography used for the Stargate sequence. The visitors' museum experience of this work stands in contrast to the visual and sensory experience in a movie theater. While cinema has traditionally been regarded as the triumph of the disembodied gaze, the museum experience is better characterized as an embodied vision intertwining the visitors' haptic mode of perception with their movements through the gallery. The Kubrick Exhibition presents a composite idea of the cinematic apparatus, projecting the filmmaker's practice onto a visitor's embodied vision. In one instance, upon entering the reconstruction of the room and corridor from one scene in *The Shining* (1980), the visitor is drawn into Kubrick's signature tracking shots, which navigate space in the film. In this reconstruction,

Figure 14.3 Section for demonstrating visual effects for *2001: A Space Odyssey*, The Stanley Kubrick Exhibition. Photo: Seoul Museum of Arts.

the exhibit's configuration both conserves and reconstructs the memory of cinema experience and the apparatus used to construct the experience—a concept that has been explored in greater detail by Bruno (2002: 236).

Dialectic of Specificity and Impurity: Film's Intermediality

From another perspective, the cinematic apparatus is dialectical, uniting its components into a single viewing experience. The components of film, however, register an affiliation with its neighboring media and the arts that existed before its invention. In this sense, cinema has its own form and also has a dialectical relation to the idea of impurity because of that affiliation.

We can refer to this as cinema's intermediality, a concept that refers to cinema's inclusion of the material, technical, and aesthetic registers of other arts and media.

The arguments of defining the essence of cinema in comparison to—or by drawing upon the analogies with—its neighboring arts (painting, architecture, music, theater, etc.) can be found in the classical film theory of the early twentieth century. As early as the 1920s, avant-garde film was characterized as "sculpture in motion" or "painting in motion" (see, for example, Abel 1993), or as S.M. Eisenstein suggested, the art of montage (1991). In his reflection on the ontology of cinema, philosopher Alain Badiou (2005) argues that cinema's establishment as modern art lies in turning its inherent impurity into the idea of art for art's sake. "In cinema, nothing is pure. Cinema is internally and integrally contaminated by its situation as the 'plus-one' of arts" (86). This view is consistent with a similar argument by Robert Stam (2005) in his description of cinema's intermediality, which proposes that the cinematic image incorporates the tradition of painting and the visual arts, while its soundtrack inherits the history of music, dialogue, and sound experimentation (5). As cinema matured in the mid-twentieth century, directors were driven by a self-reflexive impulse to expose and investigate film's multilayered and rich alliances with other arts. For example, Bergman often referenced theatrical forms or proto-cinematic devices while Godard explored his fascination with painting that encompassed classicism, impressionism, and pop art.

In reconsidering this history with a view to exploring the cinema as it enters the museum context, I argue that the Kubrick Exhibition takes a self-reflexive approach to expose how film's intermediality is reflected in his films. Kubrick disavowed the idea of cinema as pure art. In several interviews, he stated that montage is the only domain unique to cinema, while cinematography is derived from photography and mise-en-scène from the conventions of painting and theater.[7]

The set designs and props for *A Clockwork Orange, Barry Lyndon,* and *Eyes Wide Shut* demonstrate that Kubrick considered them to be key elements of his mise-en-scène in those films (Figure 14.4). The publicity poster for *A Clockwork Orange* and the lenses used for *Barry Lyndon* remind visitors of the relationships that Kubrick's mise-en-scène has with the history of painting (specifically, *A Clockwork Orange*'s relation to contemporary pop art, while *Barry Lyndon* drew heavily on the romantic painting traditions of the late eighteenth century, typified by landscape paintings by Constable and Turner). These references to the intermedial nature of film are punctuated by

Figure 14.4 Set design and props for *A Clockwork Orange* (1971), The Stanley Kubrick Exhibition. Photo: Seoul Museum of Arts.

curatorial reminders that the film, in its final, produced form, is an assemblage of other art forms. The Kubrick Exhibition also makes a point about an intermedial link between cinema and music by punctuating the visitors' exploration with soundtracks from the key films in his oeuvre played in loop in a separate room, as if the music appreciation were a standalone art form, not simply part of the final work.

In summary, a key curatorial strategy of the Kubrick Exhibition is to deconstruct the elements of literature, theater, painting, photography, and music from Kubrick's films to offer the visitor a walk through the many art forms that constitute film. In his discussion on the implications of Ingmar Bergman's entrance into the museum, Elsaesser (2009) writes: "These apparent incompatibilities . . . that can be itemized or 'problematized' between these respective *dispositifs* [apparatuses], are precisely among the theoretically most fruitful and in practice most productive factors about the fine arts and visual culture today" (5). This strategy for activating the visitor's awareness of cinema's intermediality is a useful way of preserving Kubrick's films, despite the contradictory—even antagonistic—institutional and ontological differences between a cinema experience and a visit to a museum.

Conclusion

The "exhibition of cinema," of which the Kubrick Exhibition is exemplative, has reconfigured and revivified three ideas relating to/about cinema—film auteur, exploration of the cinematic apparatus, and cinema's intermedial relationship with other, more pure, art forms. Despite the clarity with which they illuminate auteurism and intermediality, "cinema exhibitions" fail to fully realize the technical and material complexity of the cinematic apparatus within the museum's temporal economy. The perspective taken by a viewer of this deconstructed approach to an actual film contradicts concepts of time. It disrupts the concept of narrative as seen through the duration or a film and its experience in the theater. The common aspect of their apparatus lies in the uncomfortable cohabitation of fragmentary film projections inside the "black box" and the display of objects associated with film directors and their filmmaking inside the "white cube."

In his proposal for the film program of Documenta 12 in 2007, Horwath (2007) has declared, "The location of film at Documenta 12 is the movie theatre."[8] His declaration provides an ideal model for the "exhibitions of cinema," because Documenta 12 offered its visitors not simply a variety of moving image installations variously transforming and repurposing the forms, techniques, and histories of cinema, but also the rich outputs of the "only cinema" that encompass art cinema and experimental film. It is worth noting that the Kubrick Exhibition exemplifies Horwath's model. Each city that hosted the Kubrick Exhibition since its opening in Frankfurt, including Berlin, Paris, Los Angeles, Amsterdam, Seoul, and London, simultaneously opened a retrospective screening of Kubrick's films at the museum's movie theater during the exhibition.

The Documenta 12 model further suggests two points concerning the coexistence of the "exhibition of cinema" and the film theater. On the one hand, the museum gallery and the movie theater produce divergent faces of the past, present, and future of cinema in their convergence. On the other hand, the ineluctable limitations of exhibiting cinema inside the white cube suggest that the art institution and film culture should run parallel to each other while maintaining their own territories and missions.

The coexistence of limitations and possibilities suggests that both apparatuses, cinema and the museum, are in flux. Just as the postmodern transformations of the museum have propelled it to dissolve established boundaries between its traditional objects (treasures, relics, and artworks) and cinema, so the crises of the traditional filmic image, medium, and experience have created conditions that allow these artifacts to be "relocated" within the museum walls. The result is a commitment to preserve the rich history of film as an art form for the re-enchantment of cinephiles.

I have sought to emphasize the possibilities for reviving the three ideas of cinema (auteur, apparatus, and intermediality) by stressing that despite the fundamental differences between the experience of cinema and the museum visit, the "exhibition of cinema" presents the visitor with provocative opportunities to explore both apparatuses, an experience that is a key consequence of the post-cinematic condition. Considering Elsaesser's insight into the "productive factors" that enable and necessitate new kinds of encounters between cinema and the museum, I argue that the Kubrick Exhibition—more broadly, the "exhibition of cinema"—provides contemporary museum visitors and cinephiles with a rich space of possibilities for rethinking the status of the museum and that of its objects in the context of the museum's technological, curatorial, and institutional transformations. What we witness from this post-cinematic phenomenon in the museum is the dynamic archive of cinema's past, a continual reminder of what and where cinema is. As such, the museum becomes its own apparatus for saving and reconstructing the film medium, and the idea of cinema as art, in ways that may also shift the understanding of the future of cinema.

Notes

1. This chapter is a revised and updated version of my publication of the same title in *Curator: The Museum Journal* 60(4) (2017); 227–47.
2. The whole Estate's archive itself has been relocated to London's University of the Arts Center, where it is now open and available to scholars and the public.
3. For an excellent summary of the discourse of the "death of cinema," see Jovanovic (2003). And for the most recent and systematic studies of the "post-cinema" discourse, see Casetti (2015) and Gaudreault and Marion (2015).
4. These critical terms were proposed by French critics/scholars such as Jean-Christophe Royoux and Raymond Bellour.
5. Sontag's now-famous lamentation of the "decay of cinema" goes as follows: "The reduction of cinema to assaultive images, and the unprincipled manipulation of images (faster and faster cutting) to make them more attention-grabbing, has produced a disincarnated, lightweight cinema that doesn't demand anyone's full attention. Images now appear in any size and on a variety of surfaces: on a screen in a theater, on disco walls and on megascreens hanging above sports arenas. The sheer ubiquity of moving images has steadily undermined the standards people once had both for cinema as art and for cinema as popular entertainment" (Sontag [1996]).
6. Stam (2000) summarizes this project of the auteur theory as follows: "Filmmakers like Eisenstein, Renoir, and Welles had always been regarded as auteurs because they were known to have enjoyed artistic control over their own productions. The novelty of auteur theory was to suggest that studio directors like Hawks and Minnelli were also auteurs" (87).
7. Kubrick's own words on editing as the only hallmark of cinematic medium specificity are as follows: "Editing is the only aspect of the cinematic art that is unique. It shares no connection with any other art form: writing, acting, photography, things that are major aspects of the cinema, are still not unique to it, but editing is" (Strick and Houston 2001: 135).
8. Horwarth's full remark is as follows: "The location of film at Documenta 12 is the movie theatre. This is a very simple answer to the recent debates on how to adequately present moving images in the context of art. In the course of its existence, the film medium has not only given proof of its capacity to function as art (besides several other capacities) but has also developed a strong presentation format and a strong social space: the cinema. This format and space are based on the physical and technical characteristics of the medium. They allow film to be perceived on a specific level of intensity to which it owes its historical success."

Works Cited

Abel, Richard., ed. 1993. *French Film Theory and Criticism: A History/Anthology, Vol. 1, 1907–1929*, Princeton, NJ: Princeton University Press.
Badiou, Alain. 2005. *Handbook of Inaesthetics*, trans. A. Toscano. Stanford, CA: Stanford University Press.
Balsom, Erika. 2013. *Exhibiting Cinema in Contemporary Art*. Amsterdam: Amsterdam University Press.
Bellour, Raymond. 2013. "Cinema, Alone"/Multiple "Cinemas." *Alphaville: Journal of Film and Screen Media* 5. http://www.alphavillejournal.com/Issue5/HTML/ArticleBellour.html (accessed December 1, 2015).
Bellour, Raymond. 1975. The unattainable text. *Screen* 16(3): 19–28.
Benjamin, Walter. 1938[2003]. "The Work of Art in the Age of Its Technological Reproducibility, Third Version," in H. Eiland and M. W. Jennings (eds.), *Walter Benjamin, Selected Writings, Vol. 4, 1938–1940*, trans. E. Jephcott et al. Cambridge, MA: The Belknap Press of Harvard University Press, 251–83.
Bruno, Giordano. 2002. "Collection and Recollection: On Film Itineraries and Museum Walks," in R. Allen and M. Turvey (eds.), *Camera Obscura, Camera Lucida: Essays in Honor of Annette Michelson*. Amsterdam: Amsterdam University Press, 231–60.
Casetti, Francesco. 2015. *The Lumière Galaxy: Seven Key Words for the Cinema to Come*. New York: Columbia University Press.
Casetti, Francesco. 2013. The relocation of cinema. *NECSUS: European Journal of Media Studies* 2. http://www.necsus-ejms.org/the-relocation- of-cinema (accessed December 1, 2015)
Castle, Alison., ed. 2016. *The Stanley Kubrick Archives*, London: Taschen.
Ciment, Michel. 2001. *Kubrick*, trans. G. Adair and R. Bononno. London: Faber & Faber.
D'Alessandro, Emilio, and Filippo Ulivieri, 2016. *Stanley Kubrick and Me: Thirty Years at His Side*, trans. S. Marsh. New York: Arcade Publishing.
Eisenstein, S. M. 1991. *Sergei Eisenstein: Selected Works Vol. 2, Towards a Theory of Montage*, ed. M. Taylor, trans. M. Glenny. London: British Film Institute.
Elsaesser, Thomas. 2009. "Ingmar Bergman in the Museum? Thresholds, Limits, Conditions of Possibility." *Journal of Aesthetics & Culture* 1: 1–9.
Gaudreault, André, and Marion, F. 2015. *The End of Cinema?: A Medium in Crisis in the Digital Age*, trans. T. Barnard. New York: Columbia University Press.
Heath, Stephen. 1981. *Questions of Cinema*. London: Macmillan.
Horwath, Alexander. 2008. "Film as Artefact and Museum Object," in P. C. Usai, D. Francis, A. Horwath and M. Loebenstein (eds.), *Film Curatorship: Archives, Museums, and the Digital Marketplace*. Vienna: Austrian Film Museum, 83–106.
Horwath, Alexander. 2007. "Second lives—the Documenta 12 Film Programme," http://www.documenta12.de/787.html?&L=1 (accessed December 1, 2015).
Jovanovic, Stefan. 2003. "The Ending(s) of Cinema: Notes on the Recurrent Demise of the Seventh Art, Part I," *Offscreen* 7(4), http://offscreen.com/view/seventh_art1 (accessed December 1, 2015).
Krauss, Rosalind. 1999. *A Voyage on the North Sea: Art in the Age of the Post-medium Condition*. London: Thames and Hudson.
Naremore, James. 2007. *On Kubrick*. London: British Film Institute.

O'Doherty, Brian. 2000. *Inside the White Cube: The Ideology of the Gallery Space*, expanded edition. Berkeley, CA: University of California Press.

Osborne, Peter. 2013. *Anywhere or Not at All: Philosophy of Contemporary Art*. New York: Verso.

Païni, Dominique. 2002. *Le Temps exposé: Le cinéma de la salle au musée*. Paris: Cahiers du cinéma.

Pantenburg, Volker. 2014. "Temporal Economy: Distraction and Attention in Experimental Cinema and Installation Art." *Millennium Film Journal* 59: 44–50.

Philips, G. D., ed. 2001. *Stanley Kubrick: Interviews*, Jackson, MS: University Press of Mississippi.

Rodowick, D. N. 2007. *The Virtual Life of Film*. Cambridge, MA: Harvard University Press.

Sarris, Andrew. 1962[1999]. "Notes on the Auteur Theory in 1962," in L. Braudy and M. Cohen (eds.), *Film Theory and Criticism: Introductory Readings*, 5th edn. New York: Oxford University Press, 515–18.

Sontag, Susan. 1996. "The Decay of Cinema." *New York Times*, February 25. https://www.nytimes.com/books/00/03/12/specials/sontag-cinema.html (accessed December 10, 2015.).

Stam, Robert. 2005. *Literature through Film: Realism, Magic, and the Art of Adaptation*. Malden and Oxford: Blackwell Publishing.

Stam, Robert. 2000. *Film Theory: An Introduction*. Oxford, UK: Blackwell Publishers.

Strick, Philip, and Penelope Houston. 2001. "Modern Times: An Interview with Stanley Kubrick," in G. D. Philips (ed.), *Stanley Kubrick: Interviews*. Jackson, MS: University Press of Mississippi, 126–39.

Walker, Alexander, Ulrich Ruchti, and Sybil Taylor, 1999. *Stanley Kubrick, Director: A Visual Analysis*, New York: W. W. Norton.

Wollen, Peter. 1978. "Cinema and Technology: A Historical Overview," in T. de Lauretis and S. Heath (eds.), *The Cinematic Apparatus*. London: Macmillan, 14–22.

15

The Dead Kitten: Sacrifice in *Barry Lyndon*

Alexander Nemerov

A serious house on serious earth it is . . .
—Philip Larkin, "Church Going"

Representation can sometimes be found dreaming of its own endeavors. At its most outlandish, it even entertains fantasies of what it can achieve. One such fantasy is as follows: representation, to create the real, must expend massive amounts of energy; it must throw heaps of goods on the fire; it must burn down whole towns if it is to produce one small scrap of life itself. This compact that representation makes with the real is a sacrifice all the way around: for life itself, having been conjured in these elaborate rituals, is no sooner created than it too is flung in the fire.

In *Barry Lyndon* (1975), one scene pursues this burning bargain. The upstart Barry hosts an afternoon of chamber music at his wife's estate, hoping to impress aristocratic guests in his bid to become a lord. Amid the beautiful Bach music and the sweet attention of Barry's dignified guests, the plans go awry when his hated stepson Viscount Bullingdon, played by Leon Vitali, walks into the room in the company of his half-brother and Barry's true son, Bryan. In a moment adapted from William Thackeray's 1844 novel, the two half-brothers stride in side by side, the teenage Bullingdon in his stocking feet, Bryan, some seven years old, clomping in wearing Bullingdon's large shoes[1] (Figure 15.1). Bryan smiles at the loudness of his stomping feet, each pace progressively more annoying until the guests and, finally, the musicians themselves can no longer ignore the disruption and the elegant performance comes to a halt. "Don't you think he fits my shoes well?" Bullingdon addresses his mother in a tremulous adolescent voice, condemning his stepfather for having usurped his rightful place as heir to the Barry name and fortune—the young boy Bryan being now the one, evident to all, who wears the proper heir's shoes. In a moment, all hell breaks loose. Lady Lyndon upbraids her son and tearfully spirits young Bryan from the room. Then Ryan O'Neal's Barry Lyndon himself sets upon the hated Bullingdon, thrashing him so severely that half a dozen bewigged gentlemen are needed to restrain him. Barry's hopes of a title end there.

Figure 15.1 Viscount Bullingdon (Leon Vitali) and Bryan (David Morley) enter the recital. (*Barry Lyndon*, Stanley Kubrick, 1975), copyright Warner Brothers.

How is the scene a sacrifice? Most directly, it is a scene not of sacrifice but disruption, of best-laid plans destroyed. The boys' entrance into the room wreaks havoc on all the powdered care and refinement. But it does not take much to see the scene another way. The musicians actually play to summon the appearance of Bullingdon and Bryan. The violinists at their instruments, Lady Lyndon at her harpsichord, The Reverend Runt at his flute—each appears successively in a slow swiveling camera movement that shows their orientation to the attentive listeners, yes, but also to the door through which the half-brothers will enter. In the most elaborate and refined way, the scene calls forth its own destruction, sacrificing itself to the disruptive principle it has summoned into the room.

More than chamber music is needed, however, to accomplish this purpose. The politeness of the guests partakes of incantatory ritual as much as the timbre of string and key. It is as if they knew their decorum were itself necessary to call forth—as it were, out of nowhere—the destructive element. Not a cough must go unsuppressed; not a bored rustling of fan or movement of foot must be allowed to break the composure of a delicate rite bringing forth the smashing of all delicacy. The same goes for the paintings that bank the walls of the famous Picture Gallery at Corsham Court, where the scene was filmed. Genuine Old Masters owned by the diplomat Sir Paul Methuen (1672–1757), who brought them to Corsham from his overseas service, the paintings double in the film as those Lady Lyndon and now the pretender Barry have assembled, the better to certify Barry's social prestige. Amassed on the walls in much the same way that the chamber music fills the room, the paintings suggest accumulation in another fashion: as a principle of sheer excess, stack upon stack of picture, each of the right pedigree, all gathered so that a sufficient number of goods might be present to call forth, again, the disruption that will damage all. It is as though a smaller number of paintings—a number, at any rate, that did not extend edge to edge from floor to ceiling of the room—would not call forth the disaster that will proclaim all the decorum a lie. Sacrifice in abundance—dozens of paintings, a lavishing of music and attention, in short, a *critical mass* of representation—is what is required, so it seems, to make the room's double doors swing open and chaos ensue.

But why? Here we turn to Henry James, no stranger to the principle of representation in question. As a boy growing up in Manhattan in the 1850s, James met Thackeray, a visitor to the James home on 14th Street during an American lecture tour. (Thackeray, whom James would later praise as one of his favorite writers, told the shy youngster to approach him so he could see his "extraordinary jacket.") As he came to write his own novels starting in the 1870s, James mastered the art of the set piece: the elaborate scene, often set in a garden park or other formal location—akin to the picture gallery in Kubrick's film—wherein no detail is too small and no refinement of language and plotting is too insignificant to help create, suddenly, a disconcerting note of evil or duplicity. James called the crafting of these set pieces "making a scene," with the double-entendre clear. The writer's perfect scenic design would deliver a hysterical and embarrassing revelation. *A scene would be created*, a truth would appear.[2]

In James's *The Ambassadors* (1903), Lambert Strether enjoys a long day of leisure in the French countryside in which, nonetheless, the dilatory calm feels permeated by a tense and rampant sense of expectation. When at the chapter's end Chad and Madame de Vionnet round the river's bend in a small boat—their secretive affair at last confirmed for Strether, who watches amazed from the shore—the reader feels that every moment in the whole chapter has predicted this stunning and serendipitous discovery. Almost with malevolence, James makes every blade of grass bend and blow, every cloud scud across the beatific French sky, only so that a revelation at the end can lay waste to all this nicety and order.[3]

Or think of the meticulous description of Gilbert Osmond's Florentine villa in the chapter that introduces that evil character in James's *Portrait of a Lady* (1881). There again—even as every object is perfectly described, even as the sunlight and shadow of the late morning spread in delicate patterns that make the very stones of the walkways exhale a contented breath—we sense that the place is a trap, that not a bush of lavender or azalea exudes its fragrance without taking part in a design that says: beware.[4] The representational principle at issue is *expenditure*, the tremendous build-up of detail, of care, everything having been polished with the utmost refinement, so that an immaculate cathedral can lead to the calamity it is made to enshrine. Naming this principle of James's fiction in a passage that certainly hurt his friend's feelings, H. G. Wells wrote that a James novel

> is like a church lit but without a congregation to distract you, with every light and line focused on the high altar. And on the altar, very reverently placed, intensely there, is a dead kitten, an egg-shell, a bit of string . . . (in Edel 1985: 701)[5]

James's Religion of Art delivers a precious sight at the altar, a revelation small, anticlimactic, yet "intensely there." But the revelation does something else that Wells did not articulate. It crumbles the sacred edifice required to produce it. James, admonishing his friend in the last letter he ever wrote to Wells, issued a resounding definition to this effect: "Art *makes* life, makes interest, makes importance." In short, it creates the feeling of life that, by its sheer force, beggars mere art, mere fiction. This is, for James, the power of art, "the force and beauty of its process" (in Edel, 702).

Art *makes* life. Art builds itself up in layers and layers of artifice—in cathedral terms, it requires masons and glassmakers to contrive clerestories and columns and windows—all so that it can deliver us into the realm of the real. Without the painstaking design that began on the architect's table, without the execution of a million finicky details, the structure would collapse of its own volition long before the signal event it aims to produce does the demolition itself. A James novel, though assuredly meant to endure, to be a glimmering bastion in the darkness, on a deeper level *sacrifices its energies*, painfully creating minute effect after effect, so that the moment that is and is *not* a representation—call it a Moment of Truth—can emerge. And that moment, once it appears, is not art. It is hostile to art.[6]

Nothing underwrites this idea about representation; nothing says it must be so. A novelist or filmmaker could conceive other ways to "*make* life," for example in a groove-for-groove smooth delineation whereby, mirror-like, every faceted angle of a lived experience finds its correlate in a similar shine of words or pictures. Such a model of mimetic accuracy informs *Barry Lyndon*, which notably quotes poses from eighteenth-century paintings such as those of William Hogarth and George Stubbs. But Kubrick seems to have shared with James a superstitious respect for difficulty and even for some great god of representation, standing before the lairs and laws of life, whose appetite must be sated before the holy keep is revealed. The conception and execution of a film, or even of individual scenes in a film, must appease unknown gods if, down out of thin air, the principles that will cause a scene to reverberate as more than art—as indeed shockingly real—will visit the set. The film critic David Thomson wrote that Kubrick knew a great deal about films, but less about life (2013: 538). But maybe knowing a great deal about films was, for Kubrick, the only way to make life appear.

In this sense, the making of *Barry Lyndon* was a superstitious ritual. A scene that took seventy-five takes was more than just an exercise in perfection—it was a sacrificial offering, an expenditure of time, money, and labor, all lit so brightly by burning self-destructive energies that the pyre could be seen from outer space. The effort was more, much more, than necessary—even to achieve perfection itself. When after the seventy-fifth take of one scene Kubrick finally told Murray Melvin, who played The Reverend Runt, "OK, Murray, I can do something with that," the actor's repetitive chant had been the incantation of a high priest before an altar. Some god of representation loomed above these maddening perfections, waiting to be appeased in this and other propitiations. When production designer Ken Adam resigned, citing the endless arguing with Kubrick as an active detriment to his health, he was another of the film's offerings, more goods thrown on the fire. The whole film needed to be struck and scarred, brutalized like a saint tied to a post. Even the many filming locations were a part of this. Kubrick's decision to film in Northern Ireland led to disputes with unionized film workers in that country and ultimately to an IRA death threat to the director, causing the remainder of the movie to be shot in England, where English soldiers (even eighteenth-century redcoats) could conduct drill and parade without offense to the native population.[7] This too was a sacrifice, part of the great trail of effort and time on which, presumably, a deity gazed and was pleased.

The recital scene was a special offering. In Tony Zierra's documentary *Filmworker* (2018), which details Leon Vitali's extraordinary career as Kubrick's long-time assistant, Vitali recalls that the recital scene took thirty takes. "When I walk in with Bryan," Vitali says in *Filmworker*, "we did it over and over and over again. Once we found the pulse, the emotional center of the whole thing, we just let everything go, with never a cut; we just kept doing complete takes with the whole speech." These complete takes included O'Neal striking Vitali. "I hit him," O'Neal recalls in the documentary, "and Stanley said, you're not hitting him hard enough. I'm looking at Leon, you know, oh Leon. We did it thirty times; and I know I hurt him, I know I hurt him. I didn't want to, but this was Stanley. Again, again." The punishment anticipated the torments Vitali would gladly endure for the next several decades as Kubrick's chief assistant. As Matthew Modine puts it, "What Leon did was a selfless act, a kind of crucifixion of himself."

It makes no sense that a movie set in the Enlightenment would envision filmmaking as a religious ritual. But the paintings in the recital scene suggest otherwise. Many of them depict biblical topics, such as Bonifacio Veronese's *Adoration of the Kings* and Carlo Dolci's *Christ in the House of the Pharisee*, which appear to either side of the door as Bullingdon and Bryan enter. Although we understand that such paintings stand broadly and secularly for taste and money—at the one point when Barry comments on a picture, his remark is bland and ignorant—they exert a strong religious effect upon the recital scene. Of these paintings, one is undoubtedly the star: Dirk Van Baburen's *Tobias and the Angel*, which appears in several shots, notably when Bullingdon kneels down to address Bryan and when Lady Lyndon exits with her son (Figures 15.2, 15.3). The painting neatly states the religious freight of a seemingly secular scene.

Portraying a story from the apocryphal book of Tobit, Baburen depicts the angel as a taller boy leading a small one, Tobias, by the hand—just as Bullingdon leads Bryan into the room. In the painting, the angel leads Tobias to cure the blindness of his father—again a story with plenty of resonance to *Barry Lyndon*. The key however is not these thematic parallels but that Baburen's picture—like all the religious paintings in the room—attests to the lurking presence of ritual, myth, and magic in the film itself. In this sense the Picture Gallery at Corsham Court is a hothouse laboratory, a condensed image-bank, revealing the row upon row of mythic and superstitious sources on which the recital scene draws.

The pictorial etymology of this operation is basic. Kubrick relies on late-eighteenth-century portraits such as Henry Raeburn's *Allen Brothers* for his portrayal of Bullingdon and Bryan (Figure 15.4). In turn, Raeburn and Kubrick rely on scenes such as Baburen's to conjure their respective worlds. Both the eighteenth-century portraitist and the twentieth-century director understood that secular scenes derive from a deep substrate of religious imagery. In that sense even the most un-religious of scenarios—Bullingdon's dispute about inheritance—emerges out of biblical and

Figure 15.2 Lady Lyndon (Marisa Berenson) and Bullingdon with Dirk Van Baburen's *Tobias and the Angel* in the background. (*Barry Lyndon*, Stanley Kubrick, 1975), copyright Warner Brothers.

Figure 15.3 Lady Lyndon and Bryan with Baburen's *Tobias and the Angel*. (*Barry Lyndon*, Stanley Kubrick, 1975), copyright Warner Brothers.

apocryphal tales. Neither Bullingdon nor Bryan carries amulets or special healing talismans, as Tobias carries the fish in Baburen's painting, but such fantastic religious themes lurk in the eighteenth-century culture of which *Barry Lyndon* is such an exacting replica. And Kubrick, the creator of that replica, presumably understood the deep, if hidden, religious basis of the era he chose to depict. His film, in turn, aligns itself with this religious feeling that, in the recital scene, comes to the fore—where

Figure 15.4 Henry Raeburn, *The Allen Brothers*, ca. 1790. Oil on canvas, 60 x 45 ½ in. Kimbell Art Museum.

it is boasted and asserted on the walls, in full acknowledgment of the film's basis in religious representation, in fantasies of faith and miracle.

What is the reality miraculously revealed in *Barry Lyndon*'s recital scene? It is that some people in the world are sacrifices. The world takes them, eats them, and claims them. Bryan is brought into that room to die, as surely as a virgin dragged kicking and screaming before the throbbing drums at the apex of a jungle temple. His death does not occur literally in that scene—his mother hurries him to safety, but not before he takes a backward glance at the mayhem his foot-stomping has induced. The clip-clop of his oversized shoes foretells Bryan's actual death, which happens soon enough when he falls from the thoroughbred horse his father has purchased for him as a birthday present. The clattering of the animal's hooves strikes its own ominous note—the horse is simply too big for him to handle—and so the footsteps fall hard in the recital for the boy who will fall harder still. When Bryan is thrown from his mount, his killer is not the horse, and not his father or his step-brother, who has beaten him savagely in a study-room fit of pique not long before the recital. It is not even the sadistic Kubrick himself, though he is the one who writes out the orders dictating the boy's demise, just like the depraved generals Mireau and Broulard in *Paths of Glory* (1958) who sacrifice the three enlisted men.

What kills Bryan is some sense of fate, of *this is the destiny of some people in the world*, that Kubrick feels himself in the thrall of, and that he must exercise all of his own infuriating vexation and pictorial capital to conjure forth as a truth. Heaps of artistic and actorly glories must be thrown upon the altar so that a single fragrant stream of incense will rise in a mystic perfume. What it smells of is this: the world commits these cruelties, the world even consists in them. Rituals reveal these truths in the way that whips and chains make scars and welts. There might be other ways to show that the world is cruel, that it consumes innocent victims, that its sacrifices enter on cue to the overture that augurs the destruction of music and innocent trespasser alike. But this is Kubrick's way.

The impulse behind this demonstration was likely not philosophic. It may actually have been childishness incarnate, as of boys playing with matches in the most flammable of places. But the puerility of the motive does not cancel the grandeur of the accomplishment. We are indebted to art for making life, for occasionally giving it to us in the raw. If one aspect of that life should be the fact of cruelty, it is fair for advanced artists to wonder how to make it present. Yes, a painter might paint the jawbone of an ass, coloring it in tonalities partly of calcium and partly of grisly flaming light. And Iago's face might distill the fierce gaslight that floods his features, so that the coldness of a Victorian night, replete with the flowing of the Thames, seems one with the blood in an actor's veins. But these can be only surface effects, just technical achievements. Something more magical is required.

Go down therefore into the laboratory of representation. There, where the magicians pour their elixirs, a crazier recipe emerges. Filming *Barry Lyndon* by candlelight, intent on being the first to make a film by such a method, Kubrick overcame the low light, the large lens, the stench of the animal-fat candles and the search for the sweetness of the tapers made mostly of beeswax (Baxter 1997: 283). He got a kind of light that was beyond accuracy, beyond his own designs, though only his fanatical accuracy could have made such an otherness. Lords and ladies are the sum of their pores—at times, we do not know if it is the actors or the lights that glow—and to this day, Bullingdon's pheromonal youth is a source of sticky light. But we also sense that the film itself is a grand votive candle offered to the night, to the supernal gods, out there in the zones of chance and luck, who design the constellations of the stars. Votively blazing from within, the film aspires to burn itself down, as if it were possible to ignite itself from the inside. No smoldering or smoking truly crisps the edges of the celluloid frames, but a warmth and a smell of frying is palpable. A principle of sacrifice—of burning the whole film down, as a bravura show of strength, of stating how many castles, actors, pictures, and green fields can be *expended* to make a moment of truth—remains the heart of the movie's fantasy of representation.

* * *

An essay such as this one cannot simply point out this phenomenon, however. To produce its own credible version of the real, it must build up its evidence, mount its claims, and torch itself in order to produce its own moment of truth. It does this by burning its scholarly credibility—which it does, with one strike of the match, by irresponsibly perceiving a kinship with the scene in question, a scene that becomes therefore not merely a "topic" or "subject" but strangely—indeed, impossibly—a portrayal of the writer's own life. In short, only by envisioning the scene from the inside, *by recognizing himself within it,* can the critic see the "real life" that Kubrick has gone to such sacrificial pains to create.

The personal connection for me works as follows. Leon Vitali's appearance as Lord Bullingdon, notably in Kubrick's close-ups during the impassioned speech, reminds me of Diane Arbus's *Puerto Rican woman with a beauty mark, N.Y.C. 1965* (Figures 15.5 and 15.6). *Puerto Rican woman* appeared in the Aperture monograph of her work published in 1972, the year after her suicide, not long before the filming of *Barry Lyndon*. Later, it would be Vitali himself, having taken on the role of Kubrick's jack-of-all-trades assistant, who cast the twins for *The Shining* (1980), doing so (even though the script did not call for twins) because he recognized that a pair of twin sisters at the casting call evoked Arbus's haunting photograph *Identical Twins, Roselle, N.J. 1966*. Kubrick, who started out as a photographer in New York, loved Vitali's choice for self-evident reasons.[8] Like the director, Arbus now seems to have operated by some Faustian bargain. She too sought to push further and further, going past known limits, past thresholds before which many other artists would have stopped, in quest of a wisdom that she sensed lay only at extremes. But Bullingdon's face, with its resemblance to the one in Arbus's photograph, is also personal for me because she was my aunt.[9] I realize now that when I chose to write about the recital scene—having been mesmerized by Bullingdon's face, among other things—I did so for personal reasons I did not then grasp.

Figure 15.5 Bullingdon, close-up, in recital scene. (*Barry Lyndon*, Stanley Kubrick, 1975), copyright Warner Brothers.

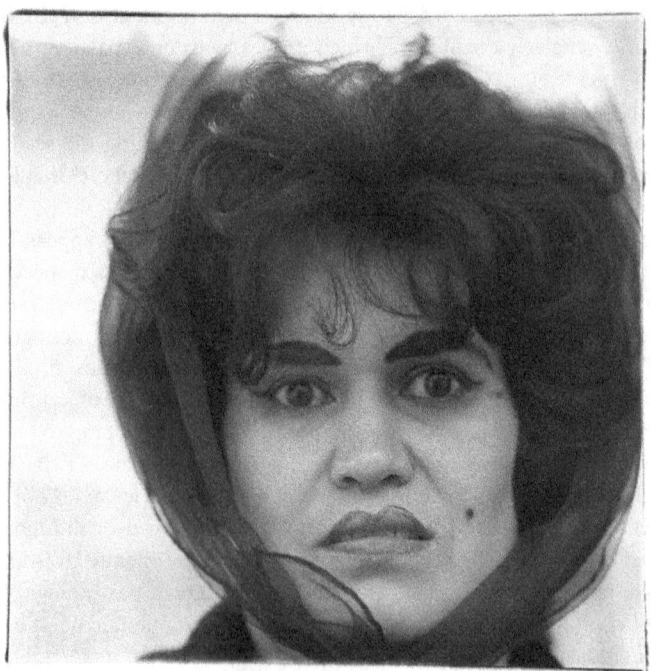

Figure 15.6 Diane Arbus, *Puerto Rican woman with a beauty mark, N.Y.C. 1965*, copyright Arbus Estate. By permission.

In fact, the subliminal presence of Arbus's photograph in *Barry Lyndon* only confirms some deeper private feeling I experienced on first seeing the film in early 2018. Of course she would be there, I find myself thinking now, because the recital scene is so thoroughly personal for me— notably in its portrayal of two young brothers in the 1970s. It brings back how my younger brother Jeremy and I would sometimes walk into a roomful of adults at dinner parties at our house. We were little boys then—I was born in 1963, Jeremy in 1965—and though not as far apart in age as Bullingdon and Bryan (and not half brothers), we were rivals who stood side by side (Figure 15.7). Sometimes, we would stroll into one of these grown-up parties in adult clothes, causing all of the party-goers to stop their entertainment and politely turn their heads. I believe Jeremy wore our mother's clothes, though perhaps I did sometimes too. We both wore shoes way too large for us.

It was not just this memory that the recital scene brought to mind, however. It was an event of much more recent vintage—the beating to death of Jeremy in Leavenworth Penitentiary in 2014. He had just arrived there the day before, having been transferred from another prison, while serving a term for drug trafficking. A long-time drug addict and thief, he had finally run out of bail and luck when our mother died in 2011, leaving him with few resources to escape his own habit, his numerous creditors, and eventually the law. At Leavenworth, other inmates beat him to death because they suspected he

Figure 15.7 Margaret Nemerov, *Howard Nemerov, with sons Jeremy (middle) and Alexander* (private collection of the author).

was a snitch, and because they enjoyed exacting gratuitous cruelty on other human beings. Thinking back to having first seen *Barry Lyndon* in early 2018, I realize now that I was moved by the recital scene not only because it shows two young brothers of the early 1970s entering a roomful of adults, but because it shows the severe beating of Bullingdon.

I wonder now: Who in the scene is me, who is my brother? In one sense, Bryan is my brother—the young boy's fall from his horse and subsequent deathbed scene suggest his violent fate. In another sense, Bullingdon himself is the spitting image of my brother's rage and grievance. Jeremy's furious demands were never as eloquent, but the sheer ferocity of his frequent calls for money—his sense that he was being bilked or cheated out of what he needed to survive—is a dead ringer for Bullingdon's (though in reality it was my brother who was himself stealing the money he was furious about being deprived of). But Bullingdon also reminds me a great deal of myself in those years, since I was just as proud and resentful, just as androgynous and self-consciously articulate. The only difference is that I did not actually seek to sacrifice my brother, any more than I myself was sacrificed. But now the recital scene makes me wonder.

I mentioned that I saw the film only recently. This is because for many years I chose not to watch it even though I knew I would like it. Finally, in my fifties, I have done so—the invitation to contribute to this volume having been the impetus. Now, as I look back, the deferral strikes me as important. I wonder if the reason I did not watch *Barry Lyndon* for all those years was because I was waiting for myself to catch up to the film, waiting for my own mind to pull even to the demands I sensed it would make upon me. These demands, I somehow knew, would be disturbing, close to home. Even before my brother's murder in 2014, which long post-dated my years of slowly coming around to watching *Barry Lyndon*, I knew there would be plenty for me to see and flee from. The murder only somehow confirmed that—time out of time—my brother's death had already occurred in the film I spent years not seeing.

There is the cathedral and, in it, the high altar with something furry placed on it. The movie palace, *Barry Lyndon* itself, the Picture Gallery at Corsham Court—these, too, are holy places bedizened with beauty, into which the humble visitor meekly enters. He is there because he is one of those who, as Philip Larkin says in his poem "Church Going,"

> will forever be surprising,
> A hunger in himself to be more serious,
> And gravitating with it to this ground,
> Which, he once heard, was proper to grow wise in, If only that so many dead lie round. (Larkin 1988: 63)[10]

What the visitor finds, however, is only himself, alone in the vacant shrine. And there, it is not the open doors, not the noise of footsteps, nor all the pictures on the walls that prepare him for the strange note of his own voice, which falls, just then, on deaf ears. The truth any interpreter encounters is his own. It echoes only for himself. But it is the silent empty church, perfect in every detail, that holds and redoubles the sound.

Notes

1 "'There was a great crowding and tittering when the child came in, led by his half-brother, who walked into the dancing-room (would you believe it?) in his stocking-feet, leading little Bryan by the hand, paddling about in the great shoes of the elder! 'Don't you think he fits my shoes very well, Sir Richard Wargrave?' says the young reprobate: upon which the company began to look at each other and to titter; and his mother, coming up to Lord Bullingdon with great dignity, seized the child to her breast, and said, 'From the manner in which I love this child, my lord, you ought to know how I would have loved his elder brother had he proved worthy any mother's affection!' and, bursting into tears, Lady Lyndon left the apartment, and the young lord rather discomfited for once." (Thackeray 1967: 273–74)
2 See James 2011: 151–53.
3 See James 1964: 300–7. The section in question is Book Eleventh, Part III, Section 30.
4 See James 1986: 278–94. The chapter in question is 22.
5 Edel quotes from H. G. Wells's *Boon, The Mind of the Race, The Wild Asses of the Devil and The Last Trump* [1915].

6 Wells had his own way of creating ceremonial rituals of sacrifice. The great German blimp armada in his science fiction novel *The War in the Air* (1907) assembles in a vast circle of dirigibles high over the Atlantic Ocean to witness the execution of a crew-member found with matches on his person (forbidden on the hydrogen-inflated blimps). With deft care, Wells describes how the man drops from the gondola with a long rope around his neck; notes still further how, at the end of his tether, the man's body abruptly jolts to a stop that causes the head to pop off. The body and head then race each other to the ocean far below—tiny details yet central, "intensely there," amid the huge pomp of the vast and encircling armada that witness and create the one human fate that destroys—that deflates—their grandiosity. The dirigibles are not Jamesian cathedrals, but the pay-off is like that of the Master: a mighty summoning, a great gaseous inflation, sure of suture and streamline, all so that something minuscule and unforgettable will drone into the viewer's mind, destroying the art that—in ecstasies of discipline—created this singular and utterly undoing vision. See Wells (1997: 63).
7 See Baxter, 288, 282–83, 291, 286–87, 289–90.
8 Vitali relates the story of the casting call, the twins, and Kubrick's reaction to his choice in Zierra's *Filmworker* (2018).
9 See Nemerov (2015).
10 Larkin (1988: 98).

Works Cited

Baxter, John. 1997. *Stanley Kubrick: A Biography*. New York: Harper Collins.
Edel, Leon. 1985. *Henry James: A Life*. New York: Simon & Schuster.
James, Henry. 2011. *A Small Boy and Others*, ed. Peter Collister. Charlottesville, Virginia: University of Virginia Press.
James, Henry. 1964. *The Ambassadors*. New York: Norton.
James, Henry. 1986. *The Portrait of a Lady*. London: Penguin.
Larkin, Philip. 1988. "Church Going," in Anthony Thwaite (ed.), *Collected Poems*. London and Boston: Marvell Press and Faber and Faber, 98.
Nemerov, Alexander. 2015. *Silent Dialogues: Diane Arbus and Howard Nemerov*. San Francisco: Fraenkel Gallery.
Thackeray, William Makepeace. 1967. *Barry Lyndon*, London: Cassell.
Thompson, David. 2013. *The New Biographical Dictionary of Film*. New York: Alfred A. Knopf.
Wells, H. G. 1997. *The War in the Air*. New York: Penguin.

Appendix
Interview with Gaspar Noé

Pip Chodorov

This interview was conducted in person by Pip Chodorov, with additional questions by Jeremi Szaniawski, at the Cannes Grand Hotel, May 18, 2018. It was edited and translated from French by Jeremi Szaniawski.

* * *

At the 2018 Cannes film festival, Gaspar Noé received an award in the Quinzaine des réalisateurs selection for *Climax*. But the filmmaker was also excited by the prospect of a 70mm screening of Stanley Kubrick's *2001: A Space Odyssey* on the occasion of the fiftieth anniversary of the film's release. Pip Chodorov and Jeremi Szaniawski took the opportunity to ask him questions about Kubrick's Sci-fi classic.

Pip Chodorov: Gaspar, we are at Cannes, this is the fiftieth anniversary of *2001: A Space Odyssey*, and it just got screened in 70mm. You are an avid fan of the film, do you remember when you first saw it?[1]

Gaspar Noé: I was around seven years-old. It was in Buenos Aires. I went to see it with my mother and my father. I came out of the movie transfixed. I was under the impression that I had enjoyed it far more than my parents did. And I remember very well, wondering at the time "what was that baby with a huge head . . ." And my parents explained to me "you know, babies, when inside the womb, have a huge head." And so they had to explain both fecundation and birth to me by the same token. So in one go, I got to realize what a psychedelic trip could be, where life came from, and how it was conceived. The origin of life. I was so fascinated by the movie . . . it got rereleased every summer, maybe every other year, and each time, I went. Without my parents, even though I was little. I would go with schoolmates, and then as a teenager I would go by myself, and I kept seeing it, in high school, in film school . . . and I have never stopped since. I must have seen the movie fifty, maybe sixty times by now.

Jeremi Szaniawski: Are there other Kubrick movies that matter as much to you?

GN: This one stands alone, above all the others. And I am flabbergasted when critics tell me that Kubrick's greatest film is *Dr. Strangelove or: How I Learned to Stop Worrying and Love the Bomb* (1964). I have seen that film once. But *2001* . . . I just can't get enough of it. I even watch it sometimes when I am on an airplane. People tell me "come on Gaspar, there's tons of new films," but I say "they are showing *2001*, I am going to watch it one more time."

JS: Your film *Enter the Void* (2009), with its "ultimate trip" dimension, its colour patterns, the way it deals with death and resurrection, its camera movements, is very ostensibly influenced by *2001*. But in general, your whole oeuvre seems to be informed by the film. For instance, in *Irreversible* (2002), the red tunnel, the poster of *2001* on the protagonists' bedroom wall, the flicker at the end of the film, revealing a subliminal outer space and the black monolith . . . and I have a sense that your oeuvre as a whole engages with a phenomenology of drugs, just as *2001* clearly engaged with the effects and hallucinations of psychedelic drugs . . .

GN: The poster at the end of *Irreversible* has to do with the fact that the Vincent Cassel character is a cinephile, but the film was also shot in the year 2001, so it's a reference to that, a way of dating the film . . . and also a way of announcing that Monica Belluci's character is pregnant: we see the Star Child, a fetus, on the poster on the wall. The camera pans and we can see the characters and the poster in one movement. I have this poster at home, by the way, and it's my favourite of all the many *2001* posters that have been released. I believe I have the largest collection of *2001* posters and publicity paraphernalia in the world. It felt good to be able to put the poster in the film. We got the clearance to do that . . . but indeed, for me, the influence of *2001* is more explicit in *Enter the Void*, this tendency toward experimental filmmaking and psychedelic representations…

JS: Would you say that there is a Kubrickian tradition in your cinema?

GN: I am not fascinated by Kubrick's oeuvre as a whole. I am fascinated by R.W. Fassbinder, by Kenneth Anger, . . . and then, there are distinct films that I am obsessed with. *Salò* by Pasolini (1975) is one. *2001: A Space Odyssey* is the other big one. I just am the opposite of Kubrick. . . . I am incapable of doing anything serious . . . even if I wanted to do a serious documentary or psychological drama. . . . I can film people getting beaten to a pulp and it's always derisive in the end, it ends up being funny one way or another. What I make will always be closer to a Buñuel than a Kubrick film.

PC: When did you start collecting posters of Kubrick's film?

GN: I always had this drive to collect. It's a mental disease. Since I was a child, I collected stamps, comic strips . . . it's pathological. I don't know, it's as if in order to possess something, you had to have the totality, the product as a whole. The latest and longest lasting manifestation of this *maladive collectionitis* in my case is my obsession with *2001*. That is clear.

JS: In Kubrick's films, in *2001* particularly, there is a worldview, a philosophy. Do you think that your films have a philosophy, a worldview?

GN: I am a dwarf . . . a flea . . . compared to the giant. . . . You can't compare. Kubrick made THE film. The film where you can wonder how could someone do something so utterly majestic and ahead of its time. When you see *Metropolis* (Fritz Lang, 1927) you know it's the major, the ultimate work of art made by a filmmaker. When you see *King Kong* (Merian C. Cooper and Ernest B. Schoedsack, 1933) you ask yourself: "How is it possible to accomplish something so perfect technically, with such special effects, at that period in time?" When you watch *2001*, made in 1968, it's sublime. It's unthinkable that someone managed to pull off a film like that, before any form of CGI. . . . It was a period when people still believed in cinema. This film is the absolute and ultimate manifestation of the power of the mind over matter, over technology. In cinematic terms, *2001* is that manifestation. I was fortunate enough to meet Douglas Trumbull, who was only twenty-four when he did the effects on that film. I did an interview with him for *Premiere* magazine. His work is a feat, an intellectual, but also an existential feat. The whole film is. It is visionary. And deep, so deep. It's a mix of depth and lucidity in the analysis of the past, but also of the future.

JS: Is there a final goal, a *telos* in Kubrick, in your view?

GN: When he spoke of his films, they were almost all on the same level. He conceived of them as a continuity. And indeed there is a continuity in his approach, an approach you can see in the evolution he describes in *2001*, of man as animal, even a reptilian creature, evolving to a higher stage. But the film also deals with many more things, it is far broader in its scope, it deals with the inner world as much as with the outside world. We spend one-third, maybe even more, of our life sleeping. So there's conscious and unconscious life, and to me, the last third of *2001* deals with the unconscious, the great, vast unconscious, as vast as outer space . . .

PC: Is there a final goal to your cinema?

GN: In Kubrick's, there is. In mine, no.

JS: Would you like to express something about Kubrick's legacy? What's the most important aspect that he has left behind him in our life?

GN: When you make a film, the film is the most important thing. That's it. After that, to each their own method, their relational approach. Kubrick would seek isolation, even on the set, he was reserved . . . he used to say that it was a great weakness to get upset on the set, to show your emotions. He would play chess with people and would keep calm to get the best of everyone. I learned that from him, from an interview where he said this: "It is a weakness to get upset with your collaborators."[2]

PC: Do you think young viewers today understand and respect the legacy of Kubrick?

GN: I don't know if it's a question of respect. . . . People simply have moved away from cinema . . . from the *temple*. The temple of cinema that we used to know. I was born in 1963. I knew the time before the DVD, even before the VCR, no Blu-Ray, no Internet. When you wanted to see a film, you would go to this place, often majestic, called a movie theatre. Today, you can see your films on your smartphone. Kubrick's films, and particularly *2001*, don't do well on small screens. You have to see *2001* on the big screen. It's a sign of the times . . . all films are accessible, in a way that is just so far less majestic than fifty years ago.

PC: Peter Kubelka said the same: You can't own a film. Nowadays, people say they buy, own a film, meaning they acquire a piece of plastic that is the DVD. But Kubelka has memories from his childhood, seeing a great film, and then lying in bed and just thinking about it, and reliving the film, this fugitive experience, which you can't "own" . . .

GN: [In the theater] you are sitting in the dark, among many other people. When I make a film nowadays, Vincent Maraval from Wild Bunch, who produces and sells my films, tells me that 95 percent of people see the film on their laptop or their smartphones. So the perception is different. And so a film composed mostly of long and wide shots, with few close-ups, registers differently, and to the detriment of the film, because, at the end of the day, surface matters.

PC: Do you change your approach to filmmaking based on this factor?

GN: I don't change mine, because I conceive my films to be seen in a movie theatre, but mine may be a *vintage* state of mind and approach.

PC: Anything else you would like to say about *2001*?

GN: Everything has been said and written about *2001*, and yet the film retains its mystery. It took me at least forty years to sort of get what the film was about, I read all the interviews by Kubrick, articles in magazines. . . . . I bought a VCR of a documentary that your father made, Pip, where Keir Dullea explains the film . . . it's terrific stuff.[3] That's how we met! You should put that stuff on the net, it's terrific. It should be on a DVD/Blu-Ray bonus of the film, when they release it in 4K or 8K.

PC: Have you read the book *The Astral Fetus* (*Le foetus astral: essai d'analyse structurale d'un mythe cinématographique*, Dumont and Monod, 1970)? It's a structuralist, Levi-Straussian analysis of the film. For example, the authors explain how at the beginning of the film, everything is craggy, nothing is straight, no straight lines except for the monolith. At the end of the film, it's the other way round—everything is straight, smooth and geometrical, except for the broken glass. There's symmetry and inversion. At the end of the film, Dave Bowman loses his spacecraft, then his suit, then the broken glass . . . it's the last layer of technology, the last surface of glass that gets shattered.

GN: And you can't tell his age either, he is outside of space and time . . . is he in a Martian zoo, perhaps? That amazing Louis XVI space, lit from underneath . . .

JS: The final membrane, as Deleuze taught us, is the brain . . . and so all of Kubrick's cinema is a mise-en-scène of the brain, of the *noosphere* as Deleuze put it. . . . Enter the brain.

PC: I also have a theory about the construction of the monolith, the music by Richard Strauss used in the film, *Thus Spake Zarathustra*, is tonic: 1, 5, 8 . . . very tonic. Harmonics. And the geometry of the monolith is 1, 4, 9. One squared by two squared by three squared. Strauss's music comprises in itself the three phases of the film: the ape, the man, and the superman. And in Nietzsche you have a similar three-stages evolution of man.

GN: You are being a bit Kabbalistic!

PC: Maybe a little bit. Every person has an interpretation of this film.

GN: For me it's about evolution . . . at first animal species, with a reptilian brain, then they develop a mammal's brain, and then a neocortex . . . the human brain. And so we have three brains, with the neocortex, which is a bit like a computer. And so perhaps the ultimate stage of evolution is when we are only left with a neocortex under dematerialized, digital form: artificial intelligence, in short. A superior form of intelligence would be man without the animal. But then there is the danger of the glitch, or the bug. Computers bug and crash. They go psychotic, like HAL 9000. Humans do, too . . . and more often, perhaps.

Notes

1 The film was shown in the frame of the Cannes Classic section, at the Debussy Theater, on May 13, 2018. In the end, however, the announced remastered print didn't make it to Cannes, and a slightly scratched print was shown instead. The Cannes program announced that the remastered print would have a running time of 2h44, meaning this would be the longer, original release version, which Kubrick later discarded in favor of a shorter, 2h29 version.
2 Still, in the making-of of *The Shining* directed by his daughter Vivian, Kubrick is seen losing his temper on the set, getting mad at Shelley Duvall, who has recounted working on the film as an often difficult, even traumatic, experience.
3 Gaspar Noé is talking about *"2001: A Space Odyssey" explained with film excerpts; hosted by Keir Dullea*, a film written by Stephan Chodorov for the Camera Three CBS weekly show, and broadcast in 1971. It includes some behind-the-scenes information and references to material not included in the final cut of the film.

Contributors

Jeremi Szaniawski is Assistant Professor in Comparative Literature and Film Studies at the University of Massachusetts, Amherst. He is the author of *The Cinema of Alexander Sokurov: Figures of Paradox* (Wallflower, 2014) and the coeditor of *Directory of World Cinema: Belgium* with Marcelline Block (Intellect, 2014), *The Global Auteur: The Politics of Authorship in 21st Century Cinema* with Seung-hoon Jeong (Bloomsbury, 2016), and *On Women's Films Across Worlds and Generations* with Ivone Margulies (Bloomsbury, 2019). He is currently editing another collection, on the influence of Fredric Jameson in film studies, *Fredric Jameson and Film Theory: Space, Representation and Allegory in a Globalizing Age* with Keith Wagner (Rutgers University Press, 2020). He is also writing a short monograph on mud in cinema, *L'attrait de la boue* (Yellow Now, forthcoming). He has translated into French the books *Film Theory: An Introduction Through the Senses* (Thomas Elsaesser and Malte Hagener, Presses Universitaires de Rennes, 2011), *V Tsentre Okeana* (Alexander Sokurov, L'Âge d'Homme, 2015), and *Contemporary Romanian Cinema: The History of an Unexpected Miracle* (Dominique Nasta, forthcoming).

Nathan Abrams is Professor in Film in the School of Music and Media at Bangor University, UK. He is also the Director of Impact and Engagement for the College of Arts, Humanities and Business at Bangor University as well as the lead director for the Centre for Film, Television and Screen Studies. He is the cofounder of *Jewish Film and New Media: An International Journal*. He is the author of *Eyes Wide Shut: Stanley Kubrick and the Making of His Final Film* (with Robert Kolker, Oxford University Press, 2019), *Stanley Kubrick: New York Jewish Intellectual* (Rutgers University Press, 2018), *Hidden in Plain Sight: Jews and Jewishness in British Film, Television, and Popular Culture* (Northwestern University Press, 2016), and *The New Jew in Film: Exploring Jewishness and Judaism in Contemporary Cinema* (IB Tauris; Rutgers University Press, 2012).

Pip Chodorov is Associate Professor of Cinema Studies at Dongguk University in Seoul. Originally from New York, he is also an experimental filmmaker, and the director of the feature documentary *Free Radicals: A History of Experimental Film* (2011). He is founder of the Re:Voir DVD label and the Film Gallery and he is cofounder of L'Abominable, do-it-yourself film lab, all three based in Paris, France.

Adrian Daub is Professor of German Studies and Comparative Literature at Stanford University, where he directs the Clayman Center for Gender Research. He is the author of six books, including *Four-Handed Monsters: Four-Hand Piano Playing* *and Nineteenth Century Culture* (Oxford University Press, 2014), *Tristan's Shadow: Sexuality and the Total Work of Art after Wagner* (University of Chicago Press, 2013), and *The James Bond Songs: Pop Anthems of Late Capitalism* (Oxford University Press, 2015, with Charles Kronengold). His writings on popular culture, film, technology, and politics have appeared in *n+1, The New Republic, Longreads* (in the United States), *The Guardian* (in the United Kingdom) *Die Zeit* (Germany), and *Neue Zürcher Zeitung* (Switzerland).

Mircea Valeriu Deaca is Associate Professor at the University of Bucharest, where he teaches film analysis and theory, film history, and contemporary Romanian film at the Department of Cultural Studies and the Doctoral School. He holds a PhD thesis on the carnival tradition and Federico Fellini's films from Paris 3 - Sorbonne nouvelle. He has been writing and publishing articles on cinematography since 1983, and is a member of the Romanian Association of Film Critics. A key focus of his research is cognitive approach to film studies. His books include: *Le Carnaval et le Film de Fellini* (Bucharest: Libra, 2009), *Camera secunda* (Timisoara: Brumar, 2011), *Cinema postfilmic* (Timisoara: Brumar, 2013), *Anatomia filmului* (Bucharest: Bucharest UP, 2013), and *Investigatii in analiza cognitiva de film* (Timisoara: Brumar, 2015). He recently published a study about the New Romanian Cinema (Cluj: Mega, 2017). He has been organizing the annual international conference *Cinema: Cognition and Arts* since 2016, and was editor for the 2018 issue of *Ekphrasis* dedicated to cinema and cognition.

Pansy Duncan is Senior Lecturer in the School of English and Media Studies at Massey University, New Zealand. Her articles on film affect and aesthetics have been published in a number of venues, including *Screen, PMLA, Cinema Journal, Cultural Critique,* and *Feminist Media Studies,* and her book, *The Emotional Life of Postmodern Film,* appeared with Routledge in 2016. Her current book project, *A Natural History of Film Form: Film Aesthetics through Animal, Vegetable and Mineral Matter,* is an eco-materialist counter-history of early popular Euro-American film aesthetics, told through the lens of the raw materials of early photographic film stock (cellulose, silver, and gelatin). It is funded by a Marsden Grant from the Royal Society of New Zealand.

Thomas Elsaesser is Professor Emeritus at the Department of Media and Culture, University of Amsterdam. From 2006 to 2012, he was Visiting Professor at Yale University, and since January 2013 he teaches part-time at Columbia University, New York. Among his recent books are *The Persistence of Hollywood* (New York: Routledge, 2012), *German Cinema—Terror and Trauma: Cultural Memory Since 1945* (New York: Routledge, 2013), *Film Theory—An Introduction through the Senses* (with Malte Hagener, 2nd revised edition, New York: Routledge, 2015), *Körper, Tod und Technik* (with Michael Wedel, Paderborn: Konstanz University Press, 2016), and *Film History as Media Archaeology* (Amsterdam University Press, 2016). His latest book is *European*

Cinema and Continental Philosophy: Film as Thought Experiment (London: Bloomsbury, 2018). He is also the writer-director of *The Sun Island* (2017), a documentary essay film produced for German television ZDF/3Sat (https://sunislandfilm.com/).

Daniel Fairfax is Assistant Professor in Film Studies at the Goethe Universität-Frankfurt, and an editor of *Senses of Cinema* (www.sensesofcinema.com). His research focuses on French film theory in the post-1968 period, and his monograph *The Red Years of Cahiers du Cinéma (1968-1973)* is forthcoming from Amsterdam University Press.

Marta Figlerowicz is Associate Professor of Comparative Literature and English at Yale, where she is also affiliated with the Film and Media Program. She is the author of two books, *Flat Protagonists* (Oxford University Press, 2016) and *Spaces of Feeling* (Cornell University Press, 2017), and is currently at work on two new projects, both on the changing forms of reflection and self-fashioning of the digital age. Her writing has appeared in academic as well as nonacademic venues, ranging from *New Literary History* and *Film Quarterly* to *Cabinet*, *Foreign Affairs*, and *The Washington Post*. She has co-organized over a dozen seminars, colloquia, and conferences at UC Berkeley, Yale, and Cambridge University, on topics ranging from the history of encyclopedias, atlases, and museums, to contemporary critical theory and the shifting political discourses of Eastern Europe.

Pierre-Simon Gutman is associate editor of the magazine *L'Avant-Scène Cinéma*. After making several short films, he defended his thesis in aesthetics and image semiotics, dedicated to the cinema of Michael Cimino, at Paris VII Denis Diderot University in 2009. He has published, among others, in *Raisons Publiques*, the *French Journal of American Studies*, or *Éclipses*, as well as given talks at UC Berkeley, and Amiens. He has taught cinema studies at Paris VII and Nancy II Universities, and currently teaches at ESRA Paris and Brussels. A regular jury member on such international film festivals as Jerusalem, Morelia, or Moscow, he has also been a member of the feature film and short film selection committees of the Critics' Week at the Cannes Film Festival, and he currently sits on the board of administration of the Syndicat Français de la Critique de Cinéma.

Rodney F. Hill is Associate Professor of Film in the Herbert School of Communication at Hofstra University. He holds a PhD from the University of Kansas and an MA from the University of Wisconsin–Madison. He is coauthor of *The Encyclopedia of Stanley Kubrick* (New York: Facts on File, 2002) and *The Francis Ford Coppola Encyclopedia* (The Scarecrow Press, 2010), coeditor of *Francis Ford Coppola: Interviews* (Jackson: University of Mississippi Press, 2004), and a contributor to several other books, including *The Stanley Kubrick Archives* (Taschen, 2005) and *The Essential Science-Fiction Television Reader* (The University Press of Kentucky, 2008). Hill's essays on the Coen Brothers have appeared in *Cineaste*, *Senses of Cinema*, and *Post Script: Essays in*

Film and the Humanities. He also has been featured in video essays for several DVD/ Blu-ray releases by the Criterion Collection, including Kubrick's *Dr. Strangelove* and Coppola's *Rumble Fish*. His current projects include a book-length study of the recent films of Francis Coppola and an edited collection of essays on the cultural and scientific impacts of the Apollo 11 Moon landing.

Seung-hoon Jeong currently teaches at the Korea National University of Arts, Seoul. A former Assistant Professor of cinema studies at New York University Abu Dhabi, he has mostly worked on film theory and critical issues through film, with a specific focus on global cinema related to multiculturalism, abjection, catastrophe, in a network with biopolitics, ethics, psychoanalysis and philosophy. Jeong received Korea's Cine21 Film Criticism Award (2003) and the Society for Cinema and Media Studies Dissertation Award (2012). He is the author of *Cinematic Interfaces: Film Theory after New Media* (Routledge, 2013), co-translator of Jacques Derrida's *Acts of Literature* into Korean (Moonji, 2013), coeditor of *The Global Auteur: The Politics of Authorship in 21st Century Cinema* (Bloomsbury, 2016), and guest-editor of a special issue of *Studies in the Humanities*, "Global East Asian Cinema: Abjection and Agency" (2019). He is currently writing *Global Cinema: A Biopolitical and Ethical Reframing* (Oxford University Press, 2020).

Jihoon Kim is Associate Professor of Cinema and Media studies at Chung-ang University. He is the author of *Between Film, Video, and the Digital: Hybrid Moving Images in the Post-media Age* (Bloomsbury Academic, 2018/16), and his essays have appeared in *Cinema Journal, Screen, Camera Obscura, Animation: An Interdisciplinary Journal, Film Quarterly*, and *Millennium Film Journal*, among others. He is currently working on two book projects, *Documentary's Expanded Fields: New Media, New Platforms, and the Documentary* and *Post-vérité Turns: Korean Independent Documentary in the 21st Century*.

Alexander Nemerov is the Carl and Marilynn Thoma Provostial Professor in the Arts and Humanities at Stanford University. He is the author of many books and essays on American art and culture, including *Silent Dialogues: Diane Arbus and Howard Nemerov* (Fraenkel Gallery, 2015) and *Icons of Grief: Val Lewton's Home Front Pictures* (University of California Press, 2005).

John Pitseys is a lecturer in political philosophy at the Université catholique de Louvain, Belgium and at the Université catholique de Lille, France. His research interests include democratic theory, deliberation, transparency, and governance. He has published articles in *Global Environmental Politics, Ethics, Politics and Society, Revue française de Science Politique*, and *Droit et Société*. He recently authored *Démocratie et Citoyenneté* (CRISP, 2017). In May 2019, John was elected to the Brussels Regional Parliament, representing the Belgian francophone Green party, Ecolo, and was thereafter appointed State Senator.

Rick Warner is Associate Professor and Director of Film Studies in the Department of English and Comparative Literature at the University of North Carolina, Chapel Hill. He is the author of *Godard and the Essay Film: A Form That Thinks* (Northwestern University Press, 2018) and coeditor, with Colin McCabe and Kathleen Murray, of *True to the Spirit: Film Adaptation and the Question of Fidelity* (Oxford University Press, 2011). His essays have appeared in several edited collections as well as in *New Review of Film and Television Studies*, *Quarterly Review of Film and Video*, *Adaptation*, *Critical Inquiry*, *Critical Quarterly*, *Post-Script*, *The Cine-Files*, *Senses of Cinema*, *La Furia Umana*, and *Journal of Popular Film and Television*. He is working on a monograph that examines contemplative styles in global art cinema from 1945 to the present.

Index

Alcott, John   46 n.2, 47 n.16
Aldiss, Brian   19, 34, 47 n.18, 151
   Super-Toys Last All Summer Long   19, 34, 151
Allen, Woody   31, 32, 64
   Take the Money and Run   31
   Husbands and Wives   65
Altman, Robert   31, 32, 132
   M*A*S*H*   31
Anderson, Lindsay   30, 33
   If...   33
Anderson, Paul Thomas   1, 10, 11, 14, 16, 18, 22, 42–4, 108, 119–22, 125, 127, 132–5, 142 nn.13–15, 166, 173, 175, 176, 183
   Magnolia   132
   There Will Be Blood   44, 119, 120, 127, 132–5, 140, 142 n.15, 143 n.22, 175, 183, 184, 190
   The Master   142 n.15
   Phantom Thread   44, 120–2
Antonioni, Michelangelo   7, 32, 141 n.8
   Red Desert   141 n.8
   Identification of a Woman   141 n.8
Arbus, Diane   9, 10, 12, 206, 289–90
   Puerto Rican woman with a beauty mark, N.Y.C. 1965   289, 290
   Identical Twins, Roselle, N.J. 1966   289
Aronofsky, Darren   12, 15, 56, 62, 63, 64, 65 n.7
   Pi   12, 62, 63
   Requiem for a Dream   12, 62
   Black Swan   62
   Noah   63, 64
   The Fountain   62–4
   mother!   12, 63, 64
Ascher, Rodney   3, 55, 90, 106, 195–208, 229 n.4
   Room 237   3, 13, 90, 106, 195–208, 210 n.14, 229 n.5

[Ashby, Hal]
   Harold and Maude   165
Aster, Ari   14
   Hereditary   14

Bardem, Javier   64, 81
Barenholtz, Ben   68
Barthes, Roland   4, 47 n.14, 209
   Sade, Fourier, Loyola   4
   Pleasure of the Text   209
Bataille, Georges   260 n.2
Beethoven, Ludwig van   30, 35, 171, 249, 250, 251, 257
   Pastorale Symphony   171
   Ninth Symphony   250, 251
   "Ode to Joy"   250
Begley, Lewis   34, 47 n.18
   Wartime Lies   34, 47 n.18
Berenson, Marisa   106, 286
Berg, Peter   183
   Deepwater Horizon   183
Bergman, Ingmar   32, 135, 266, 267, 270, 275, 276
Berlioz, Hector   33, 172
   Symphonie fantastique   172
[Besson, Luc]
   Lucy   159
Blomkamp, Neill   257, 258
   District 9   258
   Elysium   257
Bong, Joon-ho   257
   Snowpiercer   257
Bowie, David   1, 2, 24 n.1, 65 n.7
   Space Oddity   1, 65 n.7
   Scary Monsters... Super Creeps   1
   Blackstar   1, 2
Boyle, Danny   10, 11, 37
   Trainspotting   10, 37
   Sunshine   10, 38
Brahms, Johannes   135, 173, 175

Brecht, Bertolt   37
  Mann ist Mann   37
Brown, Garrett   46 n.2
  Steadicam   17, 33, 69, 88, 179, 185
Buñuel, Luis   116, 296
Burgess, Anthony   24 n.1, 80
Burke, Edmund   106, 139, 140, 143 n.21
Burstyn, Joseph   68
Bush, Vannevar   148

Cameron, James   6, 7, 11, 21, 102–4, 109
  Piranha 2: The Spawning   102
  The Terminator   21, 102, 103
  Aliens   6, 7, 11, 25 nn.8, 9, 103
  Terminator 2: Judgment Day   103
Camus, Albert   243, 244, 259 n.1
Cantwell, Colin   25 n.6
Carlos, Wendy   24 n.1, 26 n.18, 172, 173
Carpenter, John   6, 139, 141 n.1, 143 n.20, 181
  Dark Star   6, 143 n.20
  Halloween   34, 141 n.1, 181
  The Thing   6, 139, 141 n.1, 143 n.20
Carrière, Jean-Claude   116
Carruth, Shane   12, 42, 102
  Primer   42, 102
  Upstream Color   12, 42
Ciment, Michel   3, 15, 20, 23, 26 n.19, 29, 46 n.7, 67, 71, 72, 73, 101, 104–7
Clarke, Arthur C.   80, 101, 171
  "The Sentinel"   171
Clay, Thomas   25 n.11
  The Great Ecstasy of Robert Carmichael   25 n.11
Clouzot, Henri Georges   141 n.1
  Diabolique   141 n.1
Coen, Ethan and Joel   15, 16, 17, 26 n.16, 42, 43, 59, 60, 61, 62, 67–84, 90
  Blood Simple   59, 67, 68
  Raising Arizona   16, 59, 67, 69, 72, 73, 74, 76, 78, 84 n.2
  Barton Fink   16, 59, 60, 61, 62, 67, 69, 73, 75, 76, 81
  Miller's Crossing   61, 67, 69, 71
  The Hudsucker Proxy   67, 70, 78
  Fargo   73, 79
  The Big Lebowski   60, 61, 73, 77, 78, 82, 83
  O Brother, Where Art Thou?   60, 61, 76
  The Man Who Wasn't There   60, 76
  Intolerable Cruelty   77
  The Ladykillers   77
  No Country for Old Men   69, 75, 78, 81
  A Serious Man   17, 60, 61, 82, 83
  Burn After Reading   60, 77, 78
  True Grit   67, 78, 81
  Inside Llewyn Davis   67
  Hail, Caesar!   67, 77, 81
  The Ballad of Buster Scruggs   67
Colman, Olivia   17
Conrad, Joseph   35
Cooper, Merian C   297
  King Kong   297
Copland, Aaron   167
Coppola, Francis Ford   73
  The Conversation   76
  Apocalypse Now   34
Corbet, Brady   25 n.14
  Vox Lux   25 n.14
Cosmatos, Panos   7
  Beyond the Black Rainbow   7
Crawley, Lol   25 n.14
[Cromwell, John]
  The Prisoner of Zenda   169
Cronenberg, David   12, 37, 64, 90, 188
  Shivers   37
  The Brood   188
  Naked Lunch   37
  Crash   37
  eXistenZ   37, 64
Cruise, Tom   91, 132, 223
Cuarón, Alfonso   258
  Children of Men   258
  Gravity   235

Darabont, Frank   183
  The Mist   183
Day-Lewis, Daniel   44, 132, 134, 175, 183, 184, 190
Deleuze, Gilles   3, 11, 18, 38, 39, 40, 44, 90, 104, 107, 109, 113, 115, 120, 124 n.7, 143 n.23, 205, 260 n.4, 298
Dellsperger, Brice   24 n.2, 267
  Body Double 22   267

De Palma, Brian   7, 182
    Carrie   182
Desplechin, Arnaud   99
Dolci, Carlo   285
    Christ in the House of the Pharisee   285
Donner, Richard   6, 141 n.1, 188
    The Omen   6, 34, 141 n.1, 188
Douglas, Kirk   31
Dreyer, Carl Theodor   138
    The Passion of Joan of Arc   138
Dullea, Keir   16, 60, 128, 149, 298
    "2001: A Space Odyssey" explained with lm excerpts; hosted by Keir Dullea   299 n.3
Dunne, J. W.   110
    An Experiment with Time   110
Duvall, Shelley   15, 53, 64, 104, 125, 185, 196, 299 n.2

Elkind, Rachel   172, 173

Faber, Michel   117, 127–9, 154–6, 162 n.17
Farrell, Colin   87, 88, 91, 95
[Farrelly, Bobby and Peter]
    Me, Myself and Irene   260 n.4
Fauré, Gabriel   173
Fellini, Federico   32, 135, 240 n.3, n.5
Fessenden, Larry   183
    The Last Winter   183
Fincher, David   26 n.17, 37
    Fight Club   37
Flanagan, Mike   90
    Doctor Sleep   26 n.18, 90
Flaubert, Gustave   35
[Fleischer, Richard]
    Dr. Dolittle   30
Fleming, Victor   199
    Gone with the Wind   169
    The Wizard of Oz   47 n.8, 199
[Ford, John]
    The Man Who Shot Liberty Valance   215
Freud, Sigmund   95, 127, 151, 223, 247
    Nachträglichkeit   34, 104
    Uncanny/unheimlich   95, 127, 134, 223

Friedkin, William   31, 188
    The French Connection   31
    The Exorcist   31, 34, 188

Garland, Alex   21, 139, 149, 154, 158, 160
    Ex Machina   21, 149, 151, 154, 158, 159, 160, 161
    Annihilation   139, 140, 143 n.24
Glazer, Jonathan   16, 18, 43, 44, 65, 108, 115–18, 127–32, 135, 136, 141 n.5, 142 n.17, 149, 154–7, 168 nn.18, 19
    The Universal   116, 141 n.5
    Sexy Beast   65, 116
    Birth   16, 44, 65, 116, 119, 141 n.5
    Under the Skin   16, 44, 117–19, 127–32, 136, 140, 141 n.8, 142 nn.12, 17, 143 n.22, 149, 151, 154, 156–8, 161, 162 nn.18, 19
Godard, Jean-Luc   23, 99, 266, 275
    Alphaville   233
    Le livre d'image   23
Gondry, Michel   26 n.15
    Believe   26 n.15
    Be Kind, Rewind   26 n.15
Gorecki, Henryk   173
Grandrieux, Philippe   128
    Sombre   128
Greengrass, Paul   258
    Jason Bourne   258
Greenwood, Jonny   11, 119, 121, 132, 133, 134, 135, 142 n.14, 175, 184
    Popcorn Superhet Receiver   133
Guerra, Ciro   11
    Embrace of the Serpent   11

Handel, Georg Friedrich   30, 172
Haneke, Michael   4, 128
    Funny Games   4, 128
    Funny Games US   4, 128
Harlan, Jan   2, 31, 47 n.18, 69, 206, 210 n.14
    Stanley Kubrick: a Life in Pictures   2
Harlan, Veit   16, 31
Harris, Bob   11, 121
Hawks, Howard   32, 67, 143 n.20, 271, 278 n.6
    The Thing from Another World   143 n.20

Herr, Michael 101
Herrmann, Bernard 167, 169
Herzog, Werner 11, 138
   Aguirre, the Wrath of God 138
Hitchcock, Alfred 2, 7, 8, 14, 31, 32,
   67, 68, 76, 125, 126, 135, 136,
   141 n.1, 197, 213, 266, 267, 271
   Vertigo 7, 126
   Psycho 76, 125
   The Birds 125, 126
Hogarth, William 284
Holst, Gustav 173
Hooper, Tobe 181
   The Texas Chainsaw Massacre 181
Hopper, Dennis 32
   Easy Rider 32, 165

Ives, Charles 173

James, Henry 283, 284, 293 n.6
   The Ambassadors 283
   Portrait of a Lady 283
Jameson, Fredric 3, 5, 6, 7, 13, 33–5, 44,
   47 n.17, 77, 102, 104, 106, 107,
   182, 207, 208, 222, 229 n.6
Joanou, Phil 8
   Final Analysis 8
Johansson, Scarlett 16, 117, 118, 128,
   129, 131, 155
Johnson, Diane 127
Jones, Duncan 1, 259
   Moon 1
   Source Code 259
Jonze, Spike 65
   Her 159
Joyce, James 33, 35
Jünger, Ernst 37
   Storms of Steel 37

Kael, Pauline 30, 46 n.7, 48 n.19, 69
Kant, Immanuel 39, 83, 106, 137, 138,
   139, 140, 142 n.19, 143 n.21,
   221, 239
   Categorical imperative 39, 83
   Sublime 9, 106, 127, 137, 139,
      143 n.21, 239
Karel, William 13, 206
   Dark Side of the Moon 13, 206

Kaufman, Charlie 65
[Kelly, Gene]
   "Singin' in the Rain" 30, 35, 78, 249,
      251
   Hello, Dolly! 30
Kelly, Richard 102
   Donnie Darko 102
Khachaturian, Aram 7, 167, 168, 171
   Gayane 7, 167, 168
Kidman, Nicole 16, 17, 87, 90, 91, 95
King, Stephen 26 n.18, 69, 90, 217
Kosinski, Joseph 25 n.6, 259
   Oblivion 25 n.6, 259
Kubelka, Peter 298
Kubrick (Harlan), Christiane 62, 195
Kubrick, Stanley
   Fear and Desire 36, 62, 64, 68, 105,
      227, 243, 271
   Killer's Kiss 22, 60, 62, 68, 93
   The Killing 6, 18, 58, 63, 64, 65, 79,
      80, 96, 105, 116, 141 n.9, 227
   Paths of Glory 6, 17, 26 n.17, 32, 36,
      62, 64, 90, 96, 227, 243–6, 250,
      256, 257, 288
   Spartacus 5, 31, 63, 64, 92, 167
   Lolita 11, 17, 29, 36, 37, 41, 53, 60,
      65 n.4, 67, 76, 78, 120, 121, 122,
      135, 147, 159
   Dr. Strangelove, or, How I Learned to
      Stop Worrying and Love the
      Bomb 12, 16, 17, 36, 52, 55, 59,
      60, 69, 73, 74, 90, 124 n.7, 138,
      147, 148, 214–25, 243–51, 254,
      257, 295
   2001: A Space Odyssey 1, 2, 5, 6, 7,
      8, 10–12, 16, 19, 23, 25 n.6,
      26 nn.15, 16, 29–38, 43, 44,
      46 n.7, 52, 54, 55, 61, 63–5 n.7,
      67, 69, 70, 75, 80, 81, 88, 90,
      97, 100 n.6, 104–19, 125–40,
      141 n.2, 142 n.15, 143 n.20,
      147–54, 159, 161 n.9, 162 n.13,
      165–77, 195, 205, 231–9,
      259 n.1, 260 n.3, 267, 274, 295–9
   A Clockwork Orange 4, 10, 17–19, 22,
      23, 24 n.1, 25 n.7, 30–41, 52, 54,
      55, 64, 67, 72, 77, 80, 90, 92, 96,
      105, 116, 120, 122, 123 n.3,

141 n.7, 142 n.10, 147, 172, 226, 245, 248–50, 259, 275, 276
Barry Lyndon   5, 10, 14, 16, 17, 18, 22, 25 n.7, 26 n.14, 33, 34, 48 n.23, 54, 55, 64, 65, 67, 80, 88, 92, 105, 107, 110, 111, 115, 116, 120–2, 143 n.21, 172, 214–22, 225–8, 229 n.10, 269, 275, 281–92
The Shining   2, 4, 6, 8, 11–18, 22, 23, 25 n.7, n.8, 26 nn.15–18, 33, 34, 35, 36, 37, 38, 40, 52, 53, 54, 55, 59, 61, 64, 65, 69, 73, 76, 80, 84 n.2, 88–90, 95, 103–7, 116, 120, 125–40, 141 n.1, 2, 4, 5, 7, 9, 142 n.11, 172, 179–92, 195–209, 214, 217–26, 229 n.6, 255, 274, 289, 299 n.2
Full Metal Jacket   4, 8, 18, 23, 25 n.9, 26 n.16, 34, 36, 37, 40, 47 n.18, 55, 59, 64, 65 n.6, 70, 71, 76, 80, 92, 93, 105, 115, 119, 141 n.2, 172, 245, 252–9
Eyes Wide Shut   9, 13, 16, 17, 22, 23, 26 n.14, 36, 40, 41, 53–6, 59, 64, 65, 76, 80, 90, 91, 93, 95, 105, 115, 119, 132, 141 n.2, 5, 213, 214, 218, 222–4, 229 n.8, 267, 275
Artificial Intelligence   19, 20, 21, 34, 37, 47 n.18, 123 n.2, 149, 151–4, 161, 272
Napoleon   30, 53, 97, 98, 123 n.2, 266, 272
Aryan Papers   34, 47 n.18, 210 n.14, 266, 272
Kubrick, Vivian   15, 54, 55, 172, 205, 299 n.2
  as Abigail Mead   172
  Making "The Shining"   15, 299 n.2
  Stanley Kubrick Exhibition, The   2, 24 n.2, 56, 263–78
Kurosawa, Akira   105
  Lacan, Jacques   248, 255, 256
  objet petit a   214, 255, 256

Lang, Fritz   296
  Metropolis   296
Lanthimos, Yorgos   17, 18, 87–99, 100 n.7

Kinetta   96
Dogtooth   17, 88–90, 96–9
Alps   88, 96, 98
The Lobster   17, 87, 88, 92, 94, 95, 98, 99
The Killing of a Sacred Deer   17, 87, 88, 90, 91, 92, 95, 96, 99
The Favourite   17, 87, 92, 93, 94, 96, 99
Larkin, Philip   281, 292
  Church Going   281, 292
Leigh, Mike   15, 56–9, 64, 65 n.2
  Hard Labour   56, 57
  Secrets and Lies   57, 58
  Two Thousand Years   57
Lester, Richard   33
Ligeti, György   128, 129, 133, 167, 168, 170, 172
  Requiem   167, 168, 170
  Lontano   128
  Lux Aeterna   167, 170
  Atmosphères   133, 167
Liman, Doug   258, 259
  Bourne Identity   258
  Edge of Tomorrow   259
Linklater, Richard   107, 123 n.2
  Dazed and Confused   107
  Before Sunrise   107
  Before Sunset   107
  Before Midnight   107
  Boyhood   107, 123 n.2
Lipsky, Oldrich   123
  Happy End   123
[Logan, Joshua]
  Paint Your Wagon   30
Lucas, George   25 n.6, 31, 34, 107
  THX 1138   25 n.6
  American Graffiti   107
  Star Wars   25 n.6, 31, 34, 47 n.18
Lumet, Sidney   132
Lynch, David   8, 9, 10, 37, 45, 73, 76, 90, 123 n.4, 126, 127, 135–8, 142 n.15, 266
  Eraserhead   8, 135–40, 142 n.15
  Blue Velvet   37
  Wild at Heart   8
  Twin Peaks   135
  Twin Peaks: Fire Walk With Me   135–40

Lost Highway 8
  Mulholland Drive 142 n.15
  Twin Peaks: the Return 8, 127

McCarthy, Cormac 81
McTeigue, James 258
  V for Vendetta 258
Mahler, Gustav 167, 168
  Symphony 3, 167
  Maimonides 59
Malick, Terrence 10, 11, 42, 43, 136, 166, 173–6
  Days of Heaven 173
  The Thin Red Line 11, 173
  The New World 11, 173, 174
  The Tree of Life 10, 136, 173, 174
  To the Wonder 173
  Song to Song 11
Mamet, David 15, 56, 58, 59, 65 n.4
  House of Games 59
  Homicide 59
  Heist 58
Mann, Anthony 31
Mann, Thomas 35
Marker, Chris 7, 266
  La Jetée 233
Mendes, Sam 258
  Skyfall 258
Metz, Toba 62
Mitchell, David Robert 14, 42, 43, 45, 213, 214, 224
  Under the Silver Lake 14, 45, 213, 214, 219, 222–5
Modine, Matthew 285
Mostow, Jonathan 257
  Terminator 3: Rise of the Machines 257

Nabokov, Vladimir 37, 122
  Lolita 122
Nash, Ogden 171
  "One Touch of Venus" 171
Neumann, John von 147
Neumeier, Ed 21
Niccol, Andrew 257
  Gattaca 257
Nichols, Mike 31
  The Graduate 31

Nicholson, Jack 4, 6, 15, 16, 26 n.16, 32, 54, 60, 61, 69, 132, 134, 184, 189, 196, 199, 201, 207, 229 n.6
Nietzsche, Friedrich 106, 113, 167, 244, 250, 254, 260 n.6, 299
Noé, Gaspar 11, 12, 18, 42, 43, 44, 45, 108, 109–15, 123 n.6, 124 n.8, 295–9
  Irreversible 11, 18, 44, 45, 108, 110, 111, 114, 115, 124 n.7, 296
  Enter the Void 11, 23, 45, 111, 112, 114, 115, 296
  Love 115
  Climax 11, 44
Nolan, Christopher 5, 16, 18, 19, 21, 43, 108, 109, 110, 111, 123 n.4, 231–40, 257
  Memento 18, 108, 110
  The Prestige 108, 109
  Inception 108
  Interstellar 18, 19, 43, 108, 109, 231–8, 257
  Dunkirk 43, 108
Nolan, Jonathan 123 n.4
North, Alex 166–71
Nyby, Christian 143 n.20
  The Thing from Another World 143 n.20

O'Neal, Ryan 60, 106, 281, 285
Ophüls, Max 23, 24, 123 n.3
  Le plaisir 23

Pärt, Arvo 173, 175
  Fratres 175
Pasolini, Pier Paolo 296
  Salò 296
Payne, Alexander 26 n.16, 257
  About Schmidt 26 n.16
  Downsizing 26 n.16, 257
Peele, Jordan 141 n.7
  Get Out 141 n.7
Penderecki, Krzysztof 7, 8, 11, 25, 132, 133, 134, 135, 136, 141 n.7, 142 n.14, 179, 184, 185, 190
  Threnody to the Victims of Hiroshima 136
  The Awakening of Jacob 25, 132

Penn, Arthur   31
   Bonnie & Clyde   31
Pennebaker, D.A.   24 n.1
   [*Ziggy Stardust and the Spiders from Mars*]   24 n.1
[Pfister, Wally]
   Transcendence   159
Polanski, Roman   14, 31, 64, 73
   Rosemary's Baby   14, 31
   The Ninth Gate   64
Pollack, Sydney   65, 69
Preisner, Zbigniew   174
   "Lacrimosa 2"   174
Proyas, Alex   237
   Dark City   237
Purcell, Henry   30

Raeburn, Henry   285, 287
   The Allen Brothers   285, 287
Rafelson, Bob   32
Raphael, Fredric   46 n.2, 48 n.20, 59, 65
Rashi   82
Rautavaara, Einojuhani   173
Reeves, Matt   8
   War for the Planet of the Apes   8
Reisz, Karel   30
Reitz, Edgar   9, 10, 14
Respighi, Ottorino   173, 174
Richardson, Tony   30, 34
   Tom Jones   34
Rodriguez, Robert   258
   Alita: Battle Angel   258
Romanek, Mark   26 n.15
Rosenberg, Stuart   141 n.1
   The Amityville Horror   141 n.1
Ross, Steve   31
Russell, Ken   11
   Altered States   11

Saint-Saëns, Camille   121, 173
Sanders, Rupert   259
   Ghost in the Shell   259
Schlesinger, John   30, 33
   Billy Liar   33
Schnitzler, Arthur   23, 53
   Traumnovelle   23, 53
   Rhapsody   59

Schoedsack, Ernest B   297
   King Kong   297
Schumann, Robert   173
Scorsese, Martin   31, 69, 73, 132, 266, 270
Scott, Ridley   5, 6, 25 n.6, 128
   The Duellists   5
   Alien   5, 141 n.6
   Blade Runner   6, 128, 235, 237
   Gladiator   5
Semel, Terry   31, 47 n.12
Senior, Julian   31
Shiman, Jennifer   4, 25 n.4
   Kubrick's The Shining in 30 Seconds (and re-enacted by Bunnies)   4
Shyamalan, M Night   139
Sinclair, Upton   133, 183
   Oil!   133, 183
Smetana, Bedrich   173, 174
   Vltava   174
Smith, Patti   25 n.4
   M Train   25 n.4
Sobotka, Ruth   62
Soderbergh, Steven   12, 25 n.13, 42, 43, 128
   Unsane   43
   The Return of W. De Rijk   12, 128
   Logan Lucky   43
Spielberg, Steven   19, 20, 21, 25 n.7, 31, 34, 37, 46 n.6, 64, 90, 149, 151–3, 209, 233, 257
   Close Encounters of the Third Kind   31, 233
   E.T.   37
   Indiana Jones and the Temple of Doom   25 n.7
   Empire of the Sun   37
   Schindler's List   31, 34, 47 n.18
   Jurassic Park   37
   A.I. Artificial Intelligence   19, 21, 37, 149, 152, 154, 159, 161
   Minority Report   257
   Ready Player One   19, 90, 209, 235
Steinkamp, Jennifer   24 n.2, 267
   Stiffs   267
Stone, Emma   17, 87, 96
[Stone, Oliver]
   Platoon   34

Stone, Philip 25 n.7, 55, 76
Strauss, Jr., Johann 167, 172
   The Blue Danube 35, 170
Strauss, Richard 19, 109, 114, 167, 170, 171, 174, 176
   Thus Spake Zarathustra 19, 109, 167, 168, 170, 177, 298
   Der Rosenkavalier 19
   "Im Abendrot" 176
Stubbs, George 284
   Tarantino, Quentin 12, 37, 105
   Reservoir Dogs 37
   Pulp Fiction 37, 105
   Jackie Brown 105

Tarkovsky, Andrei 139, 267
   Stalker 139
Tartt, Donna 25
   The Goldfinch 25
Tavener, John 173
Thackeray, William Makepeace 281, 283
Truffaut, François 99
Trumbull, Douglas 136
Tsangari, Athina Rachel 87
Turkel, Joe 6, 55, 76

Unkrich, Lee 2

Van Sant, Gus 42
   Gerry 42
Verhoeven, Paul 21, 23, 258
   Robocop 21
   Starship Troopers 23, 258
Veronese, Bonifacio 285
   The Adoration of the Kings 285
Vezina, Richard 142 n.16
   Blue Shining 142 n.16
Villeneuve, Denis 25 n.6, 258
   Arrival 25 n.6
   Blade Runner 2049 258
Vitali, Leon 92, 281, 282, 285, 289, 293 n.8

Vogt-Roberts, Jordan 8
   Kong: Skull Island 8
Von Trier, Lars 10, 42, 166, 173–6
   Melancholia 10, 174, 175

Wachowskis, the 257
   The Matrix 257
Wagner, Richard 10, 173–5
   Das Rheingold 173
   Parsifal 173, 174
   Tristan und Isolde 174
Weill, Kurt 171
   One Touch of Venus 171
Weir, Peter 22
   The Truman Show 23, 233
Weisz, Rachel 17, 62, 64, 88, 93
Welles, Orson 2, 105, 197, 278 n.6
Wells, HG 283, 284, 293 n.6
   The War in the Air 293 n.6
Wiener, Norbert 147, 148
Williams, John 177
Williams, Ralph Vaughan 167
   Scott of the Atlantic 167
Wilson, Jane and Louise 24 n.2, 267
   Unfolding the Aryan Papers 267
Winterbottom, Michael 176
   The Trip 176
   The Trip to Italy 176
Wise, Robert 6
   The Haunting 6
Wyler, William 167
   Ben Hur 167

Yeaworth, Irvin S. 183
   The Blob 183

Zemeckis, Robert 102
   Back to the Future trilogy 102
Zierra, Tony 285, 293 n.8
   Filmworker 285, 293 n.8
Zimmer, Hans 19, 109, 173, 177

www.ingramcontent.com/pod-product-compliance
Lightning Source LLC
Chambersburg PA
CBHW070015010526
44117CB00011B/1587